Freud in the City

David Freud, the great grandson of Sigmund, entered the City in 1984 as the revolution triggered by Big Bang got under way. He had spent the first 11 years of his career as a journalist and never envisaged working in the financial markets. But a stint on the Financial Times' Lex Column led to a job in the securities operation of the leading UK investment bank, Warburg, now known as UBS. He stayed at the sharp end of the business through his 20 year span, conducting transactions in no fewer than 19 countries, and retired as vice chairman of investment banking at the end of 2003.

'Freud in the City' tells of the desperate struggle to float Eurotunnel against the backdrop of Black Monday; the battles over the Disney theme park in Paris; and the unaccountable rise and politically fraught fall of Railtrack. At the heart of the book is the hitherto untold story of the breakneck expansion of the Warburg Group, the leading beneficiary of Big Bang, which ended in humiliation and collapse.

David Freud was born in London in 1950, is married and has three children. He is currently the chief executive of the Portland Trust. Also, as a result of his independent report on reforming the welfare system, launched in 2007, he has been appointed adviser to the Government on welfare-to-work.

'He is a natural storyteller with an ability to write about complicated financial issues in plain English...Frankness is one of the many merits of this engaging and amusing autobiography...City investment banking changed over Freud's career to a far more competitive, fast-paced business where individual talent was increasingly important. He captures the chaos, cut and thrust and sheer comedy of this world.'
Financial Times

Perhaps David Freud's greatest respray job was the stockmarket flotation of Eurotunnel. Not only did he come up with a clever way to make shares in Eurotunnel plc seem more than a wing-and-a-prayer speculation, he managed to flog the stock at the height of the stockmarket crash of 1987...It was not particularly surprising that John Hutton, the Work and Pension Secretary, should turn to this particular ex-banker when ordered by Tony Blair to come up with something snappy on welfare reform.'
The Independent

Only rarely does literature about the world of finance break out of its "special interest" bracket and grasp the imagination of the wider public... It is before Freud reaches the pinnacle of his career that his account is at its best, offering an intimate insight into the workings of an investment bank in the 1990s.'
The New Statesman

I asked David Freud to float easyJet for me because he was one of the best bankers in the City. Now he has written a fascinating, and accessible, insider's account of the place - all about the mega-deals, the egos, the greed and the chaos. And it's very funny."
Stelios Haji-Ioannou - Founder, easyJet

Freud in the City

At the sharp end of the global finance revolution

—

by David Freud

Bene Factum Publishing

Published in 2008 by
Bene Factum Publishing Ltd
PO Box 58122
10 Elm Quay Court
Nine Elms Lane
London
SW8 5WZ

ISBN 978-1-903071-19-9 (1-903071-19-4)

First published in Great Britain in 2006 by Bene Factum Publishing Limited
ISBN 1-903071-10-0 (978-1-903071-10-6)

A CIP catalogue record of this is available from
the British Library

Designed and Typeset by 01:01 Design Consultants, Putney, London

Printed and bound in China

To Cilla

In memory of Nick Verey

CONTENTS

Introduction
So You're the Banker

⌒

"So you're the banker?" said the Deputy Prime Minister as we shook hands.

It was the end of a difficult meeting and the observation was clearly not a compliment.

I was absolutely stumped for an answer. "Yes," I began, easily enough, and paused. What on earth was it appropriate to say next?

John Prescott, the Deputy Prime Minister, was responsible for the UK transport portfolio, among other responsibilities, and I was one of a five-strong delegation asking him for more money to save the company which ran the railway service to the channel tunnel.

We had asked for a lot more money.

£1.2bn to be precise. Otherwise, as we had explained to him, the company could not afford to build the new high-speed line, as it had promised to do.

John Prescott was habitually treated as a figure of fun in the newspapers. Indeed, when he retired some nine years later, it was with an apology for an affair with his diary secretary which had been the subject of unrestrained joy in the media. At the time of our encounter, however, his political image had been shaped by nothing more then a tendency to mangle the grammar of his public utterances which strayed perilously close to buffoonery.

That evening in late January 1998 was the first time I had come face to face with the man and I had been rather impressed. He had subjected us to a careful and extended cross-examination, clearly understanding our answers despite their technical nature and following them up with precision. None of the sizeable entourage in his office had uttered a word through the whole process.

Admiration ran, however, very much second to the main emotions I was feeling - embarrassment and fear. The investment bank for which I worked had assembled a consortium to build a key piece of the country's infrastructure, the Channel Tunnel Railway Link. That consortium had won the concession to build the link by making promises about how it could raise finance in world markets. Now we were saying we had got our sums massively wrong.

I could just imagine the thoughts going through Prescott's head. For a politician whose instincts were decidedly suspicious of international capitalism, here was a prime example of why the private sector could not be trusted. We could not deliver our promises and now we were trying to hold the Government to ransom for an eye-watering amount of money. If he turned down our request, it was more than likely that the Government would have to abandon hopes to build the link at all for the foreseeable future. It must have seemed a combination of incompetence and malevolence to confirm every left-wing prejudice.

I was the person at my investment bank responsible for the project, with the job of advising the company. As such, I hardly represented an advertisement for the effectiveness of financial experts. Indeed, should Prescott decide against helping us, he would inevitably need to blame someone. He would turn the full fury of a vengeful Government against both me personally and my bank at this evaporation of the financing we had said would be available. I expected to be personally vilified to an extent that would make it impossible to continue my career.

After the interrogation we had been sent out of Prescott's office so that he could discuss the decision with his officials. We waited in a side-room with growing apprehension as the minutes ticked by. At last we were summoned back.

It was bad news.

"We would have liked to provide support," Prescott said, "but the amount of shortfall involved is simply too great. It's too much. We can't do it."

With that, abruptly, the meeting was over. All hell would surely break loose in the days to come.

His parting courtesy as he shook my hand with a somewhat calculating look was therefore hardly a neutral pleasantry: "So you're the banker?"

"Yes."

Suddenly I knew what to add.

"Sorry."

I doubt if many six-word exchanges between strangers have been so packed with unspoken meaning.

In fact, Prescott's rejection was not as final as it seemed at the meeting. It sparked a period of frenzied manoeuvring which allowed the project to survive in a new form. The part we played in effecting this reorganisation meant we avoided the looming repercussions. Indeed, far from destroying my career, as seemed likely on that late January night, the Channel Tunnel Railway Link was to provide it with a very substantial boost. The experience demonstrated, not for the first time, how thin can be the dividing line between success and failure when one operates in the financial markets.

My education in walking this particular tightrope had begun 14 years earlier, in 1984, when I abandoned my career as a financial journalist and joined one of the leading brokers in the London stock market. Little did I know it, but my timing was highly fortuitous. When I made my career switch, the London markets were essentially a series of specialist domestic enterprises, each dominated by a distinct and inbred coterie of niche players. Twenty years later, when I retired at the end of 2003, London was one of the core locations of a unified global financial system, its institutions incorporated into giant financial conglomerates with interests across a series of markets right around the world. Market activity had exploded in volume and nature, while the separate domestic markets had been dragged – often brutally – into an international system. By luck rather than judgement, I found myself again and again at the cutting edge of where these transformations took place.

The inspiration for this book is a profile that a shrewd financial journalist, Alistair Osborne, wrote about me in the Daily Telegraph when I retired. He played the piece for laughs, based on a series of anecdotes that I had reeled off when he interviewed me. It occurred to me that I could write the story of my experience focused on the humour and the drama, with the aim of showing what it felt like to work in the London financial markets as the global revolution took place. I wanted to write something that was accessible to the general reader, not solely the financial specialists (most of whom don't have much time to read anyway). I also felt that the experience had been so interesting that, as a former working journalist for 11 years, it would have been almost sinful to have closed the door without doing my best to leave a record.

I was a somewhat unlikely recruit to the City. My parents were both immigrants. My father lived in Vienna till Germany invaded Austria in 1938 and only escaped because he was the grandson of Sigmund Freud, the inventor of psycho-analysis, and could accompany him out of the country. He met my mother after the war, in her home town of Copenhagen, when he was working as a British army officer in the War Crimes Commission. They settled down in the UK, his adopted country, where he pursued a career as a chemical engineer. I was the first of three children and was brought up, conventionally enough, as an English middle-class aspirant, educated at Whitgift, the public day school in nearby South Croydon. However, possibly because of my origins, I always retained a streak of stubborn rebelliousness. I was suspicious of authority, irreverent and cocky, all the hallmarks of an outsider. Short, dark-haired and bespectacled, I was also extremely self-confident – not to say over-confident – and I enjoyed nothing more than working out what was wrong with the conventional and trying to improve on it. By the time I was fourteen I had decided that I wanted to be a journalist, a job tailor-made for the critical approach of the loner. Somewhat to my surprise, since I had been a disappointing scholar till I was fifteen, I won a place at Oxford University, where I studied mainly politics, and from which it was relatively straightforward to win one of the few journalistic training places for graduates. By accident, almost, I subsequently joined the Financial Times, the newspaper that was written for market professionals. In my last four years on the paper I was working in the team that prepared its heartbeat product, the daily commentary on developments in the financial markets, called the Lex Column. This was my sole education in finance, and while I had not received an academic training in financial theory, there was little to rival the breadth of coverage and access to experts across the market that I enjoyed in those years.

This, then, was my intellectual equipment when I started working for a City firm just as the global revolution took off. Over the twenty years of my experience, I was to see a complete transformation in how I worked and who I worked for. By the end of the 1990s I found myself, rather to my surprise, running a large and successful team which operated right around the world.

Success brought rewards in terms of title – I was promoted to vice chairman of the investment banking department – as well as pay. It did not really change how I thought of myself or how I operated. I still lived in the house in Highgate I had bought as a journalist; I still cycled to work (when I wasn't catching some dawn flight from Heathrow); I still wore off-the-peg suits from Marks & Spencer (to my secretary's amusement). I was still seen, I suspect, as eccentric.

Any book on the financial markets must, inevitably, contain some financial concepts. The language in which these are expressed is, like the jargon in all specialist professions, designed to mystify the outsider. For this period the terms used are doubly difficult to understand, because the meanings changed over the two decades, reflecting the transformation that was taking place. The confusion covers my basic job description as well as the type of institution I worked for.

My initial title of broker rapidly became submerged as my employer broadened its activity in the share market to become a securities house. The group, however, also touted for business from companies and Governments and had a department that managed investments for these bodies; so it became labelled an investment bank. Since I was marketing for the business of companies, I was then described as a corporate financier. However, this term went out of favour, since it implied I wasn't interested in Government work (hardly an optimal marketing stance during the privatisation boom). The usual substitute became investment banker, often shortened to banker, which had nothing to do with working for a commercial lending bank. That is what Prescott meant when he categorised me as 'the banker' for the Channel Tunnel Railway Link transaction. The overlap between the name of the giant financial corporations that now dominate the world's markets – the investment banks – and the executives who work for a particular division within those companies – the investment bankers – is one of many linguistic quirks that remain.

The regular takeover activity also resulted in a series of name changes. Even though I stayed with the same firm, I worked under no fewer than eight different corporate titles – from Rowe & Pitman to S.G.Warburg to UBS. Nor was my own company particularly unusual. Most financial organisations were juggling their nomenclature with similar aplomb. In this book I tend to call the company at which I worked 'Warburg' through the whole period, except where the specific name is relevant, to allow readers some relief.

I have confined my account in the main to what I experienced myself. Events are depicted as they appeared at the time, although I have taken the liberty of incorporating afterthoughts, reflecting information I learned later. The one period in which I have expanded this brief was that dealing with the collapse of Warburg, where I have interviewed many of the participants to build up a picture of what really happened. Otherwise, since the decision to write the book was something of an afterthought and I had not kept a diary, I have relied on my notebooks and appointment diaries, as well as notes made after meetings. In the interests of continuity I have divided the chapters by the main themes that dominated each particular period, rather than providing a strictly chronological account.

Finally, to maintain the immediacy of the experience, I have used direct speech, wherever I remember it. Many of the quotations are extraordinarily vivid and I can still picture the speaker's expression as well as their words. However, I have not relied on my own memory alone, but have painstakingly reverted to the speakers wherever possible. Most of the quotes have been cross-referred to the speakers for comment and in the bulk of cases they have accepted that this is what they said, in substance and spirit if not in exact phraseology. Indeed, the main effect of my cross-checking has been for speakers to request that their expletives (usually acknowledged) are toned down, so the language in the book is a little less colourful than it actually was.

ACKNOWLEDGEMENTS

I am extremely grateful to all my former colleagues, who gave so freely of their time, both to correct my own memory and to let me know the things that were happening of which I was unaware. I was also generously helped by bankers from rival institutions and by former clients.

Among the former colleagues, I have leant heavily on insights and information from, in no particular order, Sir David Scholey, Lord Cairns, Bob Boas, Stuart Stradling, Maurice Thompson, Rodney Ward, Michael Cohrs, Ken Costa, Robert Jennings, Robert Gillespie, Piers von Simson, Nick Wakefield, John Littlewood, Peter Wilmot-Sitwell, Chris Reilly, Sir Derek Higgs, Mark Nicholls, Richard Holloway, George Feiger, Robin Budenberg and Colin Buchan. At Mercury Asset Management, I am grateful to Peter Stormonth Darling, Stephen Zimmerman, Carol Galley, Andrew Dalton and Leonard Licht. Other colleagues who helped me were Anthony Brooke, Phil Raper, Tom Cooper, Lucinda Riches, James Garvin, Wyn Ellis, Peter Twatchmann, James Sassoon, Chris Brodie, Andrew Barker, Jason Katz, Stephen Paine, Sebastian Bull, David Hobley, Tom Hill, Raymond Maguire, Paul Hamilton, Erling Astrup, Peter Hardy, Michael Gore, David Charters, Nick Hughes,

Miko Giedroyc, Ian Dembinski, Sara Shipp, John Goodwin and Freddy Taggart. Among clients, 'rivals' and other contacts, I need to thank Peter Ratzer, Sir Steve Robson, Gerald Corbett, Richard Lambert, Derek Stephens, David Pascall, Gerry Grimstone, Gary Wilson, Lord Marshall, Bob Ayling, Joe Perella, Steve Waters, Phil Duff, Jon Foulds, Adam Mills, Sir Derek Hornby, Rob Holden, Rudolph Agnew, Dinah Verey, Sir Bruce MacPhail, Klaus Zumwinkel, Edgar Ernst, Martin Ziegenbalg, Karl Kley, Wulf Bernotat, Michael McGee, Roy Griffins and Carinna Radford. Ricard Anguera was kind enough to cast an eye over my Eurotunnel figures, while Francis Ronnau-Bradbeer at Precise-Media was assiduous in turning up obscure cuttings.

I also owe a debt to a third group of 'non-professionals', who were kind enough to read the text for sense to the general reader. I am particularly grateful to Jocelyn Ferguson, William Winter, James and John Illman and my cousin, George Loewenstein. I am indebted to Rachael Davenhill for the title of the book. Alan Ogden was an incisive editor; Anthony Weldon an inspiring publisher.

I profoundly regret being unable to verify in person my conversations with Nick Verey and Sir Alastair Morton, both of whom are now dead. Where possible I have double checked with another person present; I have tried my best not to abuse their inability to reply.

February 2006

1

An Accidental Career in the City

Recruitment into the City – 1983 -1984

"Are yo

"Yes," ou?"

The uestion. "Can you talk freely?" h

"Yes,

"My ive search agency MSL and I am City institution which would li with you. Are you interested

It w working as a journalist on the red newspaper which concentrated on matters of interest to businessmen round the world and to those working in the financial markets of the City of London. I had received job offers from City firms before, but not from a head-hunter, which certainly made the approach more flattering.

Tim Neame must have found the pause before I replied peculiarly extended. Was I interested in working for a City firm? My life flashed briefly before my eyes. How on earth had I arrived at this possibility?

"Yes," I said finally and made the first step towards a radical change of career.

I had never intended to go into the City. From childhood it had seemed an alien place full of establishment figures and norms concentrating on the sordid business of making money.

Early in my teens I had decided I wanted to be a journalist and, after the Guardian published an article[1] I wrote in my gap-year in 1968 before I started at Oxford University, specifically a Guardian journalist; certainly not a financial journalist, for which I had poor credentials. At Oxford I read Philosophy, Politics and Economics, but my grasp of calculus was so shaky that I dropped the Economics after the first year (having failed the initial exam, Prelims, first time round with an unambiguous nought in the two maths questions). After Oxford, with a rather more successful result in Finals, I became in 1972 a Thomson graduate trainee in journalism, learning my trade at the Western Mail in Cardiff, a newspaper that somewhat grandly called itself The National Newspaper of Wales. I was there for three years, the period for which it was then obligatory to complete one's indentures in the provinces before applying to a national newspaper.

Timing is all, and in my case I could not have chosen a worse moment to complete my training. By 1975 the UK was in full-blown recession, following Edward Heath's three-day week and the oil shock of the previous year. My job interview with the Guardian was cancelled when the newspaper announced the closure of the Manchester newsroom. "Regrettably, we will need to re-absorb these journalists into the London office before we can recruit from outside," I was told. Nor was the story any more encouraging from the other traditional Fleet Street newspapers to whose offices I laid epistolary siege.

The only expanding newspaper was the Financial Times and they needed sub-editors, journalists who tidied up, cut to length and headlined copy provided by the correspondents. At my interview, the editor, Fredy Fisher, told me that my stint as a sub-editor would last for two years before release – a promise he kept. In 1978 I was moved to reporting on developments in industry before I was told, to my surprise and no small consternation, that my next assignment was as the deputy economics correspondent. Luckily mathematical expertise for this job did not require more than a facility with percentages, so I rather enjoyed my stint there. I was able to write a series of features on topics as diverse as employment and poverty, the black economy and tax avoidance.

Then the bombshell; I was to transfer to the Lex Column. This was the intellectual heart of the Financial Times, a column that judged the impact of financial developments on companies and markets. It was opinionated, witty and perceptive. I had no problem with this in stylistic terms; my problem was that I had not the first idea about finance.

On the first morning, in November 1979, I was welcomed by Richard Lambert and Barry Riley, who together ran the column. "You can sit over there," said Richard. "I'll think of something for you to write for today." Richard was a tall, sprawling man with a shock of sandy ruffled hair and a shirt-tail invariably hanging outside his trousers. Towards junior journalists he presented a disconcerting combination of diffidence and authority. Some 12 years later he went on to become the editor of the newspaper and subsequently, in 2003, a member of the UK's interest-rate setting body, the Monetary Policy Committee.

I found a desk and typewriter. "I'm a little shaky on financial analysis," I told him: one of the great understatements. But I didn't have long to wait before Richard had my topic. "Why don't you do a piece on how the Amsterdam Traded Options Exchange is doing? It'll be fascinating. Make it a decent length, say 350 words; subject needs a bit of depth. Deadline, 6.30pm."

I went back to my typewriter. As tests went, this seemed comparable with the more awkward Labours of Hercules – collecting Cerberus from the Underworld, for instance. First I had to work out what on earth a traded option was. Once I had struggled to a rough understanding of this instrument, it was rather more straight-forward to grasp the competitive position of the exchange itself. A few calls to the Netherlands gave me the story; volume at the exchange was lamentable and break-even was still way off. At 6.30pm I had the 350 words. Richard read the copy through. "Fine", he said. "Fascinating. We're full for tonight's column. We'll use it Monday[2] ."

That first day was an invaluable lesson. I had learned that any topic that Richard did not want to write about himself, given his abounding enthusiasm, was inevitably complex and a straight-forward conclusion would be difficult to reach. In my four years on Lex thereafter I always made sure I had a topic of my own to cover

3

rather than waiting for one from him – or one of his successors.

The team on Lex was then made up of four journalists, who had to fill a column of about 1,000 words. It doesn't sound much, 250 words each, but great compression was required. I would come in at about 11.00am each morning, research the topic to be written about, and by mid-afternoon I would need to know enough about the subject to write an extended feature. From about 5.30pm I would start to distil all this information into a succinct, punchy comment. As a journalist one needed to build from a base of accurate analysis to develop an angle that had not been written before. In the early months my lack of knowledge of the financial markets made it a genuine struggle. I was constantly nervous of making an elementary mistake from which all the fancy writing in the world would not protect me from being ridiculed on publication the next morning.

There was plenty of help. A whole industry had built up to assess the significance of company and other business developments. Stockbrokers made a living by encouraging their clients to trade shares. By the late 1970s, several of the larger brokers had built up research departments consisting of analysts who would research why a particular company's shares should be bought or sold. This research would be used by the sales-force maintained by each broker to persuade their clients to trade – and place their orders with them. So whatever the topic, I could ring up the acknowledged experts and they would invariably be keen to pass on their analysis. This was hardly surprising. If, for instance, a stockbroking analyst was telling his clients that a particular company was cheap and worth buying, his credibility would be reinforced if Lex echoed his views. In practice, the main difficulty was disentangling all the conflicting arguments at the end of the day.

Gradually, as familiarity grew, the job got easier. We covered an enormous amount of ground and would switch the subject matter about. One week I would be commenting on how all the banks were performing as the main UK clearers reported their results for the latest half-year. As the early Thatcher recession bit, I would record its impact on the hard-pressed engineering sector. Later, as I grew in confidence, I was able to pick up the annual report of the UK computer company ICL and work out that it was going bust, a note that was headlined 'Computing ICL's cash drain'[3] . I wrote about pharmaceuticals one day, property the next and retail stores the day after. At this stage there was relatively little interest in financial developments abroad, even though the FT had launched a European edition in 1979. In financial terms, Continental Europe was regarded as something of a vacuum. However, as far as UK developments were concerned, I covered takeovers, company flotations and monetary policy – I wrote about every sector, virtually every large company, during my four-year stint.

There were two by-products of this experience. The first was that I got to know a wide range of people in the financial and corporate world. The second was that I had received a broad education in financial issues, the equivalent of attending a Business School and doing an MBA. It was this latter asset that was to draw me into the City, because by 1983 the firms in the City found themselves critically short of trained personnel and were attempting to recruit anyone with remotely relevant experience.

How had the City got itself into this pickle? The roots went back to the mid-1970s. At the time I found it impossible to get a job in Fleet Street, the markets were in a desperate state. The 1972 bull market had turned into a savage bust over the next two and a half years as a combination of the oil shock, the Conservative Government's losing confrontation with the miners, burgeoning inflation and the secondary banking crisis precipitated the worst-ever decline in the stock market. By early January 1975 the FT Index had fallen 73% from its peak in May 1972. People still described the experience in terms reminiscent of the Black Death.

One of my school-friends had gone into the stockbroking firm James Capel in 1972. "It was dreadful," he told me. "There was simply nothing to do. There were no orders, no transactions, no activity. We trainees sat around day after day playing shove-ha'penny.

"The firm held on to us as long as they could, but in the end their nerve snapped and all four of us were fired." He went off to get his articles and became a solicitor. Nothing would induce him back to the City. It was a common experience. The most reliable estimate for employment in this period is provided by John Littlewood (who appears in person later in the chapter). His researches show that the number of people who worked for the stock-market related firms in the UK (most of them in the City) more than halved from the 35,000 peak[4] in May 1972. Indeed, such was the trauma that the numbers went on declining for two years after a sharp recovery, hitting the lowest point of 16,200 as late as February 1977. A young partner described his experience in 1974 to me. "I made partner at the beginning of the year, after a decade's hard slog. I remember going out to celebrate with my wife that evening and discussing buying a better house on all the earnings we were going to make. I told her we would have to wait a bit, because as a partner I did not get a monthly salary any more, but was paid a share of the earnings at year-end.

"Unfortunately, for 1974 all the partners had to take a share of the losses, which meant I had to borrow money from the bank to pay in my share. After that experience I, and my colleagues, were pretty careful about putting on extra costs, I can tell you."

The personal liability inherent in the partnership structure imposed by Stock Exchange rules meant that by 1983 the number working for the stockbroking firms had risen only modestly – even though the value of the shares quoted on the market had increased more than 10 times. And now, as the 1980s progressed, another challenge loomed: Big Bang.

In July 1983 the Stock Exchange had accepted that its system of fixed prices for trading shares would have to go. It was either that or face a legal challenge for restrictive practices. The move, which would come into effect over the next three years, was widely expected to have a similar impact on activity in the City as that seen when the financial markets of New York were liberalised in 1975. Since that transformation, known as May Day, employment had soared. New York, a city on the skids, had regained its dynamism.

So it was not surprising that a trained Lex writer got the occasional call. The first was from Alan Kelsey at a mid-ranking stockbroker picturesquely called Kitcat & Aitken. Alan specialised in transport stocks and he invited me round to lunch one day when we had finished our phone conversation on who would end up taking over P&O, one of the last quoted remnants of the British shipping industry.

The lunch was a full-blown assault. Alan had assembled five or six colleagues, who surrounded me enthusiastically. "You must come and work for us," he declared. "You'd have a wonderful time: lots of action; great colleagues; fun."

It seemed a bit vague. "What would I do if I worked for Kitcat?" I asked.

"Why, research. That's the game at the moment. All the institutions want to know what stocks they should be buying. We bone up the info and tell them. You can come and join my sector, transport. Always action there." I thought about it briefly and politely declined. There were no fewer than 40 stockbrokers among the contacts I used for writing my comments, and Kitcat was well down the list in terms of scale and impact. But the lunch certainly planted a seed, and I tried to learn more about the prospects of the various firms as Big Bang loomed.

Alongside the stockbrokers, the second group of member firms working within the Stock Exchange were the jobbers. I had very little direct contact with them on the Lex Column. Their sole function was to trade shares with the brokers. They would make a book in a series of companies' shares and move the price up and down so that the volume of buy orders matched the sell orders as closely as possible. This was a fairly technical job, in which it was easy to lose money and for which I suspected I would have little facility. Some of the best jobbers came from the East End of London, with street-market trading in their blood.

Outside the formal structure of the Stock Exchange were the merchant banks, with which I had much more to do. These were complex and highly-respected institutions, usually with long pedigrees, the nature of whose business changed with the markets. From origins managing trade finance in various forms they had moved on by the time I was writing Lex to specialising, in particular, in merger and acquisitions work. This was the business of advising companies how to take over other companies. The merchant banks had also muscled in on the business of raising money for companies. Although they could not communicate directly with investors about new shares (a prerogative of the stockbrokers), they could – and did – take responsibility for the prospectus that described those shares. Famous institutions like Rothschild and Barings were still in the top rank, although I found myself writing more about two relative newcomers, Morgan Grenfell and S.G.Warburg, which seemed to have emerged as the two highly competitive leaders of the takeover market.

The final group in the market I was writing about were the investors. These were no longer private individuals – who held less then 30%[5] of stocks by then. Collective investment dominated the market, in particular the pension funds that companies provided for their staffs. They were known as institutional investors, or the institutions for short. The funds employed professional managers to make sure that the investments were properly looked after. It was with these fund managers that the stockbroking sales desks maintained a day-by-day, hour-by-hour, dialogue.

The nature of stockbroking seemed most interesting to me at that time and one meeting in particular proved valuable. We had invited a team from the stockbroker Cazenove to one of our regular Lex lunches. Two partners showed up, in the shape of Mark Loveday and Charles Cazalet. Cazenove was a City legend, founded in 1823 and the leader in raising money for companies in the form of new shares. It was manned by the product of the major public schools and was extremely cautious in talking to the Press. On the Lex team, we did not know them well. We were puzzled at how they were going to survive when their share of everyday trading of shares was barely 2% of the total and they rarely bothered to publish research recommending investment strategies for their clients.

Mark was one of the partners responsible for liaising with the firm's corporate customers. He was unfazed by our questioning. "We're not interested in secondary trading for its own sake," he explained. "Our skill is placing shares with the investing institutions on behalf of companies. That way we stand in between the two groups. The companies need us to raise funds; the investing institutions need us to get access to new shares. We don't need research to trade with the investors. We know what stock they've got and their attitude to it, because we sold it to them in the first place."

Here, it occurred to me, lay the real position of power in the financial markets. I took a lot more interest in corporate broking thereafter. So I was immediately interested when Nick Verey called up from Cazenove's main rival, Rowe & Pitman, to introduce himself and tell us about the latest 'Dawn Raid' that the stockbroker had conducted.

"Well, it looks as if we've got the stock again," he told me. The 'Dawn Raid' was a Rowe & Pitman innovation by which they launched the takeover of a company with a concerted burst of stock buying from the institutions. "How long they will go on selling out to us, God only knows," Nick admitted. After all, it was more rational for the institutions to wait for the sign-posted takeover offer, which would inevitably come at a higher price. Indeed it was not long before the 'Dawn Raid' ceased to work for this precise reason.

Nevertheless, when Tim Neame, the head-hunter, told me that he was calling on behalf of Rowe & Pitman, I was instantly intrigued. "What job are they proposing?" I asked.

"Well it's somewhere between research and corporate finance. Tell you what, why don't you pop over to see Nick Verey, and he can explain it to you."

So a little later I turned up at the Stock Exchange tower, where Rowe & Pitman were based on the sixteenth floor. While I had spoken to Nick on the phone, it was the first time I had met him face to face. I took to him immediately. He was a tall, distinguished-looking man with an elegant head of greying hair despite being only 40. He had a relaxed style and a completely unpompous way of talking, delving into issues and engaging in genuine dialogue with real enthusiasm. After the opening pleasantries he got straight to what he wanted. "Here's the problem. We are summoned to a merchant bank, which has been working on a transaction for months. They explain it to us and want our view on how investors will respond, almost instantly and certainly within a day or two. Then we have to go into the market and sell the proposition the next morning. We're fine on general market sentiment and appetite. The trouble is, we don't have a clue how to judge complicated situations.

"Habitat was our worst puzzle. Two years ago we very successfully floated the company for Terence Conran. It was a specialist retailer with a real edge based on style and affordability. So when the company decided to take over Mothercare three months later we didn't know how the market would react. Would they think that the move from niche specialist to conglomerate retailer would spell disaster, or would they see Mothercare as another opportunity for Terence to work his retail magic? In fact, the deal fairly flew along, much to our relief. Next time we'd prefer to know in advance.

"So that's the job. We want you to research our corporate deals. We want you to be in a position to tell us how the investors are likely to react, to price the transactions and then to work out how to sell them in the market. Do you think you can do it?"

It was a good question. As a journalist I could rely on collecting all the views out of the marketplace before reaching a conclusion. With this job I would need to rely on my own knowledge and judgement. At that point the senior partner, Peter Wilmot-Sitwell, wandered into the room. He had a slightly hunched way of moving, as if he was preparing to plunge himself into a rugby scrum. He was affable and relaxed, prone to see the humour of every situation and to greet it with a short, appreciative laugh. Later I would see the steel behind the charm and the incredible support he would offer to a member of his firm when it was required. On this, first, occasion he chuckled as Nick reprised the Habitat Mothercare experience.

"They've gone on to buy half the High Street since," he observed, "Richard Shops, Heals.

"The markets can be very cruel. You price a deal wrong by a penny and you can be left with all the shares. If it's a penny cheap the shares go out the window and the price soars, leaving you looking ridiculously conservative."

So there it was. I didn't know whether I could do the job. Further, if I made a misjudgement it wouldn't be a matter of mild embarrassment over what I had written but full public humiliation, with a transaction collapsed around my neck and cascading losses all round.

It was irresistible.

"I think I can make the transition," I said, injecting an air of as much cautious confidence as I could muster. It wasn't for years that the extent of the risk that I (not to mention Rowe & Pitman) was impetuously prepared to take became apparent. Very few journalists in practice managed to establish themselves in the investment banks, as they emerged in the UK over the subsequent two decades. Since in my experience the average financial journalist was smarter than the average stockbroker or merchant banker, my only explanation rests on elementary psychology. The journalist absorbs and assesses information; a stockbroker or banker uses it to sell a proposition.

Meanwhile I was learning more about Rowe & Pitman. It was one of the three stockbrokers that specialised in corporate finance, running second to Cazenove and ahead of Hoare Govett. This triumvirate had developed in the post-war period, when the merchant banks had muscled their way into the business of issuing shares for their corporate clients. The 1948 Companies Act laid down that when a company wanted to issue a large number of shares, it needed to circulate a document to shareholders, or potential shareholders, detailing all the relevant information about itself. In the case of a company issuing shares for the first time, this document was called a prospectus; when further new shares were sold, a new issue document was required. The corporate stockbrokers' main responsibility was to arrange for the shares to be sub-underwritten by the institutional investors, so that if too few buyers turned up, the shares would still find a home, of sorts. Having seized the responsibility for preparing the documentation, the merchant banks had used the position to win the bulk of the fees. In the fixed commission world of the financial markets the banks generally took 0.5% for organising an issue of shares and taking on the primary underwriting risk. The brokers took half of that, or 0.25%, for selling on this risk by arranging for it to be sub-underwritten by the investing institutions. The compensation for the three main corporate brokers was that the business became increasingly concentrated into their hands. Nick was doubtful how long the structure would withstand the pressures of Big Bang.

"Merchant banks and stockbrokers are bound to get together. In fact you shouldn't be surprised if we've made some interesting moves in that direction by the time you find your desk." It was a heavy hint and I did not miss it. "Once they do, I don't see how merchant banks will be prepared to work with a broker which is part of a rival organisation." The analysis narrowed the options. For many of its clients, Rowe & Pitman worked in combination with Morgan Grenfell. Based on common relationships, Schroder Wagg was second in line. From my somewhat privileged vantage point on the Lex Column, talking to all the market participants, I thought that Cazenove would inevitably team up with S.G.Warburg, or possibly Kleinwort Benson, on the same logic.

"On the other hand we may start to claw back the ludicrous amount of the fee that goes to the merchant bankers for writing pretty descriptions."

When I returned a few days later to close, Nick had fleshed out the job description. "First of all you must be ready to value and sell any transaction we need your help on. Clearly in some of the areas we are building up specialist analysts, who should be able to do the job, but most of the action seems to take place in new areas, where we are uncovered. We particularly want you to concentrate on flotations in those new areas. For instance, we are broker to British Airways, which is planning to float in the next couple of years. By the time it does I want you to know everything about it. If a client asks about some problem on the South African route, you need to be able to address it.

"Finally, since we don't have a deal every day, we'd like you to look after a few sectors as a straight-forward analyst in your spare time. You can do the banks and other financial institutions, the transport companies and the leisure sector. You should aim to build up teams to help you.

"You'll report to me on corporate finance matters and Nick Whitney, our new head of research, on the every-day research."

I certainly wouldn't be under-employed.

Next I went to see John Littlewood, who ran the administration of the firm. This was the third of the senior partners I met at Rowe & Pitman before joining and his pedigree was very different to those of Nick and Peter. Both of them had gone to school at Eton – as indeed had most of the senior Rowe & Pitman partners – and showed all the self-confident charm and courtesy typical of this top public school's output. John Littlewood had attended a grammar school and his acceptance into the senior ranks of the firm probably owed a good deal to his Blue for golf at Oxford University, where he captained the team in 1959. He had been a pioneering research analyst, building a team covering insurance companies that was ranked the best in the City. Two years earlier he had switched into the administration role. He was intensely thorough and thought carefully before speaking. When he did, his response would invariably be both original and considered. He was to retire in 1991, and subsequently published a post-war history of the London stock market. His book, 'The Stock Market: 50 Years of Capitalism at Work', provides the best analysis of the institution I have seen (and from which I have drawn some of the data I have used on the Big Bang era).

All this was many years in the future. At our first meeting in October 1983, he set out the terms of employment. I told him how much I was earning as a journalist: £23,000 a year. He explained that Rowe & Pitman paid out a bonus. I was immediately suspicious.

"It was 40% of salary last year," he said, "and we expect it to remain at much the same level next year." I was startled to learn that it was paid in a lump sum in the spring, when the annual earnings had been established. For a unionised worker in the newspaper industry, it all seemed somewhat far-fetched.

"I don't trust the bonus," I said. "Just match the basic £23,000, and I'll take the bonus as it comes." Little did I know how central, how time-consuming, how divisive, the annual bonus would become in the years ahead. John was happy to concede the amount. He was much more worried about my membership of the National Union of Journalists. "We want to buy you out of all your writing roles. What will you do about the NUJ?"

"I'll leave, of course. Once I stop being a journalist I won't be able to keep my card anyway."

And with that, the deal was done. I had switched from journalism to the City at the same basic rate of pay (plus unspecified bonus).

While I worked out my notice at the Financial Times, the revolution in the stock market suddenly exploded.

"So why on earth are you buying a jobber?" I asked the merchant banker on the other end of the phone.

He prevaricated. "Well, with Big Bang in the London Stock Exchange, we'll be able to do all sorts of things together with them."

"Such as what?"

A long pause.

"All sorts of things," he repeated confidently, if unspecifically. I was speaking to Simon Cairns of S.G.Warburg, which had just announced plans to take over one of the two leading jobbers in the City, Akroyd & Smithers. Simon was head of the bank's corporate finance department, responsible for the transaction – and for talking about it to the press. As far as I was concerned, writing the Lex Column, he was not doing a desperately impressive job. It was November 1983, and the announcement by these two leading players in the market was major news. I wanted to explain the precise rationale in the column.

Simon was too wily, however, to provide anything of interest - or value - to rivals, so he adopted a lordly and practised air of vagueness to conceal the bank's strategies. In fact, S.G.Warburg had moved with great skill to snap up a scarce institutional resource. Jobbing was a risky business and the number of leading firms had fallen to a bare five by 1983, of which two were flattered by their placement in the 'leading' category. So, even though the merchant banks had no direct relationship with the jobbers, by taking over one of the two leaders, S.G.Warburg had booked its place in the post-Big Bang world and could pick up a suitable stockbroker at its leisure. On the Monday it was announced, I took out my frustration with a somewhat peevish Lex note, which took a side-swipe at Simon Cairns' vague noises about the synergies. The bank "is emphasising the potential benefit to its Eurobond operation, though why it needs Akroyd's help here is hard to fathom"[6].

Although I could not have known it at the time, Simon Cairns was to have a decisive influence on the course of my, and indeed many other people's, careers in the City. Another Old Etonian, he had specialised in development economics at Cambridge University before starting his City career in one of the broking houses, Scrimgeour. Here he had worked on one of the major transactions of the time, the sale of shares in BP in 1977, for which he was credited with creating a structure which allowed the sale to take place simultaneously in the US and UK. He switched over to Warburg in 1979 and became a driving force within that institution for creating an integrated house. Years later he told me: "The merchant bank didn't have a clue what it was selling, or who it was selling it to. The broking house couldn't offer first class service because it didn't have the corporate finance skills.

"I certainly wasn't going to give any of our strategy away to our competitors through Lex."

I worked my notice through till the end of the year and took a skiing holiday to St Moritz and Davos ahead of the 30 January start date. While I was in Davos, Nick's hint took public form. I read in a borrowed copy of the FT that the Rowe & Pitman partners had, indeed, made a corporate move. They had sold 29.9% of the firm to the mining group Charter Consolidated, which clearly represented a purely financial deal. More significantly, they had set up a joint venture called Rowak with the broker Akroyd & Smithers, to trade international equities. This threw them straight into the ambit of S.G.Warburg, which had agreed to buy Akroyd. I was mildly surprised that Rowe & Pitman was veering towards Warburg rather than Morgan Grenfell.

However, the announcement did not catch me completely by surprise. During the recent round of Christmas drinks parties, I had run into Richard Webb, one of the directors of Morgan Grenfell. I had asked him how they were planning to respond to Warburg's aggression in teaming up with Akroyd, and which stockbroker they were in talks with. He looked at me confidently. "You know, when everyone is rushing around doing deals at breakneck speed it's incredibly easy to get caught up in the rush and do something one will regret. Perhaps the brave thing to do right now, is to do nothing." I did not know it at the time, but desultory feelers between Morgan Grenfell and Rowe & Pitman had recently come to nothing, as the stockbrokers realised that Morgan had no intention of paying up.

"They weren't even in the ballpark on price," Peter Wilmot-Sitwell, the senior partner who had held the meeting, told me later. "They were very grand. They told me they would take us over and sort us out."

Similarly, S. G.Warburg had got nowhere with the stockbroker with whom it shared most clients, Cazenove, whose partners were determined to remain independent. In the months ahead Akroyd, I learned later, became a matchmaker for a deal between Warburg and Rowe & Pitman, since contacts between these two firms were sparse. "We told the Warburg guys, why don't you go for them? They're a good firm, top quality operation," one of the directors at Akroyd described later. And that is exactly what S.G.Warburg did, the deal being announced the following August. Indeed, while many in Rowe & Pitman did not immediately accept the implications of the Rowak deal, to me, still then an outsider, it looked inevitable. So, as I prepared to join the City, it looked as if my employer would be powerfully positioned in the markets, combining a leading merchant bank, jobber and broker. I skied the gentle 10-mile run down to Kublis that Tuesday afternoon with the smugness of those who experience unplanned good fortune.

As for Morgan Grenfell, they did not stay brave for long. In the New Year their nerve broke and they started to look for vehicles with which to operate in the markets. But by then they were too late and all they could find were some scraps. In April they bought a small jobber, Pinchin Denny, to which they added Pember & Boyle, a second-tier broker specialising in trading not company shares but the very different business of Government fixed interest stock.

My first morning was the normal blur of administrative activity; documents to sign, P60 tax forms to hand over. I was shown the trading area, taking over half the floor in the Stock Exchange tower. The salesmen were working the phones with their investment clients. My own desk was down a corridor from this area at the end of a rectangular office that housed about 12 research analysts. By 12.30pm I was clear of the greetings and chores and returned to my desk. It was bare. By now, in my old job I would be well on the way to getting my teeth into some controversy or issue. What was I to do here? I felt a moment of despair.

Luckily Nick Whitney, the head of research, was taking me out to lunch. We went downstairs to a noisy, crowded bar on the first floor of the Stock Exchange. It was full of ebullient stockbrokers off the floor of the exchange, and Nick filled me in on his plans for transforming Rowe & Pitman's also-ran research position.

When I returned there was a file on British Airways sitting on my desk. I picked it up and started to read through the background material.

I never managed to clear my desk again.

---

[1] Beer and Hash at Leo's Place, The Guardian, 21 December, 1968

[2] European options, The Lex Column, Financial Times, 12 November, 1979

[3] Computing ICL's cash drain, The Lex Column, Financial Times, 9 January, 1981

[4] The Stock Market:50 Years of Capitalism at Work, by John Littlewood, Financial Times Pitman Publishing, 1998. p 267

[5] Ibid p442

[6] Akroyd moves into Mercury's orbit, the Lex Column, The Financial Times, 15 November, 1983

2

Equity is funny stuff

Learning the trade – 1984 - 1986

~

"What the fuck do you think you're doing?" exploded one of my new colleagues. Paul Hamilton worked in Rowe & Pitman's small corporate broking office, and I had put my head round the door to let him know the outcome of a telephone conversation. They were the first words he had directed at me apart from the polite generalities exchanged on my introductory tour of the office earlier in the week. "What the hell do you think you're doing, talking to McDonald? What right do you have to talk to him?"

I grovelled reluctantly. "I didn't know you had visited him last week," I explained. "It was just a check, that's all."

On my ski break in Switzerland I had been alerted by a northern acquaintance to a fast-growing private company called Polypipe, run by Kevin McDonald, based in Doncaster. "He's really going somewhere, that guy. You should put in a call. Here's his number; let him know I recommended you should get in touch."

It sounded an extremely long shot. Nevertheless I put in the call and found it surprisingly easy to get through. Kevin McDonald was extremely friendly as I started to introduce myself and explain the reason for the call. Suddenly there was a long pause. "Are you a colleague of Paul Hamilton?" he asked. I said that I thought I was, but did not yet really know him.

"This is most embarrassing," he confessed. "Paul and a colleague were up here last week to discuss running our flotation on the London Stock Exchange. I was just about to ring him to explain that we had decided to use some-one else." There was not much more to be said. My northern friend had certainly alerted me to a live prospect; unfortunately rather too live and, indeed, a little too late.

So this hardly represented the smoothest of introductions to Rowe & Pitman's corporate broking department. I had broken one of the cardinal rules of operating in the City, which was to respect one's colleagues' contacts, and I had become the classic bearer of bad news to boot. When Paul's fury had subsided enough I explained that I had no idea that Polypipe's plans were so immediate and that I had only intended to do a little long-range reconnaissance. Ironically, this was the only time I can remember the essentially good-natured Paul Hamilton losing his temper with me, or indeed anyone else, for the next 19 years. Paul was six years older than me and had been working his way steadily up the hierarchy of the firm to stand on the threshold of a partnership. Infuriating him was not a good start in a job meant to combine corporate activity with research. I would be regarded with deep suspicion by the whole department for months thereafter as a direct result.

The Rowe & Pitman I joined was changing under my eyes from an old-fashioned partnership to the core securities division of a newly-created investment bank. Indeed, I represented some of the new blood imported to allow the transformation to be made. Not surprisingly I, and the other newcomers, were regarded with deep suspicion by the older partners, who could see their roles withering away over the next couple of years.

For two and a half more years, till the formal date of Big Bang in October 1986, broking was to remain essentially unchanged. In Rowe & Pitman the heart of the operation was represented by an open-plan floor full of salesmen calling up fund managers who ran money for institutions such as the pension funds, insurance companies and unit trusts. Each salesman would have a list of perhaps 10 clients whom he would call several times a day. Most of the time they would be discussing the pros and cons of buying or selling particular stocks. Every now and then they would call about a larger transaction.

As a corporate stockbroker, Rowe & Pitman was regularly called on to sell blocks of shares worth tens or even hundreds of millions of pounds. These placements, as they were called, could be fraught affairs with each salesman working his client list to achieve the target. If the deal was on a knife-edge, a passive recipient of the stock could make all the difference.

"You'd always know when it was tight, because you'd hear the call: 'Let's stuff the Nannies'," Peter Wilmot-Sitwell recalled later. "The Nannies (the Royal National Pension Fund for Nurses) did very well out of it. The call would go up that all the stock had been placed and the share price would immediately go up. They made a fortune." The sales floor – with salesmen each facing a bank of telephone lights – was a relatively recent introduction.

"Until a few years ago we all sat out in the main room with the salesmen," Nick Verey, my new boss, explained to me early on. "But now we share this office." He was describing the room in which the four most senior partners sat. They were responsible for the other key set of relationships, with the most important companies for whom Rowe & Pitman acted as stockbroker and the merchant banks that generally awarded these roles. "There's just too much sensitive information being dealt with to risk the salesmen knowing."

The corporate broking department, of which Paul Hamilton was a member, was also a fairly recent development. "The rules and regulations for companies on the London Stock Exchange have grown like topsy," explained Nick. "So now we need a team of specialists to tell companies what they are." In early 1984 the team numbered five and was run by Stuart Stradling. They were experts on the 'Yellow Book' – the Stock Exchange rule book which laid down what information quoted companies should tell the marketplace, when directors could deal in shares on their own account and a myriad of other requirements. In practice the team conducted much of the day-by-day relationship with the companies, as they arranged to put out announcements and discussed what should be in them. And, not unnaturally, Stuart Stradling increasingly came to regard his team as the main corporate link with the companies, with a role extending well beyond the provision of purely technical assistance. Here lay a potent source of rivalry with Nick Verey who, sitting in the partners' room, was wedded to the coverage model of senior partner supported by a 'technician'. My position as Nick Verey's recruit was, accordingly, reason for the team to look on me with the greatest suspicion, regardless of my unfortunate contretemps with Paul.

Nick Verey believed that the best way to become close to a company was to understand its business. "If you understand what makes them tick, you can explain it to the investors," he told me. "That's much more important than instructing them that they have to put out a circular to shareholders when they take over a company of a certain size." Accordingly we set off on a tour of the companies that fell within my research remit, both quoted and those looking to become quoted.

First off was a visit to Britannia Arrow, where Nick introduced me to Stuart Goldsmith, the chief executive. This was a company for which Rowe & Pitman acted as stockbroker.

"This is a fabulous business," Stuart Goldsmith told me. "We are sitting on a savings boom and money is pouring in." Britannia Arrow was originally part of the Slater Walker empire, that go-go conglomerate of the early 1970s boom which came to grief in the secondary banking crisis of 1975. The business about which Stuart was so enthusiastic was fund management, particularly of its unit trusts. "Every time we sell a unit trust we collect an upfront charge, and we've just raised the charge from 5% to 5.25%. Straight profit."

Afterwards I said to Nick, "I think I know the topic of my first research piece. I'll do it on the fund managers. There are seven quoted companies; four have come to market over the last year; no one's covered them." And so I set out to put together a piece on the fund managers.

Initially I covered only five of the companies, gathering my material by going to see the finance directors. I concluded that they were all cheap, because of the savings boom, but working out how they were valued relative to each other was a puzzle. I needed to build a picture of the different types of funds that they specialised in – unit trusts, investment trusts, pension funds, or foreign funds of one kind or another. I decided to value each type of fund by running an equation of each company's fund mix against the other companies' mixes.

But how – against a tight print deadline and moving share prices?

When I first joined Rowe & Pitman, I had insisted on having a computer. I got my way, up to a point, and was allocated a terminal off the mainframe used by the fixed interest department. At least I could use this for basic word-processing but it would be a major production to try and run my equations through it. In the end I sat down with a paper and pencil one evening in May when the market had closed and worked through the sums with a calculator. It took several hours. There was no way to print this overnight, so it only went out to the investment managers – ironically in this case several of the very same people whom I was writing about – a day later. Within a couple of years, as computers became ubiquitous, it would have been the matter of a few moments to input the share prices into a prepared spread sheet and churn out the answers.

What would the Rowe & Pitman salesmen make of this research? Every morning at 9.00am the research analysts would stand up and present them with a series of two-to-three minute presentations on why a stock or a sector of the market should be bought or sold by fund managers. The salesmen would pick and choose which idea to present to which fund manager on their list – or indeed any ideas of their own they might have. It was a relaxed system that made Nick Whitney, the head of research and my other boss, furious. "There shouldn't be any choice about it," he would fulminate. "The salesmen should just sell the product. If you're a Coca Cola salesman you sell Coca Cola. You don't sell Pepsi."

I used to enjoy strolling round the salesroom and listening to the different techniques. My favourite was employed by one of the more senior salesmen. He would nestle the phone on his shoulder and cover his mouth conspiratorially. "I can't go into this in any detail for obvious reasons," he would mutter to his client, "but you really should make sure you pick up a few 'company x'." The completely bogus implication that he had picked up a trace of inside information was often irresistible to the fund manager on the other end of the phone.

For a more substantial piece of research, such as my 'Fund Management comes of age', which was all of 35 pages long and dressed up in Rowe & Pitman's light blue cardboard covers, the research analyst would brief the sales team the afternoon before launch. So on 23 May we found a meeting room and I took the twenty-strong team through it. Although it was an extremely small sector, the subject matter meant that the salesmen were fascinated and wanted an extremely detailed explanation. The next morning they would, after all, be telling their clients about their own industry, so they would need to be on top of the topic. Indeed, while very little trading was done on the next day, because the total value of the stock quoted in the five companies was less than £300m, I gained considerable credibility with both the sales-force and their clients.

I learned one other lesson from my coverage of this sector. After publication Britannia Arrow produced a poor set of figures for the first six months of the year. Stuart Goldsmith, the chief executive, sat across the desk from me poring over his budget figures for the full year. "You've got to pull your forecast down to £12.4m or so," he told me.

"You'll make much more than that," I argued. Fund management was one of those rare industries in which one could derive the profits of a company by making some fairly simple assumptions about growth and stock market performance.

"Not according to these figures," he said.

Grudgingly I pulled down my forecast. Grudgingly, because the closeness of an analyst's profit forecast to the outcome was one of the main measures of his competence, and my figures were much higher than those in Stuart's budget. However, we were the broker to the company and I could see there would be a row if I held firm. So in the November follow-up research my forecast was pulled down to £12.4m, though I inserted a firm caveat: "Britannia's unit trust operation is highly geared and two good closing months to the year could boost the expected outcome by £1.5m." The actual outcome, inevitably, exceeded even my caveated forecast. This was my first taste of the tension between providing accurate advice for investors and acting for companies as their broker. Company executives were often keen to use the 'house' broker analysts to put out modest profit forecasts so that the announced figures would 'please the market'. Even worse were the occasions when they were keen to keep the 'house' analyst at unrealistically high levels in order to fend off an admission of poor performance for as long as possible. In practice the analysts would get round the problem by publishing the official line in their research documents but tell their investment clients and the salesmen what they really thought on the phone. The tension would intensify as the Warburg group came together as a full-service investment bank.

The big stocks in the financial sector were the banks. Here the competition from long-established research analysts was intense, especially as they were concentrating their efforts on the sector and I was dipping in and out. My first success came during a conversation about one of the banks with a young, formidable, fund manager from Morgan Grenfell, John Armitage. "Right," he said abruptly. "Price and size." I could tell this was a sign-off of some kind and ran round to the sales-floor for urgent help.

"George," I asked the ever-helpful head salesman, George Pilkington, "what do I do now?"

"Well, we'll have to get price and size, won't we?" George flipped a switch to open a line to our box down below, a small office alongside the stock exchange trading floor. "Tom, could we have price and size in Barclays," he called out. That was the signal for one of our team to cross the floor to the jobbing pitches and ask the same question. The jobber would not know whether our client wanted to buy or sell and quoted a wider price for a larger volume. A minute or two later the broker downstairs called up through the open line. "50 to 60 in a 100, a point out in a quarter". This meant the jobber would buy up to 100,000 shares at 350p each and sell the same amount for 360p. If the client wanted 250,000 shares it would cost him a penny more, or 361p. If our client was a seller he would only get 349p.

I went back to John Armitage with the information and got an order to sell 100,000 Barclays. A few minutes later the floor broker called up to let us know that the deal had gone through. George then copied it down onto his dealing sheet to record the transaction and I let John Armitage know that he no longer owned his Barclays shares.

But I was a million miles from becoming a real bank analyst. Then I received an enormous fillip from, of all people, the Chancellor of the Exchequer, Nigel Lawson. His 1984 Budget speech on 13

March cut the rate of Corporation Tax from 52% to 35%. It was enough to set the stock market surging to record highs as he spoke. Less remarked on, because much more complicated, was another change to Corporation Tax: a transformation of capital allowances. No longer would companies be able to offset all their investment costs against taxable profits in the first year; within three years the amount would reduce to a quarter. On the day the market ignored this technicalia.

However, I leapt like a scalded cat. "This is a disaster for the banks," I called out to anyone on the sales floor who cared to listen. "They will get creamed."

"By how much?" asked George Pilkington, steering me with all his normal delicacy towards providing something that might be of some use to the sales-force.

"I haven't a clue," I confessed. I scurried off to work out the implications.

Years before at the Financial Times, while covering tax matters for the paper, I had developed a real interest in, and deep suspicion of, the leasing industry. In 1979 I had co-written a feature on the industry titled 'Leasing on the Treadmill'. It described how leasing was the financing method whereby companies (and in particular banks) avoided tax. By buying capital goods to the value of their profits, they would obtain a 100% allowance. They would then lease on the goods to a manufacturer. All well and good, but the article went on to point out that leasing only postponed the payment of tax, and the only way to go on postponing payments was to go on leasing. "This is the so-called tread-mill of leasing," we wrote. We then pointed out that the banks were also assuming they would never pay the tax, and had therefore declared profits on this basis. If the treadmill stopped, we implied, they would be hard hit.

And now, as I listened with the rest of the sales team to Nigel Lawson on the radio, it occurred to me that the change in capital allowances would have exactly that effect. The treadmill had been stopped. Banks could in future not expect 100% allowances and therefore could not go on assuming that the tax would never be paid. There were going to be casualties.

I became a prophet of doom. And, amazingly, I had the position to myself. Leasing was such an obscure area that the other analysts took time to get up to speed with the bombshell. Within a few days I had worked out that the four big banks, Barclays, NatWest, Midland and Lloyds would probably have to transfer about £1.5bn out of their reserves, put it into a deferred tax provision and eventually pay the amount over as tax to the Inland Revenue. It would make them uncomfortably low on capital, particularly Midland.

The salesmen did not at first take me too seriously. After all, weren't the analysts at all the other broking houses calling the sector a buy on the back of the Budget, mainly because a much-feared tax levy on the banks had not emerged? Within 24 hours, however, concern grew over the impact of the changes and the shares turned tail. The sales force, with some credible data at their elbow and a consistent story-line, steadily pulled out the sell orders from their client base over the succeeding weeks as the bad news dripped out. After this exploit, when it came to the bank sector, the fund managers listened to what Rowe & Pitman had to say. Quite how much they were to listen I would find out later in the year.

I had another piece of good fortune in the first months, this time on the corporate side of the business. In March I took a call from Cyril Stein, the chief executive of Ladbroke, the doyen of betting companies in the UK. "I see you've moved to Rowe & Pitman," he said. "I had to track you down. You should have told me." I got on well with Cyril Stein. I had written about his company's fortunes a few times on the Lex Column. In fact my first note on the company in April 1981 came a couple of years after an explosive fracas in which the Gambling Commission had banned it from running casinos for impropriety. He had received a most vicious pasting in the press that generally concluded that Ladbroke would inevitably be taken over. In my Lex note I ran through the impressive post-ban performance of the company and by not mentioning the possibility, implied it would escape this fate. Cyril Stein was grateful, not least I suspect because it was the first positive article written about the company for years.

"Good firm, Rowe & Pitman," Cyril Stein congratulated me. "I'd like to get closer to it."

"How do you mean?" I checked. "Research coverage or corporate?"

"Corporate, of course."

So in early April he came to our offices in the Stock Exchange tower with his finance director, to meet Nick Verey, Peter Wilmot-Sitwell and me.

Cyril was never one to waste time on indirect approaches. "How would you propose to look after Ladbroke? Who would do it? What service would you provide?"

Nick volunteered to be their main senior contact, while I would provide research coverage. Peter outlined how the liaison would work on Stock Exchange announcements and how we would make sure they saw the right institutional investors on a regular basis. Our payment for this would be the right to distribute Ladbroke's equity issues to the market when they were needed. I had learned as much from the answers as the Ladbroke team.

The meeting ended on a warm note. "All very satisfactory," said Cyril. "We'll be back to you shortly." This was presumably code for time to dismiss their existing broker.

"I do believe they're going to appoint us!" said Peter afterwards, in almost stunned disbelief. I suspect it was one of the easiest wins Rowe & Pitman had experienced, with none of the normal preparation and marketing. The casino debacle was now fading into history and with shares worth more than £500m – its market capitalisation – it was a substantial company for the corporate client list. Within a fortnight we were indeed appointed and Nick and I were starting to arrange a series of meetings with the various subsidiaries of the company.

Peter Wilmot-Sitwell was a classic member of the establishment. When I joined Rowe & Pitman he was in his late 40s. After Eton, the Coldstream Guards and Oxford, he floated into Rowe & Pitman on the recommendation of his then girlfriend's father, a good client of the firm. He became a partner almost immediately, in 1960, aged just 25 and had succeeded as the senior partner two years earlier, in 1982. He spoke with a clipped assurance that was presumably a heritage from his time in the Guards. He was blunt, forthright and straight-forward; deceptively modest about his own achievements. He was extremely supportive towards me – which was just as well, since in the early years I fell into one hole after the other. "I thought your appointment was very clever," he told me years later. "You brought an entirely different perspective to our business."

Later that April, after the Ladbroke meeting, Peter called me into the senior partner's office on another project entirely. "This one will tax you," he said cheerfully. "We've got to value Morgan Grenfell. They're planning to sell some shares to the institutions and need to know the price." Nick Verey lifted his head from his desk across the room and looked at me sympathetically. Morgan Grenfell was then considered the leading merchant bank in London, although it was not quoted. It had a complicated set of businesses, several of them in obscure financial specialities. Nor would imprecision be advisable, given the financial literacy of the Morgan Grenfell partners who wanted the answer. "The plan is for us and Cazenove to provide the valuation next Tuesday afternoon. You need to work out the figure with the Cazenove analyst and give us a briefing in the morning."

I set to work with my Cazenove counterpart to put the figures together. We had to disentangle all the different operations and value them separately. We used comparisons from the fund managers and other financial specialists; for the main merchant banking operation the best comparison was their main rival, the Warburg group, which was quoted on the Stock Exchange. We then had the tricky job of assessing the value of the hidden reserves, which we had been shown. It was fiendishly complicated.

In the morning we briefed Peter and his equally charming counterpart at Cazenove, Anthony Forbes. It was a tough assignment for anyone to come to cold. "Good luck," I said at the end of the meeting. Peter glanced over at Anthony Forbes. "I think you might come with us, David," he said casually as we got up to leave.

At 4.00pm we walked round to Morgan Grenfell's Georgian-style offices in Great Winchester Street. The ushers took us straight up to the board room. Peter paused as he stepped over the threshold. Down one side of the table ranged seven or eight of the most senior partners of the bank, all household names in City terms. Roger Seelig sat down the far end. My friend Richard Webb was there, as was

Graham Walsh, while Christopher Reeves, the bank's chief executive, sat more centrally. It was a formidable group.

Peter sat down opposite Christopher Reeves at the centre of the board table. I sat down next to him, near the door. I expected Anthony Forbes to walk behind us to flank Peter but, to our surprise, he sat down next to me, even closer to the door. So this had suddenly become a most odd arrangement. We were slightly off-centre to our hosts and I, the most junior person there, was sitting in the middle of the broking team. I suddenly felt most uncomfortable. Rightly.

The first question was straight-forward and Peter answered it in the confident tones which he employed so effectively on such occasions. The next was a stinker and everyone in the room knew it. As if on cue, all the eyes on the other side of the table slid from Peter to me. And now the grilling began. Every figure, every assumption, and every assumption behind that, was questioned, challenged, disparaged. Serious money was at stake for these Morgan Grenfell partners and they were not going to let anything dubious in this valuation past them. I have never been more thoroughly cross-examined. All the time I was desperate that they did not uncover some basic mistake in the figures. If they had, it would clearly have been a rout. Luckily nothing emerged and I toughed out all the attacks on the assumptions, with Peter in staunch support. It went on for a full hour, attack after attack. For my part I was deeply grateful at how Peter reinforced me so firmly through the meeting, even though he had not had the time to master the figures. He bulked his body up, nodded vigorously at all the telling points, came in instantly where he couldn't be challenged. "The market view is that there's little to choose between Warburg and Morgan Grenfell," he declared stoutly as we defended the similar valuation I had put on the two companies. When we emerged into Great Winchester Street we both practically collapsed against each other in relief that we had escaped without humiliation.

The pressures on the old-style partners grew in those early months, as they struggled to come to grips with an increasing need to provide analytical advice to their corporate clients. One of them asked me to help him value a prospective client. I had only just settled into the task when Nick Verey sauntered over and asked me what I was working on. He went white with fury when he saw the task. He marched across the office to the unfortunate partner and yelled, "Find some-one else to do your work, you lazy sod. No one told you that you could lumber David. Just lay off." It was a humiliating put-down in full view – and hearing – of the sales floor. It was the first time I saw Nick's impatience with the weaker members of the broking team, which earned him a mixed reputation within the firm and a nickname of Rhino. As his recruit I could hardly avoid being associated with his intemperance. On this occasion his outburst certainly proved an effective way of making enemies. Some months later I arrived in the lobby of our offices, still dressed in the rough gear I wore to cycle to work in. The unfortunate partner passed, dressed in his immaculate pin-stripes and stiff, old-fashioned, shirt collars. "What on earth have you got on?" he exclaimed. "Disgusting."

Nick was not the only senior partner to make life uncomfortable for the more amateur members of the firm. Stuart Stradling, the head of the corporate broking department, was also deeply professional in his approach. He stood in sharp contrast to the Old Etonian group that dominated the upper echelons of the firm. Aged 40 when I began work, he had qualified as an accountant before joining Rowe & Pitman in 1969 in what was then called the new issues department. With no independent resources behind him he was almost forced to leave in the dark days of 1974 and the firm made special arrangements to keep him through the period. He effectively ran the department from early 1975 and became a partner in the following year. He spoke only when necessary, much to the bemusement of clients accustomed to the energetic fluency of a growing number of bankers and brokers. When he did talk he could sound stumbling and hesitant, fixing an unblinking gaze on whomever he was addressing. But when a crisis erupted he was in his element, calm and methodical as he put together the necessary steps to sort out the problem. The rivalry with Nick Verey that would explode later was still incipient in my first months in the firm.

So when Stuart asked me – with Nick's full support – to provide a valuation for the flotation of the luggage company Antler, I got straight down to work. It was fairly uncomplicated. While there were no other quoted luggage companies to provide a direct comparison, there were a reasonable number of branded goods manufacturers - such as Wedgwood, the porcelain producer - whose rating would be a close guide. I prepared a short table summarising the values and brought it along to the committee.

The partner in charge of the float was asked the price he planned to bring the stock to market at. "Well, it's very difficult," he flannelled. "There are no other luggage companies so there's nothing to compare it with. We thought we might ask a few institutions how much they . . ." he faltered at the frowns round the table, "or we might use a market average."

Stuart looked over at me. "David's got a few thoughts."

With mixed feelings I handed round my piece of paper. I felt like an instrument of nemesis for an older generation. "Well," I said, "while there are no luggage companies there are a reasonable number of quoted branded goods manufacturers, and they all trade on very similar ratings. So Antler should slot pretty well into the middle of this list."

"Right," concluded Stuart. "That seems pretty straight-forward. We'll go with David's figure." The look of pain on the face of the responsible partner has haunted me ever since.

By the summer I was beginning to feel thoroughly comfortable with research. The main challenge was the speed of response required. An event, or set of figures, would be published on the screen and the sales-force would want to know the implications within minutes. Did it mean the stock was a buy or a sell? With only a fraction of the full set of information I would have to reach a judgement, and be prepared to stick with it. The required impetuosity appealed to me. Nor was it an option to come to a sotto voce view. Every year the fund managers voted on the best analysts in various surveys. "Low profile is no profile," Nick Whitney, the head of research would insist, so all the calls had to be made as forcefully as possible.

In October we made the long-planned move out of the Stock Exchange tower to the top floors of a brand new office block, the first building of what was to become the Broadgate complex. Now I was brought out of my niche in the farthest corner of the office onto the new main sales floor, sitting next to Nick Whitney on the top floor of 1 Finsbury Avenue, overlooking the car-park outside Liverpool Street station, a permanent building site for the next few years. The strategic position of my desk reflected an acceptance that I was successfully making the difficult transformation from journalist to broker. I was far from being a safe pair of hands but I could certainly make an impact, sometimes greater than intended.

Soon after the move I finished some work on the banks. I had been taking a close look at the Midland, whose capital was seriously depleted and whose share price had been tumbling through the year. Even though it looked extremely cheap, I could not work it out to be worth holding, especially as I thought there was more bad news on the way.

I strolled down the open-plan office to the group of desks arranged in a horse-shoe that housed the sales-force. I handed out copies of my figures and conclusions.

"I don't like the Midland," I announced." I think it's an outright sell. Even though the shares have fallen to the lowest point in modern times they still have further to go." I spelled out a few of the negatives and concluded. "Remember, normal companies get taken over at premiums. Banks don't. They tend to get rescued on poor terms in a deal arranged under the auspices of the Bank of England. The Midland does not have an independent future. Tell your clients to get out now."

Even before I had finished the salesmen were reaching for the phones. Something about the story, helped no doubt by my earlier accuracy on the banks' leasing problems, sparked a chord with the fund managers. Soon the sell orders were pouring in. And as they did so a secondary effect took over. Fund managers who were quite happy with their Midland shares could make out, from what our salesmen were telling them, that a pile of sell orders was building up, which meant the stock was only going one way - downward. So they added their sell orders to the stack. The close proximity of the salesmen created a competitive cauldron as they phoned up and down their client lists, talking about how the Midland price was collapsing under our pressure.

And collapsing it was. The pre-Big Bang market structure was highly responsive to one-way volume on this kind of scale. When the two main jobbers saw the Rowe & Pitman floor brokers coming over for yet another Midland quote they did not need much imagination to work out whether they were being tested for a buy or a sell order, not after the first couple of transactions. So they moved the price down dramatically to protect themselves. After all, they didn't want to end up with millions of Midland shares at the wrong price. Within half an hour, the price had fallen significantly.

Now it was my turn for the phone to ring. Analysts at other houses wanted to know what was happening. What piece of news did we have that they didn't? Then it was the turn of the journalists. What was going on? Was the Midland going bust? I did my best to explain that it was just an everyday sell call based on no more information than was readily available in the market. This was beginning to have an ominous feel to it.

The next morning a leading financial story discussed the attack on the Midland, carrying liberal quotes from me. I had hardly settled at my desk when Peter Wilmot-Sitwell summoned me into the senior partners' room.

"I've just had a call from the Bank of England," he said. "They want to know why we've been trying to start a run on the Midland Bank." He paused. "Have we been trying to start a run on the Midland Bank?" This was now looking very serious. In normal trading no one would take a second look at the price of a bank going down a bit. But a sudden collapse, of the kind seen the previous day, could indicate that the market thought Midland was going bust. If this became a more general fear Midland Bank customers might start to panic and withdraw their money from the bank. Such a run could bring the bank to its knees, and at the same time undermine the whole UK financial system, exactly the kind of crisis which the Bank of England was designed to avert. My trading call on the Midland had run grotesquely out of control.

"I just put out a sell on the stock," I explained to Peter. "I think I under-estimated the power of the sales-force."

"Are we broker to any of these big banks?" Peter asked.

"No."

"Well serve them right then." He turned to Nick Verey. "The Bank wants him to go round to see the Midland to sort it out," he said. "You'd better go with him, otherwise they'll hang him by his thumbs from the top floor."

Nick and I went round to see Michael Julien, the finance director of the Midland Bank. I grovelled appropriately and, far from threatening my thumbs, Michael Julien spent an amicable hour with us. With considerable charm he laid out the plans to turn round what he admitted was a difficult situation at the bank.

I was privately unconvinced. However after the shock of the previous day I had anyway resolved to keep my mouth thoroughly shut on the Midland Bank for the next few months. We parted with mutual good wishes.

Michael Julien did not stay long at the Midland. After selling its loss-making US subsidiary, the Californian Crocker Bank a year and a half later, he moved over to the post of deputy chief executive of Eurotunnel in the autumn of 1986, a job he only held for a matter of months. As for Midland Bank, its independence was indeed short-lived. In 1987 The Hong Kong and Shanghai took its first stake in the bank, completing a full merger four years later.

Meanwhile I was beginning to recruit to bulk out our research position in the sectors I had kicked off. A young graduate, Tom Hill, joined me in November and he concentrated his attention on the transport and leisure companies. I poached a well-ranked young analyst from Hoare Govett, in the shape of Martyn Ralph, to work on the financial services companies. The next year I found an able strategist at the Midland Bank, Chris Ellerton, who moved over to pick up the banking sector. This meant that we could start to ensure regularity in our coverage of these sectors. It also freed me up to concentrate full-time on special projects and transactions.

It was towards the end of my first year at Rowe & Pitman that I won my first flotation. While the transaction was to prove highly traumatic, I was to learn many lessons from the experience. The first was that equity is funny stuff.

In a flotation one sells shares that at one level are simply financial instruments awarding the holder the right to dividend payments. At another level the shares represent the soul of the company itself; ownership of the endeavour is tied up with the shares in a way that is not the case with other financial instruments, such as bonds. The equity investors need to know what the company is and where it is going. When one is in charge of a flotation one becomes responsible for establishing an image of the company among investors. It is a complex marketing challenge.

The company on which I cut my teeth was a computer leasing company called IBL. We had won the role of broker to the float on the back of my high-profile call on the banking industries' leasing problems. Phil Coussens, the self-made chief executive of the group came to our offices in early November, and I was convinced that he was running an impressive company. Phil had a devastating and unusual marketing technique. He would start every meeting in a state close to incoherence, thus lowering the guard – indeed, almost arousing the pity – of his audience. As the meeting progressed, however, he gained astonishing momentum and fluency and swept all opposition away. I saw him successfully apply this trick again and again.

The main problem with floating a company in this sector was its rivals. In particular we regarded the largest of them, Atlantic Computers, as a rogue elephant. "We have to create a cordon sanitaire round Atlantic Computers, or our company will be dragged down when it goes bust," I warned our team. My plan was to write up our views on the industry before the IBL float, with piece of research that would cover the competition. Derek Bainbridge, the electronics analyst, and I wrote a report on the industry, covering all the quoted companies, including Atlantic. Derek had the privilege of covering Atlantic itself, whose profits we regarded with some suspicion. The company, under its aggressive chief executive John Foulston – nickname in the market, Captain Foulenough – had invented a financing technique that took our breath away. It would lease a computer to a client for seven years and book a profit based on the full period. Many clients, however, had a break clause after four years, so would almost inevitably return the machine in order to upgrade at that point. In practical terms this 'flexlease' structure allowed Atlantic to take seven years profits rather than four for each IBM mainframe leased out. In the research we published in April we judged Atlantic overpriced and its accounting policies "cavalier". This was a serious accusation from a major broker and the Atlantic share price came under immediate pressure.

John Foulston's reaction was to complain vehemently to Peter Wilmot-Sitwell and to launch an attack on us in the Sunday Times. This latter backfired when John Jay, the journalist involved, checked with me and I explained our concerns. Instead he ran a short neutral story on 5 May, 1985, in which I was described as "disappointed by the quality of cooperation ... from Atlantic in preparing the circular, despite repeated requests". Five days later Derek and I went round to Atlantic's headquarters where John Foulston raged at us.

If anything the controversy helped to stoke enthusiasm for the float of IBL, which took place later in May and valued the company at £100m. Building the marketing success was like recreating the layers of an onion. An enthusiastic project team at the core would transmit their views to the next layer, the sales-force, who in turn would pass on their genuine confidence to their clients and thus the market as a whole.

On this occasion I fell into the trap lying in wait for those promoting a deal that subsequently goes sour. Many of the salesmen became so enthusiastic about the float that they applied for large amounts of stock for themselves – as they were then perfectly entitled to do. Initially this was no problem; over the first half-year the price gently moved ahead from the 140p issue level to peak at about 160p in February 1986. In early June IBL was due to announce its figures, but during the previous week Phil Coussens warned us that the figures were going to be down on the £12m we had expected. "It'll be somewhere around £10m," he told us. "We took some trading losses in France. We're still debating £1m up or down with the auditors." This was bad news. Investors in a company's equity were rarely forgiving when it disappointed with its first set of figures. I could also expect a deeply negative reaction from the sales-force and a substantial dent in my reputation with them. Nevertheless, I consoled myself, £10m would still be a healthy increase on the £7.5m recorded in the previous year.

Phil still could not tell us the figures on the evening before the planned announcement. The discussions with the auditors were taking longer than expected and now he didn't expect to know the outcome much before their release the next morning. "But I'm pretty confident," he assured me on the phone.

Shortly after I arrived at my desk the next morning, he phoned again. "We've just finished," he said. He sounded absolutely exhausted. "We've been battling the auditors all night. It's bad. The figure has come down to £6m. I'm sorry."

This was appalling. I ran over to Stuart Stradling's desk to let him know the news. While I had run the day-by-day marketing of the float, Stuart was in overall charge of the account.

"I don't believe it. I don't believe it," I repeated to myself. Derek Bainbridge, who had run over with me, was muttering imprecations to the Almighty.

"Calm down," ordered Stuart. "We need to decide what to do next, not sit around like moaning ninnies." He called the Stock Exchange and arranged for the shares to be suspended. At least the share price would not move around before we had time to find out the real reasons for the debacle. When the announcement was put out at the end of the week – laying the blame heavily on French problems – the share price collapsed to below 70p, or half of their float value. IBL never recovered and was later sold to the Swiss company Inspectorate. I don't think the salesmen, who had invested so heavily in the stock, ever forgave me.

It was a painful lesson. But already, as Nick Verey and I surveyed the opportunities, the prime targets were yet more flotations. The privatisation of state assets was now picking up enormous momentum under Thatcher's Government.

---

[1] Leasing on the Treadmill, David Freud and Michael Lafferty, Financial Times, 10 July 1979

3

Thatcher's revolution
Privatising the UK – 1985 - 1988

⁓

I entered a large room at the International Press Centre in London's Holborn with some trepidation. Sitting at the middle of the table, flanked by most of his board, was the chairman of the TSB, Sir John Read. He was a powerfully-built man in his late sixties, with a purple face, and he looked as irascible as his reputation suggested. He looked up at the disturbance. "What is it now?" he demanded. It was August 1986 and he was obviously fed up with the flotation mechanics that the board was reviewing.

Tony Carlisle, the leading public relations expert on flotations who had brought me into the room, explained.

"We thought it would be valuable if David ran through some of the questions you will be facing from the institutions and journalists."

"All right, all right. Get on with it then."

I moved into a chair in front of the boardroom table. Tony had briefed me outside the room. "We want to make sure that Sir John deals with the press smoothly. He's liable to lose his temper, so if you give him a taste of what he'll be facing he'll be prepared for it. Just ask the questions in the way you would when you were still on Lex."

Although I had been working on the float of the TSB Group for more than two years, I had never before met Sir John. He had been the chairman of the EMI music group when it had been taken over by Thorn in 1979, a humiliation that had clearly not improved his temper. In 1980 the Government had arranged for him to take on the task of combining the disparate Trustee Savings Banks into a floatable vehicle and now, after an unexpected delay, the transaction was about to be launched.

I cleared my throat. I decided it would be worth explaining the process again, to avoid any misunderstandings. "Sir John, I'm going to ask you these questions in the way that a difficult journalist or suspicious fund manager might put them. Just to familiarise you with the tone.

"Now you mustn't take it as me asking these questions. I'm your broker. It's just for the purposes of rehearsal."

"I asked you to get on with it. We haven't got all day."

I launched straight into the first question on my sheet of paper. "What are you going to do with all the money?" I asked bluntly. This was a particularly nasty question. Somehow Sir John had persuaded the UK Treasury that nobody owned the TSB. So all the money raised would be retained by the bank and, it was widely forecast, promptly wasted on ill-founded takeovers and investments. Sir John was well aware of the criticism.

There was a short, ominous pause.

Then. "How dare you ask that question? This is outrageous! I will not tolerate this kind of behaviour. Get out. Get out now."

I looked round the roomful of bankers, board members and consultants of one kind or another. Everyone seemed stunned into silence. Nor was anyone prepared to risk extending the outburst by attempting to mollify the man, persuading him that the exercise was worth pursuing.

I stood up and walked out of the room, followed by Sir John's glare, closing the door quietly behind me.

That was the sole extent of his preparation for the next week's press conference, at which the first question asked was, naturally, "What are you going to do with all the money?" As might have been anticipated, Sir John's response was to harangue the questioner and I heard reports back (I thought it wiser not to attend in person) that the event turned into a bad-tempered shambles.

Two and a half years earlier, in February 1984, Nick Verey had taken me round to the TSB, a bare month after I had started work at Rowe & Pitman. Its head office was conveniently situated half-a-mile across the City from ours, in the picturesquely-named Milk Street, in practice an ugly post-war office block. This was the first time I was to meet Derek Stevens, the finance director, an executive I was to get to know increasingly well in the years to come and for whom I was to work on a series of transactions spanning my whole career. Rowe & Pitman had already won the broking mandate, so this was a relaxed meeting at which Derek explained the main issues facing the bank and the timetable for the flotation.

"This is, of course, not a privatisation at all because it has been decided - for reasons that are beyond me - that nobody owns the banks. Not the customers, not the Treasury, not the management. That's what we expect to be in next year's Act of Parliament anyway. So even the most useless broker shouldn't have a problem selling it, not of course that I'm implying that Rowe & Pitman is a useless broker. After all, for anyone who subscribes for shares it will be like buying a purse and getting your money back in it."

Nick chimed in, "But we've all decided that it's important for the future of the company that it gets a good following in the stock market, with lots of keen investors. So the plan is to treat the issue like a privatisation: lots of advertising; lots of stock going to private individuals; a proper marketing campaign.

"We want some good research," said Derek. "Something that explains the stock to the investors and gives it a good start."

"That's your job," said Nick. We looked at the timetable. The most likely outcome was a float date in early 1986. "On that basis you should publish the research the previous November. I'm sure Derek will arrange a 'get to know the company tour' for us next summer."

In the following 16 months I was able to put the TSB firmly on the backburner as I learnt how to be a research analyst. It was not till June 1985, with the Act of Parliament safely on course, that Nick and I set off on our tour. In Manchester we learned how many of the bank managers were still finding it difficult to cope with making loans, introduced only eight years before. The next day we toured the branches round Newcastle. Finally, on the Wednesday, we travelled down south to Andover in Hampshire to the headquarters of the life insurance company. Here we learned that the TSB's salesmen sold 40 policies a month, compared with the industry average of six. Presumably the high rate was due to the way the TSB managers recommended their clients to be approached.

"That's not cold calling," observed Nick, "that's warm calling."

Over the following months I assembled the research report. We set the day for the release of the research on 12 November and invited all the financial journalists for 11.00am. This was the first time Rowe & Pitman had adopted such a high profile launch of its research. Notionally research was produced for the institutions with whom we dealt as broker. However, by distributing it to journalists, and encouraging them to report on it, the conclusions would become much more widely disseminated. In this way the research would effectively become the first step in a campaign to raise the profile of the company among the wider investing public. Rather than sending the piece out to the journalists and talking to them individually, Nick and I decided that a press conference would create the greatest impact.

That morning I was understandably nervous. Then, around 10.00am Nick picked up a call from the company.

"It's been stopped."

"What?"

"Everything's been stopped. A Scottish judge has ruled that the TSB is owned by the depositors."

By now the news was on our screens. There was no way a company could float while such a legal issue was unresolved. The February flotation date was history, which meant that the research was coming out too soon.

"We can't pull it," I told Nick. "It's already on the desks of the fund managers. And the journalists will be upstairs in less than an hour. We'll just have to put a brave face on it."

It was an extremely well-attended meeting for a piece of research, with more than 20 journalists making the trip to the seventh floor of our Broadgate office.

I explained the implications of the judgement, which the company had hurriedly briefed us on. "The float will be delayed until there can be an appeal. If the TSB is successful the float will go ahead as quickly as possible. If it loses, the company will have to consider the implications." I then did my best to go through the findings in the research. In the event the journalists were pretty sympathetic to this spectacular piece of bad timing. The next day's press naturally concentrated on the legal story, but there was a kind word or two about the research tucked at the bottom of the articles.

It was not until July 1986 that the claims of the depositors were rejected by a unanimous decision of the House of Lords. I was already at work on producing a pricing recommendation. Lazard, the merchant bank advising on the float, sent over a long complicated paper. By now I had a computer with a spreadsheet programme.

"This isn't easy," I told Nick.

"Course it is," he replied. "Just read across the ratings of the other banks and put them on a bit lower."

"If I do that they're worth about £750m."

"Fine, we'll tell them they're worth £750m."

"Ah yes, but if they raise £750m, they keep it. As Derek says, 'It's like buying a purse and getting your money back in it.' So then they'll be worth £1.5bn. But if they raise £1.5bn, they'll be worth £2.25bn and so on for ever."

"What's the solution?"

"I'm afraid it's very rude. You can only solve the equation on the basis that they are going to waste the new money. If they waste half of it, for instance, they can raise £1.5bn and add the unwasted half, £750m, to their underlying value of £750m."

"Will they waste half of it?"

"I'm sure. The pressure to spend their capital will intensify all the time. There's no way they can spend that kind of money efficiently."

"We'd better find a way of putting it more diplomatically," observed Nick. "But £1.5bn is the figure."

"We'll call it 'expected market price discount to net tangible assets'. How does that appeal?"

"That'll do fine."

Given these financial dynamics this was one float that was

virtually indestructible, however bad-tempered Sir John Read, the chairman, became at the questions from journalists and fund mangers. The price shot away on the first day of trading from 50p to 85p. Sadly my calculation proved all too accurate. The TSB bought the ailing merchant bank Hill Samuel at an over-inflated price the following year, as well as an insurance company, Target Life. It never recovered from the blow to its reputation and was taken over by Lloyds Bank in 1995.

Although the TSB was not formally a privatisation, it was structured as if it was. The UK privatisation programme of the 1980s and early 1990s was one of the most popular policies of the radical Conservative Government that came to power under Mrs Thatcher in 1979. For better or worse, it profoundly changed the business climate of the country as well as transforming the City's financial markets. It would be widely copied round the rest of the world.

The revolution was almost completely accidental.

The programme started as an exercise in financial housekeeping, with the disposal of Government stakes in commercial companies like BP and Cable & Wireless. At this stage the sales were essentially directed at the City institutions, which would underwrite and buy the majority of the shares. The stakes being offered were relatively small and in those first four years, while I was still writing Lex, Government proceeds never exceeded £500m a year. The main tussle was over the City's issuing practices, which the Government felt – rightly – put it over a barrel. Under the traditional process, the Government would ask its bankers to underwrite the stock at a certain price. This meant the bankers would own the stock if there was inadequate demand. The bankers would immediately commission the appointed brokers to place this underwriting risk with the investing institutions, the so-called sub-underwriters. Only after this exercise was completed would the stock go on sale – at the sub-underwritten price. There was a conservative bias built into every stage of this process. The bankers didn't want to be left with the stock, and the brokers did not want to fail in the sub-underwriting. The sub-underwriters had limited incentive to be enthusiastic since they were the end-buyers anyway, and would naturally prefer cheap stock to expensive stock. The conservatism was underlined by the way the price was set before there had been any marketing and so there was limited feedback on what the investors might be prepared to pay. When the Government came to sell Amersham International in 1982 it was stunned to see the fixed offer price of 142p a share soar to 188p on the first day of dealings. The reaction of Nigel Lawson, then the Energy Minister tasked with selling Britoil later that year, was to offer the shares by tender – a strategy that backfired miserably when a falling oil price left the issue stranded.

The battle with the City issuing system became a sideshow in 1984, when the Government decided to privatise British Telecom. At £4bn, this was the biggest issue that had ever been seen anywhere in the world – five times bigger than the previous record, for the already-quoted US telecoms company AT&T. "We told them it couldn't be done," Nick told me. "There simply wasn't the capacity in the City to absorb more than £2bn of it." Not surprisingly, after delivering this message at the formal presentation, Rowe & Pitman failed to win any role in this transaction. While S.G.Warburg obtained the junior advisory position of representing the company, the glamour role of advising the Government was enjoyed by Kleinwort Benson, one of the major merchant banks at the tail end of the pre-Big Bang era. Nor was Rowe & Pitman the only cautionary voice. So Kleinwort and the Government developed a plan to sell it to the general public as well as the institutions.

Thus was established a set of issuing procedures which were designed to generate universal public awareness. Widespread media campaigns, incorporating extensive television advertising, were introduced to alert the general public. Brokers were allowed to publish research ahead of a float, even though they were working to secure the success of the issue. Discounts and other incentives were introduced for the retail investor, so that the shares would be cheaper for the general public than for the institutional fund managers. Finally, the shares would be offered on a partly-paid basis, with further instalments due in subsequent years. This had the side effect of sharply increasing the potential early premium that the shares might trade at. So if, as in the case of British Telecom, the first payment was only 50p of the full 130p price, the partly traded price would soar by 86% to 93p on the first day of trading. In truth this was only a premium of 33% on the full value of the stock, but it made many investors fortunes – particularly those who managed to get large allocations of stock through the institutional route.

The embarrassment of the first day premium was negligible when measured against the success of the offering. The Government had established it could market offerings of unprecedented size. Indeed, there was demand for nearly ten times the stock on offer. All the press excitement about profits for the stags – those who sold out immediately – would mean that subsequent issues would also see an enthusiastic public response. For Kleinwort Benson, the architect of the structure, it was a triumph that gave them a head start in winning other business.

Popular capitalism, as it became known, came to represent a very different tradition to that prevailing elsewhere, particularly in the US, where 'conditioning' the financial market ahead of an issue was absolutely forbidden. There could be no press coverage, let alone advertising, before the formal prospectus was launched for a company. As for research, the sponsoring house could not publish any at all till months after the event. In the years ahead I would find myself working directly within this easier regulatory structure and, indeed introducing it elsewhere round the world. I would also be closely involved in the search for a solution to the problem of embarrassing first-day premiums, a problem that would take nearly a decade to solve.

Meanwhile, British Airways was scheduled to be my first formal privatisation. Indeed, Nick Verey had tasked me with handling the research and marketing the issue at my original interview, when he told me we had been appointed the company's broker. I did not admit it at the time, but this was a task I took on with some nervousness. I had not had an easy relationship with the company while writing about it on Lex. Martin Taylor, my colleague on the column, had started off the process with a vicious conclusion on the logic of privatising the company at all in October 1982. "The Government seems determined to stuff that weary-winged lame duck, British Airways, with hefty sums of cash . . . and tow it down the privatisation runway," he declared robustly, ahead of the announcement of its figures.

Two days later the company announced a net loss of £454m, the largest in British corporate history. I turned up at the lavish press event held in one of the City livery halls, with attendance from transport and finance specialists, as well as general and television reporters. On the podium was Sir John King, the chairman of the company, who took the opportunity to announce a major turn-round plan. Indeed, the scale of the loss was directly related to this plan, since it incorporated massive provisions to fund all the changes and redundancies. In financial terms the key issue, it seemed to me, was to discover whether these provisions had been exaggerated in order to improve profits in subsequent years and flatter the performance of the management – a typical business strategy. I sat in the second row and waited for the circus to begin.

Sir John (later to become Lord King of Wartnaby) was a formidable man, fairly short, grey-haired, with a piercing glare. He set off with a vigorous presentation in which he lambasted a previous management that operated as if money grew on trees. When it came to the questions he quickly realised that I was the writer of Lex and he began to glare at me ferociously, no doubt reflecting his fury at Martin's article. He hardly shifted his eyes from me for the next hour, neither while I asked my series of questions, nor when someone else was holding the microphone. As intimidation it was not particularly successful, although at the end of the Press conference I thought my image must have become imprinted on his glowering eyeballs. So I wondered how he would react when I turned up as his broker, especially after my somewhat sceptical conclusion in Lex: "There is no sign that the company has got its operating structure right."

When I did meet him, of course, there was no acknowledgement whatsoever that he had any recollection of our last encounter. But that was well in the future. By the time I was at work at Rowe & Pitman, the airline's fortunes had been well and truly turned round by the team King had brought in. A third of the workforce had been fired, taking the numbers from 59,000 to 37,000 and in the latest financial year the airline's net profits had reached the genuinely impressive level of £216m. I attended the first formal meeting of the brokers and bankers that took place in mid-April 1984 at BA's rundown Heathrow headquarters, Speedbird House. It was chaired by Keith Wilkins, then BA director of planning, who introduced the meeting by telling us, "We need to be pretty flexible about timing. It looks as if British Telecom will go in late autumn and we'll follow early next year. But if BT slips we may take this year's slot." With a bit of rough and tumble I managed to make sure that the research that I planned would be published last, as close to the issue as possible, with output from the other company broker, Phillips & Drew, and one of the Government brokers, Wood, Mackenzie, coming earlier in the marketing campaign.

However, I had hardly dipped my metaphorical pen into the inkwell when the first of a series of delays emerged. The Civil Aviation Authority began calling for a wholesale restructuring of the UK aviation industry, while the Law Lords ruled against BA over the collapse of the rival Laker Airways. The February target became increasingly irrelevant as the legal problems over Laker grew, particularly in the US. At lunch with us in August, Colin Marshall, the chief executive, confessed that he thought that the float would be delayed until July 1985.

It was not, therefore, till January of that year that I began work on what Nick and I had decided would be the definitive piece of work on the airline, and one that would leave the output of the other two, more established, research houses in the shade. It was an ambition that the airline, in the shape of the finance director Gordon Dunlop, supported vigorously. So, with my new young graduate Tom Hill in tow, I set off on a tour of the departments of the airline. Roughly once a week from the end of January we would travel out to BA's scruffy Speedbird house to interview one of the executives in charge of part of the route network. Geoff Nolan explained the operation of the Far Eastern routes to us, Alan Beaves told about the "Kangaroo route" between the UK and Australia; John Meredith, the US; Joe Goasdoué, UK domestic; and Tim Phillips, Africa. Rod Lynch was responsible for the charters and southern Europe, while Andrew Grey was responsible for northern Europe. We learned about the competitive, commercial and demographic factors on every single route; from how many businessmen travelled on a route, to the political sensitivities surrounding it, to the currency of the ticket sales. Each of the executives could rattle off the figures and information while hardly referring to a single document. It was eye-opening. I have never before, or since, come across a more effective group of executives.

With this information base it was easy to put together a dense and definitive piece of work, 100 pages long, which analysed every substantial route on an individual basis. We tied it up with some more conventional analysis on comparative valuation and the economics of the aviation industry. Then Tom and I could indulge in the fun of sorting out the cover. Here we piggy-backed on the new Saatchi and Saatchi advertising slogan 'the world's favourite airline', which leant on the fact that BA carried more purely international passengers than any other carrier. Our title was: 'The World's Favourite Route Network', superimposed on a dark map of the world showing shining route lines spreading across the globe from London. It was designed to emphasise the power and scale of BA's market position.

All we had to do now was wait for the appropriate moment to publish. And wait. July 1985 came and went. BA was still struggling to agree a settlement with Laker through the summer. By the time the suit and the class actions were settled it was late in the year. 1986 had hardly opened before another bout of anti-trust legal action was launched in the US against the airline. Yet another target date was set as this problem emerged, although Nick and I regarded the new timing of July 1986 with considerable cynicism.

As it turned out, we were right. This time the problem was neither political nor legal. In April the Soviet nuclear power-station at Chernobyl went out of control, spewing a plume of radioactivity across northern Europe, while the US military bombed Libya from their bases in the UK. "You would have thought that Tripoli was a suburb of Bournemouth, given the way the Americans have reacted," lamented Colin Marshall, the chief executive, when next we saw him. "Our US volumes have collapsed." In fact traffic was down 21% on these critical routes in the April-June quarter. But with recovery in summer the go-ahead button was again pressed. The two other broking houses published their research in the early autumn on the agreed schedule. I updated all my figures and circulated the draft to the company first, then the full marketing committee. In early November I attended the committee meeting to formally clear the document for publication.

At the head of the table sat Anthony Newhouse, a partner at Slaughter and May, the lawyers acting for the Government. "I'm sorry," he said. "There's too much information in this document to put out in its present form at the present time."

I was incredulous. "What?"

"He's been working on it for two years," pointed out Bob Ayling, BA's legal director (and future chief executive).

"I'm afraid it's just too close to the date of the launch of the prospectus. We can't take the risk that investors will rely on the information in it."

"We could take out some of the tables?" I suggested. We played around with different types of emasculation for a few minutes.

"I'm afraid it won't do the trick," he concluded.

I tried one more time. "This has been set for this slot, approved by everybody here, since April 1984. What on earth has changed to make you want to ban it now?"

There were several more "I'm sorries" but the net effect was unchanged. The research could not be published until after the float.

Worse was to come. A month later I picked up the phone to find John Phelps, a financial journalist from the Sunday Express on the line.

"David, I've just heard from a good source that your research has been banned for being too bearish.'"

This was horrific. A story that a company's own broker was too bearish, or negative, on the stock to publish would have genuine repercussions for the success of the float.

I attempted to put him right. "Can I talk to you off the record? Nothing to do with being bearish, John. It was banned for legal reasons. Of course I'm feeling pretty unhappy about it, but what can you do?"

I put the phone down, modestly confident that I had killed the story. That Sunday I did not hurry out of bed. When I did, I thought I'd just check what the outcome was and popped down to the newsagents for a copy of the Express. It was worse than anything I could imagine. The story was the lead in the financial section. It carried sidebars quoting me saying "I am sick and jaundiced" (a flippant observation that worked much better in 'off the record' conversation than cold, bold print). For good measure, after it went through my explanation of the legal problem, it still carried the claim that the research was banned for being too bearish – and outlined a few reasons for being bearish.

I phoned up Mark Wrightson, the partner running the deal at Hill Samuel. He took it remarkably calmly, all things considered.

At work the next day Peter Hardy, head of equities, said to Nick Verey, "I hope you've thoroughly bollocked him."

Nick replied, "I don't think I need to."

The float eventually did go ahead, the following January, albeit in a desperate stop/go rush. The Sunday Express story had the perverse effect of making all the fund managers want to see me, so I was rushed off my feet going to meetings to explain the key points in the banned research.

"Shall we invite the press into our office for the first day of trading?" I asked Nick. "Normally they would go to the London Stock Exchange, but that's been abandoned now. It would be great publicity."

By January, following Big Bang, all of the trading had migrated from the London Stock Exchange onto the individual trading floors of the new securities houses.

Nick was as enthusiastic as I. "I'll have to persuade our colleagues. They're not used to seeing press photographers running round the trading room. They'll be worried that something may go wrong in public."

"Tell them nobody can work out anything going wrong unless smoke comes out of the computer screens," I advised.

The apprehension of the equities team proved justified. Trading was to start at 2.00pm prompt on 11 February to coincide with the opening of the New York market, where the company was also listed. It was the first big flotation we had been involved in since the market transformation, so nerves were running high. The huge new trading room was now to be tested. As the minutes ticked down, the head trader, Ken Pitcher, stood behind his dealing desk against the window. All round him and extending down the room were the salesmen and sales-traders, many of them also standing, with phones in their hands. They were already connected to their clients and planned to call out their orders to Ken as soon as trading began. Model airplanes, Boeing 747s and Concordes, were scattered across the dealing desks. At the far side of the room, facing Ken, was a circus of media, television cameras and photographers. Despite our best efforts to limit the numbers, there were at least fifty onlookers, including Lord King, the chairman of British Airways, and Michael Spicer, the Aviation Minister.

2.00pm

"Buy 200," called the salesmen. "Sell 500." "Buy; sell". Ken Pitcher scanned the room calmly, hardly moving his head. He nodded first at one salesman and then another, acknowledging their orders. Across the room the photographers scurried for position. Television cameras focused on Lord King and Michael Spicer, as they conducted interviews across the salesmen's desks. It was pure pandemonium. Onlookers at subsequent first-day launches were much reduced.

The launch behind us, we did eventually publish the research - in March - hurrying it out before the Government broker Wood, Mackenzie could stop us. "Sorry," Nick told them, when they phoned up to prevent publication. "It's just gone out."

"Oh, dear. Well, I suppose that it'll be all right."

Even then I couldn't get the timing right.

"You've caused a run on the shares just before they are going to fix the base price for our options," complained Keith Wilkins, the BA director of planning, only half-jokingly, when I met him at the celebration of the launch at London's Savoy hotel mid-month. It had taken more than seven years for the Conservatives finally to float the company and I had been working on this frustrating account for three of those years.

Luckily, I had been able to use my new-found knowledge of the airline sector much earlier, in 1985. It was to lead to my first completed privatisation, which involved a company far from the heartlands of Thatcherism - in Singapore of all places.

In April of that year, two colleagues approached me to discuss a transaction we had been awarded. John Walker-Howarth, a director in the S.G.Warburg corporate finance division who specialised in the Far East, explained that we had been mandated to sell Singapore Airlines in Europe in a privatisation of the company that was planned later in the year.

"The bulk will be going to employees and local investors, but there will be tranches in the US and Japan, as well as Europe."

There was just one problem. "Half the profits come from selling second-hand planes, so the price they are talking about looks outrageously expensive." John Walker-Howarth was referring to the fact that investors would not regard such profits as repeatable and therefore would disregard them for valuation purposes.

The head of the Far East sales desk, Richard Bonsor, concluded: "We want to do the deal, David, but only if we can sell it. Let's see what value you come up with."

Over the summer I played around with the problem. In 1985 the financial markets were still extremely localised, as were accounting standards. This meant that a company in one country would report completely different profits if it was located elsewhere. It was difficult to compare values of similar companies in different countries for this reason alone. The US investment banks were making heroic efforts to pretend that a thriving international equity market in new issues was developing; the reality was that in 1985 the volume of genuine deals was still minuscule. Those stocks that were distributed abroad in a new issue - more often than not UK privatisations - were often sold straight back to locals in the following weeks. Investors simply did not trust what they were buying.

I studied all Singapore Airlines' accounting policies. Suddenly I saw it. They were depreciating the aircraft to virtually nothing over about nine years. The other quoted airlines were using 15, 16 even 22 years. No wonder the reported profits were lower and the profits on sales were high. The depreciation charge was twice that of other airlines – hitting the profit line - and so when they came to sell the aircraft they would make an apparent profit on the over-depreciated assets. I made a rough and ready adjustment to the profits of a selection of quoted airlines round the world using the same depreciation rate of 15 years for aircraft. The comparison showed a huge jump in underlying profits at Singapore Airlines.

"How much are they talking about selling it for?" I checked with Richard Bonsor.

"They seem to have fixed on S$5 a share."

"That's a total steal," I whistled. "This company is making money hand over fist."

In mid-October I flew out to Singapore to see the company and write a research report. I was joined by the analysts from Goldman Sachs, who were handling the US distribution, and Daiwa, who were selling the stock in Japan. The company strategy and figures were explained to us by senior management on the Tuesday morning and then we were taken on a tour of the base. At one point we studied the new Boeing 747 Megatops in the hangar from a gallery. They represented the launch order for this generation of planes.

I saw an executive at the side of the gallery and went over to him. He seemed to have a particularly proprietary smirk on his face as we gazed through the glass divider.

"They look pretty impressive," I commented.

"Yes," he said. "We ordered these planes at the exact trough of the recession and got some rock-bottom prices. Boeing was desperate for a launch order. We got round to selling the planes they were replacing a couple of months ago. Times are much better now, of course; even so we were pretty pleased when we sold them for more than we paid for the Megatops, even though they were seven years old." I was not surprised to learn that he was responsible for the company's plane purchasing strategy. No wonder the airline was so profitable when it could upgrade its fleet in this way at no cost whatsoever.

There was one more thing to check. I spent my last day visiting a couple of local brokers in the heart of Singapore's financial district, in their modern high-rise office blocks. What I learned dampened my enthusiasm somewhat. The Singapore market seemed to have climbed to dizzying levels. The brokers projected yet further rises and dismissed my cautions in the way typical of participants in all booms. I did not understand the particular and beneficial conditions Singapore was enjoying.

When I got back I wrote a note for our Far East investors that concluded that Singapore Airlines was a great purchase, even though the local Singaporean market was undoubtedly heading for a crash.

John Walker-Howarth was worried again. "We've got the senior management coming round next week to see the big investors one by one. The trouble is, we don't think the investors have the first clue what to ask them about. If the meetings go badly, we'll get the blame."

So it was agreed that I would go round to see all the investors ahead of the management. The main purpose was to make sure that all of the fund managers had interesting questions to ask. And, indeed, when the series of London meetings took place the reports we got back suggested that they had indeed gone well.

"We've held our end up with them," concluded a relieved John Walker-Haworth.

From then on the practice of sending an analyst round the investment community ahead of the management team 'roadshow' became standard. The purpose became to build up interest in the offer and persuade investors of the value of the company. Little did the analysts involved in later years realise that the practice originated in an acute concern within a corporate finance department to avoid embarrassment in front of a company's management.

We sold our allotment of shares with great ease. But my

concerns about the state of the Singaporean market were validated far sooner and far more dramatically than I had imagined. Almost immediately after the offer had closed a major diversified conglomerate in Singapore, called Pan-Electric Industries, collapsed. Its fall revealed a web of forward share dealings based on borrowed money and threatened a mayhem of collapsing confidence in the over-extended market. The Singaporean authorities promptly shut the market for three days to limit the repercussions of the worst financial crisis ever to hit the country. When it opened on 5 December the shares hit the floor.

"Singapore Airlines is now down below S$4," Richard Bonsor told me on the phone.

"What?" I exclaimed. "That's incredible. We should pile in."

The sales-force got the bit between its teeth and organised a series of meetings for me with the fund managers who had originally been most enthusiastic about the stock.

"You don't often get a get a chance like this," I told them. "The stock is completely undervalued. It doesn't matter what happens to the local market; Singapore Airlines effectively trades on international traffic flows." My recently published warning of incipient collapse added greatly to our credibility. The London investors started vacuuming up loose stock, sucking it out of the US and Japanese markets. Soon the price burst back through S$5 and kept on moving upward. By the end of February 1986 it was nearly S$7 and the price doubled again within eighteen months. It was the dramatic start of a long involvement for Rowe & Pitman – shortly to be renamed Warburg Securities – with the airline industry on the world's stock markets.

After the success of the British Telecom privatisation, the Conservative Government realised that there was no practical limit as to which assets might be transferred to the private sector. At the end of 1985, with the Singapore Airlines flotation freshly negotiated, I wrote a Christmas piece for our fund manager client base in our regular weekly Equity Briefing. For the occasion it was renamed 'Very Important Equity Briefing' and lampooned the conversation between a salesman and his client on the next big privatisation:

"Fund Manager: So what's the name of this new delight?

Stockbroker: you really mustn't worry about the name, Ron. It's coming early in the New Year, and whatever happened last time, this one is really going to be bargain basement stuff. P/E of 4. Honest.

Fund manager: Historic or prospective?

Stockbroker: Hang on, hang on, I reckon that must be historic. Fantastic fixed asset base. £8bn, it says here. And we're selling it for £1.5bn.

Fund manager: The name, George? The name.

Stockbroker: According to Bill, you know, Biggs, the projections are excellent. I can't tell you those. Not formally anyway. I could give you a bit or a steer though, maybe, informally.

Fund manager: Look George, all I want is the name.

Stockbroker: Oh all right. British Sewers plc."

The piece had gone down rather poorly with the sales-force, who read it with stony faces on the Thursday before Christmas.

The last laugh was on me though, because a few weeks later, in early February 1986, the Government released a White Paper on privatising the UK water industry, responsible for both the supply of water and the management of the sewerage systems. An idea that had appealed as fantasy had become reality with blinding speed. The water industry was to be divided into 10 separate companies, all to be floated off as soon as they had established individual identities and track records.

I immediately set to work finding out as much as possible about the industry. A fortnight later I was sitting at my desk working up our pitch to the industry when I was suddenly disturbed.

"And what are you working on?"

I turned round to see Queen Elizabeth, the Queen Mother. I knew, of course, that she was due to be shown round our offices that morning, but was not involved in her reception and had hardly expected her to arrive at my open-plan desk. I was a little taken-aback.

"I'm working on our presentations on the water companies," I explained. "For the planned privatisation."

"How interesting," she replied. "And do you think that privatisation is a good idea?"

That was a stinker. I opened my mouth, "Well . . .," I hesitated.

John Littlewood, her host for the morning, was ready with an instant reply, "We do think this approach has great benefits, Ma'am."

"Fascinating, fascinating," she replied, disguising any disappointment at this courtier's response.

In March we pitched to win the brokership of Thames Water - failing to be selected. Two months later we missed an appointment as stockbroker to Southern Water, so my record in the water industry was soon looking pitiful. The S.G.Warburg corporate finance department did slightly better and managed to pick up an advisory role for one of the smaller operators.

We had better luck a couple of years later, in February 1988, when we pitched to the Department of the Environment for the role of the Government's stockbroker. This was to be an extremely contentious transaction, with sustained hostility in the media. Nevertheless, it proved to be the plum appointment, and at the end of the following year we distributed all 10 companies in a package, at £5.2bn, of which £4.2bn was undertaken in the UK, the largest issue achieved by a single house till that time. On the first day of dealings, the complex basket of companies traded out at a 44% premium on the partly-paid price. Indeed, in retrospect it seems to have been the most successful of the UK privatisations in which I was involved – confounding my hesitation in front of the Queen Mother.

By the late 1980s, our patchy record in privatisations and large flotations was well and truly behind us, helped immeasurably by the successful flotation of Eurotunnel after the market crash in November 1987. Indeed the Government awarded us a second major stock-broking mandate early in 1988, in the shape of the privatisation of British Steel. While my role in the water industry was effectively limited to preparing the presentation, with some subsequent marketing oversight, in the case of British Steel I took full responsibility for managing the marketing campaign. However, on this occasion I was not required to write the research, especially as Warburg Securities - as we had now become - had transformed its research position and employed a leading analyst in the engineering sector in the shape of Ewen Cameron Watt. Instead, this became the first time I experienced the full weight of the committee work involved in a Government privatisation.

The key marketing challenge facing us was how to put some excitement into a company that operated in a distinctly unglamorous and old-fashioned industry in which over-capacity was endemic. These factors threatened to overwhelm the management's track record in pulling the company back into profitability. A tour of the company's facilities at the end of March provided the solution. There was nothing in the industrial world that could match the sheer drama of the steel production process. At the Port Talbot steel works in South Wales I watched in awe as a huge vessel filled with molten steel was tilted and the liquid metal within poured out. Sparks arced from the fiery mass and the noise of roaring and bubbling was overwhelming.

So in early July we took the first group of 20 fund managers from London's Paddington station in a private train carriage to Port Talbot. On the train, the management was able to spend more than an hour going through background information about the company and the industry background, as well as showing a video of the steel-making process. Once in the plant we went almost straight to see the Basic Oxygen Steelmaking (BOS) process that had so entranced me. It certainly had a similar effect on the fund managers, and their attitudes to the company softened significantly. We were taking a rather larger risk than we realised, because on one of the later tours, the fund management group had only just left the BOS plant when there was a mini-explosion with molten steel flying all over the shop. Wiping out a substantial proportion of the investor base would have been a novel approach to marketing.

In the event the £2.5bn flotation in December was a "close run thing", as Wellington observed after Waterloo, even with all the institutional investors still intact. The shares were subscribed only three times over and ended their first day of trading barely above the issue price.

I was involved in one other substantial UK float in the 1980s, for Abbey National, which converted from building society status and became a bank, issuing new equity in July 1989. Like the TSB, this was not formally a privatisation, but it had many of the hallmarks of this kind of transaction, with a huge advertising campaign to the retail public, in this case the 5.6m customers of the bank who would be allocated free stock. It had one other characteristic in common with the privatisations; the inordinate time between appointment and completion. In this case I first went to meet the finance director, James Tyrrell, in November 1985, just three days after the embarrassing launch of my TSB research. I had gained the introduction through a research colleague at work, whose wife worked as his secretary.

"That's classically the wrong way to meet people," Nick Verey had pointed out. But in this case it wasn't, because James Tyrrell proved to be a most uncharacteristic director of a financial institution, having recently moved from running the HMV record store chain. We spent much of that first meeting discussing the magnificent hi-fi system installed in his office in Baker Street. It was not until the middle of the next year, however, that we were formally appointed broker. And then it took a further three years before the float itself was completed.

By the end of the 1980s the first stage of the UK privatisation boom was visibly nearing completion with only the electricity industry left to float. By now we had established firm credentials in the privatisation arena, although the Government had never selected both sides of our firm – stockbroker and adviser – to act together. Nor was it especially attractive business in terms of profits. The Government took pride in pushing down fees at each transaction and other users of the market took their cue from this. For instance, for distributing more than £4bn of water stock in the most complex multi-company transaction seen anywhere in the world, our earnings as the Government's sole stockbroker were probably less than £3m.

It was time to turn the undoubted prestige these roles gave us, and our hard-won knowledge, into more profitable business. The international arena beckoned, especially with Governments round the world hurrying to copy the British privatisation model. Here we would come up against the US investment banks which were determined to take this business for themselves.

If we were to fight them successfully on neutral ground, we would have to change our whole approach to take advantage of the revolution created by Big Bang. Already at the beginning of 1986, Nick and I had started to work on those opportunities and in the next few years I would spend my "non-deal" time working on a series of projects designed to transform the way we operated.

---

[1] John Phelps, Sunday Express, 14 December 1986

4

All Together Now

Big Bang – 1984 - 1990

"We're not calling them handcuffs," Nick Verey told me. "They're too comfortable for that. We're calling them golden cufflinks." On 14 August 1984 it was finally announced that S.G.Warburg would be taking over Rowe & Pitman. It was hardly a surprise. Just before I arrived in the Stock Exchange tower Rowe & Pitman had tied up with the jobber Akroyd & Smithers for international business. Since Warburg had taken over this jobber in the previous November it had seemed almost inevitable that a three-way merger would be agreed. Indeed, in the end it was a four-way deal, since the Government gilt broker, Mullens & Co, was incorporated. This was the result of a discreet Bank of England 'suggestion', since Mullens would no longer have a role post Big Bang, when the Government would stop using a broker to sell its stock. The new combination was to be called the Mercury International Group.

The partners did their best not to exult too publicly over a substantial windfall. A total of some £46m was shared out between 36 partners and 12 near-partners, or 'Associate Members'. Part of the proceeds would be payable only to those still with the firm three years later, to encourage the partners to stay with the firm. These were the so-called golden handcuffs. To celebrate, Nick had a pair of gold cufflinks made up decorated with small handcuffs. In retrospect, and in the context of the payments made to City professionals over the next two decades, the payment was small beer: an average of less than £1m per partner or associate.

All over the City the picture was repeated as the partnerships sold out. The fifty Scrimgeours stockbroking partners sold out to Citicorp for a reputed £50m; stockbrokers Grieveson Grant received £44m from the merchant bank Kleinwort Benson; Barclays was reckoned to have paid up some £42m for the stockbroker de Zoete and £100m for the jobber Wedd Durlacher. John Littlewood took a keen interest in developments, both at the time and later. He wrote in his book, The Stock Market, "Never before had so many sellers run headlong into so many willing buyers[1]." Later he told me, "I reckon that the top nine stockbroking firms went for £450m, the five main jobbers for £300m and the smaller stockbrokers got another £400m."

I had been too late for any of this largesse. Nor was I particularly concerned. As Nick put it, "They're being paid for their position in the market. Actually, most of them won't be wanted in the Big Bang world, so it's a redundancy cheque. You shouldn't worry; you'll make your fortune by performing in that world."

The key rule change for the Stock Exchange concerned the nature of trading, which was not due to take place till October 1986. Meanwhile, the next two years represented a period of phoney war. The pieces were in place; the planning was under way; but the surface activity remained unchanged. At the end of 1984 I wrote a piece for Rowe & Pitman's institutional clients, in my capacity as the financial analyst, describing the Big Bang process. Entitled 'Pandora's Box in the UK Stock Market', it endeavoured to explain why the lifting of a seemingly arcane rule within the Stock Exchange had sparked "an extraordinary spate of corporate deals by the groups whose business is based on the UK stock market.

"The pressure for change seems to have its roots in two main developments. Firstly, the increasing concentration of capital in the hands of the institutions and secondly the growing internationalisation of capital markets, with the abolition of exchange controls in 1979 throwing the UK into the midst of this process.

"The US stock exchange restrictions were lifted in the mid 1970s, and the result has been the creation of a handful of well-capitalised, highly profitable securities houses. The greater interest of US funds in foreign securities is taking them abroad and their more competitive rates have enabled them to win international business out of London, taking it away from the UK firms which might otherwise have hoped to gain the business."

I was deeply pessimistic over the outcome for many of the houses. "Given the speed with which the process has taken place it would be surprising if a large number of the deals were not found to be failures and abort prematurely."

Privately I had come to the view that the only real strategy was to try to build up an equivalent business structure to that of the integrated US securities firms. I did not believe that the clearing banks could succeed in this and wrote off Barclays as a result. That left only two real contenders with adequate starting scale; the Warburg group for which I worked and Kleinwort Benson, which started a long way behind without a jobber and a broker with little experience of corporate work. The other leading merchant bank, Morgan Grenfell, was left standing in the blocks. With the benefit of hindsight there was only one thing wrong with my pessimism: it was too limited.

I had never met Siegmund Warburg, the founder of the firm for which I was now to work. He died in 1982 when I was still finding my way in financial markets as a journalist. But his achievement in building a leading merchant bank post-war was the subject of widespread commentary and, indeed, myth-making. A German Jew from a well-established European banking family based in Hamburg, he saw the writing on the wall early and fled Germany in April 1934. (This prescience reflected a sharp contrast with my own Jewish family, from Vienna, which did not flee till after the Anschluss of May 1938.) While many of the merchant banks were founded by foreigners – Rothschild, Hambro, and Kleinwort Benson, to name but three – those origins all lay in the nineteenth century or earlier. Warburg was the only independent twentieth century start-up of a major house. The small operation he founded in the 1930s, called the New Trading Company, was renamed S.G.Warburg and Company in 1946 and only joined the front rank of merchant banks as a member of the Accepting Houses Committee in 1957.

His success has been attributed to many factors. Warburg and his largely immigrant colleagues worked long hours and hard – an unusual trait compared with the relaxed norms of established rivals whose work-patterns descended from those devised for the convenience of the Victorian upper class. Siegmund Warburg was a rigorous and unforgiving taskmaster, who would scan all the communications coming in and going out of the firm. A secretariat to allow this information to be examined and shared was at the heart of the operation.

These performance standards were clearly important in the rise of the house of Warburg but they did not account for it. The key factors were an ability to innovate, born out of necessity, and a personal talent for effective marketing. "He was discreet and subtle and had the capacity to fascinate," recalled David Scholey, his successor at the bank, many years later. According to another executive whom he recruited, Simon Cairns, "He was more a philosopher than a banker." Siegmund Warburg maintained an astonishingly wide network of contacts which he maintained assiduously and his personal image and charm enabled him to work those contacts to win new business.

The two break-through innovations were in corporate finance and in the credit market. In 1958 he initiated the first 'hostile' takeover when he acted for the US-based Reynolds Metals Company of Virginia against the British Aluminium Company. An established corporate finance technique in the US, 'hostile' in this context meant proposing a transaction direct to the investors of a company which was not – initially, at least – supported by that company's board. When the investors preferred the Warburg offer, against an array of opposing merchant banks, the firm was suddenly a major player in corporate finance and was able to build up its list of clients on the back of its new-found prestige.

The second major break-through took place five years later, in 1963, when Warburg was commissioned by the Italian state entity responsible for reconstruction, IRI, to launch a eurobond for Autostrade, the motorway concession company. This $15m bond recreated the pre-1914 international bond market by targeting foreign currency held outside the owners' countries of residence. As such it was a market unbound by the exchange controls and other constraints of the national debt markets. It took off rapidly after this pioneering start and became a market of billions of dollars employing many thousands of highly paid financial professionals. As an originator, S.G.Warburg was able to gain a major position in this market and one of the most important departments of the merchant bank, the Financing Division, was filled with a cadre of foreign bankers whose job was to solicit eurobond mandates from companies round the world.

By 1984 the Warburg image was sharply defined. It was austere, as exemplified by a tradition of running two lunch sittings every day; by repute the less important clients were invited to the first sitting and the most valued to the second. (Neither were offered any alcohol other than perhaps a glass of beer.) It was thorough and careful. Advice was offered only after full consideration. Internal mail was classified either as secret, ephemeral (and typed on flimsy yellow paper) or suitable for the mail list. This last category of note was summarised daily and circulated to all corporate finance directors. Late hours reflected a hardworking culture and there were apocryphal stories of executives caught leaving a spare jacket hanging on their chair in the evening to disguise early departure.

Siegmund Warburg's successor was David Scholey, who became joint chairman of the bank in 1980, two years before the founder died, and was in charge when I arrived. David came from a City family. His father had worked at the small merchant bank Guinness Mahon and David spent seven years learning the ropes there before being recruited into Warburg in 1964. At the time of the merger he was in his late 40s. He shared several of Siegmund Warburg's characteristics. In particular, he was a phenomenal networker, meeting business contacts for breakfast, lunch and dinner, where he exercised his considerable charm. He displayed an intensity of interest in those he was meeting, occasionally feigned but more often, I thought, quite genuine. The driven quality of this regime led to two consequences. The first was personal; David was a tall man and his knife-and-fork-led marketing resulted in him building up considerable bulk in this period. The second was that he found it difficult to drag himself away from whomever he was talking to. As a result he was invariably late, sometimes extremely late, for the next meeting. This tardiness was adopted throughout the bank, and it was a rare meeting at Warburg that began within half-an-hour of the scheduled time. Clients would be driven to fury by the perceived discourtesy. In the latter part of the 1980s I was to have regular contact with him and he would always treat me with extreme courtesy even though I tended to the bumptious. "You were provocative, if not provoking," he summed up my endeavours many years later.

Soon after the takeover of Rowe & Pitman, I ran into another key figure at Warburg – Simon Cairns, then head of corporate finance. I had crossed swords with him on Lex, when he had done his best to disguise the rationale for the takeover of Akroyd & Smithers.

"I've been reading about your forebears in a dirty book," I told him.

"Which one was that?" he asked with a grin.

"There's a story in Frank Harris about an actress and a proposal of marriage that blew up." The Frank Harris book, My Life & Loves[2], was an explicit account of a late Victorian adventurer's progress through the social and sexual ranks of the period.

"Ah yes," he said, shaking his head, "That was my great uncle. He fell for a lady in the front row of the Savoy theatre and was foolish enough to propose in writing. When he changed his mind after a couple of evenings, Frank Harris put the lady up to suing. My great-uncle's father was the Lord Chancellor, the first Earl Cairns, who paid her half of everything my great-uncle stood to inherit. He later died of drink, having blown most of the Cairns' modest fortune."

When I first met him Simon was known as Lord Garmoyle, later inheriting his father's earldom and title as the sixth Lord Cairns. (In this book I have used the latter title throughout). Like most of the senior Rowe & Pitman partners, he had been schooled at Eton, going on to specialise in development economics at Cambridge University. He had then spent 17 years working at the stockbroking firm Scrimgeour. It was at this time that the relationship with David Scholey was established, when both were working on what was then the world's largest-ever equity offering, the Labour Government's £564m sale of BP stock in 1977. In retrospect this was a transaction that would have profound repercussions for Warburg. It was this deal, more than any other, that shaped the strategy for Big Bang and provided the bank with the leadership cadre with which to tackle the crisis of the next decade.

In David Scholey's words, "The Bank of England had appointed me personally as the representative of the banks and brokers on the deal. Simon was head of corporate finance for Scrimgeour and I was impressed by his individuality. He came at everything from a slightly different angle. He devised a way of co-ordinating the UK and US public offering systems, which was a complete breakthrough."

According to Simon, "It was during that deal, working with the US investment banks, that I worked out that if you are going to play in this league you've got to have the combination of skills or you will lose."

David cast his fly over Simon with great skill. "Would you ever take time to see Siegmund?" he asked at a subsequent meeting, in 1978. "I sent the letter you kindly wrote to me to our graphologist, and she rang Siegmund and said here was someone he should meet." Siegmund Warburg was famous for his use of graphology in recruiting. Simon described, "Against that bait, how could I say no? So I had two or three conversations with Siegmund. We didn't discuss business at all, we discussed anything but business – the arts, politics, commercial relations. Eventually I said OK." He joined Warburg at the beginning of 1979 and became an increasingly influential figure at the bank, seizing the opportunity to take over Akroyd & Smithers in 1983 when they came to him for advice.

While Simon was hardly a member of the haut riche (thanks in part to Frank Harris), he appeared almost a caricature of an aristocrat. He spoke in a languid drawl, with ironic quips and word-games, doing his best to disguise the intelligence behind the quizzical, amused, exterior. "Some people understood it and could go along with it," said Derek Higgs, one of his closest supporters at the bank. "It left others wondering what planet the bank was on."

Simon was also an influential figure when it came to deciding strategy for the division of the bank dealing with fund management. This was a third area of innovation, besides corporate finance and eurobonds, that was proving to be of great financial value to the group, although Siegmund Warburg himself did not appreciate it. The fund management department, called variously Warburg

Investment Management and later Mercury Asset Management (MAM), had grown into one of the leading operations in the market. I was to meet the management of this area quite quickly, since with my publications on fund management I had become one of the leading analysts in this highly specialised part of the market. In early July 1985 I was invited to their offices to discuss the value of the division. I explained the methodology and told them they were worth, on this basis, about 1.25% of their funds under management, or £125m. The eyes of Leonard Licht, one of the directors, lit up at this. "Do you think the market would be interested in a minority in us, if we were floated," he asked.

"Absolutely," I replied. "The sector's growing like topsy and there's very little stock out there. With £10bn under management you represent one of the leaders of the industry. They would snap you up."

This was all a very far cry from the recent past, when Siegmund Warburg was reputed to have tried to dispose of the division. According to David Scholey, "The reason he didn't like it was because the performance was so visible. There was no room for justification. No wiggle room." Peter Stormonth Darling describes in his witty book City Cinderella[3] how when he was appointed chairman of the business in late 1978, Siegmund told him to "get rid of it". Approaches were made to two rival merchant banks – Robert Fleming & Co and Lazard & Co. According to Peter, the price Siegmund Warburg indicated to Lazard was – in retrospect – a derisory £100,000. However, both banks seemed to consider that any offer from Siegmund Warburg was bound to be a poisoned chalice and politely declined.

The divisional management was pushing on an open door when they argued that some of their shares should be quoted. Simon Cairns explained, "There were accusations we used the shareholdings for the bank's purposes where we were the adviser and MAM was a big shareholder. This came up most invasively in the Lonrho v House of Fraser deals. I spent time in front of the Department of Trade inspector, which is not a particularly pleasant exercise when you don't know what the other side has said. 'Do you mean that you used the very large shareholding that your investment side had in House of Fraser automatically to be on your side? Do you mean to say, Lord Garmoyle, that you do not do that? Now I've got some bits of paper here that suggest you might have done.' In fact we got the cleanest bill of health you can get. But in all the big takeover battles MAM tended to have what might be the decisive shareholding so, firstly I was keen on the separation of MAM and secondly I was in favour of a quote for some shares in the subsidiary to indicate a further degree of separation."

It took nearly two years to float the 25% minority and by then it was clear that the fund management division was a major asset for the group. Immediately after the April 1987 float it was valued at £240m, a substantial proportion of the group as a whole. Whether the sale of the minority was in the interests of the rest of the group would become a topic of sustained argument in the following decade. In 1994 the separate quotation threw a logistical hurdle in the way of the entire group's strategy and was a factor in its subsequent collapse.

As 1985 progressed I met more of my new Warburg colleagues. Typically this was in meetings to discuss potential transactions, but they were relatively few and far between. The most dynamic group were in the Financing Division, who were keen to see how they could capitalise on the success of Rowak, the jobber/broker combination that had seized a large market share of the international share business in London. The Financing Division grew out of Siegmund Warburg's initiative in originating the eurobond, now a huge international market in which the incredible sum of $800m a day was being raised. Unfortunately, with the big banks, particularly the Japanese, muscling into the market, margins were appalling and it was impossible for a bespoke business like Warburg's to make money any more. The executives in the Financing Division were keen to see if they would have better luck in the international equity markets, which were then in their infancy. In fact the deal with Singapore Airlines in which I had been involved was one of the first genuine transactions in this market. In early April 1986 Rodney Ward, the executive responsible for financing business in North America, dragged me out to Montreal to meet Air Canada executives and talk about how we might help them privatise in the light of our

Singapore experience. It was the first time I had experienced Rodney's 'drop everything and jump on a plane' attitude – a lesson I was to take to heart in my subsequent career.

Rodney and his colleagues had proved forceful in other ways too. They insisted on leaving the main headquarters of their S.G.Warburg colleagues on the London Bridge end of King William Street and decamped en masse to our Broadgate building. "If we're going to do business in the markets, we damned better be near the traders," Rodney explained the move to me. "What's the point of sitting around with all those deadbeats?" This was an unkind reference to the corporate finance division, and probably senior management too, given Rodney's genius for casual abuse. He was in his early 40s when I first met him, a hyperactive bundle of energy towering a full six foot five inches, constantly looking at ways to drum up business. A Cambridge rowing Blue, he had spent much of his time at Warburg in the US, where he worked for the eight years before returning to the UK in early 1985. "Move those cheeks," he would summon his secretary when an urgent letter needed to be dictated, in days when the concept of sexual harassment was still unformulated.

Outside the Financing Division, however, Warburg seemed much less dynamic. There was little evidence of innovation, while marketing for new customers seemed an alien concept. The corporate financiers seemed content to rely on their reputation and methodical reliability in executing transactions.

"They're like a whisky production line," said Nick Verey. "All they worry about is making sure that the whisky is excellent. In fact they should be worrying about the image of the whisky and the marketing strategy." Nick had chosen this particular analogy because he and, to a much more limited extent, I had been working as brokers for Argyll in its bid for Distillers. Nick's thought processes always became permeated with whatever transaction he was currently working on. It was Saturday 19 April 1986 and we were sitting in his office in our casual clothes, trying to plan the future. Nick was baffled by Argyll's defeat in the battle for Distillers, which had been announced the day before. "I don't know how Cazenove did it. They simply outgunned us; we couldn't match the price that they drummed up. It's the Mayhew Magic," he sighed, referring to the senior partner at Cazenove, David Mayhew, who two days earlier had beaten our side's bid for the critical Distiller's stake held by our sister company, Mercury Asset Management. "You can't blame the MAM boys. They managed to get absolutely the top price for their clients." In the years to come we were to learn that the 'Mayhew Magic' was of the black variety as the full details of the Guinness scandal emerged. It was a scandal that was to see many of the participants serve prison sentences and to trigger the fall of Morgan Grenfell. David Mayhew himself was cleared of any wrong-doing. On that Saturday afternoon, however, we had little inkling of these repercussions. After chewing over our failure we got down to the purpose of the session. Nick was casting around for a role in the new group, stung by the success of his senior colleagues. Peter Wilmot-Sitwell was the chairman of the new Securities division and on the Board of the parent company, as was John Littlewood, who had become head of administration for the whole group. Peter Hardy was in charge of the equities trading floor, while Stuart Stradling remained responsible for corporate broking. Nick had been appointed a senior director of the division, but a fortnight earlier First Boston had offered him a job, flying him over to their New York headquarters to make the offer, and he admitted that rejection had not been a straightforward decision.

"We've got a major problem," I said. "The Warburg Securities broking operation and the S.G.Warburg corporate finance department have got about 350 clients in total. That's great. The trouble is - they only hold nine of them in common." I had been analysing the client lists of the two firms. A decade earlier Rowe & Pitman had fallen flat on its face in placing a bond for a Warburg client, a Canadian paper company. Warburg had been left holding the bulk of the debt and ever since had steered its clients away from the broker – explaining the almost complete lack of overlap.

"On the other hand, it's a major opportunity, since we can warm call more than half the leading companies in the country," responded Nick.

"None of which want an integrated adviser and broker," I pointed out. There was considerable propaganda in the market that clients' best interests were served by choosing a separate adviser and broker. It was an argument promoted strongly by the merchant banks without an effective distribution arm – which meant most of them.

"And that toad Stradling is doing his best to encourage them," Nick said bitterly. The rivalry between the two of them was growing, and now it was developing a structural base, as Stuart fought to maintain his broking empire. I did not know it at the time but Nick had argued strongly that he should take over corporate broking within a remodelled coverage department. Stuart Straddling, naturally, had been furious. Later he told me, "I got on fine with Nick until he tried to steal my job." With Straddling successful in fending Nick off, Rowe & Pitman, as the small corporate broking department would still be called, would work for as many merchant banks as possible. Nick, meanwhile, was tying his flag to the integrated mast.

In the privacy of his office we laid into both S.G.Warburg and Rowe & Pitman. "Neither side knows how to market. The systems are obsolete. There are far too many generalists where there should be specialist functions. The trouble is that Siegmund was a brilliant marketer and he recruited executioners to transact his deals. Now that he's gone the executioners are running the show."

"We don't even collect price data, for Christ's sake," I expostulated. When Peter Wilmot-Sitwell or Stuart Stradling – or for that matter you – are with a client who asks for a piece of advice you pluck an answer from the air. If the client wants to know the right discount on which to launch a transaction Peter answers that he 'feels it in his water' that 14% is the right level. No analysis of the level at which other recent deals have been done, and how they performed. We simply don't know. Mind you, Peter says it absolutely brilliantly."

"Right," said Nick, "We need to recruit somebody to record all this data. We'll call it 'Scoreboard'."

"And another thing. The brokers are spending half their time responding to queries from the companies about what the investors think about them and how they should address those concerns. The brokers do their best, but it's not their specialism, and they don't get paid for the work. So they skimp and leave the client unhappy."

"What's your solution for that?"

"We should set up a specialist investor relations service, for which clients pay, having agreed a specific contract."

"Exactly," agreed Nick, "People only value what they pay for and if they pay the true cost of the service we will be able to afford to provide it."

"We're going to need a marketing data base for the whole bank, if we are going to try and approach corporates from both the broking and advisory sides," I added. "And we'll also need decent presentation materials. At the moment we seem to rely on typed up letters to make our proposals – usually delivered weeks after the originating enquiry to make sure it is absolutely perfect."

We both found the Saturday session deeply cathartic, and they became a regular feature of our working lives, with more and more attendees over the years as our team expanded. For Nick had now found a role in the new organisation and he began to discuss with David Scholey how he might drive forward the detailed task of integrating the group.

Before those talks reached fruition, in summer 1986, Stuart Stradling summoned me to his desk. "The idea is, you see, that you join the corporate broking department. Peter thinks that we need your marketing flair full time, and I agree with him." I already knew about Peter Wilmot-Sitwell's plans and was pleased to agree. Stuart was clearly concerned about my close relationship with Nick, however. "You do understand, don't you," he said, "that you will be working for me, now." Again, I was happy to agree, although in the free-wheeling atmosphere of a securities house in those days I found it difficult to understand what that meant in practice. To Stuart, I suspect, it meant that I cut my ties with Nick. To me, it meant that I would work more with the broking team and Stuart personally, which I was happy to do. I had recently completed the float of the computer leasing company IBL under his overall charge and found him easy to work with.

However, as Stuart saw little sign of change in my relationship with Nick, I suspect he regretted accepting me in the corporate broking room almost as soon as he made the invitation. The first problem was my computer.

"Well you can't sit with us if you're going to bring your

computer in here."

"Why on earth not?"

"It hums. It will distract us."

"But we're all going to need computers. We won't be able to function without computers."

"Speak for yourself. I can function perfectly well without one. You'll have to sit over there, next to the secretaries. Then we won't hear it."

The corporate broking room hierarchy was expressed by how close one's desk was to Stuart's. My position behind the door was about as far away as it was possible to be, while still in the room, reflecting a status somewhere between typist and outcast.

"I want to recruit someone to help me in all these marketing projects," I explained.

"Fine. If you feel you need to."

"She's called Julia Land. She's been an audit manager at the accountants Arthur Andersen & Co."

"I'm not sure there's going to be enough room for her."

"There's a spare desk next to mine. She can use that."

So Julia arrived and joined me next to the secretaries. But not for long. I was searching for an appropriately qualified youngster to set up 'Scoreboard', the market information source that Nick and I had decided was essential to allow us to be coherent in front of clients.

"I would like to recruit Caroline Speck for this role," I explained to Stuart. Caroline was a graduate who had spent three years with the rival bank County NatWest. A second female for this all-male bastion was clearly pushing the boundaries of acceptability.

"If you're going to employ girls, you really can't sit in here," Stuart exploded. "You'll have to find a place outside."

Stuart's fury was probably driven by the uneasy feeling that Nick had outflanked him. Early in July David Scholey had put out a note to the bank announcing that Nick had been appointed to run a Corporate Development Group that would span both the merchant banking and securities groups. He would be responsible "for developing new clients, new ideas and new products". I would be working directly for him, as the director of Corporate Development, effectively as his chief of staff and ideas generator. With a network of senior participants from across the group, and a place on the board, Nick would have the weight to make sure our ideas were pushed through. Stuart, who pointedly was not in this group, could only resent the flood of initiatives, especially as I am sure he believed that existing arrangements were entirely satisfactory.

Our first challenge was to organise the way in which corporate clients were covered. This was an issue that was to remain a top concern of all investment banks for the rest of my career. As Nick put it on one of our Saturday sessions: "All our top people spend their time doing transactions. In the future the top bankers will spend their time talking to the clients and persuading them to use us for their transactions." We wrote a paper recommending a matrix style approach, with executives from different parts of the bank liaising under a senior relationship holder.

"Ouch. That's going to be political," I said to Nick. "Who's going to decide who's a senior relationship holder and who's in a support role? And it's going to need some pretty sophisticated computer programming if everyone is to have access to what the other members of the team are doing."

"I'll sort out the politics," said Nick. "You can sort out the programming. I thought you liked computers."

"Isn't that a bit ambitious. After all, I'm just about the only corporate financier in the bank with a computer at the moment."

"This is our chance to get a computer on every banker's desk," said Nick. And so I spent the next two years working with the IT department to build a programme that would disseminate information about our clients. We called it the Group Client Information System - GCIS for short - and it became the Trojan horse that in 1989 was to computerise the whole investment banking department.

"How are we going to cover small companies?" I asked. "It's no good having an elaborate coverage model for them because it will cost too much. We should have a dedicated team of young bankers and brokers working together to float fast-growing companies."

"We should call it the Acorn Unit," decided Nick, who set about organising a team to realise the vision. This was an idea that was better in contemplation than execution. The first company floated by the unit was called, suitably enough, Babygro; the manufacturer of a stretch romper suit for infants. Unfortunately, rather like IBL, it blew up shortly after flotation and left the Acorn Unit's reputation in tatters.

The formal date of Big Bang was Monday 27 October, when the new trading system, Stock Exchange Automated Quotations – or SEAQ – went live. This was a real-time system under which market participants could see the competing quotes of their rivals; more to the point so could the investing institutions. A brand new trading floor for equities had been assembled on the fifth floor at Finsbury Avenue. It stretched right across one side of the office block and round the atrium. Here there was room for the traders, salesmen and research analysts to work together. It was not clear yet whether the Stock Exchange floor would continue to function or whether all the activity would migrate to the trading floors of the major securities firms. John Littlewood, in charge of the transformation, had made contingencies for a full transfer. We held a rehearsal of the new system well before its launch, on Saturday 12 July. Here the salesmen were challenged to complete orders. These might be put through on an agency basis, in which we would still receive a commission for finding the best price in the market for our client. Alternatively we tested how to handle a net order, which represented a sale straight from our book in which no commission was payable. Phil Ellick, the salesman running the show, threw a test at me: "Right, David, one of your corporate accounts wants 5% of its rival, company X. Will you charge commission?"

"I'd like to," I said.

"In that case can you afford to let the market find out what you're doing by only going to the firm offering the best price?"

"I don't know."

"No. Neither do I. I guess we'll find out later."

Big Bang, when it happened, was an anti-climax. Our systems stood up, as did SEAQ for most of the day – although it was suspended for a little over an hour while a computer glitch was sorted out. The main fall-out was in the Stock Exchange building itself, which steadily emptied as the traders and brokers migrated to the new trading floors each of the aspiring securities houses had built round the SEAQ screens. By January, the Stock Exchange floor was abandoned by the last of its supporters, the former jobber Smith New Court.

"If we're not careful, they're going to eat our lunch," Nick said in one of our Saturday sessions. He was referring to the US banks. "They're coming over here and they know what they're doing. They've had a decade to organise themselves. You'd better go over to New York and see what you can find out."

At the end of March 1987 I flew over to see a wide array of US bankers – somewhat amazed that they would spend the time to see a nascent rival. Goldman Sachs, Morgan Stanley, First Boston and Shearson all opened their doors to me. I spent most of my time learning how the US banks handled new issues of equity and how they managed their relationships. In both they had great advantages over us. In a new issue they would typically collect between 5% and 7% of the amount raised – dwarfing the standard 0.75% which was the amount normally shared by the UK adviser and broker. Of this commission, up to 70% would be kept by the lead bank, the book-runner.

There was nothing particularly new about how the US banks managed relationships with clients – except that they were extremely focused and well-established, while our own structure had only just been agreed in principle. "We've spent $60,000 on software to make sure that we have a proper call reporting system," the managing director at First Boston told me.

"They've got to make the calls, and they've got to record them," said the executive at Shearson. "I fined one of my best producers $50,000 last year because he didn't record his calls."

"Wow," I said, "That's serious money."

"Yup. He only got $750,000 as a result." It was a different planet. In that year I had earned less than a quarter of this amount. And that was after a two-year period which began shortly after I joined the firm during which my salary was raised every half-year, reflecting the competitive pressures in the build-up to Big Bang.

I returned to the UK more determined than ever to push

through our project to re-engineer the bank. Nick had assembled some powerful allies in the endeavour to turn the bank into a marketing-led operation. Chief among them was Derek Higgs, whom David Scholey had asked at the time of Big Bang to head up an integrated corporate finance division, including the Rowe & Pitman broking team. Derek had made his own way in life. His father had seen to that. A self-made businessman, he had left all his money to charity, which Derek administered. After Bristol university and a spell at the accountants Price Waterhouse, he joined Warburg in 1972, aged 28, attracted in part by the egalitarian and meritocratic culture of the bank. Derek was a breezy, cheerful individual who eschewed airs and graces. He had a tendency to search for complicated solutions and to describe them in even more convoluted language. This trick probably stood him in good stead when he was negotiating a merger and the objective was to obscure differences. As a management technique it was less satisfactory and many times I would leave his office wondering what, exactly, we had agreed. Nor was I alone.

Nick and Derek assembled a group from the other divisions. Laboriously through 1986 and the first part of 1987, they allocated responsibility for corporate marketing to teams across the bank. On paper it was a fine system. In retrospect it had a major flaw. Whereas the US banks were recruiting, promoting and measuring people on their ability to win business, Warburg was still dominated by experts in execution, many of whom regarded marketing as irredeemably vulgar. Nothing Nick or Derek did in this period shifted the balance of personnel towards the new model.

In large part this was due to the management approach adopted by David Scholey, who exercised extreme caution in effecting the four-way merger. The senior Rowe & Pitman partners were delighted with this style. Peter Wilmot-Sitwell, chairman of the securities business, told me later, "David took the view right from the beginning that he had bought a business for a lot of money and he wasn't going to run their business."

John Littlewood, head of administration for the group, told me, "I thought David Scholey was incredible - charismatic, cultured, thoughtful and demanding. He took people as he found them. He ran the group in a collegiate style, but he forced us to take decisions. I was chairman of three committees and he used to say that the other members of the committee were there to help me, but I had to take the decisions."

While David's consensual approach was certainly instrumental in ensuring the success of the merger, drawbacks became more apparent when it came to building on that success. With the benefit of considerable hindsight, Derek Higgs later expressed his frustration to me. "The board had 30 people on it, compared with the seven that Morgan Stanley had. It was simply hopeless. Fairness was paramount for David and there was too much respecting the past institutions. There was a sub-current of trying to keep things unchanged. We should have gone harder for the integrated service and if people were not committed to it they should have been allowed to go somewhere else." Part of that frustration reflected Stuart Stradling's obstinate success in maintaining the independence of his broking operation.

David preferred to encourage change from below rather than impose it from above. To that extent, he provided very considerable support to the Corporate Development team. Nick would obtain semi-automatic approval for all the schemes we developed. David would refer to us as his 'hit squad', looking to us to effect the change that was essential if we were to compete globally. However, much as I relished this opportunity to be at the heart of a revolution, in retrospect David should have relied less on this form of guerrilla management and more on central direction.

My next project was to go one step further in coverage, by promoting what I called in a paper written in May 1987 'Industry specialisation in investment banking'. In the paper I argued that corporate clients would appreciate knowledge of their industry and business. "A research-based understanding of the industry concerned will help us think up and recommend deals as well as create financing products." As a first step I set about creating a team to cover the banking sector, recruiting John Reizenstein out of the corporate finance division to head up this effort. In practice his team became the first of the sectors established by S.G.Warburg. From the mid-1990s, the sector approach was to become general right across the European investment banking industry. Indeed, in the fullness of time I was to become a sector banker myself, and to put into practice the approach I developed in 1987.

Not everybody appreciated my efforts. In September Nick Verey called me into a room with a look close to despair on his face. "David, I have some terrible news. You've been turned down for a full directorship."

I had not been aware that I was being considered, so I was less upset than he had expected.

"Stuart Stradling and Nick Whitney opposed you strongly," Nick told me. "Peter didn't feel he could push it through against their opposition."

That did make me more upset. "Did they say why?" I asked.

"They said you weren't a safe pair of hands. But that's bollocks. It's an attack on me as much as you."

I had paid the price for my run-ins with the press over the Midland Bank and British Airways. But actually I was not particularly disconsolate at this reverse. I was simply too busy with all the projects and by now I was deeply immersed in the rescue of Eurotunnel. Given the high profile nature of this transaction, and the pivotal role I was taking on, my place up or down a rung of the ladder of the Warburg hierarchy hardly seemed to matter.

In fact Peter Wilmot-Sitwell did not let me stew for long. The following May it was announced that I had been appointed a director of Warburg Securities. He sent out a curt note apologising for the fact that there had not been time to consider this appointment at a full committee meeting of directors. The time-table would be re-adjusted so that this omission would not happen again. Certainly, as far as I was concerned, Peter would not let the infighting between Stuart and Nick have any further repercussions.

By the autumn of 1988 it was time to take stock of our position post-Big Bang and how the group should move forward. A planning exercise, conducted by John Littlewood and completed in October, made interesting reading. The S.G.Warburg Group (as we had now renamed ourselves) had emerged as the largest of the investment banks to be based in the UK. Headcount totalled 3,630. We had strong market shares in corporate finance, at about 15% and in the equities market with 15% in market making and 8% in distribution. Big Bang had transformed our research position; up from an also-ran in the previous year to third, according to the most reliable survey, run by Extel. But the financial analysis made more sobering reading. Only three major business lines were profitable: the traditional UK corporate finance business, UK equities and fund management. Eurobonds were loss-making, as was fixed interest, while the cost of building businesses in Japan and the US from scratch also tore a hole out of the profits. As a result international equities had pulled down the group's pre-tax profit of £111m in the year to March 1988 by nearly 20%.

While it was the largest investment bank in the UK, with capital and reserves of $1.1bn at the end of 1987, Warburg was dwarfed by the competition, lying thirteen in a league table made up of powerful Japanese and US securities houses. Salomon and Merrill had three times our capital. There was also a powerful group of commercial banks with substantial resources; Citicorp, UBS of Switzerland, Deutschebank, Credit Suisse and J.P. Morgan each had capital and reserves five times and more the size of ours.

The paper concluded - tentatively - that we should look for growth businesses in three areas: Europe, cross-border M&A and derivative products.

"The real trouble," said Nick, as we leafed through the final report, "is that Big Bang has transformed S.G.Warburg from a nimble international business into a big and decidedly UK one. I hope it hasn't killed the entrepreneurial culture of the business, although I fear it has."

I was to see the discomfort at our narrow earnings base at first hand the following June, when Warburg released its figures for the year to March 1989. In my capacity as the executive responsible for our press relations, I joined David Scholey for his briefing of journalists. We saw representatives from each of the major newspapers for an hour each through the Tuesday morning.

"How much commission income did you make abroad?" asked the Financial Times.

"Well it depends how you define abroad," David prevaricated. He launched into a long theoretical explanation about how we might categorise particular bits of business that left the two journalists sighing in exasperation. Later in the day I phoned all the newspapers to give the journalists a clear (and naturally favourable) interpretation of the results. David was characteristically and immediately grateful. "I thought that you prepared, prompted (and in some cases even wrote) the press comment excellently yesterday. Well done and thank you," he wrote in a note. The morning had been a dramatic pointer to David's dislike of showing the world our true performance. The merchant banks had been accustomed to providing a smooth profit progression through the use of hidden reserves, which meant their figures had been indicative at best, if not complete nonsense. In the post-Big Bang world there was no such hiding place and the bank was culturally unprepared for it. This was a discomfort that would assume vital importance when profits collapsed in 1994 and led directly to the crisis that engulfed the bank.

Whatever lay in the future, our position was infinitely preferably to that of some of our rivals, whose businesses were now rapidly unravelling. Morgan Grenfell announced in December 1988 that it was shutting its equities division as the costs of building a business from scratch overwhelmed it. The firm was struggling with the aftermath of the Guinness scandal and within a year it had sold itself to Deutsche Bank. County NatWest and the UBS-owned Phillips & Drew were both badly damaged by another City scandal, when they misled institutions over the level of their secret holdings of shares after a failed placement of the recruitment agency Blue Arrow in August 1987. Rumours were rife that losses at Kleinwort's equity business would inevitably lead to closure – although in practice the management refocused the strategy of the business in the following year and kept going. My gloomy predictions of 1984 were becoming fulfilled in spades.

As far as the Corporate Development team was concerned, the last two years of the decade saw the transfer of many of our initiatives into the operational mainstream. Computers were, at last, put on all executives' desks. An investor relations service was growing into considerable scale, and independence, under Julia Land. Now we set to work to modernise the presentations made to clients. We bought an Apple Mac and my secretary, Heather Jane, went on a training course on how to use it. Before long I found myself without a secretary as all her time was taken up in producing presentations. In the years to come Heather's one-man effort was to expand into a major department. It would span the world with some 200 operatives churning out the flipbooks and slide shows that were to become the staple output of the investment banking world. It was to be the essential base for our dramatic success in the international equity market in the early 1990s.

Almost unconsciously we were closing down our efforts. My assistant Julia Land moved over full-time into Investor Relations, building up a team and reporting to corporate broking; the 'Scoreboard' monitoring process had migrated to the relevant business areas; seminar management was hived off. I found more and more of my time taken up with transactions. So when Nick told me in early 1990 that he was being sent out to the New York office, to act as chairman there, it seemed natural to close down the Corporate Development operation. It had served its purpose. We had set up the systems necessary for effective marketing; now it was up to the bank to apply them effectively.

I would have to find a new role. However, I suspected that wouldn't be a problem. Parallel with my work in Corporate Development two transactions – Eurotunnel and Euro Disney – had propelled me towards the newly opened international equity markets. The next chapters tell the dramatic story of those two experiences.

---

[1] The Stock Market:50 Years of Capitalism at Work, by John Littlewood. Financial Times Pitman Publishing, p324

[2] My Life and Loves by Frank Harris in five volumes. Grove Press reprint of Bookthrift edition. Volume Two, p331.

[3] City Cinderella, The Life and Times Of Mercury Asset Management, by Peter Stormonth Darling. Weidenfeld & Nicolson, 1999. Chapter 13.

5

Tunnel Vision
Eurotunnel – 1986 - 1994

~

Alastair Morton was bristling with rage. "Who the hell leaked that story to the Standard?"

"I did," I admitted reluctantly.

It was late November, 1987. Alastair Morton was the co-chairman of Eurotunnel and we were the lead brokers to the flotation, meeting to assess the level of applications. They had indeed fallen short, as the Evening Standard had suggested they probably would.

"And who the hell authorised you to talk to the press?" he demanded.

"He's been talking to the press every day for the last four months," Nick Verey pointed out. "We wouldn't be here today if he hadn't been talking to the press."

Our involvement with Eurotunnel had begun nine months earlier, and had been a roller-coaster experience, from despair to elation to despair again. We had taken on the transaction only with the greatest hesitation.

My own awareness of the project dated back to the previous summer. We had had no involvement in the Channel Tunnel competition whatsoever, let alone the winning consortium, Eurotunnel, so my interest was confined to a cursory look at newspaper coverage every now and then. It all seemed remote and somehow fantastical: a company that did not exist raising £1bn in the equity markets.

My indifference was punctured by the S.G.Warburg project

finance team, in the shape of Nick Wakefield and Kit Beer, who I first met in the spring of 1986. They were extremely interested in whether equity could be raised out of the stock market for infrastructure projects – hardly surprising, since it would open up new levels of activity for their business. Project finance was an esoteric part of the financial markets, dominated by a handful of major commercial banks. Typically these lent long-term money on the collateral of future earnings that would be generated from a project. The business received a big boost in Europe in the 1970s with the opening up of North Sea oil reserves using this type of financing. As the financial structures involved became more sophisticated, a wider range of banks became interested in the area. Nick and Kit had been separately recruited from the giant US bank, American Express, at the end of the 1970s to lead the Warburg effort. This concentrated on advising companies on how to structure and fund projects that they did not want to finance themselves. Until then, the main emphasis of such project finance specialists had been on assembling various forms of debt for each project. The equity involved was usually extremely modest and typically provided by the sponsors of the project. My vague disinterest in exploring the potential in the quoted equity market did not satisfy them at all.

"Come on, David. I thought you were meant to take up all the new opportunities round here. I challenge you to think about something bigger than getting market equity into infrastructure. There are billions of dollars of projects going on all the time, all over the world," said Nick Wakefield. Nick always showed immense drive when it came to persuading others to help him in any particular endeavour. I was to be closely involved with him on several major transactions in the future.

They had an ulterior motive. "We're trying to get a role in this Thames Crossing at Dartford, and market equity would give us the edge. Would you help us take some market soundings?"

I couldn't really refuse. So the next week I went with one or the other of them to see a handful of institutions to find out whether they would be interested in investing equity in the Thames project. The responses were unambiguous. They were put most expressively by MAM, who could afford to be blunt, since it was the in-house fund manager of the Mercury Group and our sister-company.

"We don't like investing in building projects, because UK contractors always over-run and hold you to ransom," said Carol Galley, reinforcing her team's disinterest at a lunch I had with her shortly afterwards. Carol was in charge of UK investments at the asset manager and was to become well-known for her clear-headed approach to the task, an approach that was to earn her the soubriquet of 'Ice-Maiden'. She ticked off the points on her elegantly manicured fingers.

"The return isn't enough for this level of risk. We need a return of at least 25% a year to compensate for the risks. You're offering below 20%.

"Besides, we wouldn't come in early. We can wait till your bridge opens and the dividends start to flow. Nothing will happen to the stock till then anyway. And yes, I know that if everyone decides to wait you won't have a hope in hell of launching an Initial Public Offering. That's markets for you."

As soundings go, this one had the virtue of clarity. The other institutions were equally negative. It was quite clear that the dream of Kit and Nick of using the equity market was premature, at best.

"Mind you," said Nick, as we shook hands after our brief post-mortem, "our problem is minuscule compared with that of Eurotunnel. We can always stick to loans. They have committed to raising a sixth of their funds in equity, as a condition for obtaining their debt. After what Carol said I'd be impressed if they got £50m, let alone the £1bn they're going to need. No wonder they are in trouble."

From that May I began to take more than a cursory interest in what was happening to Eurotunnel. And it was not pretty.

Eurotunnel had won the competition to build the cross-channel link in January 1986, after a four-way competition. Its pure rail solution was chosen despite the Prime Minister, Mrs Thatcher's, preference for a road-based option. However, it was seen as the safe alternative, with a proven technology, reliable cost estimates, as well as extensive financial and contracting commitment from both sides of the channel. Eurotunnel was effectively a 50/50 partnership between a French and British company, each of which consisted of some of the leading contractors and banks in the country.

Mrs Thatcher's other main requirement was not so easy to overturn. Over French objections she insisted that the tunnel was built only with private finance. While this was a requirement that could be absorbed in the more centralised financial organisation of France, with its nationalised banks, it was a major challenge in the more open UK market. And the company faced this challenge when the effort of putting together such an extended consortium and winning the highly complex bid seemed to have exhausted it.

Through the spring the company developed its financial plans. In the critical London market its financial team was weak. The advisers were Morgan Grenfell, not a major issuing house however powerful in M&A, and the boutique merchant bank, Flemings. Its brokers were Fielding Newson-Smith (in the process of changing its name to County Securities), the securities arm of NatWest, and Scrimgeour, a subsidiary of Citigroup. Neither were recognised corporate brokers. Seeing their livelihood at stake, the ferry operators had created an organisation called Flexilink to attack the rationale for a tunnel. Its vocal opposition produced extremely effective propaganda against the project.

By June expectations were beginning to build up. Investors had been approached and the official prospectus for raising £206m in what was called Equity 2 was due. The official launch of the campaign was announced in mid-June. The strategy was to raise the money, mainly in the London and Paris markets, in the form of unquoted equity. This would keep the company going till a substantial issue of £750m in the quoted equity markets a year later, which would in turn trigger the ability to draw down £5bn of loans from the banking consortium.

Week after week went by, and still no prospectus. No explanation either. The level of negative comment in the media began to build up. By July the company was forced to announce a delay, to general derision. It emerged later that one of the major factors holding up the process was a battle between the banks and the contractors over where the financial risks should lie. When the row was settled the pathfinder prospectus was released in late

September. The opposition was well prepared. Flexilink held a press conference to ridicule the whole operation. Richard Hannah, a young transport analyst at Phillips & Drew, concluded in a research paper[1]: "These returns are low by venture capital standards". Richard was in the process of discovering that overt opposition to Eurotunnel was the quickest road imaginable to publicity and a high profile in the market.

The returns of the project in the pathfinder prospectus were stated to be 16.7% a year[2], a figure seized on by commentators and deemed by the institutional investors to be too modest. It was probably the single issue that caused most discontent among those being asked to invest.

There is nothing more soul-destroying than watching a placement fall apart in your hands. Institutional investors are polite to your face, but slow; and finally, eventually, negative in their indication of interest. This was the fate of the County/Scrimgeour team as they anxiously counted up their commitments day after day and saw the figures inevitably coming in short.

At this stage the Government, for all its protestations about leaving the project to the private market, took a very direct involvement, through the Bank of England. It began to move on two fronts. Firstly, to sort out the management of the project and, more immediately, to make sure that Equity 2 was completed.

One of the County/Scrimgeour team described the experience to me afterwards. "It was horrific. We were told to go to the war-room and wait by the phone. We weren't required to join the Bank team in contacting the institutions. In fact, we never found out who from the Bank was doing the rounds. Some-one clearly was, because every fifteen minutes or so the telephone would ring and one of the institutions, which had point-blank refused to invest up till then would say through gritted teeth, 'Put me down for £1m, then', and slam down the phone. Bloody effective equity raising, mind; Bank of England Broking Services Limited, they should go into business".

When it was revealed that the first stage shareholders, contractors and banks (as well as two of the sponsors), had to put their hands in their own pockets to contribute a further £18m or so in order to complete the issue, any sense of achievement in the outcome was effectively dampened still further. The main legacy of the process had been to build up real dislike for the project among those institutions forced to invest in it. The challenge facing the company in raising £750m within nine months of such a public rejection and in so hostile an investing environment was steeper than anything I had seen previously. Most companies need to convert indifference into enthusiasm to get their floats away. Eurotunnel's starting point would be overt contempt.

It didn't get easier for the company after Equity 2. The Bank of England juggled with the management team, and rumours about new financial advisers periodically emerged. Round the turn of the year Stuart Stradling rang me up. "I've been asked whether we want to become the broker for Eurotunnel," he said. "Doesn't seem very attractive to me. What do you think?"

"No way," I said. "The whole thing's a shambles. Everyone hates them. It doesn't add up financially," I concluded, with the certainty of someone who has done negligible detailed work. Stuart hardly needed much persuading, however, to turn the opportunity politely down.

In February 1987 the UK Eurotunnel management, painfully assembled over the previous months, imploded. The chairman stood down, then Nigel Broackes of Trafalgar House left, followed by the deputy chief executive, Michael Julien. Another discreet feeler as to our level of interest came through.

"You should probably take a look," suggested Nick.

On the first Monday of March, I went to the Stag Place offices of Eurotunnel to see the Treasurer, Peter Ratzer, and some of his colleagues. They looked remarkably relaxed for a team that had been through turmoil and faced worse. "We do hope you come on board," said Peter, "We need some extra guns." He showed us various models and pages full of figures.

"A return of 16.7% is simply not enough," I told him. "The institutions are talking about 25%-plus for a risk project."

Peter replied that in practice this was a high return for a project that had a fifty year life. "There should be good capital returns for investors once the tunnel is built," he argued. He showed us a table with the equity value soaring at least four times over the next eight years. And if investors were happy with average income of 10% a year from 1995 onwards, the equity would soar more than nine times, he explained. I was a long way from being convinced. It did not solve the Carol Galley challenge: Why should investors buy at the issue, rather than waiting?

"Look, I really don't understand how all these internal rates of return and dividend discount models and share price values inter-relate," I admitted, exaggerating only slightly. "And I can assure you that none of the equity investors and salesmen understand it either. The concepts are simply not used in the equity market."

I was more intrigued at the opportunity to use one of the Government's new tax vehicles, the Business Expansion Scheme, as a way to appeal to private investors; but that was a thought inspired by desperation.

Halfway through the meeting I had been joined by one of the most formidable advisory directors at the bank, Bob Boas. Bob had worked at S.G.Warburg since the mid-1960s and had been involved in the channel tunnel scheme abandoned in 1975. Ever since he had remained enthusiastic about the project. He was a legendary figure in the world of corporate takeovers, for his determination and intellectual horse-power, not to mention a deceptively casual style. One young Warburg banker recalled sitting next to Bob at the urgently-called crisis meeting of a client on the receiving end of a hostile bid. The chairman launched into a rousing speech of defiance, designed to rally the company team. As he reached a crescendo, Bob's companion realised with dismay that his eyes were shut and he seemed asleep. Discreetly he nudged his boss in the ribs just as the chairman turned for confirmation to his senior advisor: "Isn't that right, Bob?"

Without missing a beat, Bob opened his eyes and confirmed: "Absolutely, chairman," and proceeded to engage himself in the business of the meeting.

Now Bob decided that Eurotunnel was worth taking up.

Shortly afterwards, David Scholey called Nick and me over to his office. "We've been approached on Eurotunnel". He held up his finger to stop me interrupting with my account of our recent meeting. "Really," he added. "I think we have to take it quite seriously." David was on the board of the Bank of England and neither Nick nor I was in any doubt as to why we had to take it seriously. Bob Boas was also lobbying him hard to take an interest.

"We're only going to go for this if we think we can do it successfully. I'm also disposed to do it on an integrated basis, broker and adviser. But there's no point in getting involved if it's going to end up in failure, whatever our efforts. It looks as if Alistair Morton will become the joint chairman shortly. I'll set up a meeting for you to see him."

A few days later I travelled over to the Warburg offices in King William Street to see Alastair Morton. I think Scholey had scheduled me somewhat anonymously as the individual who would handle the marketing of Equity 3. Be that as it may, Alastair clearly was not expecting to meet me, because he looked genuinely startled when he walked into the meeting room. The last time we had met had been unpropitious. I had been writing the Lex Column comment on the Guinness Mahon figures soon after he had become the company's chief executive in 1982 and concluded that there was little point in keeping all the various bits of this boutique merchant bank under one roof. Nor had his humour been improved by the facetious headline we had put on the column that day in tribute to singer Neil Sedaka, "Breaking up is Hard to Do". He had summoned me to lunch the subsequent week and we had had a vigorous debate on the subject. I think Neil Sedaka rankled most.

Alastair recovered quickly from his surprise, and with a brush of the hand, we got down to business. He had other things to worry about than historic insults. Alastair was a tall and imposing presence, then aged 49. He had been brought up in South Africa and came to England to study law, staying in the country thereafter. He came to prominence as managing director of the British National Oil Corporation in the late 1970s and solidified his reputation as a trouble-shooter at Guinness Mahon, which he saved from bankruptcy, despite my unkind Lex note. Alastair was incisive, direct and combative. He could be explosive in meetings when he disagreed with what was being said. He became well-known for generating spectacular rows with almost everyone he encountered, contractors, journalists or advisers. I suspect he did it more out of a conviction that this was an effective business technique than any personal animus. On a personal level he could be charming and built great loyalty within the Eurotunnel team. In relative terms, my relationship with him proved pretty harmonious.

On that afternoon, he spelled out the challenges for the company. It had to ensure the Anglo-French treaty establishing the concession was ratified; it had to conclude the debt negotiations; it had to establish a coherent management team; it had to make sure the contractors were organised to start work the moment the funds were obtained; and it had to raise £750m in the public equity markets. "I've already announced that we're going to delay the float into the autumn, but we're looking at doing a mini rights issue to keep us going meanwhile. What do you think?"

"It'll be pretty messy," I said diplomatically. "There needs to be a really compelling story for people to put in more money willingly, and then you'd have to give yourself time to sell it. From my perspective, I can't even work out what the story would be at the moment, let alone go out to shareholders with it."

"How long will it take you," he asked.

"I've got some ideas, but I'll need to do some more work. I'll need a couple of weeks." I was still extremely dubious.

It took another few days for the penny to drop.

"It's no good just saying that capital returns will be good," Bob said. "You've got to produce the figures to show how the share price might perform in practice, especially in the early years."

This was the challenge. Peter Ratzer had shown us how the value of the shares should – in theory – jump when the project was completed, but the Eurotunnel team had not had time to develop the analysis from theory to practical application. In particular there was no justification for the precise level they might jump to. Without specific numbers the institutional investors would be, and indeed had been, unimpressed. To pin down the answer I turned to some financial theory that had been little used in the markets. This aimed to assess the returns that investors required from different types of shares. If I could work out what return investors would want from the stock when the tunnel was functioning, I could fix a value for the company at that point, based on the projections for profits.

Nick Wakefield and Kit Beer lent me their project finance assistant, in the shape of Tina Ruygrok, whose skills in what was still the relatively new art of computer modelling were exceptional. With the minimum of fuss she knocked up a simple model of the cash flows from the company for me to play with, designed so that I could try to establish what the share price might be at different stages.

A few evenings later I was manipulating the figures at my desk, which was then in a corner of the main equity trading floor. Nick Verey was sitting in his office behind me. Suddenly the figures began to move into shape.

"Nick," I called out, "If these cost and revenue projections are right, some of these returns are really very, very sexy."

"How do you mean?"

"Look at this. If you invest £100 in a project like this tunnel you'll want a return of, let's say, at least £30 each year during the risky building phase, right? That's what they mean by a 30% discount rate."

"Right."

"When the project's built it will produce nice steady returns, with very little risk. You'll want a bit more than your bank account, won't you, and probably a bit less than you'd expect to earn in the equity market. People putting £100 in the equity market today seem to be expecting to earn about £12-50p a year, partly in dividends and partly in share price gains."

"OK, try it out on £12 a year."

I input the 12% figure into the model.

"I've put in that investors will want £12 a year from 1993 onwards." I gaped at the figure that popped up in slight amazement. "On that assumption the value of the shares in 1993, when the tunnel opens, will be £7bn. That compares with £1.1bn when we issue them. Between 1987 and 1993, that's an increase of more than six times - more than 40% each year. Now is that a story, or is that a story?"

"Wow," said Nick. "Bugger the 16.7%. We'll offer the hot investors 40% for the high risk phase and then they can sell on when it becomes a utility to the utility investors, who'll want the 12%."

It was a pure Eureka moment. I had taken an academic theory and turned it into a specific valuation, which was relatively easy to understand. The Eurotunnel team had played with a theoretical analysis during Equity 2 which had left investors unconvinced. This simple model pinpointed how the share price should behave in practice. I subsequently used it to show how the share price would move through the tunnelling phase itself. As the perceived risks of construction changed, the value of the shares should move – and in a relatively predictable way. So obvious, in retrospect, that it was amazing no-one had thought about analysing how to split the rates of return in this way before. The reason, presumably, was that there had never been an issue for which this approach was relevant. Suddenly, researching Eurotunnel moved from being a chore, or at best an academic investigation, into a real prospect. We started to clear our diaries.

A few days later Nick and I went over to see David Scholey and Bob Boas.

"We think we can sell it," said Nick. "We'll need a free hand and to use every trick in the book. And time. No way can we do anything in the markets before we've had a chance to work on the sentiment."

David wanted to know how we were going to deal with the opposition, in the shape of the ferry operators' lobbying consortium, Flexilink. "After all," Bob pointed out, "this will be the first contested IPO in history" – a reference to the standard contested takeover jargon of the merger and acquisitions market.

"We'll just have to match them head on in the press," I said. "Story by story, claim by claim. We'll simply have to outgun them."

"How?"

"Research will give us credibility and then we'll need to talk to the journalists all the time."

"Right," said David. "Let's do it. And you better bloody make sure we succeed."

Nick and I met Alastair Morton on the following Friday, at the end of March, to confirm that we would like to take on the role of leading broker to the company. There were two principal issues to deal with. Should the company go ahead with a rights issue from the long-suffering Equity 2 investors to tide it over, or should it raise bridging finance to carry it through to an autumn issue? We were very keen to avoid the bad feeling that a further small issue would inevitably create, as was Alastair. He planned on the bridging route, if at all possible (an outcome that was successfully adopted a few weeks later).

The second issue was control. "We need to run the marketing as tightly as possible," explained Nick. "We can't afford any mixed messages." That meant shutting down the other brokers, County and Scrimgeour. "It's not that they've been doing bad work or that they're incompetent. They've just lost all credibility as a result of Equity 2. Besides, it will be impossible to remain coherent if everyone is talking in public."

The upshot was that all marketing meetings arranged by the other brokers were to be stopped. A new marketing committee was formed, made up of Nick, Tony Carlisle at the PR consultants Dewe Rogerson, Martin Hall, director of corporate affairs at the company and Rory McNamara, an advisory banker on secondment to the company from Morgan Grenfell. We thought it unnecessary to formally pronounce our role as lead broker.

"It will just create ill-will with the others," Nick said. "In practice we will be quietly slotting ourselves into the position through our control of the marketing process."

That was the politics taken care of. Now we had to perform.

I wrote a note to the team on how best to handle the research. "In order to maximise the research interest in Eurotunnel," I wrote, "we should switch tactics in producing research. Instead of a single blockbuster, as in the case of British Airways and TSB, we should produce a series of short reviews dealing with particular features of the product. This will allow us to receive regular coverage in the media." The three topics chosen were traffic patterns, building the project and valuation.

At the end of the month we got down to work with the first of several meetings with the traffic consultants, who were led by Alastair Dick. This was designed to gather information for our first piece of research, which we were to call "Eurotunnel: The impact on European Traffic Patterns". Our base was a set of forecasts produced by the consultants two months earlier. This had concluded, "If for any reasons the revenue figures were to differ from those given, they are more likely to be higher than lower"[3]. This was a pretty promising starting point from my perspective. Tom Hill, my research analyst on the transport sector, was working with me on the note. I explained to him what the objective was. "We need to seize the agenda with this note. We need to get people talking about the point of the project, about the transformation in travel behaviour. And we need to start concentrating people's minds on the upsides here. The equity investor likes nothing more than a bit of blue sky upside.

"And by the way, if we're going to succeed here, it's got to be fucking good. People have got to decide that we are absolutely the most credible transport gurus in town." Tom, to his credit, blenched only a little, stiffened his shoulders, and got down to work.

We split the tasks. The finished product[4] was a crisp 38 pages and contained two key messages. We argued that the traffic consultants had been extremely conservative in making their projections. Furthermore they had taken only limited account of the traffic that would be created as a direct result of the provision of the new link.

By the end of July we were ready to launch. Until then the press had been indifferent to hostile, apart from a handful of stories centring on Alastair's appointment and early initiatives. Over the Wednesday evening and following morning we briefed each of the heavy-weight newspapers one by one.

Our timing was fortuitous. The day before Mrs Thatcher and M. Mitterand had – at last – ratified the Treaty at the Elysée Palace. The main railway and banking agreements had been agreed. The supportive press coverage the next day was full of references to light at the end of the tunnel and the tide turning. We had achieved our purpose. The journalists had seen us establish our presence and were able to envisage how our campaign was likely to unfold. Now whenever Flexilink or a hostile analyst, typically Richard Hannah, put out a negative story, we would get the chance to counter it. From that point on, there was barely a day when I did not have to deal with one or more journalists running a Eurotunnel piece. Furthermore, with the salesmen briefed, we also had a base from which to talk to the institutions – informing, countering, reassuring.

Research was only one part of the campaign. At a meeting soon after appointment Nick, Bob and I pooled all the ideas we could think of. "The institutions have got to become comfortable with it," Nick said. "That means meetings, contacts, visits. But we've got nothing to show them, no reason to get them out of their offices and spend time on this."

"Apparently there's a plan to take a group of institutions on a rail trip to Switzerland," I told him.

"How the hell does that stand up?"

"Well we can see the tunnel at Lötschberg. It's a shuttle tunnel like we're planning. And the food is good in Switzerland."

"Fine. Let's do it. But it's not enough. We'll need a model railway."

"What?" said Bob and I, aghast.

"A big one. Showing how the tunnel will operate. Trains and shuttles whizzing round. People love that kind of thing. We'll put it in an office in the middle of the City and invite the institutions for meetings and dinners. They'll all come to see a model railway."

"OK," we said, acquiescing in an investment of, I am sure, well over £500,000.

"It should feel like a privatisation," said Bob. "All the normal paraphernalia. A big retail advertising campaign, a share information office, Dewe Rogerson at full tilt."

"Discounts for retail investors?" I asked, somewhat disingenuously, since I knew the answer already.

"No discounts," said Nick. "It's not like selling off a state asset cheaply. It would just be a transfer to retail from the institutions, who would be deeply pissed off."

"Then it will just have to be travel perks," said Bob. "Big ones. We can fine-tune them when we get a better feel for how the marketing is going."

With the ground rules set, we got on with the programme. Bob probably had the worst of it. He had to obtain a consensus out of the unwieldy two-headed organisation to produce a coherent prospectus. Following his experience of designing a joint UK/US issue for Reuters, he also had to harmonise the very different sales processes of the French and UK capital markets, representing a significant step forward in creating a global market for issuing equity. Later he told me, "Mind you, the real nightmare of the whole thing was to get the French to organise their selling effort. They left all the detailed work to some young American lawyer. It was only right at the last moment that they suddenly realised they had to make a serious selling effort in France and started looking closely at what we were doing."

Nick, meanwhile, was making sure the model railway was built, ready for the formal kick-off of the campaign with the opening of the Share Information Office in Winchester House on London Wall at the beginning of October.

The plans were in place, but we were under no illusions about the extreme difficulty of the task. Eurotunnel was still a widely distrusted animal. And a significant portion of the burden of turning that sentiment still fell to me and, in particular, whether I could sell the valuation approach sketched out in March. Distraction and stress made me more than usually poor holiday material that August with my family in Brittany. One morning I reversed the car out of the field next to the house we had rented. My children, Andrew (aged 6) and Emily (4) together with their cousin Robbie (6), were in the back seat, the sunroof open. I backed straight into a small, but prolific, apple tree. The apples came cascading through the sunroof to the utter delight of the children, who whooped with laughter. It was the high point of their holiday. I felt like charging Eurotunnel for the damage to the car.

When I came back at the end of the month, Phil Raper was in the final stages of the second research note dealing with the building of the project, "Eurotunnel: The Construction of the Fixed Link". This note was not designed to excite anyone about the project; it was essentially defensive, to demonstrate that it was likely to be built to time and budget. There had been a series of attacks launched on Eurotunnel based on the unreliability of the construction industry. In response Phil leant heavily on the dramatic improvement in UK contracting performance since 1981 analysed by the National

Economic Development Office.

However, all was not going smoothly with the note. In particular the company, and the contractors behind it, were worried about the high level of confidence being expressed in the summary. The compromise introduction emerged as: "We believe the balance of probability is that Eurotunnel will be completed both on time – May 1993 – and to Budget."[5] At the time, neither Phil nor I (nor indeed anyone on the team) saw anything more in it than the protectiveness of lawyers.

On 8 September, we reran the briefing process for the main papers. This time we were up against a renewed campaign by Flexilink, which had issued a financial model claiming to show the extreme vulnerability of the project. We could sense our momentum next day as our story overwhelmed their case. The Independent concluded: "Warburgs' circular makes a good case against Flexilink's pessimistic scenario for construction costs and timing."[6]

So far, so good. Now it was over to me and the valuation note. I had been battling it out over the summer, helped by Caroline Speck, who was responsible for collecting market data. We had been gathering comparable discount rates for projects round the world, and built up a picture of Eurotunnel's projected cash flows. We also aimed to calculate the sensitivity of our valuation to changing circumstances, if there was a delay to opening, for example, or traffic was lower than expected. As we moved towards the finish, however, we ran into an acute capacity problem. The projections were stored on the most powerful PC then available, an IBM AT, which could barely cope despite its 4MB of extended memory on top of the standard 640k. Whereas a few years later a PC would calculate changes in a matter of seconds, back in 1987 the computer had to be left overnight to calculate a change in the assumptions. When Steve Cupit, the modeller at Eurotunnel, saw our requests for all the different sensitivities he was horrified.

"David, I simply don't have the time to do everything for you and for the team working on the prospectus, as well as for everyone else. The assumptions are moving about all over the place and you all want different things. It takes hours and hours to do a single run."

Steve was mollified when I told him a couple of days later that we had agreed to use exactly the same methodology and sensitivity assumptions in the research as the prospectus. We would also freeze the assumptions. It still took an awfully long time to build up the relevant tables.

I was still struggling with the challenge set by Carol Galley more than a year earlier, when she argued that she could afford to wait to invest in an infrastructure project. I needed to be able to illustrate how the share price would perform. I followed the logic of the changing discount rates between the build phase and utility operational phase. Even within the build phase, investors' perceptions of the level of risk would change, I decided. The highest risk would be during the twelve-month preparatory phase, when the organisation was establishing itself. After that, assuming smooth progression, risk would reduce through the tunnel boring phase, the fitting out phase and finally the commissioning phase. At each stage risk would be seen to fall, and therefore investors would require a lower discount rate. As a result the price would jump at each change in sentiment. I also analyzed how the project might perform if it disappointed. Whichever, it promised to be a lively share in the markets on almost a daily basis. I drew elaborate graphs illustrating the behaviour.

With a week to go before publication I wrote a punchy summary and handed it over to Nick Verey for approval. "This will make you clench your teeth," I told him. He promised to read it when he got home.

He rang back later in the evening. "My teeth are all over the floor," he said.

I started working on the presentation to institutions, designing the support materials for all the individual meetings I would need to go to. Ahead of going live, I decided to test the presentation on the toughest audience there was, and set up a meeting with Carol Galley and her team after lunch on the Friday before the Tuesday 29 September launch day. If it worked there, it would work right through the market.

By the time I had finished, Carol was smiling broadly, "David," she said, "you've done it." It was the best possible boost to morale.

The launch of the final piece of research[7] went better than we could have dreamed. As before, we saw journalists from the main papers individually for an hour each through the morning and over lunch. By now, they were comfortable enough with progress to offer, in some cases, stunning endorsements. The comment piece in The Daily Telegraph by Neil Collins, by now the most influential financial commentator in the press, was absolutely unequivocal. "This looks such an attractive investment that rationing of allocations is inevitable," he concluded in a piece entitled: Tunnel as a passage to the Gold Mine. He also endorsed the analysis of share price behaviour. "Warburg has got away from the ludicrous assertion, made by earlier proponents of the tunnel, that this is an investment for our children and grandchildren; that is no more true than a purchase of Exchequer 12 p.c. 2013-17. Every share in Eurotunnel will change hands many times in its life as investors' perceptions, tax position and wealth change – that is the point of a Stock Exchange quotation, and a powerful reason for financing such projects with public equity."[8]

The Times was hardly less positive. In a City editor's comment piece entitled 'Cinderella Eurotunnel could soon be a star', Kenneth Fleet concluded: "The combination of large capital gains in the early years with the simple prospect of a first day premium on the shares seems likely to attract both the yuppie punter and the middle-aged high taxpayer wanting a retirement investment."[9]

It was the tipping point. Suddenly the Eurotunnel issue became hotly anticipated. We had been extremely fortunate. While Alastair Morton had been beating the project into some kind of shape, closing down the negotiations with the railways, the banks and the contractors, the background environment had been more than benign. The stock market was at the peak of the mid-1980s boom, relishing an expansive March Budget and the re-election of Mrs Thatcher's Conservative Government in June. The privatisations of the year, British Airways, Rolls-Royce and British Gas, had all seen large first-day premiums. The advertising for the Government's sale of a further tranche of BP was now getting underway, with a heady campaign of TV advertising. "BP – Be Part of It" was intoned in deep masculine tones nightly on TV in what was probably the most mesmerising message yet devised for a public issue. Eurotunnel was scheduled to follow close on its heels. We even derived a macabre benefit out of the tragedy of the sinking in March of the cross-channel ferry Herald of Free Enterprise, at a cost in lives of more than 150 passengers and 38 crew. With bow doors inadvertently left open, she capsized 90 seconds after leaving Zeebrugge harbour. The horrific accident undermined Flexilink's credibility in attacking Eurotunnel, particularly over safety issues.

So the marketing programme over the first fortnight of October at Winchester House was well-attended. As Nick Verey had anticipated, fund managers were keen to come and see the model railway and then stay on for a lunch or dinner. Here Alastair Morton and the Eurotunnel team would brief them on the project, describing the plans for the issue and answering questions. We had divided the institutions into three groups, with Scrimgeour, County Securities and ourselves taking responsibility for inviting the key individuals at each institution to the series of functions. By 13 October the company was briefing the analysts from outside stock-brokers on the project, so that they could write their research for clients. It was all going incredibly smoothly. One of our salesmen told me, "I'm getting loads of calls from savvy North London punters trying to get their hands on a decent swag of stock." I began to relax and switch my attention to all the obligations I had let hang while Eurotunnel had absorbed my time. The issue was moving along the standard assembly line.

On Thursday evening, 15 October, I sat in on a briefing of technical analysts at Winchester House, going through the detail of the construction programme. That night I was woken in my home in Highgate by a ferocious gale. It gusted round the exposed gable of our front bedroom and at the peak seemed about to lift off the roof. Television reports the next morning described a devastating storm. Worst hit were those further south. I got on my bicycle and wended my way to work, as usual, dodging the trees that had come down on Highgate West Hill. The office was uncharacteristically empty. Nick Verey came in later from his West London home. "It's carnage," he said. "Half the trees are down in Hyde Park. The roads are all blocked."

It was a curious, empty day. More people began to filter into the office as the morning progressed, each with a story of endeavour, but the trading floor was barely half-manned. Virtually all the telephone calls I made were unsuccessful. Nobody seemed to be at their desks. After lunch people began to filter out again, to brave an equally horrific journey home. Trading in London was at a virtual standstill but after lunch the news from the US was bleak. The steady slide over the previous fortnight at the New York Stock Exchange accelerated, with a further drop of some 5%. After what was already being dubbed the Great Storm, there was an apocalyptic feel to events. The Sunday newspapers added to the ominous tone, with warnings of big falls to come when the markets opened on Monday.

They could not have been closer to the mark. On Monday all hell broke loose in the markets. In London the FTSE dropped 11%. Worse was to come, as on Wall Street the Dow Jones index collapsed a stunning 22%. The next day in London the rout went on with a further 12% fall and after a brief respite on Wednesday the market continued to decline through the week.

At the end of that first day, later dubbed Black Monday, I went home in dark despair. It seemed that all our work to make Eurotunnel floatable had been a waste of time. After this bloodbath it would be like starting all over again.

There is nothing like an early emotional reaction for purging the system. I arrived in the office the next morning feeling resolved, and even cheerful. If I had learned one lesson from my experience in the City it was the importance of keeping going, even when the likelihood of success seemed remote. Besides, Eurotunnel was only one of the escalating problems we were involved with. We had been an underwriter of the £7.25bn BP issue, the world's largest ever equity issue, and now this was causing mounting concern. Its price had fallen to 286p by Tuesday evening, compared with the underwriting price of 330p and the foreign underwriters, who had not sub-underwritten the issue and were therefore fully at risk, were already bleating. TSB, whose flotation I had spent so much time on, was also high and dry with an offer to buy the merchant bank Hill

Samuel that now looked extremely overpriced. In the event they went ahead with the purchase at an unchanged price and thereby at one blow satisfied my calculation of the rate at which they would waste their capital. Finally, the rights issue we had launched for Ladbroke the previous month to finance the acquisition of Hilton International looked irredeemably under water. The sub-underwriters would be left with the stock here, too.

As the pattern of the market became clearer, Bob Boas agreed with Alastair Morton that we would press ahead with the Eurotunnel float in November regardless. As Bob later admitted, "We didn't have any choice, really. The company was due to run out of money at the close of the year and it would have been all over."

The attack on Eurotunnel planned by Flexilink at the end of that first week now looked highly dangerous. Before Black Monday our momentum would have allowed us to brush it aside as self-interested propaganda. With the markets in turmoil, it threatened to provide a rallying point from which increasingly negative views could be aired, a process which could easily reinforce self-fulfilling doubts among journalists and analysts over whether a flotation was still possible. Something had to be done.

In the absence of any other strategy, I turned up myself at the Friday press conference held by Flexilink at the Savoy hotel. Somewhat to my surprise I was allowed in. I sat in the second row directly in front of James Sherwood, whose company owned one of the cross-channel ferry operations and who was the leading light of the Flexilink consortium. I was surrounded by all the journalists covering the story – amused, cynical, gossipy – many of them friends. It felt like old times.

The warm-up was a doom-laden video, concentrating on the inevitability of cost over-runs where tunnels were concerned. Then James Sherwood introduced the document that was being launched: "The Channel Tunnel. Some weaknesses of the Financial Case"[10]. It was a condemnation of virtually every aspect of the Eurotunnel case, from passenger numbers to tariffs; from safety issues to contractors' penalties. Then it was over to questions.

I drew a deep breath and started up. The trick of making an impact at a press conference is to ask the first set of questions, following up the answers rigorously, asking for specific information and data. After a few exchanges the rest of the journalistic corps sits back to enjoy the show. "Why," I asked, "are Flexilink's forecasts for cross-channel passenger growth so conservative, at 6.5% a year, compared with the 8.5% seen in the previous decade?

"What is your evidence of price inelasticity for passenger volume?"

Several times I played on the differences between Sherwood's claims as leader of Flexilink and what he had said two years earlier when promoting his rival Channel Expressway project for the concession. "You claimed you could build the Expressway, with tunnels of twice the diameter, by 1991 and for only £2.5bn. Why are you so concerned about over-runs for Eurotunnel?"

This was not going James Sherwood's way at all. Clearly, as the president of Sea Containers Ltd, which owned the former BR ferry business of Sealink, he could not be expected to handle the detail. An affable, amusing man, he was becoming visibly upset as he maladroitly handed over my vicious questions to his team.

"I think it's only fair if we give some-one else a chance to ask questions," he said.

He took a question from another journalist. Then silence, as the corps waited for the fun to recommence.

I resumed my private demolition job uninterrupted.

Next day's coverage of the document was cursory. The threat from Flexilink was extinguished.

We waited another week. Maurice Thompson, one of the Warburg bankers who arranged syndicates to underwrite our international equity issues, came to find me. He was responsible for the international tranche of Eurotunnel and needed to find some underwriters – no easy task given the Chancellor's decision the day before, on 29 October, to limit severely any help given to the BP underwriters. It was a thankless and depressing round. Swiss Bank Corporation: no; Enskilda: no; EBC Amro: no. We went to see one prominent Middle Eastern institution, who received us with the greatest possible civility. "We are most flattered to be invited to participate in this prestigious offering, particularly as we are not normally on the Warburg underwriting list. However, on this occasion we do have to ask ourselves whether we are being offered a poisoned chalice." In other words: no.

We came back with a virtual blank sheet. In the event, hardly any underwriters came forward independent of the sponsors themselves and the original backers.

Peter Wilmot-Sitwell and Nick Verey had put their heads together. "We're going to have to see everyone, not just the institutions but our corporate customers too, to see if they will underwrite this," said Nick. "After all, we can tell them it's in their own interest that this thing gets built. Improves links with their European businesses."

I went to see David Pascall in BP Finance. The company was a slightly soft touch, given the historic relationship with the project. BP had been an investor at Equity 2 and the previous finance director, Q Morris, had transferred to Eurotunnel during the competition phase. He had been the architect of the financing of the North Sea Forties Field for BP – designed without exposing the company to the full risk directly – and was responsible for setting up Eurotunnel's financial plan. David Pascall was also particularly conscious of the current difficulty of underwriting, given the squealing that still surrounded the BP name. Nigel Lawson, the Chancellor, was being accused of throwing the world into another 1929 by some of the wilder commentators. "All right," he sighed, "I think we'll be able to see our way to £5m. Although I do find this most puzzling. I thought the idea was that you brokers raised money for us companies, not the other way round."

Even though the market continued to go down, the launch day was set for 16 November. But this date would signal the end of our main effort, not the beginning. David Scholey, who was shortly to reveal an £8m net loss on our BP position, was absolutely adamant that we would not launch unless we had sub-underwritten it all beforehand. "We are not going to take a single penny on our own books unless we have firm commitments to take it from us upfront," he said. Bob Boas tried to soften the diktat. "At the very least we could risk our fees?" he argued, but to no avail.

We had a week to convince the investing institutions to sub-underwrite the issue. The UK share was £353m. The three brokers went to work on their apportioned institutions, with a target of £118m each.

I went to see fund manager after fund manager to describe the investment case. They hardly absorbed a word, their eyes flicking to the Topic screens in their offices, showing the prices of the leading stocks. The figures were almost solidly red, indicating that each price was going lower. The fund managers were no longer worried about relative stock market performance; they were worried about the safety of their jobs, about whether a 1929-scale recession was looming.

Each evening we would gather to assess responses. Dickie Fulford of Scrimgeour Securities, dogged and determined; Richard Redmayne of County Securities, full of jovial confidence; Nick Verey, relaxed yet serious. They went through the lists carefully. What about that institution? How was this institution reacting? Richard was determined to inject his own determined spirit into the team. "If I'm not able to write my own personal cheque for £118m on Friday, I'm a Dutchman," he declared.

On Wednesday the market slide stopped. Blue began to appear on the Topic screens, the colour of price rises. Maybe the world wasn't ending, after all. The fund managers began to pay attention. "It's a pretty risk-free underwriting," we explained. "We've redesigned it as a retail issue, with incredible perks. Someone's only got to invest £5,000 to get free travel for life. The feedback[11] from Dewe Rogerson shows that there are still 574,000 people certain to subscribe, even after Black Monday."

Nick Verey went to see Peter Wilmot-Sitwell. "Would you call Robert Maxwell?"

Peter looked shocked.

"Why?"

"He's got a French wife," said Nick.

Maxwell – Cap'n Bob, as he was dubbed by our salesmen – had a dubious reputation in the financial markets and we generally refused to have anything to do with him. Peter put the call in and went with Alastair Morton and a salesman to Maxwell's Holborn office. They were settled in a comfortable sitting room, when a huge oil painting was flung aside and Maxwell – a huge red-faced bulk of a man – burst through.

"I'll call you at 6.30am tomorrow," he promised Peter, when he had heard their appeal. He was as good as his word. On the dot of 6.30 he rang to take £25m of the stock for two of the pension funds he controlled.   The news represented a substantial boost and inspired the whole team for a final push, the salesmen cajoling, flattering, bullying their clients. When we gathered late on Friday afternoon, Dickie Fulford could report that he had made his target; and although Richard Redmayne was well down on his, the Maxwell contribution closed the gap. Of the total, about 42% had been sold outright, as opposed to underwritten. "Well, Richard's a Dutchman," I told Nick, "a small price to pay for getting this away."

We had done it: pure jubilation, mitigated only by exhaustion. The weekend headline "Maxwell digs for Europe", hardly registered. The formal launch on Monday was a foregone conclusion. The next day I was due to fly Concorde to New York for a round of investor meetings. When I woke I could hardly move, incapacitated by a particularly nasty flu bug. I sent the car away and later in the day Tom Hill went in my place.

By the time I was back on my feet, the offer was halfway through and not progressing well. I kept a brave face for the journalists, but we were still well under-subscribed as we moved through the second week. Nick Verey reported on a desperate row between Bob Boas and Tony Carlisle at the marketing meeting over how much information on progress to release to journalists. "They were standing up across the table yelling at each other. Real heavyweight stuff, I've never seen anything like it. We were all stunned, including Alastair, who likes a good argument. I asked them whether this was a private row, or could anyone join in?"

On Friday morning I went down to the NatWest New Issues department in Princes Street opposite the Bank of England to see the offer's 10.00am close. It was a far cry from the crowded scenes at the close of some of the more popular privatisations, when queues of people would stretch far down the pavement to deliver their applications. Having delivered my own envelope in decidedly unjostled circumstances, I returned to my desk to find the Evening Standard's Michael Neill on the line. "How's it doing?" he asked.

"Please give it to me straight. We won't be publishing till way after it's all over anyway."

"OK," I told him. There was nothing to gain from being ambiguous. "We were just over halfway last night and I doubt if we've got enough to close the gap this morning."

"Oh, thanks. I'll write that it's touch and go."

That afternoon at the meeting at the Warburg office to review application levels, Alastair Morton was furious. He took me to task for leaking to the Evening Standard and it was only the intervention of Nick pointing out that I'd been talking full-tilt to journalists for month after month that calmed him down.

"I couldn't lie to the Standard," I defended myself. "You can only have a dialogue if they trust you to tell the truth."

"You don't understand that we're running a dual issue here," grumbled Alastair. "The French are furious about the story. They say it's undermining them." No-one had the bad manners to say that the French were meant to have closed their books at the same time as the British. When I dared lift my eyes from the table it seemed to me that I was in a room full of tramps. None of us had had time to visit a barber for months and our hair hung far over our collars.

Wearily we totted up the figures. We would be 20% short in the UK. And while we never achieved total certainty, we estimated that the underlying outcome was similar in the more opaque French market. After BP and Ladbroke the sub-underwriters would be receiving yet another tranche of stock from us.

"There's nothing you can do," said Peter Wilmot-Sitwell early the following Monday, before trading opened. "It's never worth setting up support operations for this kind of thing. The price has to find its own level. The market will sort it out".

We didn't have long to wait. Within minutes of opening the share price was on its way below 250p, reflecting the rush by institutions to get out of their positions. In subsequent weeks it sagged further to bottom out at 235p.

Curiously, there was no backlash. The participants in the market decided, on reflection, that it was a formidable achievement to have got the deal away at all. As an advertisement to Warburg 'placing power' it was to serve as a powerful marketing card for the group in the next few years. I, meanwhile, was the pleased recipient of a respectable volume of congratulation from colleagues and rivals. I took greatest pleasure from a cartoon by Heath in the Spectator a little more than a year later, in February 1989, which showed a bespectacled City gent in pinstripes reading our Eurotunnel research report to his son, who was fast asleep in bed[12]. My former colleague, Dominic Lawson, by then the editor of the weekly, helped me to buy the original from the artist.

The share spent the next 10 weeks flat on its back at around 240p, effectively the price at which buyers would take out the unhappy underwriters. At that price, I thought, Armageddon and beyond was taken into account. So in the more relaxed environment of the time concerning share purchases by stockbrokers, I bought a few thousand shares. In March Eurotunnel stock bounced back over £3 a share and in the summer I bought more, illustrating how much I believed my own analysis. By August I held 8,500 shares at an average purchase price just over the £3 level.

It was in November that they started to take off, crashing through the £3.50 flotation price (for the combined shares and warrants) and surging towards the £5-mark by year-end as encouraging news about the progress of the tunnelling emerged. A month later the shares broke through £6, and The Telegraph carried a story[13] reproducing my illustration of how the shares would be rerated once tunnel boring got properly underway. Amazingly, the share price surge coincided exactly with the first of the shaded areas in which I had predicted a revaluation. Within a week the shares had hit £8. They had become simply the most exciting share in the market. Salomon Brother's issued a covered warrant in May aiming to take advantage of the fever. This was the first such derivative to be offered on a UK share and gave purchasers the right to buy Eurotunnel shares at £12 in three years time. The London market was full of rumours about Salomon's sales technique. My own valuation would put the shares towards £20 by May 1993, if all went well; the equivalent figure now coming back through the gossipy salesmen was no less than £70.

Our own advice was for our institutional clients to take advantage of these prices and sell, which many did. Among the sellers was Robert Maxwell, the rescuer of the issue, who sold the shares on behalf of the two controlled pension funds which had invested in the project. Less than three years later his business empire collapsed and he drowned mysteriously off the side of his yacht, the Lady Ghislaine. He was found to have plundered the self-same funds to try to keep afloat, destroying the livelihoods of the pensioners. At least on this occasion he made a profit for his victims.

That June the price peaked at £11.64, some 45% over my estimate of where it should have traded. Alastair Morton had arranged a trip on Friday, 14 July, for the core Eurotunnel team to see the tunnelling at Folkestone. David Scholey, Nick Verey, Bob Boas, Melanie Gee and I took the train down to the coast, dressed up in protective gear and then were driven through the cliff to the underground staging area. We walked along the huge tunnel to the boring machine that was setting out for France. The machinery was deeply impressive; the level of activity seemed curiously muted.

In the train back to London I said to Nick. "You know, I really do think I should sell my Eurotunnel shares. They're way over the right price now."

Bob smiled. "Shall we put them inside, Melanie?" He didn't bother to wait for an answer. "The costs are out of control and we'll need to do a rights issue. Sorry."

That meant I couldn't sell, although in practice I was hardly being singled out. No-one from Warburg was allowed to sell the stock as the next crisis loomed. The news was released in late July. I watched my £100,000 steadily erode with as much composure as possible, although I never traded in another stock for the rest of my career at the bank.

There wasn't much fun in the Eurotunnel story from that point. It became a grisly slog to find the funds to complete the project as one disappointment after the other emerged and rows over costs escalated. An early casualty was Alastair Morton's relationship with Bob Boas, who was regularly incensed at his unwillingness to take advice on a timely basis. With David Scholey refusing to substitute a more pliable director for Bob, we stopped acting as the company's adviser in March 1990, although who sacked who is a matter for debate. We remained the lead broker however, and Stuart Stradling took over responsibility for the role on Nick Verey's transfer to the US.

The rights issue at the end of 1990 proved insufficient (although at least I was able to sell my stock at a modest profit once it was completed). A second was required in 1994, as the final blow emerged. Enough car-carrying shuttles to allow a full service would not be delivered till mid-1995. The Anglo-French safety commission had apparently insisted on widening the internal doors, a change which required a time-consuming redesign.

The 1994 rights issue was enlivened by a ferocious row with a new boy on the London investment banking scene, Swiss Bank Corporation (SBC). It had managed to become adviser to the construction group, which had insisted that the bank was given a piece of the underwriting, very much against the wishes of the established team. Some injudicious quotes to Reuters following this agreement by Brian Keelan at SBC about the timing and size of the issue brought out all of Alastair's most pugnacious instincts. He insisted that Brian was removed from the SBC team. The battle rumbled on through April, with bitter complaints from Stuart Stradling that SBC was marketing directly to institutions without any consultation with us as lead broker and then tried to pull out of its commitment at the last moment. But most infuriating to Alastair was the poor performance of the share price during the issue period, which led to a prolonged bout of finger pointing. Indeed, accusations surrounding this issue were still a topic for the French courts more than a decade later. The bad feeling surrounding the transaction was to have an ironic outcome just two years later, when SBC took over Warburg.

In the end Eurotunnel cost almost exactly twice the original projection of £4.9bn, although two-fifths of the over-run reflected the cost of delays rather than pure construction costs. In retrospect, allowing contractors to lead the process represented a fundamental flaw in the competition for the concession. They were interested in winning the contracting work and passing on as much risk as possible to a weak owner. When things went wrong Eurotunnel shareholders suffered disproportionately.

As for the traffic projections, far from being deeply conservative, as we had claimed, they proved to be wildly optimistic. Rail passengers were projected to number 21.4m by 2003. In fact the figure was 6.3m. The shuttle was hardly less shocking, at 8.6m trips compared with the 21.7m forecast. Total freight carried was nearer the mark at 18.4m tonnes, compared with the forecast of 21.1m. One important factor in the disappointment was the totally unforeseen surge in low-cost air travel, which had the effect of reinforcing the appeal of southern Europe compared with the near continent. From a standing start in the mid-1990s, the low-cost airlines such as easyJet and Ryanair were carrying some 85m passengers a year throughout Europe by 2003. An unexpectedly dogged rear-guard action by the ferry companies, which was undoubtedly economically irrational, also undermined the fixed link by depressing its traffic volumes and prices. As far as I was concerned, the experience made me deeply cynical about traffic forecasts, an attitude that was to have profound repercussions when I found myself reluctantly responsible for financing the Channel Tunnel Railway Link.

There was one other lesson for me from the Eurotunnel flotation. It illustrated the marketing power of research, but I was hardly acting as an independent research analyst. Shortly after the flotation, Martin Hall, Eurotunnel's director of corporate affairs, announced that he was leaving to join the Securities and Investment Board, the market regulator.

"What on earth are you going to do there?" I asked.

"I'm going to stop people like you doing what you do," he joked.

The comment, light-hearted though it was, increased my level of discomfort at the hybrid role I was performing as Chinese walls hardened. Indeed, the ambivalence between analysing a stock and proselytising on its behalf was widely blamed for some of the excrescences of the dotcom boom more than a decade later. When the regulatory authorities caught up, the practice was banned in the rigorous settlement imposed in New York in April 2002 by Eliot Spitzer, the Attorney General.

By the end of the 1980s, I was already working out that I

would have to find a new way of doing business, and I now moved firmly towards the corporate finance side of the divide. I was, indeed, only to write one more piece of research after Eurotunnel, for the flotation of Euro Disney.

[1] Digging Deep for Eurotunnel, Richard Hannah, Phillips and Drew, 30 September 1986

[2] Eurotunnel. Preliminary Prospectus Dated 26 September 1986. p16

[3] Eurotunnel. Traffic and Revenue Forecasts February 1987 (Amended July 1987). p62

[4] Eurotunnel: the Impact on European Traffic Patterns, Tom Hill and David Freud, Warburg Securities, 28 July 1987

[5] Eurotunnel: The Construction of the Fixed Link, Phil Raper, Warburg Securities, 9 September, 1987

[6] War of words over the tunnel, Jeremy Warner, The Independent, 9 September 1987

[7] Eurotunnel: The Investment Opportunity, David Freud and Caroline Speck, Warburg Securities, 30 September, 1987

[8] City Comment, The Daily Telegraph, 30 September 1987, p23

[9] Comment, Kenneth Fleet, The Times, 30 September 1987, p27.

[10] The Channel Tunnel. Some Weaknesses of the Financial Case. An examination of the facts by Flexilink. 20 pages, undated. Issued 23 October 1987

[11] The Eurotunnel "Equity Three" Share Sale. The Offer Campaign – Research Report. July-November 1987. Dewe Rogerson, undated. Distributed January 1988

[12] Michael Heath, The Suits, The Spectator, 11 February, 1989, p19

[13] Holders see light at the other end of the tunnel, John Petty, The Daily Telegraph, 2 February, 1989

6

Mickey does Paris

Euro Disney – 1988 - 1994

Gary Wilson blocked me into a corner of the corridor so I couldn't escape. He wasn't a particularly big man but he carried an energetic intensity that could be highly intimidating.

"David, this deal should go out at 85 francs," he insisted vigorously. Gary Wilson was the chief financial officer of the Walt Disney Company for whom we were floating the Paris-based subsidiary, Euro Disney. I was genuinely shocked. We had spent the previous 18 months battling over the value of the company and I thought we had agreed to issue the stock at Fr62 a share. This was my first experience of working for a US company and there was none of the quaint notion that we were acting as a respected adviser. Disney and Gary Wilson were at war with us to ensure that their appointed bank obtained the highest price the market would bear. I spluttered incoherently.

"David, you're being far too conservative," he stated emphatically. Having made his point he released me. It was the warm-up to the longest and most exhausting meeting to agree a price that I have ever experienced, stretching over four days in the autumn of 1989.

Our involvement with Euro Disney stemmed from the beginning of the previous year. Fresh from the Eurotunnel float I had put in a call to the company to set up a meeting in Paris in early January. Disney was facing all the same issues as Eurotunnel: how to float a company that needed to build a project and would not earn a penny for many years. Disney had reached agreement with the

French Government to build a theme park complex in eastern Paris in March 1987. The twist in the agreement was the Government's insistence that outside shareholders should hold more than half the shares. No doubt the French Government was presuming that those shareholders would be French nationals. However, membership of the European Union outlawed national discrimination. So the shares would have to be made available to investors throughout the European Community. When it happened, the flotation was to be the first to offer shares to retail investors right across Europe, representing a major step forward in the globalisation of financial markets.

Our meeting in January 1988 was with John Forsgren, the Disney group treasurer tasked with leading the European project. John provided a great deal of basic detail about the planned park. "We've managed to negotiate an incredible deal with the French Government," he told us.

"They're committed to selling us 4,800 acres at 1971 agricultural values, which amounts to a fifth of the size of central Paris itself. They're putting two motorway interchanges onto the site, a local train connection and even a station for the high-speed TGV rail line. We're also getting Fr5bn of subsidised loans."

The deal was testimony to the effectiveness of the Disney Company's negotiating ability, especially the potent use of the threat to build the park in Spain. From the French Government's perspective, the park represented an unparalleled way to revitalise the depressed eastern half of the Ile de France region and balance the hegemony of economic activity in the western suburbs of Paris. Disney played on that strategic imperative with great skill.

Our team at that first meeting included Rodney Ward, head of US coverage, and Chris Reilly, who had recently joined the small team specialising in issuing international equity. I was to get to know both of them closely as a result of our work on Euro Disney.

As the meeting stretched through the morning, we spent a lot of time running through out valuation methodology for Eurotunnel, now largely accepted by institutional investors.

"The key to generating excitement will be research and its use to get the press on board," I said. "That's the way to capture investors' imagination when you only have farmland to show."

By the end of the meeting John had become openly encouraging about our chances of becoming the lead manager of the shares to be placed outside France. "The choice lies between you and CSFB, with Morgan Stanley as a possibility," he told us.

John was a delightful character; charming and urbane, he clearly relished the cultural benefits of working in Paris on the Euro Disney project. He was completely straightforward in his dealings with us and over the years ahead was to become a good friend. Ironically, his thoughtful and considerate approach served to relax our guard as we entered into an intensive dialogue with one of the toughest management teams in the corporate world of the US.

Walt Disney had founded an entertainment empire on the cartoon character, Mickey Mouse, who debuted in 1927. The founder's death in 1966 triggered a long decline, which had reached its nadir three years earlier. In the spring of 1984 the well-known corporate raider Saul Steinberg revealed that he was buying stock. The defence involved a transaction that brought in the wealthy Bass brothers of Fort Worth, Texas, as the major shareholders, followed by the purchase of Steinberg's stake at a price that allowed him a healthy profit[1].

The new shareholders now became instrumental in transforming the management of the company, bringing in Michael Eisner from Paramount as chairman. With him came Frank Wells as chief operating officer and a little later Gary Wilson from Marriott as chief financial officer. Together with Jeff Katzenberg, as president of the film and TV divisions, this team set about transforming the company. Full feature cartoons were reintroduced, theme park revenues maximised and merchandising re-invigorated as the team set about exploiting its brand. The share price moved from an equivalent $14 at the beginning of 1984 to $60 and climbing four years later. In striking contrast to the cordial Mickey Mouse, emblem of the company, this was a team that was focused on stock market return, to an extent that was to become notorious in the years ahead.

However, such considerations were far from view as we took our next steps to win this mandate. At the beginning of March I traveled over to Disney World in Florida with a team to gather material for a detailed presentation to the company later in the month. We stayed at one of the hotels on the lake facing the Magic Kingdom Park. This park was the model for the proposed centre-piece of Euro Disney, made up of five differently themed areas – from Frontierland with its pioneer feel, to Discoveryland with its science fiction-inspired rides. The hospitality team at Disney whipped us round the park on the first morning, taking us to the support facilities tunnelled underneath, from which staff emerged into the various lands dressed in appropriate costume.

However, over our two-day visit there was little time for sightseeing. We spent the bulk of the time holed up in a meeting room going through a financial model that built up the cost and revenue profile of the Euro Disney project. Nor were we to meet anyone senior on this visit. We were still very much outsiders trying to work our way in.

On our return we had less than three weeks to put together our views and send in our presentation. We calculated that the value of the equity was about Fr3.3bn, or £330m. On this estimate it would be a small transaction, especially as far as we were concerned. With Disney holding half the shares and French investors a further quarter, the best we could hope for was to lead the distribution outside France of the remaining shares worth about £80m.

After our presentation, the dialogue went quiet for a couple of months. On the phone John Forsgren told us there was nothing ominous in the silence; the company was conducting a complete review of valuation in the light of our proposals.

"You'll never make an autumn float unless you start to move now," we warned.

"I know," he acknowledged. "We're going to miss the window, but there's too much value at stake to charge ahead."

Chris Reilly and I arranged to travel out to see him for lunch in early June, simply to keep the relationship warm as we waited for the review. Since we didn't have to be in Paris till midday, we decided to take one of the morning Air France flights from the City Airport to Charles de Gaulle; we could leave at a civilised time, too – aiming for a departure at 9.00am.

It was a foggy morning and with havoc on the roads I arrived at the airport with only a few minutes to spare, just ahead of Chris. But in those days, at the barely-used City Airport, this left just enough time for us to check in, so I bade farewell to my driver, Mike Hawkins, and scurried to the check-in counter.

"I'm sorry," said the clerk, "we've had to divert the plane to Southend airport because of the fog and we've sent the passengers down there by coach. I'm afraid you've just missed it." Chris, who had now arrived, hurried over to a pay-phone and called Mike back to pick us up. "Will the plane wait for us if we drive down ourselves?" he asked. The check-in clerk shrugged. "You can try."

Mike struggled through the fog down the 30 miles from the London docklands along the A13. Chris used the car phone to Southend airport. "We are on our way. Will you wait?"

He got only the feeblest of assurances. "If you get here in time."

Every five minutes Chris rang again. No assurances but, on the other hand, the coach had not arrived either. After an hour we were on the outskirts of Southend. Another call. The coach had still not arrived and given how close we were they finally assured us that they would indeed hold the plane for us. We started to relax.

"Chris," I said suddenly. "I've forgotten my passport."

For several minutes Chris said nothing at all. Then, "Well, we'll just have to see how we do." Chris was a couple of years older than me and able to stay calm in virtually any circumstance. His first job, for Shell, had taken him to Germany, where he had perfected his German, while an MBA at the French management school Insead had brought him fluency in French. Seven years in Warburg's international business had been followed by three years at Morgan Stanley, from which he had returned in 1987. When I asked him why he had come back he told me: "I missed the intellectual diversity and stimulation of Warburg; the emphasis on doing things in the best possible way." Chris paid great attention to detail and focused precisely on the task at hand. Years later I told him that I thought he risked a heart attack by bottling up all the tension and after that it was good to see him, once or twice, lose his temper. In the car that day, however, he seemed to remain completely relaxed and only the back of Mike's neck indicated contempt for my incompetence.

At Southend there was chaos. We arrived at the same time as the coach and were all hustled indiscriminately onto the plane. No one thought to ask for passports at an airport set up to handle only private flights, and so I passed the first barrier. At Charles de Gaulle, however, they were very much set up to examine passports. Chris, who spoke impeccable French, came to my rescue. "Monsieur," he explained, "has an important lunch."

The passport official was visibly impressed. "Ah, déjeuner d'affaires." And he wrote me out a slip that not only allowed me into the country, but would also allow me to leave later in the day.

"I think," said Chris, who by now knew I would never let self-regard stand in the way of a good story, "that you might not mention the passport to John. We are, after all, trying to impress him as competent bankers."

We made lunch, in one of Paris' better restaurants, in plenty of time. I only disgraced myself once, by asking for my filet to be "soigné" or, as John took delight in telling me, well-groomed, rather than the more conventional "saignant", or rare. Despite the lapse, John was particularly reassuring over our role. He told us that we stood well ahead of our rivals. We had clearly demonstrated our ability to market the type of infrastructure stock that Euro Disney represented, and that we were seen increasingly as the leaders of the transaction. "Mind you," he warned, "wait till you see what Gary Wilson is cooking up in terms of valuation. There's a complete revamp going on."

We traveled back to London in a state of contentment. I apologised to immigration at the City Airport for neglecting to bring a passport. The official looked at my suit and briefcase, made a brief internal calculation of the productivity of further investigation, audibly sighed, and said, "OK."

Ever since, I kept my passport in my inside breast-pocket ready for action, although the Warburg drivers delighted in checking whether I had it to hand at the start of every airport transfer for the next 15 years.

Shortly after that trip we were to meet Gary Wilson himself, when he came over to Europe to assess the rival bankers. John introduced him to us almost casually, without fanfare. He was impeccably dressed in a dark grey suit with wide lapels, from which every now and then he casually flicked imaginary specks of dust. White teeth, tan and sandy, floppy hair were all immaculate. He looked much younger than his 48 years. At that first meeting he said very little, in itself disconcerting enough, as we explained in some detail how we arrived at our valuation for the company. He was sizing us up, letting us do all the talking.

We heard nothing more over the summer. Then in October the Disney team came back with what Gary Wilson had been cooking. It was breathtaking. The valuation for the quoted equity emerged at Fr15.6bn, nearly five times our March estimate. In addition, the fees that Disney was proposing to take out had soared. At the highest level they would take 50% of the operating cash flow in what was termed an incentive fee, on top of healthy royalties. On this basis, Walt Disney Co would be receiving fees worth twice the net income attributable to shareholders. Gary had absorbed the methodology we had shown him and worked assiduously both at the strategy for developing the estate and at key assumptions in the model.

Rodney Ward looked over the figures. He showed a true investment banker's instinct. "My God," he said, "this is becoming a big deal. It's not a hobby any more, this is serious."

"We can never sell this," I protested. "It's completely over the top."

Our negative reaction during a meeting we held with the company in London had some small effect. Gary Wilson came back in November with what he called an addendum, reducing the value of the equity by 8% - still leaving it way too high in my view.

There followed a grisly series of meetings with Gary as we worked our way through the model in November and early December. By now Disney had rented an elegant office in central Paris in the corner of the Place Madeleine, in a carefully updated eighteenth century setting. In one of the meeting rooms we argued with Gary.

"You can't put a value like that on property development gains."

"Why on earth not? This piece of land is the tenderloin of the whole development. People are paying fortunes in American cities for this kind of position." Gary would argue every point with the utmost force and conviction. He was the most concentrated, determined, negotiator I had ever come across.

Now it was Rodney's turn to be aghast. "I've never heard of a tenderloin in an American city," he protested. "And the Europeans certainly won't. How can you expect us to go out and sell investors tenderloin?"

Following this encounter Rodney nicknamed Gary 'Jaws', after the metal-dentured heavy in the James Bond film Goldfinger.

Privately I said to John Forsgren, "I feel like I've been raped. He's taken all my methodology and manipulated it ruthlessly."

John was unsympathetic. "Well if you were raped, you were standing round the Place Pigalle with your blouse undone swinging your handbag asking for it," he said.

Slowly the billions came off; too slowly from my perspective. I really did not want to go round the City with an unsaleable proposition, however glamorous. One morning in December we gathered for breakfast in the Hotel Bristol in Paris.

"Rodney," I said, "I really think we should pull out. They want too much."

Rodney and Chris looked at me as if I had gone suddenly mad. Rodney said, "Steady on, David, calm down. We're just about to be appointed to this. We can't walk away now, not after all the work we've put into winning. We'll have one last push to get it to something you can live with."

In the end we reduced the figure to Fr11.9bn. "But," I said to Gary, "we'll need a decent discount for the IPO price, otherwise nobody will be interested." So we agreed. In the research I would write, the value would be set at Fr11.9bn, or Fr70 a share, but the issue price would be set some 13% below this, at Fr62 a share. The issue price would be a third below Disney's starting bid, therefore. It was still toppy, but I persuaded myself I could live with it.

From Rodney's perspective it remained a very big deal and while Gary was tough on price he was happy to pay large US-style fees. So when afterwards Chris managed to negotiate a commission of more than 5% we became set to earn more on this IPO than any before. It was an early taste of the difference between fees common in the US and in the UK. A sponsor could collect around 5% in US (and international) markets, whereas the norm in the UK was then no more than 0.5%, or 0.75% including distribution.

But now I had to perform, and the next stage was to prepare the research. We were already running late for an issue that was planned for the first half of 1989. We set up a major fact-finding expedition for the last week of January. This time, with the formal announcement of our role as bankers to Euro Disney, we were insiders and Disney threw its astonishing organisational resources at ensuring we had a productive trip. On Sunday morning we began a seemingly unending series of tours and meetings with operating executives designed to teach us how a theme park resort functions. We spent the first four days in Florida at Walt Disney World, which we were shown over in minute detail. Early on we took a helicopter tour over the site; then it was down to ground level for explanations of Disney's staff policies and training at the Disney 'university'. We learned about marketing, theme park management, the hotels and resort facilities, as well as future projects.

I was particularly struck by the Disney expertise in handling crowds. They had developed a series of logistical norms: two-way walkways should be 3.5 feet wide for every thousand people that passed an hour; cars should be parked at the rate of one a second, so fast that the next car had moved into position before the occupants of the first could open their doors. All this was clearly world-class. More than 50 million people a year were then visiting the four main Disney parks: Epcot and the Magic Kingdom in Florida, Disneyland in California and Tokyo Disneyland, an average of more than 12 million each. This represented true dominance in an industry where the next most popular theme park anywhere in the world, namely Sea World of Florida, was estimated to have attracted only 4.6 million people in the previous year. It was deeply impressive.

We were a large group. With me from the Warburg team was Markos Komondouros, a new recruit to the Financing Division working on his first deal, David Jones, the lead analyst of French companies and Joe Hall, one of the senior salesmen for European shares. We were joined by a team of four from the French bank Indosuez, which Disney had selected to run the flotation jointly with us, taking responsibility for the distribution of shares within France. It was led by Henri Chermont, the senior analyst of the Indosuez research group Cheuvreux de Virieu. We became a close-knit group as we traveled from one Disney location to the other and quizzed the executives on how the operation functioned.

On Thursday we were up at 6.00am to catch a flight to Los Angeles, to visit the heart of the Disney organisation at Burbank, spending the afternoon and evening being briefed by the engineers who created the rides. The next morning we were driven to the offices dedicated to developing Euro Disney, to attend an architectural presentation of the hotel complex. All the senior Disney executives were present, together with their support staff. Michael Eisner, the chief executive, made us welcome with an easy, almost boyish, charm. His chief operating officer and right-hand man, Frank Wells, tall and aristocratic looking, sat nearby, as did Gary Wilson, who was uncharacteristically silent through the meeting. Also there was Robert Fitzpatrick, who had been vice president of the 1984 Los Angeles Olympic Organising Committee and was now president of the Euro Disney management company.

The architectural team ran through their design, a group of five hotels laid round a lake beyond the Magic Kingdom. They were using an extremely large model that took up the centre of an open-plan floor. Robert Fitzpatrick, a former academic whose fluency in French had been important to his appointment, asked a couple of aggressive questions. The architects answered with a practiced mildness. No one else said a word. Robert Fitzpatrick was an outsider; the insiders were all watching to see how Michael Eisner would react. There was a long silence. Then he nodded. The floodgates opened. There were supportive questions here and useful comments there, but no questioning of the core positive judgment. Then the half-hour meeting was abruptly over and everyone hurried off to their next appointments.

We drove across Los Angeles to Anaheim and the original Disneyland theme park. There was not much time left on our trip, so after the obligatory photographs with Mickey Mouse, we were raced through the gates to experience a few of the most popular rides in the park. Our host, John Cora, the head of operations, had no intention of wasting time in the queues, so we were slipped in through the exit doors straight to the loading bay of the first attraction. I sat behind David Jones, our French analyst, as we were fitted into our harnesses. I had some intimation that this ride would bleach the knuckles, but David seemed not to: his body settled comfortably in the seat apparently awaiting the first soothing words from Walter Cronkite, the deep-voiced doyen of US news commentators who provided the commentary on many Disney "edutainment" rides. Instead, shockingly, we were hurled up into a narrow passageway with lights flashing all around us. I have never seen the back of someone's neck change more expressively. As it tensed, the tendons stood out at each side like steel cables. But I had little opportunity to examine David's physique further as we were flung into a roller-coaster in the dark, Space Mountain, which incorporated some of the most extreme loops and twists built until then. After an endless 2:45 minutes we came to the unloading dock through an explosion of blue lights and strobe effects. For a couple of seconds no-one moved. Then David pulled himself out of the rocket seat. He had turned a distinct shade of yellow.

On our return the pressure was extreme. Disney wanted to complete the float before the summer break, in June, which meant the research would have to be published in April, with an extensive marketing programme compressed into the next weeks. I started hammering out a draft of the first part of the research. I summarised the project; wrote a history of the theme park industry; described what set Disney apart from the competition and analysed the economic drivers of the theme parks. I also wrote a section on attendance, discovering, to my genuine surprise, that there were some 400,000 UK visitors to the US Disney parks in the most recent recorded year. This suggested that half of all British tourists to the US visited a Disney park, representing a fifth of all holiday trips outside Western Europe.

My 40-page opening section was ready within three weeks, the writing squeezed somehow between meetings in Paris, preparation of presentations for the float of Abbey National and a myriad of other meetings. I sent the draft over to the company for checking. Judson Green, the newly appointed finance director of Euro Disney sounded dubious. "It's not 'Bill Peco's' Wild West restaurant in Frontierland", he pointed out primly, "it's 'Pecos Billy'. And there's a lot of commercially sensitive data in those tables on theme park economics, which will have to come out."

Gary Wilson read it on a plane coming over to Europe. He was straight on the phone. "How did you get all that stuff? There's lots of stuff there even I never knew about. It's good. It's very good. Well done." After that, as far as Gary was concerned, I was a protected species, to be nurtured and given full freedom of action in running the marketing campaign. More importantly, it signalled a positive transformation in his overall attitude to Warburg.

Markos Komondouros wrote the 20-page valuation section at the back of the report, based on the Eurotunnel methodology, arriving at the figure of Fr11.9bn we had painfully negotiated with Gary Wilson. David Jones produced the central section of the report, covering the Disney background and brand, together with the plans for developing the hotels and rest of the site.

With the research under control, my job was to concentrate on marketing the flotation, with Rodney Ward and Chris Reilly worrying about the corporate finance side of the transaction; ensuring a prospectus was written and establishing a syndicate of banks to sell the shares. We were planning a full-blown production, based on privatisation precedents, with an offer to the general public, advertising, and extensive press coverage. However in this case the razzmatazz would extend across Europe for the first time, rather than be confined to one country (or two in the case of Eurotunnel). From the Disney perspective all this would have the valuable spin-off effect of raising consumer awareness of the park.

The press was beginning to follow the story avidly. In the run-up to the float it became a great supporter, an enthusiasm that was solidified by a three-day trip to the Florida parks with about 30 European journalists in May. Once again the Disney organisation put on a hugely effective programme, with a judicious mix of briefings, trips round the parks and entertainment, including a relaxed beach barbecue one evening on the central lake of the complex. The resulting coverage extended way beyond the French and UK newspapers, with enthusiastic features in the Dutch, Italian, German and Belgian media.

I was having a much easier time of it than Rodney and Chris, who were responsible for producing a prospectus that was both attractive and legally water-tight. Row after row ensued as they asked the Disney team to prove particular assertions in the draft document. The requests would be sent to Walt Disney headquarters in Burbank and time and again, they would be turned down.

On the marketing front, by contrast, I was having great fun. We finally released the research[2] in June, to an enthusiastic reception. The front cover made a major break from the sober norm for such documents. It featured a group of waving Disney characters against the Magic Kingdom castle and a deep blue sky, into which soared a cluster of coloured balloons. The more potent content within revealed our estimate of the project's worth, and the Fr11.9bn value was uncritically accepted across the financial press.

Within Warburg, however, a more hostile eye was being cast in our direction. Rodney Ward called Chris and me to a sudden meeting. "We've been grassed on," he said bitterly. "Scholey has just had me in the office and torn seven strips off my back."

"Why?" we demanded.

"Apparently we're letting the company walk all over us. He's none too keen on the research either. Said it was a puff piece. Didn't like the cover at all."

"Who's fed him all this?" Chris asked.

"He wouldn't let on. I reckon it's that bastard - ," he said, naming a senior lawyer involved in the transaction. "It's all been stoked by jealousy in the corporate finance department. They hate the fact that we're running this eye-popping flotation and they're not involved at all."

The upshot was that one of the younger corporate financiers with a legal background, Chris Brodie, was deputed to monitor the transaction. It was not a task he undertook with relish. "How on earth am I meant to check anything? Nothing's there to check anyway," he complained miserably to me, wisely keeping as low a profile as possible. As it was, I don't think Rodney ever forgave him for the lèse-majesté.

By now we were moving into detailed planning for the launch of the issue. In July we met the Disney marketing team to hear their proposals for supporting the launch of the prospectus. The presentation was led by Mimi Schaaf, a formidable lady from the Anaheim office with excellent connections through the Disney organisation. "On the weekend before the launch we intend to hold big outdoor parties in Paris and London for the financial communities in each City. In London we are looking into booking Battersea Park for the Sunday." she told us. "Here's a video of some of the entertainment we plan to put on. They've all been rehearsing hard for it." There followed a five-minute showcase of dancing and singing from a sleek troupe, gyrating and slithering across a stage. Even a music hall enthusiast would have found it excruciating.

When the video came to a stop there was an embarrassed silence. No-one wanted to make a lifelong enemy of Mimi. Rodney Ward gesticulated at me furiously. After all, I was responsible for marketing.

"Well," I said. "That's a wonderful show. I'm just a little bit worried about the cost of the programme, at $1m. I'm afraid it could be counter-productive with the institutions and press who will wonder why we are being extravagant. I also doubt how many will actually give up a day of their weekend to come to something like this." We compromised with a major event involving dancers, Disney characters and antique cars for the formal launch of the retail offering in October. But no weekend parties.

We did, however, organise one more extravagance, in the shape of a trip to the Florida parks for the main institutional investors in the middle of July. With the Disney organisation again on top form, this was another major success. So I left for my two-week family break in the last fortnight of August in a relaxed frame of mind. Everything was under control and I did not expect to be disturbed. Indeed, I had taken a few steps to make sure my holiday remained unbroken.

Rodney Ward, however, was feeling much less relaxed when he returned in the latter part of August from his own break. He was still exhausted from the endless rowing to produce a prospectus in which each claim would stand up to scrutiny. He was excruciatingly conscious of the eyes of the chairman on him, after the earlier encounter. He worked out that I had only a week between returning and the launch of the issue on 12 September. Were all the marketing arrangements in hand? He phoned my secretary, Heather Jane, an effective and tough individual who would later rise to a senior position within the support staff of the bank. She was intensely loyal.

"Where's David on holiday?" Rodney asked. "Give me his telephone number."

"He's in Northern Cyprus," she replied. "The Turkish bit. It's pretty remote. I don't think he's on the phone there himself. He told me not to give out the landlord's number to anyone except in the direst emergency."

"Well this is a dire emergency. You won't have a job unless you give me the number."

Reluctantly Heather read it over.

"What's the code for Northern Cyprus?"

"I don't know."

"Don't worry; we'll get it from the operator."

Rodney's secretary found this easier said than done. Rodney grabbed the phone from her. "Get me this number in Northern Cyprus, and sharp about it," he demanded.

"I can't," explained the hapless BT operator. "The UK doesn't recognise Northern Cyprus so I can't give out the code or connect you."

Rodney's temper, always liable to spill over in theatrical fury, was vented in full, with threats escalating to a referral to the BT chief executive. He got the code.

I happened to be sitting in the cool drawing room of the landlord's main house, which we had moved into, after lunch when I heard a remote tinkling sound. Looking under a cushion in the corner of the room, I found an ancient phone. To my complete surprise it was Rodney.

"I'm just phoning up because this launch date is coming up in less than a fortnight. Are you under control?" he asked. He sounded exhausted.

"Oh yes, perfectly," I told him. "See you on Monday". And I put the phone back under the cushion. We were due to climb the vertiginous medieval fortress of Buffavento that afternoon, so I had more immediate things to worry about than work.

In fact, with all the events carefully choreographed well in advance, I was expecting to take a back seat on my return, as indeed initially proved to be the case. The launch of the pathfinder prospectus went smoothly, with Mickey Mouse on hand to ensure plenty of material for the press photographers. It was followed up by two separate trips to Paris, one for journalists and the second for institutional investors, where we clambered over the muddy site at Marne-la-Vallée and enjoyed extended French lunches in a local restaurant. The management team then set about seeing the senior institutional investors round Europe, and particularly in London, to explain the project. I awaited an avalanche of calls from them about the issue and the assumptions in the research. I remained pretty nervous about our valuation and was not looking forward to being grilled.

For days there was silence. Then one young analyst from a leading fund manager called up. "How do you get to your Fr70 a share value?" he asked. I explained the methodology, but could discern a lack of interest in my response. Then, "How are we going to get hold of a decent amount of stock?"

That was the last and only formal questioning I received, and reflected a growing hysteria surrounding the issue. I was not the only one to notice. Gary Wilson had decided that such was the enthusiasm for the stock that the market would absorb a higher price than we had contemplated. It was during this period that the scene at the opening of the chapter took place, when he blocked me into the corner of a corridor and told me the right price was Fr85 a share.

Part of my incoherent shock at this re-opening of our agreement came from the forcible realisation that I had completely misunderstood the role of an investment banker in a float. My one-man press campaign had been designed to make the issue and the agreed price attractive to the market. However, I had also managed to increase the expectations of the seller. In future I would worry more about what the seller expected than what the market-place would deliver, a part of the job I had poorly-understood until this transaction brought it painfully to my notice.

A couple of days later we began to negotiate the price in a formal meeting.

"I can take this deal away from you and give it to Credit Suisse First Boston, who have offered to do it at 85 francs," threatened Gary, as he warmed up. Credit Suisse were the bankers we had displaced from the lead role and who were now lodged in a subordinate position in the syndicate as our co-lead manager.

"How could you think of taking this transaction from us after all the work and effort we have put into making it hot?" Rodney exclaimed indignantly in reply. The two of them really enjoyed the mutual battering. They were remarkably alike. Athletic, decisive and determined, each was accustomed to taking the lead role, without turning elsewhere for approval of their decisions

The positioning shots were cut short by the need to go to the formal presentation for the London institutional investors at Glazier's Hall on the River Thames. The meeting was packed as I have never seen before or since in the City. Our expected attendance of 120 was far exceeded as fund managers arrived unscheduled. Gary Wilson was the first speaker. He arrived in a car with Rodney Ward. They had rowed furiously on the 15-minute trip over from our offices. They stalked up the centre of the entrance foyer, surrounded by fund managers registering for the event, shouting at each other in total disregard for their audience. I doubt the fund managers had seen anything like it.

Gary Wilson was still in a rage when he took the podium. He snapped his way through his prepared speech over-viewing the Walt Disney Company and its role in managing the new resort.

Back in our offices after lunch, our pricing discussions went nowhere all afternoon. Gary Wilson continued to insist on Fr85. We indignantly responded that we had agreed Fr62 up front and based the whole marketing campaign round the figure. We argued vehemently that it would destroy the credibility of the whole project to price above fundamental value just because of overheated demand. With tempers raised on both sides – some real and some theatrical – we agreed to reconvene on Monday in Paris midmorning to find a conclusion.

After Gary Wilson stalked out, John Forsgren suggested we all went out to dinner with the rest of the Disney team. "But don't tell Gary. It would be unendurable to have him along in the middle of all this."

He found the row extremely amusing. As we sat at a west London restaurant he and Jon Richmond, a young Disney executive who was working on the legal issues of the flotation, waxed eloquent on Gary Wilson's negotiating style.

"You know who taught him, don't you?"

We shook our heads.

"The Chinese sugar traders of the Philippines. Devastating technique." And they roared with laughter.

Chris Reilly and I were nonplussed. We had never heard of the negotiating technique of the Chinese sugar traders of the Philippines, but they certainly sounded formidable. Gary had apparently come up against them when he worked for the Manila-based Trans-Philippines Investment Corporation.

"All the same," I said glumly, "I've never heard of a pricing meeting stretching from Friday over a weekend and through the following Monday."

And that was what it did. Joined by a large number of the syndicate we sat and argued with Gary in a Paris meeting room all day. There was plenty of theatre. At one stage I stood up at the table, opened my case and flung in all my papers aggressively and made as if to leave. Luckily I found an excuse to stay as the row went off at another tangent.

At last, as evening plane after plane took off without us and we made a series of calls to our secretaries to juggle the bookings, we reached agreement at Fr72 a share. It was Fr2 above our stated estimate of value and far from offering the customary IPO discount. But we would have to live with it.

The price was announced three days later, with the launch of the retail offer. The level was enough to persuade most serious press commentators to warn investors off, while acknowledging that the strength of demand would probably push the price up in the aftermarket. At the launch itself Mimi's team of dancers finally got to perform. In Paris they received short shrift, with demonstrators hurling eggs and shouting "Mickey go home" at Michael Eisner and other Disney executives on the steps of the Paris Bourse. French intellectuals had dubbed Euro Disney a cultural Chernobyl. In the pro-American City of London the second team of dancers was able to gyrate undisturbed in the central arena of Broadgate, outside our offices. At lunchtime Disney characters invaded the Warburg sales floor, rushing round and embracing the delighted traders.

The advertising campaign took off in France and the UK, with regular TV and press ads. The phone calls to our office began to build up. In the UK, we had been receiving a steady stream of requests for prospectuses, which would allow the general public to apply for shares, from the beginning of summer. On top of that the public could tear off coupons from newspaper advertisements requesting the prospectus. By the beginning of the marketing period more than 100,000 requests had been received by Tandem Communications, the London subsidiary of our French advertising agency, HDM, which was handling this part of the operation. We alone had passed over more than 25,000 letters.

"We're going to need some temps," said Heather Jane, as she struggled with the weight of phone calls. She set up an office with four initially, which was doubled by the end of the week.

"There's something going wrong," she told me. "The people are complaining that they are not getting the prospectuses, even though they wrote to us weeks ago."

I checked with Jane White, our contact point in the London offices of HDM. She reported that they were achieving an overnight response time for sending out prospectuses of well over 95%.

"Well it doesn't feel like it," I replied. Our room full of temps now numbered more than 25 and the conversations were extremely difficult. People would rage at our incompetence in sending out their prospectuses, when they had requested them days, weeks and even months before. With a week of the UK offer still to go, I arranged for the temps to start posting out prospectuses direct to anyone who called. I turned to Liz Vettewinkel, the young graduate who had been helping me through the year on the Disney marketing programme.

"Liz, why don't you pop round to the Tandem offices and find out what the hell is going on?" I was deeply conscious of the scandal over the posting out of Abbey National share certificates in the summer, when one of the distributors had been so overwhelmed by the volume that it had been caught burning the certificates in a skip.

Liz wasn't keen on sleuthing. "How the earth am I going to know what's happening by looking round an office?" she demanded. "I wouldn't know what a proper system was, let alone a broken one."

I was in a poor position to insist. In the spring we had travelled to Paris together for a planning meeting and got stuck in a taxi on the périphérique, the ring-road round the centre of the city. We were already running late for the meeting. "The taxi may be stuck, but we are not," I had declared, paying off the driver and climbing over the metal fence onto the side road. Liz had found the manoeuvre more difficult to perform, and split her long dress right up the back. She spent the day in Disney's Paris office with her back to a wall and ever since had taken a poor view of any nonconformist instruction I might give her.

As fate would have it, the market crashed right in the middle of the offer period, on 'Grey Monday', 16 October. Luckily we had closed most of the transaction earlier, leaving only the relatively small UK public offer exposed to changes in sentiment, with its fixed closing date of Friday 20 October.

There was no sign of any abatement in interest as far as demand for prospectuses was concerned. Jane White continued to pass on the statistics from the Tandem office showing that virtually all applications were being met immediately. But on the ground in our offices, Heather's team of temps had grown to forty strong, handling the phones and posting out prospectuses. The callers mixed fury with desperation as the closing date loomed. And their calls put an incredible strain on the Warburg telephone system, which had not been designed to handle retail volumes. On one occasion, as the calls on hold built up, it simply seemed to explode, scattering the calls through the building. Bemused executives, from David Scholey, down, would pick up a ringing phone to be ranted at by an aggrieved member of the public made still more furious by the length of time they had been kept waiting.

The team of temps managed to send out more than 40,000 prospectuses. But despite all our frenzied mailing it was not possible to keep the story out of the press, with the Daily Mirror enthusiastically lambasting our cavalier attitude to the public[3]. They printed Jon Richmond's business address in Paris as the recipient of all complaints, particularly as he rashly promised to look into every case referred to him.

At least, as we closed on Friday, we had a successful offer on our hands, in sharp contrast to the contemporaneous flotation of Hays, whose demand in the public offer had been destroyed by 'Grey Monday' and fell short by 92%. We were able to announce that the international offer, for which we were responsible, received applications 11 times greater than the shares we had available, while the UK public offer was subscribed nearly five times over. A triumph. And when the shares started official trading in the next month they soared by 22% on the first day from our Fr72 issue price to close at Fr88.5.

By now Jane White had conducted an internal investigation revealing that the statistics we had been supplied were figments of someone's imagination, designed solely to keep us off his back, and passed on by her in good faith. We were hardly surprised, given the rancour of those telephoning us. She was acutely embarrassed.

The party to celebrate the transaction was held in Paris two days after the start of official trading and, as is traditional with these events, involved plenty of congratulatory speeches and gifts. Jon Richmond took great pleasure in presenting me with a board on which he had festooned extracts from the deluge of letters he had received from disappointed Daily Mirror readers.

Their emotional outpouring reflected genuine bitterness at what was typically seen as part of a conspiracy to exclude them from any prospect of financial advancement:

"I believe you did not want any 'little' people involved in your project," wrote one.

"I bet there's hundreds getting more than their share. Then people wonder why the other half get aggravated. I don't ask for much but when I do I don't get it. I wonder why I bother," fumed another.

"I only wanted 50 shares each for my three grandchildren as a small nest-egg."

Over the following years, their outrage would doubtless have subsided along with the fortunes of the venture.

In the immediate aftermath, however, the Warburg Euro Disney team were the heroes of the hour. We had successfully launched the first truly pan-European flotation, raising £600m – the second largest IPO outside the privatisations seen till then. We had also earned more than any previous Warburg transaction. Our direct commissions totalled a cool £13m for the float. On top of this we had made a large profit from holding the shares in a transaction structured to satisfy the transfer requirements of the French Government. In addition, the equities division would have earned many millions more trading the shares in the following months. By contrast our commissions on the float of Eurotunnel had been little more than £1m, which included a special bonus for our research effort. In an organisation in which money talks, all the earlier concerns simply melted away.

Gary Wilson could be the most charming man alive when he was not in negotiation mode. The previous July, sitting on a Disney riverboat steamer during the fund manager outing to Florida, he quizzed me on airlines. "What do you think about KLM?" he asked. "Will they make good partners?" He went on to explain the deal he was backing to take over Northwest airlines. I have to confess that I did not take the project entirely seriously, so I was pretty surprised when his consortium, Wings, succeeded in completing the takeover of the airline a month later for a massively geared $3.65bn. The next year Gary resigned as chief financial officer of Disney to concentrate full time on the new acquisition.

Nor was this the only change in personnel. Judson Green returned to the US to take over Gary's role and John Forsgren became the finance director of Euro Disney. At Warburg, Rodney Ward became head of the Financing Division, into which I transferred after Nick Verey relocated to the New York office.

Our second transaction for Euro Disney took place nearly two years after the first. It was to prove a particularly tangled, even bad-tempered, mandate for reasons we could not understand at the time and only became clear in hindsight. Early on, in November 1990, we began exploring with the company the opportunity to raise money to fund further development by issuing a convertible bond. This was an instrument incorporating features of both debt and equity, on which the company would initially pay interest at a relatively low rate. If progress at the company were poor the instrument would remain debt and eventually be repaid, while if the project went to plan and the share price increased the instrument would convert into equity. The combination of protection on the downside and the opportunity to share in the upside would, we believed, have strong appeal for fund managers.

Despite our close relationship with John Forsgren, he made sure he kept us on our toes by soliciting a stream of competing offers from other banks. But this was not the source of the tension in the deal. This derived from what appeared to us his terrible indecision as to whether he wanted to go ahead at all. Through the first half of 1991 he again and again called to say that the deal was off. He seemed totally distracted by the budget discussions on building the Magic Kingdom he was having with Disney head office in Burbank and was particularly reluctant to issue a prospectus that incorporated any changes to the assumptions in the original issue.

In early June he called Rodney to say it was impossible to proceed since they could not provide a Financial Model section that provided sufficient quantitative information to satisfy the French authorities and which truly reflected the company's knowledge about the progress of the project. Rodney despatched Chris Reilly and me to Paris to rescue the transaction. At dinner that evening, John agonised over what to do. "I feel like John the Baptist," he lamented. Presumably Salome represented the option of issuing a convertible.

Over the next day we dragged some data out of the company, which was less horrifying than we were beginning to fear. The costs at the Magic Kingdom had increased by 9%, which could be explained by the decision to increase the capacity of the rides by 15%. The other main change was a big jump in the costs of the hotel complex, up from Fr3.4bn in the original model to Fr5.7bn. This two-thirds increase was more hair-raising, but we felt confident we could explain it as a redefinition of this phase of the project, taking in the entertainment centre and substantial upgrading of the hotels. With a few more twists and turns a suitable text was agreed with the French authorities over the next week[4].

Now we could all indulge in the traditional rows over the roles of the banks, commission levels and the exact terms of the transaction. Disney had switched its French bank from Indosuez to BNP for this transaction. Although we had argued fiercely to run the transaction by ourselves, John's response to Chris Reilly had been that the French banks would be outraged if a non-French house were to lead manage a French issue. "I have to live with these people," he pointed out. So we would have to act jointly with BNP, despite all our arguments about the need for rapid decision-making and single lines of responsibility for a market-based instrument. Unlike an initial offering, the issue of a convertible would take place against a live market in the underlying equity, with all the games that the market participants were prone to play – as we were to find out.

Meanwhile the battle with our French joint lead manager, BNP, went strongly in our favour, much to our surprise. For technical reasons, the issue was divided not just between stock to be distributed in France and abroad, but also between 'free' stock that could be sold immediately and 'priority' stock which had to be reserved for existing shareholders to take up if they so chose in the weeks after the issue was announced. Clearly it was far more attractive to distribute the so-called 'free' stock immediately, rather than run the risk of underwriting 'priority' stock which investors might not be interested in, especially if the underlying equity had underperformed. The BNP syndicate insisted on high fees for the French tranche, and even accepted total responsibility for distributing the far riskier 'priority' stock as the quid pro quo, albeit with considerable bitterness. This left us with the larger share of the issue, which we could distribute immediately. Chris Reilly was incredulous. "I don't think they realise what they've given away," he told me later, when he was describing the meeting. "Just shows how inexperienced they are in the convertibles game." Little did we guess the terrible revenge BNP would take when they did work out how we had wrong-footed them.

The next few days were a scramble to agree the terms of the deal and draft the prospectus and legal documents. On Monday evening we agreed the price of a convertible to raise Fr4bn – or £400m. The terms were aggressive and we became desperate to start selling immediately. But now the most obstructive factor had become Walt Disney's lawyers, Sullivan and Cromwell, whose insistence on fighting every minor point meant the prospectus was not ready for approval by the French financial authorities until the Wednesday morning. "We've lost a whole day," complained Maurice Thompson, our head of syndicate. When a bank takes on a convertible it owns the stock till it is distributed. Any syndicate head becomes nervous when such deals do not go smoothly.

That morning I sat in on the sales floor after we launched the issue. We had Fr2.3bn to distribute in the international tranche. There was a degree of well-disguised nervousness among the senior salesmen at the start as they contemplated a sharp drop in the level of the Tokyo market overnight. But, with Joe Hall and David Haysey, the head of European sales, in full flow on the phone the orders started to come in. "It's fine," said David Haysey, "a bit slow, but there's real interest there."

Then abruptly, at around 10.00am, the orders dried up. Some of those fund managers who had indicated interest withdrew their demand. Something was going badly wrong. Over on the syndicate desk in the corner of the trading room Maurice took a call from Goldman Sachs. "We've got Fr100m of the EuroDis convert here. Do you want them?" Maurice crouched over the phone to avoid anyone hearing the conversation. He licked his lips nervously. He had little choice. If Goldman were to dump the stock in the open market the price would collapse and we would never distribute our holding. But from where on earth had Goldman obtained this stock? "Fine," he said jovially. "Heave them over."

An hour later there was another call. Another Fr100m. And another. And another. By the end of the day we owned, not only the greater part of our original Fr2.3bn stock, but another Fr0.5bn out of the market, courtesy of Goldman. Later that year, when Michael

Cohrs, the syndicate manager at Goldman, switched to Warburg, he explained how the operation had proceeded. "BNP offered us a slug of stock at a good discount, so we were happy to take it and test you out. When you took it, we went back for more and slung chunk after chunk at you over the rest of the day. We took a nice little turn." BNP had clearly given in to the delicious temptation of dumping the stock on a bank that had outplayed them in their own market. We were learning the hard way why doing this kind of deal jointly with another bank was so dangerous.

Michael carried on, "Our people then tried to work out strategies to trade Warburg stock against EuroDis stock. Buy one, sell the other. Trouble is they all went the same way. If EuroDis went down Warburg would go down too - and probably go bust, in our view. After all, with way less than a £1bn of equity in its own balance sheet, Warburg couldn't afford to wipe out the best part of £250m-plus in an unsaleable convertible. Shame; would have been a nice trade." Michael was always ruthlessly pragmatic when it came to business.

I was sitting at my desk in front of Rodney Ward later in the day as the horrific news steadily unfolded. He was aghast. "What?" he exclaimed. "We've got a whole chunk back? How the fuck has that happened?" His stentorian voice boomed round the open-plan office. Everyone could appreciate that something had gone terribly wrong.

The next morning Rodney was talking to the lawyers on the phone. The conversation could, as usual, be heard right across the floor. "OK, so we don't have to tell the market we've got them, thank God.

"But we have to tell anybody we try to sell stock to about our position? That's ridiculous. No-one will buy if they know about our position. That's bloody useless." And Rodney slung down the phone in fury. We were caught in a classic Catch 22. We needed to sell out our holding in the stock, but no institutional investor would buy if the huge scale of our position became known. The market would interpret it as the result of a mispriced issue and wait for the price to spiral lower as we became increasingly desperate. As the weeks went by I became more and more surprised that the story didn't leak.

Rodney's regular phone calls on the matter were hardly discreet and most of Warburg must have known the hole we were in, a hole big enough to damage seriously the leading UK investment bank. But not a word was breathed to the press on what would have made a sensational financial story.

Over the next two months markets drifted downwards, as did the price of both the underlying Euro Disney shares and the new convertible. On paper we weren't losing much money, but the position continued to nag away. Then, in the dog-days of summer, on Monday, 19 August, we woke up to hear that Gorbachev had been deposed in a Russian coup. European markets went into an immediate tail-spin – as did the Euro Disney price quotes. Now we were losing real money. I totted it up to be in the region of £40m in the unlikely event we could sell out at prevailing prices. And it was all set to become much worse. I began to settle into a fatalistic mood. No-one's career could survive a loss of this magnitude and I suspected that everyone involved in the convertible issue would be badly damaged.

Then in the afternoon the mood began to change. Boris Yeltsin stood up on a tank in front of the Russian parliament building to defy the leaders of the coup and thousands of Muscovites were rallying to his side. By Wednesday, the coup leaders were trying to flee the country. European markets responded rapturously and the Euro Disney price soared with all the others. Soon we were looking at a substantial theoretical profit on our enforced holding of convertibles. A few days later I came back from a meeting to find Rodney beaming with relief. "They've gone," he said. "All of them." With the markets enthusiastic for fresh stock, the sales team had taken the risk of revealing the position and succeeded in quickly placing all of it at a substantial discount to prevailing prices. Even with the discount, we still made more than £5m profit on the transaction. And although no doubt this was the least of the consequences of Yeltsin's brave defiance, I have remained extremely grateful to him ever since for saving my career.

As opening day approached in April 1992 the Disney marketing machine scaled the heights. The Warburg team was invited – along with thousands of others involved in the project – to join the weekend party to celebrate. We were all to stay in the hotel complex, which was being opened on the Friday of our arrival – 12 April. Saturday would see a party for the privileged invitees in the Magic Kingdom itself, while the official opening on Sunday was expected to see an overwhelming tide of enthusiastic paying guests. Already Disney executives fretted that the motorway network in eastern Paris might congeal entirely under the pressure.

As it happened, congestion surfaced somewhat earlier, on the Friday afternoon. We arrived at the Newport Bay Hotel to find hundreds of privileged guests packed solid and immoveable in the foyer. The computer system had apparently broken down, leaving the inexperienced counter staff at all five of the newly opened hotels at a total loss how to transfer up to four thousand sets of guests to their rooms. Slowly, over the next few hours, the foyer was cleared using paper-based improvisation. "Oh, well," I said to Rodney cheerfully, "You've got to expect a few snags when you launch four and a half thousand rooms like this on one day."

And, once checked in, the party was truly extraordinary – a production as only the Disney marketing team at full stretch could put on. One by one the hotels were officially opened. Then, as the evening progressed we came to The Four Tops in front of the New York hotel. They stepped through their hits to an admiring crowd: "Baby, I need your loving"; "Reach out, I'll be there". We all sang along. Then it was time for the fireworks over the lake. Again an extraordinary event, with figures from the Little Mermaid lit up against a backdrop of explosive colour in the balmy sky.

And that was just the start. On the Saturday the Magic Kingdom was opened, with parades, rides and champagne. With temperatures in the 70Fs, we could have been in Florida. That evening there were more stars performing. We crammed into Discoveryland to see Cher on stage, followed by Tina Turner, hammering out her hits. I have forgotten the budget for this party, but it was truly staggering. I never expect to go to a better event again.

On Sunday I ran into John Forsgren at the official opening ceremony in front of the castle. He was a little apprehensive. "The French Transport Minister has been on radio warning Parisians that all the roads will be blocked and not to come," he said.

I next saw him in the middle of the morning. He was standing with a group of Disney executives at the front of the theme park. They were in intense debate and visibly far from happy. The Magic Kingdom was still relatively empty, the car parks barely half-full. I decided against interrupting them. After the euphoria of the last two days, it was clearly a deeply disappointing start.

Nor was the point lost on the financial markets. From its peak of Fr164 just before opening day, the shares fell in a straight line to Fr61 by December. The press coverage turned from ecstatic to vituperative almost overnight. Attendance in the first six months was down from the projected 7.7m to 7m, and even that figure had been boosted substantially by the free passes Euro Disney were handing out. More significant, the projected profit for the first year had been transformed into a loss of Fr339m in the first six months alone.

That December Rodney and I, together with Herman van der Wyck, a Warburg main board director, paid a visit to the Burbank headquarters of The Walt Disney Company. We were welcomed by Frank Wells, who was flanked by Judson Green – now head of the Disney theme park division – and Richard Nanula, the incredibly young new chief financial officer, then aged a bare 32 years. We were blunt. Rodney introduced the problem by stating, "The share price is a disaster."

I then carried on with some analysis that showed that outside investors were being hit far harder than The Walt Disney Company due to the lop-sided financial structure of Euro Disney. I concluded, "You should reshape the financial structure entirely. You may also wish to put in some further funds to repair the damage experienced by outside investors." I did not dare point out that the Euro Disney investors were suffering at the same time as Michael Eisner was reported to have enjoyed a $202m windfall from exercising his Walt Disney options. But the point was hovering in the background.

Frank Wells was, as ever, extremely polite, however unpalatable our message. He showed his irritation by taking a couple of side-swipes at me, but remained studiedly courteous towards Rodney and Herman, the two senior visitors.

John Forsgren reported the fallout a few days later. A task force comprising Burbank and Euro Disney executives, lawyers and Warburg was to be set up to find a solution to the crisis. "All the options will be examined, including taking the company private, a major injection of equity from Burbank or the sale of hotels from Paris to Burbank at an attractive price."

But this proved wide of the mark. The concerns I had expressed about the risks to the Walt Disney reputation in the international financial markets seemed to evaporate as the weeks progressed. A little later Richard Nanula told me, "David, we all thought you were entirely mad when you suggested that Walt Disney should inject its own funds. Whatever were you thinking of? And by the way, next time you plan a visit like that, let us know in advance. Frank thought it was just a senior courtesy visit, so we looked pretty foolish in front of him."

So by the spring of 1993 we were being tasked to organise an issue of new capital of another Fr5bn to Fr6bn for the company. Walt Disney would supply fresh funds, but only in line with the other shareholders. There would be no change to the financial structure that so favoured the parent company. In practice this meant we were to spend the best part of a month holed up in one of the hotels of the complex, the New York Hotel, trying to write a prospectus. Given the high-profile difficulties of the company, persuading the long-suffering shareholders to find further funds to support it would tax our persuasive abilities to the limit. Nor was the task helped by the steady background deterioration in the Euro Disney operating performance, which a parallel team were attempting to stem with an ambitious turn-round plan.

Every morning a roomful of lawyers, accountants, bankers and company executives would gather to work through the day on the prospectus, and then there would be a conference call with Burbank to discuss the issues that had arisen. Unfortunately the nine-hour time difference between Paris and California worked to the disadvantage of the European team, as Burbank only seemed able to devote time to Euro Disney towards the end of their day. This meant a string of conference calls extending to 3.00am, and by the end of the first fortnight we were walking round like zombies. One night in early May we had to deal with a proposal to announce a Fr4bn loss at the same time as the issue. "It's only an accounting change," said Richard Nanula. "Lots of companies do them. Go for it."

"But Richard," groaned Rodney wearily, "it will put the company into default on its debt. The banks will be able to take control. You can hardly expect us to raise new capital in those circumstances." At the last minute an announcement to launch a June issue was pulled. By the end of June, with visitor numbers and financial performance continuing to deteriorate, a full-scale restructuring involving the banks and convertible holders became inevitable.

In August Chris Reilly and I prepared a new presentation for the Euro Disney financial team on how we could help them in the restructuring. We brought with us two Warburg banking colleagues who were experts in restructuring, Don Procter and Chris Coles. I travelled over with them the afternoon before so they could have a quick look through the Magic Kingdom before the presentation. We decided to stay in the Newport Bay Hotel and I entertained them on the flight over with the story of the booking shambles on the first afternoon. It meant they were not particularly surprised when we went to our three rooms to find that each was already full of someone else's possessions. We took our plastic card keys back to reception to try again. This time Don Procter and I found our rooms appropriately empty and met ten minutes later in the lobby. Chris Coles was nowhere to be seen. "How on earth has he managed to lose himself before we've even begun the sight-seeing?" I grumbled to Don.

Eventually he sauntered across the lobby. "Where the hell have you been?" I demanded.

"Well," he said, "if you thought the first room was bad, you should have seen the second one they gave me. I opened the door and there standing at the end of the bed, framed in the doorway, was a naked woman. I don't know who was more shocked." He paused to consider the question. "Me, probably. Not the kind of thing you expect to see on a Wednesday afternoon." Clearly the hopelessly under-specified hotel computer system was still far from adequate more than a year after opening.

The presentation resulted in our appointment to advise Euro Disney in the necessary restructuring of the project. As it turned out, this was an invidious role in what became a tug of war over the next nine months between Michael Eisner's team in Burbank and the French banks which had provided all the loans, a total of more than Fr17bn. Scant interest was taken by these two parties in the position of the outside Euro Disney shareholders, whose interests we were employed to represent. As a result, we were increasingly seen as an irritant in the transaction. Nor did we endear ourselves to the Walt Disney team when we were presented with the terms of the transaction that the two parties had agreed. New money of Fr6bn was being raised at Fr10 a share from both The Walt Disney Company and the outside shareholders. In return Walt Disney would waive its royalty and management fees for a few years, but the payments would still eventually lock in. There were various concessions by both sides on debt and interest payments. We did our sums. Fr7 was the most we could calculate the shares to be worth. It was hardly an attractive deal for the outside shareholders.

"It's a dead company," I told Rodney. "Every time they start to move the profits ahead, the Disney royalty and management fees are raised and suck it all out. The share won't be worth looking at till 2020." This analysis led to our refusal to support the issue by joining the underwriting syndicate. Indeed, the issue would have collapsed and been left with the French banks if Prince Al-Waleed, the Saudi Arabian investor with a reputation for a magic touch, had not rushed in at the last moment and sucked up the loose stock. It was not one of his most distinguished ventures. The price promptly collapsed to below Fr7 a share and continued falling over the years to come.

It was a traumatic time. Devastating articles were published in the financial press blaming Michael Eisner personally for a considerable portion of the cost over-run at the park and the hotel complex[5]. In April on the Easter weekend, as the rescue was under way, Frank Wells was shockingly killed in a ski helicopter crash in northern Nevada. Just three months later Michael Eisner underwent emergency heart bypass surgery. The decade that followed was full of difficulty for the Californian company.

The transaction, combined with a series of personnel changes, effectively marked the end of our relationship with Euro Disney, renamed that autumn Disneyland Paris. It had not been a happy experience. The dreams I had of spear-heading the opening up of the equity markets to provide capital for infrastructure projects had long since died in the slow-motion wreckage of Eurotunnel and Euro Disney. Indeed, the regrettable outcome of these two transactions had still left the European public equity markets closed to projects up to the time of my retirement a decade later. In the end the promoters of each of these two projects (contractors in the case of the former and Disney in the latter) did not find it painful enough when their projections fell short; the new investors took risk that they did not share. The solution to this conflict of interest was to be found later in the 1990s in Australia, where sponsoring companies such as Maquarie Bank began to invest their own money on the same terms as the outside investors. The result has been a powerful and successful group of infrastructure companies. However, back in the early 1990s, from my own particular perspective, I had to find another role in the financial markets.

---

[1] Storming the Magic Kingdom. Wall Street, The Raiders and the Battle for Disney, John Taylor. Balantine: New York 1987

[2] A Share in Euro Disneyland, David Jones, David Freud, Markos Komondouros, S.G. Warburg Securities, 20 June, 1989

[3] Mickey Mouse Muddle, Stephen Ellis, Mirror Money, The Daily Mirror, 25 October, 1989

[4] EuroDisney offering circular. Issue of convertible bonds, p35. Developments Affecting The Financial Model. 18 June 1991

[5] Mouse Trap: Fans like Euro Disney but its Parent's Goofs Weigh the Park Down, by Peter Gumbel and Richard Turner. The Wall Street Journal, 10 March, 1994

7

World War III

The International Equity Market – 1990 - 1994

David Scholey was looking at me incredulously. "What do you mean, we can't do it? Tony Ryan was sitting in that very chair this morning offering us the job of running his float. And you think we should just turn it down?" It was two days before the 1990 Christmas break, and I was sitting in the chairman's office along with Derek Higgs

I took a deep breath. "I haven't seen any figures; but then, I don't really think their figures would tell us anything, anyway. The simple fact is that GPA is carrying a massive aircraft order-book at its own risk. Aircraft prices have collapsed about 20% since those orders were put on. Aircraft are being stacked up in the desert because of Saddam's invasion of Kuwait. The company is bust."

David Scholey's expression turned from incredulous to threatening. "That's a very big call when you haven't looked at any information at all, isn't it?"

I stood my ground. My experience with the computer leasing industry had taught me all too vividly how dangerous leasing could be. I saw very little difference between GPA, as Guinness Peat Aviation was known, and the computer leasing companies. My conviction was boosted by the dramatic way that Atlantic Computers, the company which we had attacked for cavalier accounting, had earlier that year brought down the financial conglomerate which had foolishly bought it, British & Commonwealth.

GPA had built up a huge business during the airline boom of

the 1980s by ordering aircraft from the manufacturers in bulk and selling them at the higher prices that prevailed at the time of delivery. The airlines renting its existing fleet would, naturally, chose to eliminate these aircraft rather than their own when they were downsizing. Some of the airlines might go bust. So GPA was desperately exposed to the worst airline downturn for at least a decade. It might not be able to rent out the aircraft it had ordered, and if it did the prices would be depressed; at the same time some of the fleet already rented out would be returned.

"It's not as if we have a long list of £1bn-plus flotations at the moment," David Scholey observed, "especially at international fee-scales."

"When do you have to revert to Ryan?" asked Derek Higgs.

"I think we've got a bit of time, what with Christmas coming up."

"Well, let's ask David to do a tiny bit more research and reconvene."

I had gathered reinforcements for our next meeting, which did not take place till late January. The analysts had written a sprightly piece on the collapse in aircraft values, called "Airburst", while the corporate finance team that had worked on the value of GPA for one of the owners, Air Canada, had also been negative. Another sceptic was John Mayo, who was later to embark on a controversial career as chief financial officer of Marconi. His summary view of GPA was even blunter than mine.

"All right," said David Scholey, "if that's the view I'll ring Ryan up and give him our regrets." I was both surprised and impressed. I am sure that few investment banking chiefs would have turned down the opportunity of running a fee pool of more than $50m. It was a graphic illustration of the obsessively high ethical standards with which the founder, Siegmund Warburg, had imbued the firm and which David Scholey was at great pains to maintain. Committees would be summoned to discuss (usually at great length) all new business prospects and clients, to ensure that the bank would not find itself subject to criticism when it undertook transactions. It could be a tortuous process but it did weed out many dubious pieces of business. Other banks could be much less discriminating. Indeed Tony Ryan, the dynamic chief executive of GPA, found very little difficulty in assembling a star cast of investment banks to handle his flotation. He appointed the largest Japanese broking house Nomura as the lead bank, or global co-ordinator, with Goldman Sachs and Merrill Lynch to handle the US distribution and Schroders and BZW the UK.

As Scholey had pointed out, there was not much action in the international equity markets at that time. Since the 1987 crash there had only been a handful of significant equity transactions outside the UK privatisation programme. So the competition for new opportunities was intense. All the investment banks understood that their position in this lucrative market would be determined by how many transactions they won over the next few years and how well they performed in those transactions. I might very well come to regret my role in turning down GPA, if the transaction turned out to be a triumph, whatever my views about the long-term instability of the business.

And for a time it looked as if I might have made a terrible misjudgement. The GPA public relations bandwagon rolled along, master-minded in the UK by Gerry Grimstone, a former Treasury official working for Schroders. Story after story appeared in the press extolling the company and its prospects. Particularly inspired, I thought, was a row between the company and the FT-Actuaries, an arcane body of experts who decide in which of the various indices a company should be classified. In this case they responded to a request by the company to go into the UK indices by pointing out that GPA was an Irish company and could not therefore fall within the UK categories. This meant it would be bought by fund managers specialising in European, rather than British, companies. It was sheer chutzpah to ask at all, but the disagreement generated terrific publicity and I considered that was its real purpose.

"I understand you've been saying negative things about GPA." It was Gerry Grimstone on the phone. He adopted an effective patronising tone, one that was well-worn in my case since by some bizarre coincidence he had been in the year ahead of me both at school, Whitgift in South Croydon, and at my Oxford college, Merton. He had caught me fair and square. I had, indeed, been expressing my amazement at the progress of GPA's float. Unfortunately I had done so at a lunch attended by the PR firm working on the transaction, and they had promptly reported my scepticism to the company and its bankers. The company's sensitivity to our views had been honed by some unfortunate quotes in the Financial Times from David Scholey, when his off the record comments on the real reason we had turned down the float found their way into print.

"Of course, you're totally within your rights to say whatever you like about the company," Gerry told me. "But we think it only right that, if you do, you should be properly informed. So we're inviting you over to see the company for the day, so you can get the full story."

The thought filled me with dread, especially as I was busy on several other transactions and had little time to spare.

"I'll do a deal with you," I replied. "If you excuse me the day out with GPA, I promise never to talk about them to any outsider ever again." Which deal I kept.

It didn't mean, however, that I stopped following the progress of the float. Indeed I had little choice. It was well-known that I was instrumental in our rejection of the company and as the float excitement gained real momentum in the spring of 1992 there were a few pointed remarks.

"You turned down $100m of fees," exaggerated Rodney Ward bitterly in June as the transaction was launched. "I hope you know what you're doing."

"It's bust, Rodney. How could we float something that's bust?"

"That's not what the rest of the world thinks," he pointed out, waving a newspaper with a particularly fulsome feature on the flotation in it.

A few days later I shared a car back from Heathrow with a Goldman Sachs executive. "How did the GPA investor presentation go in New York?" I asked him.

"Incredible," he replied. "Standing room only. It was the best-attended roadshow meeting I have ever seen."

I began to brood. I realised, all too late, that my stand on GPA was almost as career threatening as the near-fiasco of the Euro

Disney convertible a year earlier. I felt an icy chill on the back of my neck whenever I sat at my desk, imagining the glares of my colleagues. I realised that they would be equally unforgiving whether I lost the bank a large sum of money or prevented it from picking up a bonanza.

The news, when it came through on the Thursday morning, 18 June, was as stunning as it was unexpected. Institutional investors, particularly in the US, were not interested in owning the company. Demand was simply not there, almost at any price. Attendance at the roadshow presentation had reflected curiosity rather than enthusiasm. The evening before, when Gerry Grimstone reported the failure, Tony Ryan had exploded. "May you rot in hell. You have brought down one of Ireland's finest companies." In a night of bitter recriminations the deal was pulled. Among the wilder conspiracy theories circulating later was that Goldman Sachs deliberately destroyed the transaction to undermine any prospect of Nomura establishing itself as a leading bookrunner.

I felt overwhelmingly relieved. We had not wasted 18 months on a high-profile disaster. My own reputation was undamaged and we could continue our battle in the international equity markets without a humiliating failure to undermine our marketing efforts. For most of those bankers involved in the deal it was to prove an expensive diversion. As far as I am aware, Nomura was never awarded another big piece of equity business outside Asia.

By now I was deeply involved in the international equity markets. When Nick had left London to become the chairman of Warburg's New York office I needed a new home. It was natural to approach Rodney Ward, who had taken over the Financing Division and with whom I had worked so closely on Euro Disney. He was equally keen to welcome me into the department. So in September 1990 I moved down into their open-plan office in front of Rodney's desk. I retained my responsibilities for the Warburg PR team and for our presentations effort, where my former secretary Heather Jane was expanding a department to churn out ever-increasing volumes of pitching materials under my close eye. With good-looking output to present to potential clients, I could now devote almost all my attention to winning international equity business. This, I reckoned, was where we would win or lose the battle to become a world-class investment bank.

In retrospect I was right to anticipate rapid growth in this market. In the years between 1990 and 1995 the volume of international equity sold soared to more than $60bn. Transactions in which I had been involved in my career till that point, like the floats of Singapore Airlines in 1985, Eurotunnel in 1987 and Euro Disney in 1989, all represented significant mile-stones in the market's development. The big investment appetite for stocks from abroad was in the UK, the US and Switzerland, driven by theoretical analysis that showed financial benefit in diversifying into foreign stocks. The transactions could be initial public offerings, or IPOs, where a company is first floated on the market; secondary sales of stock, in which the owners sold more of the company, or funds raised by the company itself through the issue of new stock. The battle between the banks for this business became absolutely frenetic. The financial equivalent of World War III broke out in the international capital markets.

Fuelling the rapid growth in this period was an acceptance by Governments across Europe that they needed to copy the Thatcher privatisation strategy. As a full participant in the UK privatisation boom we were well-placed to benefit from this trend. However, we had a terrible Achilles heel. In the 1980s, a combination of UK Government policy and successful propaganda by the US investment banks comprehensively undermined the aspirant UK banks in their home market. The Government would always hand out privatisation mandates to an advisor and broker from separate houses. It would also hand out the distribution of the shares abroad to investment banks from the relevant country.

In mid-March 1991 we invited the head of public enterprises at the Treasury, Steve Robson, to a presentation at our offices. It was to prove the single most important presentation by Warburg in the decade. Our timing was both fortuitous and impeccable: fortuitous, because the invitation was the result of a casual acquaintanceship at a dining club, to which both Steve and Roger Harrison-Topham, the Warburg director responsible for international equity issuance, belonged; impeccable, because Steve Robson was feeling in a most revolutionary mood.

Steve was an unusual animal in the UK civil service; he knew what he was doing. The standard policy of three-year rotation meant that most civil servants had just got to grips with their job when they were moved on. Similarly Steve, then aged 48, had moved through various jobs in a 21-year Treasury career. Crucially, however, he had spent three years in the mid-1980s working on privatisations such as Enterprise Oil and British Gas. So when he was promoted in 1989 to head the public enterprises office he hit the ground running. He was dismayed that while the industries being floated were being forced to face up to competition, the City's issuing procedures remained hidebound.

Later Steve told me, "We were a serial user of the capital markets and we had learned a lot in the process. There were too many things in the way between the vendor and the market, like the lack of competition between the brokers and the cosy way shares were allocated to the institutions with whom the brokers had a relationship, rather than those which were keen on the stock." The issue had just been brought into dramatic focus with the Government sale of the electricity generators. The Japanese broker Nomura had leapt into the market on the first day of dealing and bought up stock to send the prices soaring.

"If only we had been able to bring that Japanese demand into the issue, the Government would have been able to price the stock more aggressively," Steve complained during the preliminary chat before we launched into our formal presentation. Our target was the sale of the next tranche of shares in British Telecommunications, which we knew the Government was likely to announce in the Budget speech four days later, on 19 March. We made three main points. We could develop a structure where the deal was priced at market rather than at the huge discounts that had so often embarrassed the Government in previous privatisations. To do this, we would need to act as a unified bank and broker in the home market and we would want control of the distribution exercise abroad. We pointed out that our share of everyday trade in UK stocks to US investors was bigger than that of the US banks – contrary to their propaganda.

Steve Robson had one more thing on his mind. "Could you let us see who the buyers are?" he asked.

There was an ominous pause. It was axiomatic that the identity of the investing institution which subscribed for shares was a closely guarded secret of the bank through which it applied. That anonymity in fact disguised all kinds of underhand activity by the banks involved. Stuart Stradling, the head of UK broking, had a most conservative expression on his face.

"I don't see why not," I broke in, braving Stuart's scowl. "I'm sure we could arrange for you to see the book of demand." I could sense that this was an absolutely pivotal issue for the Treasury. The issue of 'transparency', which the process of revealing the names and behaviour of the institutions to the vendor was dubbed, was central to Steve's thinking. Later he told me, "We had dreamed up an issuing process in the Treasury which incorporated pricing at the end of a transaction, transparency and flexibility as to where we allocated the stock, in a structure controlled by a single bank. Sadly I had come to the conclusion that no UK bank would have been game to do it. We were resigned either to abandoning the idea or using a New York bank. So this meeting was a happy chance."

In the formal presentations made a few weeks later the advisory side of the house pitched separately from the securities arm; but for the first time the Government appointed us as a unified team to run the whole transaction. It was a turning point: a revolution in how European issues were sold thereafter.

The structure proved overwhelmingly successful. In the past, UK privatisations had usually been underwritten by the institutions and then offered to the general public in a formal sale period. Uncertainty as to both the progress of the market during the sale period and the success of the sale itself meant that the institutional underwriting price incorporated a discount. In BTII we dispensed with the underwriting and priced the offer simply to reflect the demand from the institutions. The offer to the general public, conducted at the same time as the institutional process, would be at a discount to this price. The public applied for stock without knowing the price, but proved happy to do so given the discount. In sharp contrast to previous experience, the share price moved up less than 1% on the day of the issue. For one of the largest share sales ever - at £5.4bn - this was a stunning outcome.

We built an elaborate computer model for Steve Robson, which allowed him to see the applications for stock, institution by investing institution, round the world. It was not without hiccups. Our initial US bookrunner had been Salomon Brothers, but a scandal involving their manipulation of the US Treasury market in August meant they were fired midway through the process and the most aggressive of the US banks, Goldman Sachs, appointed in their stead. They seemed to take the computerised model a good deal less seriously, with the result that the US book of demand failed to materialise on the final Friday evening in early December. The senior Goldman partner on the transaction, Eric Dobkin, had flown over from the US during the day and was hauled from his bed in the Savoy Hotel in the middle of the night to re-assemble the pieces – a piece of ritual humiliation which gave savage joy to the Warburg team. "He still had his pyjamas on under his coat," one of the overnight team told me afterwards. Eric's rage when he arrived at Goldman's London office the next day was reported to be truly heroic.

The success of BTII gave us an enviable marketing platform. Well in advance of the completion of the transaction I was running round Europe describing it to Government departments. I paid particular attention to Sweden, where the conservative Government which gained power in September announced a privatisation programme modelled on the UK.

"Who do you want to see?" asked Mats Nilsson, our Swedish coverage banker.

"Everyone," I told him. "We need to see everybody who could conceivably have some influence."

Mats had an infuriating habit. When our car was due to leave for Heathrow to catch the last flight to Stockholm he would pick up the phone on his desk and make a series of calls. It meant we always set out half-an-hour late and I would spend the car-trip in a frenzy of concern over whether we would make the flight. After my third experience of this I insisted on travelling ahead in a separate car.

Bad as his time-keeping was, Mats was as good as his word in making sure the two of us saw every official who might conceivably have some influence over appointments. In particular he took us to see Per Tegner, who was working in an obscure quango.

"This is probably a complete waste of time," he confessed, "but you never know."

"Well, I asked for everybody," I said. And I ran through the whole BTII structure with Per, who was fascinated by it. He also seemed flattered by what I suspect was the sole attention he received that year from an investment bank.

The attention paid off handsomely when Per Tegner was appointed out of the blue to head the privatisation programme at the Swedish Ministry of Industry and Commerce. In January 1992 we submitted our pitch to privatise the most attractive asset, Procordia, a conglomerate with heavy pharmaceutical involvement. On 8 May the Ministry rang up to let us know that we would be appointed the global co-ordinator of the transaction.

Less than a fortnight later, on 20 May, two of my colleagues on the transaction, Roger Harrison-Topham and James Sassoon, and I put in a call to Per Tegner to discuss progress. There was an embarrassed pause. "I need to tell you some good news and some bad news," he said.

There was little good news. After a series of presentations from the US investment banks the Ministry had decided that our sole leadership role should be shared with Goldman Sachs. Protest as we might, there was little we could do but accept. "I understand how difficult and disappointing this news will be for you," said Per at the end of the conversation.

To ensure that the two banks worked harmoniously, he laid down that the commissions and fees would be shared equally between us. However this had absolutely no impact in relaxing the Goldman drive to dominate the transaction. They were less interested in the economic return on this early Continental European privatisation than establishing a record of supremacy in the business. Just as we had found a champion in the Ministry, so had Goldman, whose former employee Jan Amethier had moved to become Per Tegner's deputy. In the endless rows between us in the succeeding months we would each lobby our respective champions.

Goldman's first victory over us emerged within a week, when we discovered that they would be responsible for all the mechanical aspects of managing the book of demand. This was revenge indeed for Eric Dobkin's disturbed night. They then attacked our proposal to take responsibility for distributing the stock through Europe, while Goldman took the US.

"In the interest of fair sharing, Europe should be split between you and Goldman," Jan Amethier told Roger Harrison-Topham on the phone.

"There'll be a mood of outrage in this organisation that we are not considered the right people to run the entire European tranche," responded Roger.

"I understand your position, but I don't sympathise with it," was Jan's curt response. "A UK house has no more credibility than a US house when looking into Europe." In the end, a complicated split was agreed in which we obtained all of Europe except France, as well as Japan. Goldman obtained the US, Canada, France and the rest of the world, but they had succeeded in undermining our strategy of presenting ourselves as the European end of any transaction.

In this struggle for dominance the bank responsible for the domestic distribution, the Swedish house Enskilda, came off very much the worst. It took responsibility for the Nordic region and for advising the Ministry on Swedish matters, but was pointedly not named a joint global co-ordinator.

The battle for precedence between banks in international equity transactions by now encompassed a wide range of fronts. One of the most important was linguistic. As in all specialisms, jargon was used in a manipulative context. The equity markets had originally appropriated the roles of the banking syndicates in the eurobond market, with lead managers superior to joint lead, co-lead and co-managers. On this was grafted the concept of the bookrunner, the bank which had control of what was called the book of demand for a stock and which would allocate the shares to the individual institutions. This was clearly an overwhelmingly powerful position vis a vis the rest of the syndicate, since the investing institutions would tend to apply to the bookrunner direct for stock, rather than the more junior banks, since it was (rightly) assumed that the bookrunner would favour applications with commission income attached. It was perfectly possible to be appointed a lead manager, but still to be in a subordinate position because the other lead manager was also the bookrunner. The final embellishment was introduced at the beginning of the 1990s, probably by Goldman Sachs, with the concept of the global co-ordinator. This was an extremely clever piece of verbal gymnastics. On the surface it added nothing to the positions of bookrunner and lead manager, yet it was used to catapult the international banks ahead of their domestic rivals. Enskilda, with its local base, could not claim to have a powerful presence in markets all round the world. Goldman and Warburg could and so we seized the title global co-ordinator. By implication – and within a very short period in practice – the so-called global co-ordinators ranked above the domestic lead manager, even though these might be responsible for the lion's share of a particular transaction. At Warburg we had quickly decided that this title might also play to our advantage and in the BTII transaction we had ensured that we were appointed as global co-ordinator, as well as bookrunner, the first time the formal title had been used in a UK privatisation.

Enskilda might have been sidelined, but this did nothing to diminish Goldman's hostility as far as we were concerned. Our team had to maintain constant vigilance to prevent our role in the transaction being eroded. One of the favoured Goldman tactics was 'paper capture'. I was to experience this at first hand.

In June I began work getting to know the company and its operations so that I could work out a marketing plan. It was a complicated animal, resulting from a series of mergers, with interests that spread from its pharma business into tobacco, sweets, and mineral water. It would not be easy to present as a coherent entity to the institutions. I made firm friends with the head of investor relations, Jan Isoz, and he organised a series of presentations for us to meet the management of the different divisions.

Adapting the strategies I had used for UK companies, and Euro Disney, I then wrote a short paper outlining an appropriate marketing campaign. It laid out when we should publish research, the timing of company presentations to journalists and investors and so forth. I sent the paper to the company, Goldman and Enskilda for their consideration late one afternoon.

Next morning I was stunned to see a fax of the paper back on my desk. Only now it was presented as a Goldman paper, in their distinctive, squat type-face. The contents of the paper were unchanged, except for one inconsequential sentence added at the end – to justify the recasting. I took particular note of the time of the exercise, revealed in the computer-generated reference at the bottom of the page – 3.30am. Their team had worked through the night to turn round this paper in their format and circulate it to all parties.

"You've rattled them," said Maurice Thompson, head of equity markets. "They've been busy grabbing all this mechanistic stuff and they've only just realised that you've seized the crown jewels, the marketing campaign."

I had caught Goldman on unfamiliar ground. The US regulators forbade any marketing of an issue before the prospectus was launched, so they did not have the processes we had developed for European marketing campaigns. And in the eyes of the Ministry, master-minding the marketing would be far more visible and important than most other aspects of the transaction. Goldman's attempt to seize back the initiative by retyping was easily dealt with. Later that morning I put out the paper again. It incorporated the extra Goldman sentence and one more from me. This was alibi enough to put it out as a final, approved, version addressed to all parties, including the Ministry - this time in our typeface. I had managed to outplay Goldman at its own game; all future papers on marketing in this transaction would now be authored by us.

Paper capture was only one technique. Goldman was adept at playing the individual rather than the institution. They would target a particular member of an opposition team and subject them to criticism and ridicule with the aim of undermining the client's, and even their own colleagues', confidence in that person's judgement. Shortly after my marketing campaign coup I was naturally picked out as a target.

"How's Sigmund?" the Goldman syndicate desk would regularly mock their counterparts on our desk. "Who's he analysing now?"

This tactic back-fired rather badly when they were informed that I was indeed a close relation of the Sigmund they were referring to – my great-grandfather. My new nickname suddenly did not seem so wounding and was abruptly dropped.

In the event a collapsing equity market through 1992, followed by a major restructuring of the company in the following year, meant that the transaction was delayed till June 1994. But the battle with Goldman carried on right through to the bitter end as they used every means at their disposal to brand the sale of the company, now renamed Pharmacia, as their own. The final twist occurred on the night the prospectus was printed, when our team-member at the printers, Michael McNish, saw to his horror that the ink chosen for the text was the Goldman black.

"This should be dark blue," he told the printer. "Change it."

The printer refused to do so without authorisation from Goldman which was in charge of the printing arrangements. Goldman refused to make the change. Michael refused to allow printing to commence. Only when Michael got on the phone to Per Tegner in the middle of the night was a Ministry instruction obtained to change the ink to our distinctive dark blue.

It was not an elegant manoeuvre. The convention in conducting the infighting between syndicate banks was to let the client see as little of it as possible. One could only go squealing to mama so often. I used to dread joint appointments, which were increasingly common. It was like being put in a sack with another ferret to fight it out. Compared with a sole appointment, a so-called partner doubled the resources required to conduct a transaction.

The growing importance of the international equity market led to a series of organisational changes within Warburg. The Corporate Finance department was merged with the Financing Division, to form the Advisory and Financing Division. It was run jointly by Rodney Ward and Derek Higgs. The integration had not been without trauma as two very different management styles clashed. Rodney recalled later, "I put up a simple organogram, with a clear division of domestic and international business. He put up a matrix of cross reporting. No-one could understand what he was talking about. Luckily my version was endorsed."

The resources of the equity capital markets team were beefed up under Maurice Thompson. I had worked with Maurice since Eurotunnel in 1987, when we had tried and failed to put together a genuine international syndicate. In 1991, Maurice was in his early 30s, having joined Warburg straight from university 10 years earlier. He had spent most of that decade on the international equity side. He began running the syndicates almost by default, when it was seen as a purely organisational role. By the time of Eurotunnel in 1987 his position as the syndicate manager had been formalised and two years later, by the time of the float of Euro Disney, he was being styled the head of equity capital markets. As the volume of equity issues ballooned, he seized the chance to build up a formidable team. Maurice was tall, boyish-looking, with immense charm, and his team became steadily more dedicated to him. He showed the way with a remarkable intensity of effort. At the time of the Euro Disney convertible in June 1991, his wife Vivienne was due to deliver their fourth child, Isabel. "I told her on the Sunday that if you don't have her today, you can't have her till Tuesday." In the event the Euro Disney issue was delayed a couple of days and Isabel was delivered at 2.00am on Wednesday morning. After spending the night at the hospital, Maurice was at his desk at 6.00am to face the nightmare of Goldman dumping loose stock on us through the day.

Maurice's response – to recruit Michael Cohrs (the Goldman banker who did the dumping) to run the syndicate area within equity capital markets was a masterstroke. Michael was a high profile American, with great experience in the black arts of syndication. A couple of years older than Maurice, he had joined Goldman in New York in 1981. He switched from corporate finance to equity capital markets in 1989 and then moved over to London the following year. Compact, dark and intense, with an infectious sense of humour, Michael was known as a 'street fighter' in the market and knew all the games that needed to be played in this arena. When Michael arrived in the autumn of 1991, he formed a tight unit with Maurice within the bank whose influence steadily increased.

The final component in our response to the opportunities in the international equity market was the establishment of a dedicated team in the advisory area. This was called the Equity Corporate Finance Department. Its task was to ensure that the documentation and in particular the prospectuses required for major issues were prepared to appropriate standard. Since many of the issues were privatisations at this stage, the Government committee work required by the team to achieve this end could be formidable. The leader of this effort was James Sassoon. James had spent eight years in a leading accountancy firm before being seconded to Warburg to help effect the merger at the time of Big Bang. He switched to corporate finance in 1987 and subsequently worked on the BTII transaction. A relation of the famous First World War poet, Siegfried Sassoon, James was thin, with a shock of dark hair and a quizzical way of looking at whoever he was talking to. He was methodical, cautious and concentrated with great intensity on detail – in sharp contrast to my own impetuosity, which meant we both enjoyed working together in the years to come. I was to sit alongside his department in the next couple of years taking responsibility for our marketing efforts to win a share of the international equity business.

We were still desperately disadvantaged in competing with the US houses. The fees they extracted from corporate America were far higher than those paid anywhere else in the world. With those excess profits they could afford to subsidise their efforts to build a position in the newly-developing European market.

"How on earth do US fees stay so high?" I once asked Michael Cohrs, who had run Goldman's syndicate desk in New York. Typical IPO fees in the US ranged from 5% to 7%. By comparison we received a bare 1.1% on BTII.

"It's easy," said Michael. "The syndicate of each of the bulge bracket firms keeps a graph of all deals; size of deal down one axis, percentage fee along the other. If a deal by one of them falls outside the established spread he gets punished. Not invited for co-manager roles by the others. You can get 10% of the revenue for doing absolutely nothing by being a co-manager in New York, so the pain quickly adds up."

"Why doesn't the Justice Department break it up?"

"Can't. The US houses are too powerful. They've got people placed right across the political spectrum."

"That's quite a tax on corporate America."

"Sure is."

Much of those excess profits went into the pockets of the investment bankers who worked for the US houses. The high bonus levels fostered a level of intensity that was entirely alien to practice in London. The Warburg ethos was well-known as hard-working and dedicated. The vicious determination of these new US competitors was on another plane. In the years to come I became used to conversations that ran like this:

"How are things going?" a senior US banker would ask at a social event.

"Well, you know, not too bad - although it would be useful if the markets picked up a bit."

"That's funny. We're going absolutely great guns. Can't remember a better period for years. We're picking up mandates all over the place. By the way, how's so and so doing?" This would be a reference to a colleague who had left the US firm and joined us.

"I've only had a chance to talk to him briefly since he arrived. It's still a bit early to tell."

"I do hope it works out for him. He always had real difficulty in communicating with his colleagues. Some kind of social problem."

"How's so and so?" I would ask, referring to some-one who had moved the other way, from Warburg to the US house.

"Absolutely brilliant. He's settled in magnificently. He's having an outstanding time."

That was the pattern: everything in their own house was wonderful; all new recruits were brilliant; former colleagues damned. I must have had a conversation like this ten times through the 1990s - a mantra designed, presumably, to psyche out the competition. It felt like talking to someone who had lost their soul.

Within a year of the BTII transaction, the Government decided to sell the final tranche of the company and we received an invitation to make a presentation on 18 November, 1992. This was less than a month after I had moved into my new office next to the equity corporate finance team. The pitch had to be compressed into no more than 12 pages – a shocking contrast to the hundreds of pages and appendices in two, three or even more books that had been typical for important competitions.

"You could use very small type," suggested James Sassoon, "6-point or something."

"Bollocks to that," I replied. "We're using bloody great type that people can read and we're going to get everything worth saying in, even if it kills me."

In the few days we had to prepare the pitch I had virtually unlimited resources at my disposal as we compressed as much information as possible into colourful tables and graphics and I typed out our submission paragraph by painful paragraph. Heather Jane worked full tilt at the graphics and lay-out with me and by the time it was complete the presentation represented a radical leap forward in our whole style – one that other investment banks would be copying for years to come. In terms of content, the most revolutionary element in it was a proposal to dump the complicated arrangements allowing individual banks a virtual monopoly in particular regions and to allow all members of the syndicate to sell to institutions anywhere in the world. This concept had been developed by Maurice Thompson following discussions with Steve Robson at the Treasury during the execution of the BTII deal. The concept had undoubtedly received a boost during the shambolic weekend when the BTII orders through the regional bookrunners were assembled so late (thanks in large part to Goldman's computer difficulties) that the start of trading was almost delayed. But the core driver was Steve Robson's realisation during BTII that the 400 or 500 investors who drove an international issue were happy to talk to any major investment bank, not solely a local intermediary. "I didn't see why we had to pay banks to be in the syndicate who didn't do any work," he told me later. "By creating a small syndicate the banks involved would have a financial incentive to do some work."

The success of BTII made it almost impossible for rival banks to beat us to the next BT mandate. The £5.4bn BT3, as it was called (for some obscure reason using the Arabic rather than Roman numeral of BTII), was another remarkably successful transaction. The global syndicate structure we had recommended proved robust and effective. It was whole-heartedly endorsed by the Treasury, with the Financial Secretary, Stephen Dorrell stating on 19 July 1993: "The new shares started trading this morning at a modest premium. This is testament to the effectiveness of the Offer structure, the demand it generated and the keen pricing which resulted."

The global syndicate concept was bitterly and publicly attacked by the US investment banks, furious at a structure which opened up the US investing institutions to general approach by foreign houses. Goldman was most vitriolic of all, not least because we had taken the exquisite pleasure of excluding them from the list of 11 global managers involved in BT3. However the success of the transaction spoke more loudly than Goldman's attacks on it and over the next few years the global syndicate steadily became the standard structure. In many ways it intensified the battle-ground. There were no consolation prizes now, in the shape of lucrative regional roles. Anything less than the role of global co-ordinator and bookrunner became increasingly valueless. The fight to become global co-ordinator, either solely or in a duumvirate or triumvirate, became the focus of the intensive marketing efforts in which all the investment banks were now involved. Already it was evident that banks were spending more resources winning business than executing it and the best paid bankers were the marketeers.

Thanks in large part to the innovation displayed in the BT transactions, we were able to win a significant share of the business. Indeed, by 1995 we were the comfortable leader in the international equity market round the world, with a market share in that year of more than 15% - well ahead of our US rivals.

Not all transactions were as competitive as BT or Pharmacia. In March 1992, Nick van den Brul, a junior director in the Financing Division came to my desk to discuss a prospect in Austria.

"The directors at Vienna Airport want to float."

"Why?"

"To get the Government off their backs. They reckon they can raise new money and get a quote on the Vienna Stock Exchange."

"The only airport ever floated was the British Airports Authority, back in 1987, and everyone thinks that was because Mrs Thatcher's bonkers," I pointed out. "What do the institutions think about Austria at the moment?"

"They pretend it doesn't exist. We don't even bother to have an analyst covering the stocks."

"Who's handling it locally? Creditanstalt?"

"Bank Austria. They're a souped-up savings bank. Never done an equity issue before."

"How on earth did they get the mandate then?"

"God knows. This is Austria. They lent them some money, I think, and getting the issue was part of the deal."

"And if I remember right, the last privatisations in Austria were a total disaster."

"Yes," confirmed Nick. "Both EVN and Creditanstalt went to big discounts. That's why nobody's interested in Austria."

"So the whole thing's completely ballsed up?"

"Basically."

"I see. Well, I've only ever been to Vienna once, and since that's where my family came from, I'd like to go again. We'll take David James, the BAA analyst. He can talk about airports. When can we see them?"

"I'll set it up," said Nick. Two weeks later, on 20 March, the three of us made our presentation to the managing directors of the airport and the team from Bank Austria, led by a worried Gerhard Edelmann.

"Our soundings tell us that there is very little interest in buying this stock among Austrian investors," he pointed out.

"It'll be fine," I reassured them, with a confidence I certainly did not feel. "It's a lovely airport with a great story. We'll have the London investors frothing at the mouth to get hold of it and that's bound to translate into demand in the local market."

We were appointed virtually on the spot.

Then it became the time to translate promises into reality. To my relief, my breezy confidence at the pitch proved - rather to our surprise - absolutely accurate. In early May I placed some positive stories about the float in the main British newspapers. We followed up with a piece of research by David James and the head of European research Miko Giedroyc. Soon the salesmen were receiving serious enquiries from their institutional clients. For a small deal, at a little less than £100m, this kind of interest guaranteed success.

"What should we price this at?" I asked David Charters, who was handling the transaction on the syndicate desk.

"It's going to trade from 370 Schillings up," reckoned David. "Don't go higher than that."

Shortly afterwards, Gerhard Edelmann was on the phone in despair. "We've just had a meeting of the Austrian syndicate. They say there's not much interest locally. Creditanstalt refuses to accept any underwriting at a price above 307 Schillings."

"Throw them out, then," I said.

"What?" Gerhard was aghast. Creditanstalt was the most venerable financial institution in Austria and had enjoyed a virtual monopoly in equity issuing until this transaction. It had earned its place in the history books as the bank whose collapse triggered the banking crisis of the early 1930s.

"Throw them out," I repeated. "You can't price at 307 Schillings. They're not being serious."

"What do you mean; not serious?"

"They're playing games with you. They want to make you look stupid when the price takes off in the aftermarket. You have to be tough. Throw them out."

And, to the shock of the Austrian financial community, Gerhard Edelmann proceeded to do exactly that. However the deal was still priced well below David Charter's 370-Schilling limit, reflecting the nervousness of the domestic market. In the end we priced the stock at 335 Schillings a share, and the first day premium soared through David's figure.

For Austria it was a transformational deal. The graphic demonstration of interest in Austrian stocks by international investors meant the Government was now able to contemplate a series of privatisations in the Thatcher mode. Bank Austria seized a dominant position in the domestic financial markets; indeed, it took over Creditanstalt in 1997. We were to complete a series of transactions jointly with them; and with dedicated analysts to cover the stocks and Chris Reilly taking over the investment banking coverage of the country, Austria became an important place for us to do business.

Austria was only one of the countries to move rapidly from the periphery of the financial world into the mainstream through the early 1990s. The South East Asian countries, which had enjoyed their own economic miracle over the previous decade, were suddenly worth exploring.

In October 1990 I was in Sydney, pitching with our local Australian team to win the float of Qantas, the national airline. Chris Brodie, one of the younger directors of the corporate finance team, was with me. Chris had been the corporate finance executive deputed as minder to the Euro Disney flotation.

"Let's stop off in Thailand on the way back," he suggested.

"Fine. Why?"

"I just read in the Press that they're planning to privatise Thai Airways. We can just adapt this stuff for Qantas to make a pitch to them."

We made a follow up presentation or two after this literal flying visit and by the following April we read in the Press that we had been appointed international financial advisers to Thai Airways, alongside the US bank Morgan Stanley.

"That's how things work in Thailand, apparently," said Chris. "They don't tell you when you're appointed; it's announced in the Press."

As Warburg's first official appointment in Thailand, it represented a break-through in our efforts to position ourselves in this rapidly expanding economy. In other ways it proved rather a double-edged sword. At least a transaction was under way; the Qantas process ground to a halt and did not restart for another three years

The complexity of arranging a UK-style privatisation in such a foreign environment was deeply time consuming. Quite apart from the work involved in preparing the various papers (and rowing with

Morgan Stanley as to their content), we had to attend a series of meetings in Bangkok through the rest of the year. Finally, in late January 1992, we were ready to present a comprehensive set of recommendations to the Government, approved by the management of the airline, alongside the two local advisers with whom we were working. We proposed launching the company with proper corporate governance onto the international market, the first Thai company to make this step outside the domestic arena.

"You'll need to explain the recommendations to the 'four wise men' first," we were told by the airline management. "They'll be quite concerned about the low value you're putting on the airline and I suspect they'll be suspicious about your recommendation for an international tranche."

Painfully the four advisers spent Tuesday, 28 January, rehearsing the presentation of our formal recommendations. The next morning we filed into the committee room and arrayed ourselves before 'the four wise men'. These were some of the leading bureaucrats of the most powerful ministries. Dutifully we ploughed through the strategy.

Mid-flow the chairman of 'the four wise men' stood up. "This is completely outrageous," he said, turning round and walking out of the room.

The presentation was over.

"What was outrageous?" I asked.

"When you said that the airline management should have the power to manage the company; that's what he found outrageous."

Effectively, our role was over. Thamnoon Wanglee, the finance director, had aimed to use the prestige of two international investment banks to persuade the Government to let Thai off the leash. The bureaucrats, probably concerned that the national airforce would take even more liberties with the company if they let go, pushed back.

The transaction, when it happened two months later in March, was hurried through as a purely local deal at a price 50% above our recommendation. Due to a series of logistical difficulties trading in the shares did not start until July, and the price collapsed almost immediately. The share price, and airline, spent the next decade struggling to find a sound footing.

The resources we put into this mandate far exceeded the fee of US$500,000 we were paid. It had proved a most expensive and frustrating diversion. But in the new international equity market it was easy to chase mirages – especially when the rewards of innovation and of being an early entrant could be so great.

It was the heroic age for equity; the period in which a handful of participants made up the structures and practices of the market as we went along. Winning business was a matter of flair, instinct and luck. Success required the raw grit of a cowboy combined with the polished confidence of a Victorian gentleman. It was also hard work. I was travelling more and more. In March 1991 I was in Hong Kong working on an ultimately abortive attempt to float the money broker Exco out of the ruins of British & Commonwealth. Euro Disney required trips to Paris and Los Angeles. I marketed privati-sation in Finland and Sweden as well as Thailand. In October I was on Reg Grundy's rain-swept yacht in Juan Les Pins on the French Riviera investigating how we might float his company Grundy, the maker of the television soap 'Neighbours'; another abortive effort. I made my first marketing trip to Japan – an annual tradition I was to maintain for the rest of the decade.

In 1992 I added a further set of destinations: Vienna, for the airport; Brussels; the US; Rome; Copenhagen; Amsterdam and Singapore. The last represented a series of marketing trips to win Singapore Telecom – another deeply frustrating and expensive effort. After a seemingly endless series of pitches involving senior teams out of London, the Singaporeans selected Goldman Sachs ahead of us. Our chagrin diminished when the Singaporeans chose to auction the stock, rather than building a book of demand, in a poorly received transaction. The strategic cost of losing a transaction was wiped away if it was not seen to set valuable precedents. Indeed, we took a leading position in subsequent Singapore Telecom deals later in the decade.

It became increasingly difficult to plan a family life. If I had spent half a year or more marketing for a particular piece of business, it became impossible to write off the investment in time when summoned to attend a formal presentation or key meeting, however inconvenient the timing.

One evening in late July 1993 I said to my wife, "Cilla, it's terribly lucky we're going on holiday in Denmark this year."

"Why?" she asked suspiciously.

"Because on the last Friday I've got to do a beauty contest in Copenhagen – for the airport. We can all travel up to town in the morning and I'll do the presentation while you're sightseeing. Then we'll have a really good lunch. Of course, I'll have to rehearse with the team on the Thursday . . ."

A few evenings later the conversation was more difficult. "It's lucky that we're having the party for all our Danish relatives on the middle Sunday and not the Saturday."

Cilla didn't deign to ask why.

"I've just got to pop over to Amsterdam on the Friday evening for a pitch to KLM first thing in the morning. You'll hardly notice I've gone. I'll slip off on the last flight and be back by lunch-time on Saturday."

Shortly before the start of our broken holiday I arrived home to find a strange man sitting in the living room.

"Ah, David," said Cilla. "This is Mr White. He's an architect. He's very kindly agreed to see us at short notice."

The two of them then proceeded to redesign the back of the house with the greatest relish and at no inconsiderable cost. I had no moral authority to interfere. It was only later that I was able to draw up a balance sheet of the financial implications.

We lost the Copenhagen Airport mandate, reflecting the determination of Den Danske Bank not to allow the foreign houses onto its home turf. More positively, we were awarded a mandate from KLM to provide a fairness opinion on their proposed merger. But all we could manage to negotiate as our fee was a miserable £100,000. This approximately matched the costs of rebuilding the back of my house. It was a useful lesson. In future I virtually never allowed business to break my family holiday, although I was careful to take it in weeks in which irresistible demands for my presence were unlikely. (The fortnight straddling July and August was usually pretty safe.)

The KLM fairness opinion was the first time I had worked with

Piers von Simson, one of the board directors at the bank, and one of the wittiest and most irreverent personalities within it. Then aged 47, Piers was fours years older than me. Parallel to my own family's experience, his father had fled Hitler's Germany in 1936 only to be interned on the Isle of Man after the fall of France. Piers had a polyglot background; born in Birmingham and then moving to Luxembourg when he was eight where his father became a top European lawyer. Piers topped a traditional British education with a period in California. On his return to the UK in 1971, a family connection brought him an interview at Warburg. "What I really want to know is how hungry are you?" demanded one of his more aggressive interlocutors, probing for evidence of determination and drive at the end of a long morning.

"A spot of lunch would go down very well," admitted Piers, with characteristic insouciance. Accepted despite this gaffe, Piers spent many years in New York. By 1989 he had joined the main group board and taken a responsibility for developing the bank's European business, his fluent German and French standing him in good stead. I always found it difficult not to collapse in laughter whenever I was with Piers and the KLM beauty contest was no exception. The chief financial officer of the airline, Rob Abrahamsen, emphasised the importance of controlling our expenses in the assignment.

"We don't want to see you staying at five-star hotels in Amsterdam at our expense and limousines everywhere. The extravagance of you investment bankers is simply not acceptable here."

Piers was outraged. "I suppose you want us to take the bus?" he asked in his characteristic drawl.

The sarcasm was lost on the frugal Dutch which was just as well or we would have lost the mandate. In practice this would have been little loss. We were providing a so-called fairness opinion on a transaction that had been dubbed 'Alcazar', a four-way merger between KLM, Swissair, SAS and Air Austria. The terms had been pre-agreed in a meeting between the leaders of the four European airlines not, apparently, burdened by anything as vulgar as meaningful financial data. This made our role uncomfortable, since we would be liable to KLM's investors in stating that in our opinion the terms were fair. All our analysis suggested that KLM was worth rather more than the value put on it under the fixed Alcazar terms. Luckily, from our point of view, the deal collapsed later that year as a result of a clash between KLM and Swissair. This was based on a growing enmity between the managements of the two airlines and a disagreement over which of the partnerships with US airlines to maintain.

The summer of 1993 saw a poor run of results from our attempts to win mandates. Rodney concluded that our fundamental weakness was a lack of a powerful presence in the US, which equity owners increasingly wanted to see. I was not so sure about this. I thought that our marketing had become too general. What clients wanted to see, I thought, was real understanding of their business, not expertise in selling equity to institutional investors. Apart from anything else, they were in a position to differentiate between those claiming to understand their industry; by contrast they did not have the first idea who was stronger in the market. And if they did, by the time they saw a couple of banks they would be more confused than before. Banks became experts in manipulating the league table of performance. They would juggle the criteria so that every bank pitching would be able to claim it was No 1 in the exact qualities required by the putative client. My initiative of starting sector specific coverage back in 1989, with John Reizenstein's banking team, had been more prescient than I realised at the time.

So from the summer of 1993 on I switched my emphasis from general marketing to concentrate on a sector. The question was, which sector? The biggest were telecoms, finance and pharmaceuticals. Unfortunately none of these really interested me. Nor did I have much of a track record in them. I looked back over the deals I had completed and realised that transport featured well ahead of anything else. This meant I could go to any company in that sector and talk about the deals I had been involved in. Bragging rights were an invaluable commodity in the competition for mandates. While it was a small sector I decided that there was enough activity in it to keep me fully occupied, so long as I could win significant market share.

Sector expertise should also allow us to take the fight to the enemy. An early test leapt at us out of the blue in the shipping sector. The summer had seen NatWest Markets take advantage of a sudden surge of interest among investors for shipping stocks by floating a Norwegian tanker company called Smedvig. Would we be interested in floating another one? Our enthusiasm was doubled by the fact that the tanker company involved, called Bona, was currently advised by our arch-rival Morgan Stanley. They had irritated the parent company, Leif Hoegh AS, and the new chairman, Rudolph Agnew, who transferred the mandate to us after a reasonably competent presentation in early September.

"I'd like to extend my congratulations to you for winning this piece of business from us." It was Steve Waters, head of European investment banking for Morgan Stanley, on the phone.

"Thank-you," I replied, surprised and impressed that he had rung. Then I started to wonder what he wanted.

"May I ask whether you were looking for any publicity over this matter?" he enquired. "Of course, we'd prefer it if the transfer of the mandate was carried out in a low-key way."

"I'm sure that's right," I replied, trying to match his smooth, mature, delivery. Rapidly I calculated that a public spat between the two banks would hardly enhance our chances of a successful flotation. "We weren't planning on going public with it."

"That's fine. We'll keep our heads down too. Good luck with the float."

We needed all the luck Steve Waters could offer. Despite moving with extraordinary speed to launch the deal a bare 13 weeks after our presentation, the window of enthusiasm for tanker stocks was already closing fast. With a last minute scramble, which involved slashing the price by 10%, we were able to raise $115m from investors. Just.

Sometimes there were barely credible coincidences.

"Where have you been working lately?" asked my father in early 1994. He always took a keen interest in my travels.

"We've just done a small float in Austria for a railway points company, VAE. I went down to visit them at a place called Zeltweg."

Since my father was born in Austria he would know the geography.

"Ah, Zeltweg. That's my airport."

"I didn't realise. It's still there. There's a runway just across the fence from the factory yard."

It was a famous story in our household. My father had escaped the Nazis after the Anschluss through the good fortune of being the grandson of Sigmund Freud. He was part of the family group that arrived in the UK with him in 1938. After exile in Australia as an enemy alien and some frustrating years digging trenches in the Alien Pioneer Corps, he joined the Special Operations Executive. In April 1945 he parachuted into Southern Austria, with the triple aim of sabotage, raising resistance and establishing a British presence ahead of the Russian advance. Unfortunately he became detached from his colleague and equipment. After some days scavenging in the mountains, finding nothing to sabotage and virtually no-one fit to mount acts of resistance, he addressed the third of his objectives. With the Russian advance progressing rapidly, he made his way to the town of Schiefling. Here he strode into the mayor's office and demanded transport to the aerodrome of Zeltweg.

The mayor commandeered the only vehicle with fuel in it, the fire engine, and drove him to the airport. With astonishing bravery, my father marched into the Commandant's office and announced, "I am Lieutenant Freud of the British Eighth Army; I have come to take over your aerodrome." This was a slight exaggeration, as my father was certainly not a member of the Eighth Army.

The Commandant slumped down on his desk and started to cry: "All our efforts, all our sacrifices, all in vain."

At the meeting the next day attended by the local army and Nazi officials of the district, it was decided to send my father to Linz to confirm the takeover of the airport. Escorted by a major he was driven to the headquarters of General Rendulic at Linz, where his capture of the aerodrome was confirmed. Clearly the Russian advance had speeded up still further. But my father was not able to return to Zeltweg. On the way back the car ran into a group of Austrian army mutineers, who 'arrested' the escorting major and next day took my father to the American front line.

The capture of Zeltweg airport was the high point of my father's army career, if not his whole life.

The next time I was in Austria I told Edmund Auli, the chief executive of VAE, about my father's connection with the local aerodrome. He went back and checked in the files. At our next meeting he said, "It's absolutely true, your father did liberate the aerodrome. Bring me the Captain."

My father had always refused to return to Austria, the country that had rejected him. But Edmund Auli made the offer irresistible. So at the end of May 1994 my father and mother travelled back to Vienna. They were received as VIPs by Vienna Airport, which I had floated two years earlier, and were then whisked down to Zeltweg in a big black Mercedes. Here he was the centre-piece of a dinner to celebrate the liberation and the next morning guest of honour at a fly-past by the Austrian Airforce. I could not have got him a better present.

In the autumn of 1994 two deals were looming large in my in-tray. The first was the privatisation of Qantas, which had come back into the frame after a three year delay and which we had won in the summer. The second was the flotation of a UK cable company for the US telecoms giant Nynex. The latter was to prove a difficult and contentious transaction.

Nynex was one of the largest of the Baby Bells, offshoots of AT&T when it was split up in 1984. It was the monopoly provider of local telephony for the New York and New England areas and had the ponderous bureaucracy that might be expected from such a giant. Nynex had entered the UK cable market in 1990 by buying various franchises to become one of the leaders in the industry. Over the previous year we had gradually worked our way into advising the company on the flotation of the subsidiary, Nynex CableComms. The US bank Salomon Brothers had been brought in alongside us somewhat later. Salomon was still clawing its way back into a serious position in the international equity markets after the 1991 scandal in which it rigged the US Treasury bill market. As a result it was far more combative on joint transactions than the other leading US banks with whom we had by now reached a *modus vivendi*.

"Hi David." It was Wendy Dietze on the phone, my equivalent from Salomon on the deal. "I just wanted to let you know that I've phoned up Davis Polk and told them we don't need them. I've appointed Cravath instead."

"You've what?"

"I've appointed Cravath."

"But we both agreed on Davis Polk weeks ago. You can't just fire them out of the blue."

"Well I have."

This was my first formal encounter with the Salomon style. I had felt a sense of mild triumph a few weeks earlier when the Salomon team had agreed with our suggestion to use Davis Polk as the US lawyer on the transaction. Davis Polk was the regular firm used by Warburg and could be relied on to alert us if our 'partner' Salomon were to initiate any legal games at our expense. Cravath, by contrast, was a regular lawyer for Salomon and had worked for Wendy on their previous deal in the UK cable industry, the flotation of Bell Cablemedia. They could be expected to support Salomon against us. She had been inattentive when we slipped Davis Polk through and now she aimed to reverse the slip-up.

Michael Cohrs was adamant when he heard of the call. "You have to win this battle, David. If she wins here they'll take us apart right the way through this deal."

I phoned up Davis Polk and unfired them.

"I've thought of a solution," Wendy came back. "We'll keep Davis Polk and get Cravath to act for Nynex on this deal. Chadbourne & Park isn't up to it."

"The company are very close to Chadbourne. Charley Hord at Chadbourne has developed the whole financial structure of the cable company," I pointed out.

"Nope." She insisted. "Nothing against Hord, but at Salomon we refuse to work with Chadbourne. It's a directive right from the chairman's office. I'll tell Nynex to drop Chadbourne and appoint Cravath."

My senior team member on the corporate finance side was Adrian Haxby. "Why don't you ring Charley and warn him what's happening," I suggested. Adrian put in the call. Charley Hord did some checking of his own. Adrian was grinning when he came back into my office. "Charley is mystified about this ban on Chadbourne at Salomon," he told me. "He's done some checking around and apparently Chadbourne & Park act for Salomon on its own corporate affairs."

"Well I think we can leave Charley to defend his own position with the company," I concluded. "At least we're going to have two legal friends. I don't think Charley Hord is going to regard Wendy Dietze with great affection from now on."

This was just a warm-up for the real battle.

In late November the company rang to tell me that it had decided that Salomon would be the sole bookrunner of the CableComms deal. This was a real coup for Salomon which had used its strong relationship with the company to lever out such a dominant role. From our perspective the news could not have been worse. We would be awarded various grand-sounding titles, but the company assurance of 'joint economics' was undermined by a subsequent conversation with Salomon in which they talked of 'jump ball'. By this they meant the sales commission would go to the house that received the order. Obviously, the bulk of orders would go to the bookrunner. All the talk of partnership between the two houses had been so much hot air.

I phoned up Colson Turner, the Nynex Treasurer, a weighty African American. He was always immensely courteous and considered. "Colson," I said. "Excuse me for phoning you direct. I just wanted to let you know that we cannot act on the basis you suggest and therefore we have no other option but to resign."

It was a calculated risk. I estimated that all our work advising the company on its complex financial structure meant we could not be replaced in a hurry. On the other hand Nynex might react to such an act of lèse majesté by ridding themselves of these troublesome foreign bankers regardless. I had never tried such a high-wire strategy before and neither, to my knowledge, had any other banker at Warburg. Indeed, I was only to try this tactic one further time in my career.

Colson was clearly shocked by the ultimatum. He went through the ramifications with me in his normal slightly ponderous way. "This decision of yours is of the utmost seriousness for the company," he concluded, obviously rehearsing the arguments he would need to apply internally. "It's public knowledge that you've been advising Nynex CableComms and it will not be possible to complete the IPO to the spring timetable without you. I simply cannot imagine any other bank replacing your level of understanding of the issues in any reasonable timescale." He asked us to delay our resignation by five days to allow him time to achieve an accommodation between the two banks. I did my best to disguise the relief in my voice as I agreed to the request.

Faxes and phone calls ricocheted between the various parties. By the following Tuesday Nynex had forced Salomon back into parity. We would be joint global co-ordinators, each responsible for bookrunning our own tranche: Warburg would take Europe and Salomon would take the US. The two banks would share all the income, and risk, in the deal on a 50/50 basis. It had been an enormous effort to get us back to the position we already thought we were in. The equally traumatic completion of this transaction took place amidst the shambles of a transformation of the bank for which I worked, and is accordingly included in the account of that experience.

It was unseasonably warm for New Year's Day and the birds were not bothering to fly from their lake habitat to search for food. Every now and then the radio in my dug-out in the middle of a field would squawk into brief life: "Nothing yet."

I was being introduced to shooting in grand style on the first plantation ever established in the US, in Virginia. Our hosts were the James River Company, a paper manufacturer that we had been assiduously courting for more than three years. While I was in the field waiting for some hapless goose to arrive, David Scholey was a mile away on the riverbank looking out for duck. We had travelled by Concorde the day before to the second of what was becoming an annual ritual between Warburg and James River. As we waited for the birds to arrive I sensed from afar David Scholey's growing irritation. He was a keen shot, but he had come a long way to get up at five in the morning and sit around for five hours without so much as seeing a bird.

After our morning's sport, which left the avian population little troubled, we settled down in a well-appointed conference room in the annexe of the luxurious plantation house. A log fire was spitting gently on the grate.

Together with Tom Tullo, our New York-based account officer for James River, I launched into our presentation on how we might float the European subsidiary of the company, Jamont. It soon became evident that the company was not particularly interested.

"What are your views on how we might separate out our coated papers division from the rest on a global basis and float that?" asked Bob Williams, the chief executive.

Tom Tullo knew considerably more about paper than I did so he did his best to devise a coherent answer. We waded further and further from our set piece. The company's disinclination to float Jamont became increasingly evident.

David Scholey detached himself from the proceedings as we struggled along. Between answers I noticed him busily scrawling a note on some scraps of paper.

The meeting broke up after lunch and we travelled our separate ways. I was flying straight to Oslo for my second marketing trip of 1995. When I returned to London on Thursday I found out what David Scholey had been so pre-occupied in scribbling. He had sent out a coruscating note on our, and in particular Tom's, incompetence in sending him marketing for a non-existent mandate. Why, demanded the note, had Tom not followed up the previous year's meeting properly and why was he unaware that the company had changed its mind on Jamont?

I had never read anything quite so vitriolic from the chairman's pen. It seemed that the lackadaisical attitude of Virginia ducks to food-gathering had fuelled an enormous resentment.

"I wouldn't offer insurance on Tom's career at Warburg," mused Chris Reilly, who was one of the team-members on the account who received the note. "This is pretty terminal."

After this stinging rebuke, which would have had any UK executive looking for another job, David Scholey was nonplussed when Tom Tullo got on the phone to arrange a conference call with him and the team to deal with the issues.

The call, when it took place on the following Tuesday, was surreal. As an American employee Tom simply had not absorbed the Warburg note culture and did not realise he had been shot. He insisted on going through the criticisms in the note one by one in order to devise a marketing plan for the future. Chris and I watched as a puzzled David Scholey went along with the pretence. Whatever he was prepared to put on paper, he remained as civil and charming as ever on a face-to-face basis.

David Scholey's uncharacteristic ruthlessness at this point could be attributed to another factor entirely than the lack of duck. Suddenly S.G.Warburg was fighting for its very existence and the pressure on the chairman was mounting steadily.

The collapse of S.G.Warburg, which until then had generally been acknowledged as the leading UK investment bank, had begun. The events of the next months were to see many others, alongside Tom, depart the firm.

8

Principles of Pre-emption
The Collapse of Warburg – 1994 - 1995

"They're up to something, David," exclaimed Ken Costa. "We've got to find out what it is. We should challenge them." With typical excitability, Ken had stopped a small group of us in the corridor and harangued us on the perils into which senior management were likely to plunge us if left unchecked. He was a corporate finance director of my own age with a nose finely attuned to prospective changes in the office climate. Ken was a walking dichotomy. Short, dark-haired and tanned, he had been brought up in South Africa before coming to Cambridge University to take a masters in theology. He retained an intense religious involvement through his career, playing a leading part in the activist Anglican Holy Trinity Brompton church near his home in West London. In business he was a loner, fostering a series of one-to-one relationships with senior business executives. He invariably displayed immense enthusiasm and chutzpah, with a repartee honed to absorb all vicissitudes. On one occasion a South African client took him to task in a large working meeting for the extravagance of his fee demand. "Do you know what it takes to earn $10m?" he demanded, at the close of his denunciation. Ken merely shook his head sadly. "I'm learning," he informed the roomful of executives. "I'm learning."

Ken's antennae had started to twitch early in November 1994, as he watched one of his colleagues, Robert Gillespie, walk past his office day after day into a small, apparently disused, room on the top floor of the building. His first step was to beard one of the joint heads of the division, Mark Nicholls.

"What's Robert doing?" he asked. Mark confessed that he knew only that Robert had been diverted to a project for senior management. Ken was horrified. "You should know," he replied. "You're the head of corporate finance. You should know what he's working on."

Ken was not satisfied merely with haranguing colleagues in the corridor with his suspicions. His next step was to start requesting files on the main US investment banks from the library. "I was trying to work out how I would find out what they were looking at," he told me later. "I ordered the files on Morgan Stanley, Goldman Sachs and so on. And there was one I couldn't get. So then I knew what was going on."

Ken's investigative efforts took place after a difficult period for the bank. On the surface, the early 1990s had seen the bank go from strength to strength, building on the dominance that John Littlewood had analysed in his report of 1988. Across the European equity markets the bank now held more than 10% of regular everyday trading. It had seized a leading position in the rapidly growing business of issuing new international equity. A survey of chief financial officers in Europe put the bank in overall top place in 1992, leading the rankings in both hostile bids and in defence[1]. In the core UK market the corporate clients were almost indecently rhapsodic about the level of service provided. A piece of independent research showed that their approval rating for the corporate finance department had climbed from 25% in 1991 to 37% by 1994, with the next ranked bank, J.Henry Schroder, scoring less than half, or 17%[2]. Profitability marched in step with business success, with earnings in the year to March 1994 earnings doubling to £200m.

With Big Bang successfully negotiated, David Scholey stood down as chief executive in 1992, promoting the broker he had recruited in 1978, Simon Cairns, as his successor. David himself stayed on as chairman and few signs of change registered, externally or internally. As an exercise in effecting a smooth succession, David could undoubtedly congratulate himself. The main business impetus in this period were a series of decisions to grow the bank organically in the two main areas in which it was weak – trading in fixed interest securities and growing a US investment banking operation. This was on top of expanding in continental Europe and maintaining an expensive, and loss-making, Japanese operation. There was little sign of disagreement between the chairman and new chief executive on this strategic direction.

In retrospect, the decision to grow organically was probably key to the events that followed. At this stage the board seemed to have turned against the alternative strategy of growth by acquisition. In the depths of an investment banking recession in 1992 I had written a short paper pointing out that the value of the US securities firms had fallen so far that we could afford to buy a solid middle-ranking player. The house I specified was DLJ, which I worked out was only valued at a net $200m if its holdings in low-grade corporate debt – or 'junk bonds' – were stripped out. Naturally, we would need to pay a premium and the junk bond portfolio might be problematic, but I thought it was worth looking at. Nick Verey took the idea to the board, where it was dismissed with little apparent consideration. A few months later I asked Michael Gore, the finance director, why the board had been so negative.

"Well, David," he replied. "We were concerned that we simply did not have the management expertise to handle a US acquisition like that. We thought the management of the company would take us to the cleaners." In fact, unknown to me, Warburg had been in extended discussions with two middle-sized US house in the 1980s – DLJ itself and Wertheim – and with the collapse of those negotiations the management had lost interest in buying a mid-ranking player, accounting for the cursory treatment of my paper. The strategic issue, nevertheless, remained a burning one. Our long-term rivals were the US firms, which enjoyed much higher margins in their home market than we did. They would inevitably outplay us unless we somehow found a way to compete in the US. Possibly the 1992 recession provided our last chance of bridging the gap. In that year Warburg might have been able to build on its success in Big Bang to acquire a US arm of reasonable scale and the investing institutions would certainly have supplied funding for such a strategy. After 1992 the price of the US firms soared out of reach.

If the senior management of the bank was not able to control a

US acquisition, it was probably not capable of formulating and executing a coherent global growth strategy either. With 26 board members, the group was too unwieldy to take specific decisions and as a result growth seems to have become a competitive game between the different areas of the bank. In the US, the number employed had soared from 200 in 1992 to 600, all of them expensive investment bankers recruited from rival firms at a premium. In early 1994 the board took a second expensive decision – to build up the firm's fixed interest operation. Later, Simon Cairns reflected on how the management of the division would have come to him and argued, "We are at a scale that doesn't work. In order to give us a chance we have to be twice as big." In the heady times of early 1994, the argument was accepted, although Simon admitted, "I have never been in that business and as the verdict stands we were guessing what to do."

The 1992 recession had also pointed up the fault lines in the new advisory and financing division. With business turning down, numbers needed to be trimmed. But which heads should be cut? By now Rodney Ward had taken over as sole head of the division and he toiled at his desk drawing up lists of the weakest performers who could be placed in the ATL column. ATL stood for 'Asked To Leave'. But as soon as the list was released there was uproar. Everyone on it had a sponsor or friend at senior levels in the bank who insisted that the name should be removed. "The trouble was," reflected Rodney later, "that the old-style corporate financiers wanted to sack the international financiers, because they were less technically competent. However, they were often much more entrepreneurial. The financiers, naturally, wanted to fire the people they saw as expensive technicians, who wouldn't know one end of a marketing pitch from the other." In the end the whole exercise boiled down to the firing of a handful of wretched middle-ranking executives in early 1993, who were typically given six months or more to find themselves a new job rather than face summary dismissal. The process was dubbed by one wag 'the night of the short penknives'.

In March 1993 Derek Higgs, who had become a vice-chairman of the group, took the bull by the horns. "We are in a box," he told

David Scholey and Simon Cairns. "We have high costs and low profits in our home market which means our capital is squeezed. We can't pay our people enough."

He concluded that there were three possible solutions. "We can sell out, create a series of partnerships with powerful institutions such as the commercial banks or we can effect radical change on our own."

The meeting was enough to jolt David and Simon into action. They asked Robert Gillespie, a British corporate financier who had been seconded to the New York office to prepare a paper on the US securities industry. Robert, then in his late 30s, was a tall, thoughtful corporate financier, who came to clear, decisive conclusions, despite a somewhat lugubrious conversational style. His view on the characteristically complicated diagram Derek had drawn to reflect the partnership option was a succinct, "That is the daftest idea I've ever seen in my life." His own paper ran to 50 pages or so and he concluded that the only bank with which it made sense to combine was Morgan Stanley. Because of the difference in size the much bigger US house would, in practice, take Warburg over rather than merge with us.

In October the senior board management held a discussion on the various options. The group shied away from Gillespie's option. The paper summarising the discussion said, "Combination with a large US securities firm would sooner or later result in the loss of the Group's identity. In any case most of the likely partners believe they can achieve their objectives without combining with S.G.Warburg.[3]"

A go-it-alone strategy was tentatively identified. "It is possible that the investment bank's performance could be improved substantially by introducing more carrot/stick: pay talented, productive employees at world standard and pay underperformers less than at present or make them redundant." The night of the short penknives had shown quite how difficult this would have been to achieve.

At any rate, Simon Cairns saw little evidence of transformation and was losing patience. The strategy to build up the fixed income business had backfired dramatically when an unexpected and sustained upturn in interest rates knocked bond prices and dried up the market in new issues. On Saturday 14 May, Derek Higgs travelled down to Simon Cairns' country house in Wiltshire, anxious to wrap up the formal meeting of the day in time to watch the football Cup Final on television. He was in luck. The meeting decided relatively quickly that a radical transaction with a large US firm made sense and that Simon should explore whether Morgan Stanley might be interested. Derek was able to enjoy watching Manchester United trouncing Chelsea 4-0.

The turn in the bond markets was not the only thing that went wrong for Warburg in the second quarter of 1994. Our image was undermined when we conducted a hostile takeover that failed. In the spring we had picked up a high-profile mandate in the UK oil sector. We were acting for Enterprise Oil in its hostile takeover assault on Lasmo. At £1.6bn this was a much bigger takeover attempt than anything seen in the UK for some years. Piers von Simson, with whom I had worked on the KLM fairness opinion, was the director in charge of the attack. He went on a vigorous marketing campaign in the press over the summer, trumpeting the mandate and talking about other wins.

It seemed, at the outset, a straight-forward contest. Lasmo had a poor reputation based largely on the unfortunate purchase of another rival three years previously in the shape of Ultramar. Enterprise Oil, by contrast, had a smart management that had made a fortune for its shareholders in the North Sea through savvy buying of exploration blocks. We could hardly fail.

Only the process did not feel like that. Rudolph Agnew, for whom I had acted on Bona, had been brought in to chair Lasmo, and he put up a great fight. From day one most of the press was on the side of the underdog, and that view was reinforced in the last week of the offer by the clumsy purchase of a 10% stake bought mainly from the largest shareholder, the fund manager Phillips & Drew. The risk was that this would irritate the other shareholders.

So on the afternoon of the last day I was pretty interested in how the share commitments were coming in when I saw Michael Tory, Piers' deputy on the deal. He was scurrying between meeting rooms on the seventh floor, clutching a computer print-out of Lasmo shareholders.

"How are we doing?" I asked.

"Fine, fine," he muttered. He seemed distracted, his eyes rolling from side to side. "We're basically there," he assured me abruptly. It was clearly not a good moment to talk.

The next morning, on 1 July, the wire services carried the news. We had received acceptances for only 23% of the stock, on top of the 10% bought in the market. It was a humiliating loss, and the newspapers revelled in our embarrassment. In the tight world of M&A, where Warburg had built a reputation for reliability and judgement, the bank's credibility had been badly undermined.

On the following Monday, Piers had to describe the failure to a packed 9 o'clock meeting of the corporate finance directors.

"I considered escaping to South America and spent the early part of the weekend poring over airline timetables. But then the news came through that Andrés Escobar had been gunned down by an outraged fan when he returned to Colombia after scoring an own goal in the World Cup. So I decided it was safer to face the music at home." Piers was clearly nervous, but he maintained his languid drawl and earned a laugh from his opening sally. Characteristically, he succeeded in charming his audience and his account of what had gone wrong was received in relatively sympathetic silence. In fact there had been a large measure of bad luck in the failure, with a strong oil market, an over-confident management determined not to overpay and weakening financial markets all undermining the bid. As 'deal captain', Piers had rather honourably accepted responsibility for the failure. More than a decade later he still had mixed feelings about whether he was wise to take the public blame for a loss whose perpetration could properly be allocated to a number of parties.

Our rivals were keen to keep our embarrassment over Lasmo to the fore.

"Those buggers at SBC have told the press we're going to give £750,000 to Rwandan charities," said Richard Holloway, the public relations officer for Warburg whom I had recruited back in 1987. He was explaining the latest row with the Swiss Bank Corporation, commonly shortened to SBC, the smallest of the three big Swiss banks.

This was truly bizarre.

"What the hell for?" I asked. I was still heavily involved in our public relations, although I thought Richard was more than competent enough to operate with the barest oversight from me.

"It's this whinge they've got that we should have filled their pre-placed order with us for Lasmo when we did the market raid."

"That's all bollocks isn't it?"

"Probably. It was a set up. They placed the order to try to catch us out. I don't think they use dealers to place orders with us, they use lawyers. Now they're claiming that we've conceded their case and have agreed a payment to charity."

"We can't win," I decided. "Whatever the rights and wrongs, if we refuse to pay we look like tight-fisted bastards who also happen to be too incompetent to win a straight-forward takeover battle. Tight-fisted, incompetent bastards: not the best marketing image. We'll have to pay up. Then we'll only look incompetent. You might try to get the figure down a bit, though."

In the end, Warburg paid £250,000 to the Rwandan charities. As Jeff Randall, writing in the Sunday Times afterwards on 7 August, concluded: "In crying foul, Swiss Bank's main objective appears to have been to embarrass its rival and market leader. In that respect it scored a sneaky goal."

This public spat followed the much more ferocious row between Warburg and SBC over the Eurotunnel rights issue in the spring. The newcomer in the market seemed to have decided on a strategy of direct attack on the market leader as a way of leveraging up its position and image. It would not be long before it found a far more direct way of building market share.

It was in the following month, September, that Simon activated the decision made on Cup Final day, making contact with the chief executive of Morgan Stanley, John Mack, over a relatively casual lunch. Early feelers exploring the possibility of merging back offices quickly gave way to discussions about a full-blown merger of the two companies.

Morgan Stanley was a quintessentially establishment firm, established in 1935 out of J.P.Morgan & Co, the finest financial house on Wall Street (if not the world), when the Glass-Steagall Act forced financial institutions to decide between banking and securities business. It was acknowledged to be one of the leaders of the US investment banks - in the jargon, one of the 'bulge bracket' houses (from the placement of their names on a prospectus in larger type and more white space at the top of any list of underwriters). The dominant area within the firm was the bond business, which had been enlarged and made consistently profitable by John Mack, who had run the business for nearly a decade before moving up to lead the whole firm in 1993. John Mack took the idea to his chairman, Dick Fisher, who had run the company over the previous decade and with whom he had a close relationship. Dick was then aged 58, an urbane man of average height who played his cards close to his chest. He had suffered from polio as a child and walked with the help of two canes. He found the concept of combining with Warburg equally appealing and suddenly the negotiations were on their way[4] .

Somehow the talks survived the announcement of Warburg's figures for the half-year period to September 1994, which were a bloodbath. They showed that profits for the investment bank (excluding the Mercury Asset Management subsidiary) had collapsed from £98.4m in the same period of 1993 to a bare £5.5m. I was grateful not to be involved in explaining the figures to the press. I knew from my experience of interpreting the reported profits for sceptical journalists, that they disguised the problem at the heart of the business: the foreign endeavours lost the money earned at home - lots of it. Any company can have a bad set of figures. The problem was that these showed, however well disguised, that the group's strategy was out of control. Our break-neck expansion at a time of difficult market conditions had blown up in our faces.

I was also conscious that our management structure remained as labyrinthine as ever. Earlier in the year Simon Cairns had appointed my mentor, Nick Verey, to be chairman of the securities businesses. While it was clearly a significant step up in the hierarchy, it signally failed to ensure that there were clear reporting lines through the bank.

"What kind of job is this," he complained to me once. "I don't set Sarge's pay and anyway he's on the board. It's a muddle." Michael Sargent was the head of the securities division. Nick found his senior job title productive only of a series of stressful turf battles.

To a large extent I was inured to all this. Over the previous couple of years I had moved further and further from the corporate centre and buried myself in the competitive battle in the international equity markets. So these developments seemed to happen at one remove. I was more interested when Maurice Thompson arrived in my office in September to discuss how best to play the pitch to privatise Deutsche Telecom. This was a key mandate, which would build on our success in the BT transactions, if we could win it.

"I think you shouldn't over-prepare the presentation, otherwise you'll come out stiff and wooden," I said. "You should just know the points you want to make and then explain them naturally."

Maurice grimaced. "That's all very well, David. But this presentation is in German, and my German isn't up to extemporising. It's all incredibly formal. They film us as we talk so that they have everything on record."

"I take it all back. You'd better just learn it off by heart. Good luck."

Behind the scenes the talks with Morgan Stanley picked up pace from early November. There was cold fury as the inner team of senior management on the Warburg side learned of Ken Costa's attempts to uncover the identity of the other side by ordering library files. Robert Gillespie, working intensely on the deal directly for Simon Cairns, did his best to forestall Ken's efforts. "I ordered the files on every single financial institution from the US. Then I started ordering the Japanese and Europeans as well. Everything was out in my name." Whether or not Robert succeeded in covering his tracks, Ken's increasingly public expression of his sixth sense that something was going on inevitably gave a boost to the rumours that were now beginning to do the rounds.

On a Saturday late in November, Derek Higgs attended a management meeting for the corporate finance business. At it he was asked point blank what Robert Gillespie was working on. He stonewalled. "Robert is working on something for Simon and me, which is nothing to do with you," he is reported to have replied. "Either we can have a sensible meeting on the agenda, or we can call this meeting off." The US-based executives could recognise a smoking gun when they saw it. When they returned to New York at the end of the weekend they started making discreet enquiries of former colleagues at the major investment banks to find out if they knew anything. Time was running out.

Steadily the circle of insiders was widened. A special board meeting was called in the following week at short notice. It was widely known that Rodney Ward, who had taken over responsibility for the Asian business in May, had been forced to abandon important meetings with clients so that he could attend. So had Tom Wyman, the former chief executive of CBS, who had succeeded Nick Verey in chairing the US business. Very little hard information leaked from the board meeting.

"It's the whole ball of wax," said Michael Cohrs afterwards. "A full merger with J.P.Morgan, with us running the investment banking division." But his certainty didn't seem based on anything much more than wishful thinking. J.P.Morgan was the premier name in banking in the US and, having been excluded from investment banking in the aftermath of the 1929 Wall Street crash, was now looking to re-enter the business. Becoming their re-entry vehicle was an exciting prospect. A few days later Michiel McCarty, the head of the US corporate finance business, told me, "Tom Wyman is pouring cold water on the JP story."

Over the subsequent weekend a handful of heads of departments were brought inside and started to hold planning meetings with their opposite numbers at Morgan Stanley. Even Ken Costa was told the identity of our negotiating partner to sate his curiosity. In retrospect, as far as I can judge, the lips of all the insiders remained sealed.

By Wednesday, 7 December, the rumours were all-pervading. Early in the afternoon Simon Cairns happened to enter the lift I was in, carrying up some sandwiches for lunch. He looked incredibly relaxed. I puzzled as to what to talk to him about, given it would have been both gauche and inappropriate to ask the only question of interest. Luckily he initiated the conversation. "I had lunch the other day with your friend Rudolph Agnew", he said, referring to the chairman of Bona, the tanker company I had floated a year earlier. "He was complaining bitterly about the lack of action in the tanker market."

"At least he can't complain that we priced it too low," I replied. "It's down 10% from the level we floated it at."

Afterwards we debated the significance of Simon's relaxed state. "Maybe it means that the deal is off," pondered Chris Coles, the banking specialist with whom I had worked on the rescue of Euro Disney.

"I doubt it," I replied. "More likely it means his own role has been settled in whatever combo is being set up."

"You're probably right," laughed Chris.

Later that afternoon I ran into Maurice Thompson on the equity capital markets desk. "I think it's Morgan Stanley and a full merger," he said.

When I passed on the view to Ed Chandler that evening he was dismissive. "No, Maurice has got the wrong Morgan. It's JP. I'm pretty confident in the reliability of my source." Ed Chandler was the coverage banker responsible for our Scandinavian business - a sensible, reflective individual who was intensely loyal to the organisation. For want of anything better to do, we were sitting at his desk swapping views as the early winter evening drew on.

"It's J.P.Morgan," said Ed. "It's got to be. It would be an incredible fit." He took a file out of his drawer that was full of information on the US bank. "My father set up the clearing business there. It would be a dream combination."

"Well," I tied up the gossip-session before going home, "between all the rumours, information and disinformation, I confess to being totally baffled."

The next morning I was sitting in my office planning a transaction with a fellow director. As we discussed tactics I kept my eye on the screen showing the Warburg share price. It was really starting to motor from the 672p starting point. We went across to the regular 9 o'clock meeting of corporate finance directors to see if there would be any news.

Nothing. The meeting ran through the regular items. At the end Derek Higgs said, "There may be a statement later in the day."

By the time I was back at my desk the price was up at around 730p. A news agency report on the market rumours named Deutsche Bank, J.P.Morgan or HSBC Holdings as potential merger candidates. The banks were denying it or, in the case of JP, refusing to comment. The tension was palpable. With a share price behaving this way, the Warburg board would be forced under standard Stock Exchange rules to make an announcement – and everyone in the bank knew it.

The group of top floor offices used by senior management – David Scholey, Simon Cairns, Nick Verey and Derek Higgs – had been unkindly christened the Ceausescu Suite after the extravagant former dictator of Romania, executed by an enraged people five years earlier. In reality, the offices were only one grade above the Spartan levels found appropriate by Siegmund Warburg. That morning they were the scene of a tense meeting on the Warburg side. The Stock Exchange had called up to insist that an announcement was made by 9.30am in the light of the share price movement. The ultimatum had caught a small group of senior Warburg executives and lawyers meeting to agree a final position on the merger. Suddenly a rapid decision had to be made. Should the deal be abandoned? It was conventional wisdom, after all, that pushing such a transaction through when it was in the public eye would be much more difficult. The usual tactic when there is a premature leak is to abandon negotiations, announce that nothing is going on and quietly resume the process three months or so later. That was not the decision taken.

David Scholey later told me what happened. "We had to make a quick decision either to confirm and announce or to deny and literally call it off for a few months. We had a very rapid, concentrated talk about it. We felt it was extremely unpleasant because some substantive details still needed to be negotiated, particularly in relation to MAM. There was also the merger of UK corporate finance, bearing in mind that the Morgan Stanley team was known to be not totally compatible with ours. Nevertheless, we thought we were close enough to believing we could do it that we would be able to work our way through the unpleasantness of negotiating through the columns of the financial press. Also if you put it off for a few months we'd have been pretty close to that May announcement that would indicate what a very, very bad year we'd had. The market didn't know how bad. We had a discussion. Simon and I decided to go ahead."

The others present did not know that the decision had been taken. David and Simon left the room and quickly set up a conference call with their opposite numbers at Morgan Stanley. It was just after 4.00am New York time, but Dick Fisher and John Mack seemed to be fully alert. It was a brief conversation. "We just said that the Stock Exchange is requiring us to say something and we want to say that we're in discussions," David Scholey recalled. "They weren't going to argue at that point because it could only be to their advantage."

Robert Gillespie, the lead corporate financier on the transaction, stayed in the meeting room with the lawyers. He had agreed a standard announcement with the chief financial officer at Morgan Stanley, Phil Duff, denying that anything was happening. Now he turned his attention to tidying up the documentation, so that it would be ready when talks resumed a few months later.

"Simon and David walked back in," recalled Robert. "They said they'd talked to Fisher and Mack and that all four of them had agreed that they would announce the deal, disclosing both sides and the basic economic terms. I can remember being just gob-smacked. Nobody said anything. One of the lawyers whistled in disbelief. That was all anybody said."

After the 9 o'clock directors meeting I returned to my office and spent more than an hour on the phone with the strategy director from a company we were advising, discussing tactics. When we had finished I glanced through the window to the equity capital markets group, to see Maurice Thompson holding a meeting of the team. I went over. The announcement was out. It confirmed that we were 'holding discussions' with Morgan Stanley with a view to effecting a merger on a two to one basis.

We didn't learn much more at a Business Management Meeting held shortly afterwards at 11.00am for fifteen or so more senior directors. It was run by Mark Nicholls and David Hobley, the two heads of the corporate finance department. They had been brought into the loop over the weekend and had held meetings with their counterparts at Morgan Stanley. David was impressed by their remuneration. "Their pay levels are many times our own," he muttered. He was clearly a rapid convert. "They want to preserve our client oriented culture and they're concerned that they've moved too far from this business ethic in the 1980s," he said. "They think we'll help them move in the right direction."

They would run the Americas; we would run Europe. It had already been agreed that Mark Nicholls would run the corporate finance operation in Europe for the new company, which would be called Morgan Warburg. (This was an over-statement. I learned later that the Stanley name would have to be kept for contractual reasons.) "They've got an incredibly thorough personnel assessment system, which means the merger arrangements will be truly objective," Mark said. I glanced round the table at that, to see some uneasy glances. I suspect that it occurred to several of us that this could cut both ways – especially in the light of our own primitive system.

At lunch I caught up with Chris Reilly, my Euro Disney colleague, and asked him what he made of it. After all he had gone to work at Morgan Stanley a decade earlier and had come back after only three years because he couldn't bear it. "There's only three things that matter to them; the bottom line, the bottom line and the bottom line," he joked. "They've changed a bit, which is why they're saying they are interested in our culture. That's because they've discovered that pure bottom line can be damaging to business. So that's only another way of working on the bottom line."

Conflict problems filled the afternoon. We were pitching to be global co-ordinator for Bezeq, the Israeli telecom company for which Morgan Stanley was the adviser. The Israelis had stated that the adviser could not distribute. I grabbed the phone from Peter Golob, our telecoms banker, who was telling William Atkins, poached from us only three months before, that we would halve his salary once the merger went through. William was acting for the Israelis. "Listen," I said, "For now we need to agree that everything will go on as before in the conditions of absolute secrecy." I grumbled. "It'll be typical if we lose the distribution commissions for your lousy advisory fee."

Later that afternoon, Simon Cairns stopped by on walkabout. "Well, David," he demanded, "Is that bold enough for you then?" I had never seen him so ebullient.

Over at equity capital markets, Maurice Thompson told me: "John Downing is saying that Morgan will carve our workforce to ribbons." Downing was the head of syndicate at Goldman. "That's clearly the Goldman line. They're going to pump it out to unsettle us as much as possible."

Neil Collins, the City editor of the Telegraph called. "What is it then? Good, bad or indifferent?"

I told him that it was good – if the cultures of the two organisations could be successfully melded. I hoped I was right.

"I'd better tone down what I'm writing," he replied.

At 7.30am next morning, a Friday, we gathered in Nick Verey's office to discuss press handling for the day and to review the morning papers. Before the others arrived Nick said he was leaving the handling of the deal to Derek Higgs and Simon Cairns. "I told them: 'You do the deal and I'll sell it'".

Derek Higgs and Richard Holloway joined us, as well as some outside PR advisers: Alan Parker and David Brewerton from Brunswick and Angus Maitland from his Maitland Consultancy. We agreed the papers were better than expected and we all laughed at the report from the Sun which described the Warburg moneymen dancing round their desks at the prospect of increased pay. The press on that first day had been handled by Robert Gillespie and he had done an excellent job of it. Possibly too excellent; the deal was almost everywhere described as a merger, rather than the takeover it truly represented.

Cairns was at the 9 o'clock meeting. He was, as usual, almost conversational as he described what had happened. "This has been going on for the last two and half months. It started at a casual lunch with John Mack, talking about ways of sharing our high costs. It was almost impossible to find anything. As we talked further we did find that the fit between the two businesses was extraordinarily complementary. We went away to see if we could think the unthinkable.

"The further we went the more intriguing we found the

approach. Was there a basis with respect for each others' cultures and the management systems of each house?

"There are still a number of serious difficulties. We are in the process of refining clear commercial and contractual points and had been planning an announcement on 19 December.

"We will continue for the next 10 days to see if there is a basis for going forward. We shouldn't do it if the risks turn out to be wrong. But I believe this will make it an even more exciting place for us all to live."

There were a few nondescript questions. After the meeting I ran into Chris Reilly. He shook his head. "That's not how it works. We can't just pull out if we don't like the look of it. He hasn't got it; we're committed now."

Our vulnerability was becoming increasingly obvious. As the junior partner in the merger we were running a much bigger risk than Morgan Stanley, as we were to find out.

I spent the rest of the day in sustained and chaotic overload: clients to reassure, journalists to talk to, papers to prepare for Nynex and a Railtrack pitch to the Treasury to complete.

Before lunch I joined Nick Verey in briefing two sets of journalists: Patrick Hosking and Richard Thompson of the Independent and then Nick Goodway of the Observer. The questions were pretty run of the mill; mood of the employees, rationale, New York dominance and the position of Mercury Asset Management, the 75%-owned fund management subsidiary.

Just before 2.00pm I got through on the phone to Colson Turner, the treasurer at Nynex to whom I had delivered an ultimatum in our battle with Salomon to run the float of their subsidiary, Cablecoms. "I guess you're one of the best-placed people in the world to understand why we're doing this," I told him cheekily. "After all, there would have been no question of our ability to handle the CableComms float on our own as Morgan Warburg." He seemed duly impressed by the size of the combined firm.

I piled through the journalists. Paula Dwyer, on Business Week, told me: "The American banks are pumping out heavily negative propaganda. They're saying it won't work because Morgan is Wasp and Warburg is Jewish."

John Gapper at the Financial Times was after management arrangements; Clive Wolman at the Mail on Sunday had a story on employees receiving clearance to buy Warburg shares as late as Tuesday. This became one of the main topics of the wrap-up meeting in Nick Verey's office at 4.45pm. Ian Marshall, the company secretary, said: "I've been going frantic at the dealing requests. They've been playing cat and mouse with me to see if anything's going on. It would have given the game away if I had rejected them. One director asked for clearance to buy 100,000 shares."

"Silly clown," Derek exploded (the actual expression was rather more earthy). I had rarely seen him so bad-tempered. Employee requests to buy shares were turned down if some sensitive information was about to be released, and it would look embarrassing in retrospect if they had bought shortly before publication.

I phoned New York to catch up with Michiel McCarty, the joint head of the corporate finance business there. His secretary, Nell Dunn, told me: "Everyone is very low. They've bust a gut to build a business and now this."

Michiel sounded more phlegmatic. "A friend told me it reminded him of a pet shop with a fish tank full of exotic tropical fish at one end and piranha at the other – and somebody has just raised the barrier." He reckoned that very few of Warburg's New York employees would be retained.

I tried for the umpteenth time to get down to redrafting the summary for the Railtrack pitch. Robert Jennings, one of the corporate finance executives on the Railtrack team, called from Derek Higgs's office. "We've got a Morgan Stanley problem," he explained. "They were pitching jointly with BZW but as a result of the announcement, BZW has dumped them. Now they want to team up with us."

I went upstairs to Derek's office. "Let's go joint with them," said Derek. "It'll give us a quick result to endorse Morgan Warburg."

"I'm reluctant," I replied, "not least because the fees in this transaction will be pretty skinny."

He called up Steve Waters, joint head of Morgan in Europe, on the speakerphone. Short, charming, quirky even, Steve was a classic New York investment banker. He had helped found the M&A

department at Lehman brothers in 1980, switching to Morgan Stanley in 1988. He became co-head of the New York corporate finance department in 1990 before moving over to London two years later. Steadily over the last two years he had been working to improve the dire profitability of the European operation. It was the first time I had talked to him since snatching away the Bona mandate a year earlier. This was another difficult conversation.

"A full joint pitch may well backfire," I explained, "given our emphasis on the value of a single adviser and co-ordinator."

"Okay guys," he replied. "But can I ask you to liaise with Francis Maude on this? He's taken charge of our Railtrack effort." Francis Maude had been Financial Secretary to the Treasury in the early 1990s and had moved into investment banking in 1992, initially for Salomon Brothers and since the previous year for Morgan. In 2005, back in Parliament, he was to become Conservative Party chairman.

Robert and I braced ourselves. The meeting was set up for Sunday at 5.00pm at our offices. Francis Maude arrived with two colleagues. We were all dressed pretty casually.

"We've been working on this joint pitch with BZW since May," Francis explained. "We had sorted out the key positions of the team and we at Morgan Stanley were planning to put in extra added-value." Robert and I glanced at each other at this. 'Extra added-value' sounded like code for putting in less time than BZW.

Apparently BZW had not only sacked them, but had also abandoned the whole pitch and had no plans to go it alone. Francis concluded: "So we'd like to come in joint with you. If not, we'll pitch on our own."

We were having none of this. I said, "We're extremely confident of winning this deal and we don't want to raise any doubts in the Department of Transport's mind with a half-thought out joint approach."

Robert chimed in, "We thought we'd mention you with a light touch. That if the merger went ahead there would only be upside in having the resources of the combined firm."

"Yes, a light touch," I confirmed. I thought the phrase too glorious not to repeat.

They did not like this at all and wanted guarantees and formal agreements. We fended these off with vague talk of gentlemen's agreements and commitments to look after them if the merger fell through.

While they were checking with their powers that be, Robert and I talked to Nick Verey on the phone. He was a lot less accommodating than Derek had been on the Friday. "I don't see why we should offer them anything at all," he concluded.

Thus reinforced we went back to the Morgan team, who told us they had decided not to go it alone – although we did not believe this had ever been a realistic alternative. We agreed to send them our pitch when it was ready.

"I presume you'll want us to join you at the face to face presentation with the Department?" suggested Francis.

"Well, let's see about that," I replied, meaning 'no'.

On Monday Derek seemed quite happy with our hard line. "We're having a few problems," he hinted. He was probably referring to Mercury Asset Management, which the newspapers were already talking about as a 'hitch'[5]. There were also reports of anguish at Morgan's European headquarters in Canary Wharf as the realisation sank in that they would be sacrificed to the merger. On Sunday in New York Dick Fisher had warned Simon that the deal might have to be called off[6].

Mid-way through the afternoon Rodney Ward rang up from Hong Kong. He was in a state of real woe. "I was given no notice of the deal before the board meeting, just a 10-minute briefing by Scholey. It's all going to be far worse than anything that Derek or Simon imagine. They're just naïve. The Americans won't understand a word of Derek's matrices. They're bond traders. They'll be straight out of the room as soon as he opens his mouth. They are complete shits, without a spark of human feeling."

He didn't give much for his own position as head of the Far East, given his recent arrival in the region. "When I talked to my opposite number it was a total farce. I was saying 'we' and 'us' and all he did was talk about 'my' plans and 'my' intentions."

Later I learned that Rodney was set to become a prime casualty of the deal. After a previous battle with Morgan's head of capital markets over a transaction – business as usual – he was persona non grata with the US firm. Simon had rung him up to tell him, "You will not be on the management committee of the new entity. We're trying to find a suitable position for you." Rodney had interpreted this as the terminal assurance it undoubtedly was.

He was not the only senior executive in dismay at the transaction. One of the joint heads of the fixed interest division, Peter Twachtmann, was openly negative. When he was asked for his view of the deal he said, "It's very simple. I won't have a business to run. All our people will be fired." The public dissemination of this view threw the whole of the fixed income division at Warburg into despair.

Shortly after I had talked to Rodney, Michiel McCarty from the New York office put his head round the door. "I've written out a list of 20 'A' bankers in New York, who have to be given assurances within the next fortnight, or I can't hold them."

When I saw Mark Nicholls a little later he told me: "There've been some unfortunate conversations between juniors in London, with our guys telling theirs that they're going to be fired."

James Sassoon was less confident. "Apparently the Canary Wharf bankers are all working away assessing our people to compete for jobs. I think our sector guys will have a tough time; they've been at it much longer than we have."

The deal was now unravelling fast. The centre of action had moved from the investment bank to its subsidiary Mercury Asset Management. The exact course of developments in the next few days are still the subject of heated debate more than a decade later – with each side blaming the other. According to Phil Duff, Morgan Stanley quickly took the view that the tough negotiating stance put up by Mercury could not be dealt with in the short time-scale of a transaction being conducted in the public eye.

Dick Fisher traveled to London to meet the Mercury board on Tuesday 13 December, where he was told that Morgan would have to pay a substantial premium to buy out the 25% minority that had been floated in 1987. The management also told him that they wanted to continue running an independent operation.

That evening Dick Fisher held a small dinner at Morgan's Mayfair meeting house in Upper Grosvenor Place for three of his most senior executives in the European business. Steve Waters, the joint head of Europe, recalled, "He really wanted out by then. He was complaining about the lack of profitability in Warburg's investment banking, the lack of profitability in equities. He said there were too many people in the operation. He complained about the difficulties with Mercury."

Early on the Wednesday morning Dick Fisher held another meeting, over breakfast, with Mercury's advisers, discussing the kind of premium that might satisfy the subsidiary board. Then he hurried for the 10.00am Concorde out of Heathrow. His mind was made up. Back in New York later that day, he chaired an operating committee of the bank, which decided to pull out.

Next morning Simon received a draft fax stating that Morgan was withdrawing from the negotiations. It was in the sole name of the US bank and it was due to go out in 20 minutes. He held the paper helplessly in his hands. "Look at this," he said to Richard Holloway, head of public relations, who was sitting in his office. It was a body blow. Quickly Simon phoned up John Mack to ask for the statement to be put out in the two banks' joint names.

"There's not time to do that," Mack told him brutally, agreeing to make a few cosmetic changes. Within minutes the statement was on the screens: "While the discussions between Morgan Stanley and S.G.Warburg were proceeding on the basis of a market-for-market merger, the price and terms on which Mercury Asset Management indicated it would be willing to participate in the transaction were unacceptable to Morgan Stanley."

For Warburg the rejection was a body-blow. As one un-named bank analyst told Reuters: "It's a shambles. If it can't sell itself, where does that leave credibility with clients?" We were now 'in play'. We had told the world we did not have a strategy for pursuing an independent future and now we were seen as available to be taken over by other banking groups.

Why had Morgan Stanley acted so aggressively? Three months later – with much water under the bridge – Simon Cairns visited Dick Fisher and John Mack to ask exactly that question. "They said their London people had informed them that we were so much better at running the press than they were, that it would have been an anti-

Morgan press, rather than an anti-Warburg press, if they had not acted pre-emptively."

Dick Fisher made sure that the message was hammered home. He sent his favourite PR official, Jeanne Andrews, over to London to help Steve Waters run the press campaign. She came armed with a series of statements which were to be delivered to the press. The most explosive of these, delivered by Steve, was that MAM had always been the primary attraction of the deal[7]. Many years later he still regretted making an 'off-the-record' statement that earned him unrelenting enmity from Warburg directors. "It was not what I believed. I was a proponent of the merger," he told me. For Jeanne Andrews, at least, the story had a happy ending. Dick Fisher subsequently divorced his wife and married her.

The following morning Simon Cairns addressed the 9 o'clock meeting for investment banking directors again. It was an unhappy talk, full of regret for the collapsed transaction.

He justified the attempt by saying: "If we had been able to put the two together we would have stolen a huge march on our competitors. That was a prize worth going for. I hoped we could take it further without the glare of publicity."

The process itself had been valuable, he claimed. "We've learned a lot about ourselves, as we've explained ourselves to Morgan Stanley, and to learn about how another firm runs itself is a useful piece of competitor analysis. Don't snipe at them. We left the discussions with the highest view of them." This piece of justification was poorly-received, since many in the room felt they already understood how we operated and hardly needed to let a competitor know in order to find out.

He was also keen to stop us blaming Mercury Asset Management for the failure of the deal. "MAM was always known at all stages to be one of the issues. MAM saw its responsibilities both for its minority shareholders and its relationships. There should be no sniping at MAM. Their views were blessed and confirmed by outside advice."

As to the future: "This is not a question of feeling that we have a need to have a partner. We have no intention of doing anything other than contracting our own destiny."

It was hardly the stuff to remotivate a bemused work-force. In predictive terms, it was also to prove entirely wrong.

Simon had a more difficult ride at the Board meeting at midday when he extolled the bank's future prospects. Peter Twachtmann, one of the heads of the fixed interest division, laughed openly. He had already paid a visit to David Scholey to demand that Simon be fired. "Having just spent several days telling the world that we can't make it on our own, how are you going to explain the bright new future now?"

Angrily, Simon replied, "That is what you have to tell the workforce."

"I know my responsibilities," Peter replied pointedly. No one else on the board was prepared to be so aggressive. Shortly after the meeting Simon summoned Peter to his office.

It was a short encounter.

"There isn't room for you here any more," Simon told him.

"I quite understand," Peter replied. He left on the same day.

While I travelled with David Scholey to Virginia in the New Year, a second move was being prepared. After my return – and the surreal phone conference between David Scholey and Tom Tullo – I sat down with Nick Verey in his office on the Friday evening. He was apprehensive.

"We're going to fire them in groups of 10," he said. "There are too many to do individually. We've had the specialists in all day to train us in how to handle it."

"What on earth do you need training for? Surely you just tell them you're closing the division down and let them know the terms."

"Oh yes, wise guy, so what do you do when one of them rushes at you brandishing a chair? And what do you do if one of them collapses on the floor with a heart attack? And what do you do if one of them breaks down and starts shrieking abuse at you?"

"OK, so you need training." As the chairman of the securities operation Nick was set to play a leading role in organising the closure of much of the fixed interest division, planned for the following Monday 9 January. "By the way," I asked, "what do you do if someone does attack you with a chair?"

"You have a great big security man in the room with you and he takes care of it," Nick told me.

In the event, to Nick's relief, the workforce took the announcement with resignation rather than fury or despair, and there were no untoward incidents. But the announcement that we were cutting much of our international bond business, and firing some 180 people, was a desperate muddle, leaving the market unclear whether or not we still planned to operate in areas like UK domestic debt.

The decision to cut fixed interest threw Rodney Ward into a rage. The following week he appeared in my office, having flown over from Hong Kong for a special board meeting. He was accompanied by a fellow board director, John Stancliffe. They used my office as an impromptu base.

"What a disaster," Rodney fumed. "We made them pledge at the last board not to change the shape of the business till we had time to discuss it. Now they've gone ahead without thinking it through. It's a fiasco."

"Completely ridiculous," confirmed John.

"It's no good yelling at me," I pointed out somewhat unkindly. "You're meant to be on the board, with responsibilities for the group as a whole. If you want to do something about it, do it there. You needn't whinge at me."

Stiffened, apparently, by my lack of sympathy, Rodney took a hard line at the subsequent board meeting.

"Simon, we've made a major strategic error," Rodney was reported to have said. "We've canned fixed interest without being clear what business we're in. Are we going to be a Little England of corporate finance business? Are we getting out of international finance to be an M&A boutique? Is that sustainable?" Rodney's attack was supported by a solid block on the board and Simon Cairns was unable to provide a coherent answer to the criticism. Rodney told me later he was indifferent as to the repercussions. "I knew Simon had been ready to let me go. I had no sense of loyalty from that point." The board attack spelled the beginning of the end for Simon.

Maurice Thompson, on the equity markets desk, was not

prepared to wait for Simon Cairns to sort out a new direction for the group. As take-over reports appeared daily in the morning newspapers over January, he made his move.

"Maurice is resigning," Nick told me in early February, "and Michael Cohrs is going with him."

"Where?"

"Deutsche Bank." Deutsche Bank had bought the stricken Morgan Grenfell in 1989 and had recently declared a determination to rebuild its presence in the London securities market.

"Will we be able to hold them?"

"We're trying, but I doubt it."

Maurice and Michael shuttled up and down from their desk on the fifth floor to the Ceausescu Suite for the next day and a half.

"We wanted to see if the Germans were serious about building up London," Maurice told me in one of the interludes in the process, "so I put a call in. And, my God, they are serious."

Another time I asked Michael: "Why are you going with him?"

"I've always trusted Maurice and, you know something, he's never screwed me."

Later I heard the full story. Maurice had put in a call a fortnight earlier and seen John Craven, the former Morgan Grenfell chairman now tasked with building up Deutsche Bank's London business. Craven was immediately interested and arranged a series of meetings at the Frankfurt headquarters of the bank. Michael Cohrs went with Maurice, but was not keen on joining Deutsche whose investment banking operation was nascent. The only effect of Michael's reluctance was to increase the amount Deutsche was prepared to offer the two star equity capital market bankers.

On the first Sunday evening in February Maurice phoned to let Warburg management know they were leaving. They were asked to hold up the resignation long enough to see if the firm could put together a package good enough to entice them to stay. On the Monday evening, with Maurice and Michael waiting upstairs for the outcome, senior management gathered over dinner to decide what package could be offered.

It was fairly plain to all concerned that they would leave unless there was a large financial offer and at least one of them was offered a place on the board.

According to Piers von Simson, "We realised how damaging their departure was likely to be. All of us said they should be offered the board seat. And we dispatched Simon Cairns to impart the message."

Simon was having none of it. He told me later, "I said no, I wouldn't," (albeit probably not to the assembled company, although it had been a good dinner and people's memories are hazy). It was past midnight by the time he and David Scholey went across to find Maurice and Michael stretched out on the sofas, fed up with the extended delay. There was absolutely no mention of board seats.

"The financial offer was completely uninteresting," Maurice recalled. At that stage Warburg did not know what the Deutsche package entailed.

By the next morning there was a whiff of palace revolution in the air. Management discipline was visibly breaking down. A group of senior bankers assembled which deliberately excluded Simon Cairns and the ostensible heads of the corporate finance and securities businesses, Derek Higgs and Nick Verey, as well as Piers von Simson. Maurice and Michael were urgently asked to attend and a series of bizarre discussions took place, in which it was proposed that Maurice should become joint chief executive in Simon's place. Two of the bankers set off to deliver the message to Simon.

But Maurice lost interest in the increasingly chaotic proceedings, especially as Deutsche was putting pressure on the pair to make good their commitment to effect the transfer.

By the afternoon of Tuesday, 7 February, it was all over.

"We're off," said Michael as they arrived back downstairs after the last session. I went into a side room with them to say goodbye. It was a defining moment. "Good luck, guys," I said and hugged them both farewell. I had experienced too many cathartic transactions with each of them to wish them ill despite a sense of desertion.

The papers the next day carried a leak from the Warburg side, accurate enough, that they were each being paid £3m a year by Deutsche Bank for the next two year's work. At the 9 o'clock meeting Derek Higgs tried to explain away the loss. "The two of them found an economic anomaly and took advantage of it," he told us. The leak of the Deutsche pay-scale backfired badly. It generated a frenzy of interest among Warburg personnel, particularly among the equity sales-force, in participating in this largesse. Newspaper photographers camped out in front of Maurice and Michael's houses, trying to seize a shot of these new plutocrats.

In normal times the loss of two front-line bankers was a regular event for an investment bank. But for Warburg these were anything but normal times and the departures were seen as a judgement on the firm. They were also likely to trigger a flood of emulation as the head hunting calls to Warburg personnel went in from rival banks.

Derek was an early casualty. Two days after Maurice and Michael left, as the pressure from the divisions built up, Cairns reacted by publicly demoting both Derek and Nick Verey. They had been too closely associated with the aborted Morgan Warburg deal. He put out a statement saying that the securities division would no longer report through Nick Verey, nor would corporate finance report through Derek Higgs. The relevant executives would report to him direct. Now Nick received the punishment for selling a transaction in which he had not been involved. He had been comprehensively defeated in his battle with the securities division of which he had been in ostensible control since earlier in the year, and which had deliberately distanced itself from him.

Simon put in a call to Rodney, asking him to become the chief operating officer of the group. Rodney turned him down flat. "There was no hope being allied to Simon," he told me later. "Simon was the problem. By now I doubted that the firm would survive."

If these were attempts to shore up his own position, Simon had sadly miscalculated. That day I was making final arrangements to fly to New York for a meeting at the Nynex headquarters just north of the city in White Plains. I went over to see David Charters on the capital markets desk. With the departure of Maurice and Michael he was now in charge.

"Look, with Michael gone I think it would be valuable to have you with us at White Plains tomorrow," I said. "We're still battling it out with Salomon."

David looked sorrowful. "It's chaos here trying to keep everything together. I think I'd better stay and mind the fort."

When I entered the meeting room at White Plains the next day I encountered Bob Nau, the head of syndicate for Salomon. He held a sheaf of wire reports in his hand.

"Looks like you haven't got a capital markets desk left," he said. He showed me the reports. Deutsche Bank was trumpeting that David Charters and five others - most of the rest of the team - had followed Maurice and Michael. No wonder David had turned down the trip to New York and wanted to 'mind the fort'. An eight-hour flight was no place to negotiate one's transfer to another bank.

Somewhat to my surprise Bob did not try to take advantage of our collapsing organisation. After the meeting at Nynex he said to me: "David, we went to this dance together and we'll leave it together."

My puzzlement was lessened a few weeks later when I learned that Bob himself had abruptly left Salomon after a furious row about remuneration. He joined UBS, the largest of the Swiss banks, which was becoming known as 'the lumber yard' because it offered pay deals variously described as 2 by 2, 3 by 2 or even 3 by 3. The first figure represented the millions of US dollars that would be paid each year, while the second was the number of years for which the pay was guaranteed.

The trip to New York was but the first stage of my journey that weekend. By Monday I was due in Australia to help kick off the marketing of the Qantas privatisation. The flight from Los Angeles to Sydney is dislocating at the best of times. It takes more than fourteen hours and Saturday mysteriously vanishes as you pass through the dateline. On this occasion, locked away in a sealed capsule, I felt something very close to true despair. The firm I worked for was clearly falling apart. Would there be anything left by the time I landed?

I was not the only Warburg executive to have a bad weekend. On the Saturday that for me never was, Simon Cairns went into David Scholey's office. "I believe I've lost the confidence of the people," he confessed. "There are difficult times coming up. I don't believe that in the interests of the business I'm the right person to carry it through."

"Would you stay on and help run the client side of the business?"

asked David.

"No, the right and proper thing is to go."

At that point Ken Costa put his head round the door. "The Sunday Times wants to talk to Simon," he explained, faltering as he met the glares of the two men. Quickly he retreated.

Shortly afterwards Simon went quietly to his own office to sort out his things. When he had finished he sauntered down the corridor and put his head round Richard Holloway's office door. Richard was preparing for the press onslaught.

"Abyssinia," Simon said. It was a typical piece of euphonic word-play for 'I'll be seeing you.' Already he must have felt relief at getting out. It was probably the last word he said in the office.

---

[1] Corporate Finance, March 1992, p21

[2] Annual Broker Survey, Consensus Research International. 1991-1994

[3] International Strategy. Summary of a meeting on 25 October 1993. Draft of internal note dated 28 October 1993

[4] Morgan Stanley and S.G.Warburg: Investment Bank of the Future by James K Sebenius and David T. Kotchen. Harvard Business School

[5] Hitch in Warburg Merger, by Mark Milner. Guardian, 12 December 1994

[6] The Takeover of S.G.Warburg – Year that killed the global dream, by John Gapper. The Financial Times, 22 May 1995

[7] Warburg Talks Collapse over Price of MAM by John Willcock, The Independent, 16 December 1994

9

Swiss Roll In
SBC takes over Warburg – 1995 - 1996

~

"Winston is back," declared John Goodwin, as I listened in on a speakerphone at our office in Sydney, in some shock at how much can happen while one is airborne. John was one of the Warburg old guard and he was quoting the telegram sent round the fleet when Winston Churchill was re-appointed to the Admiralty in September 1939, an office he had last held in 1915. The 'Winston' he was welcoming was David Scholey, who had just declared to a packed meeting on Monday evening that he was stepping back into the role of chief executive.

The emergency board meeting on Sunday, 12 February 1995 to decide on what to do after Simon Cairns' resignation had been fraught and ill-tempered. An attack on David Scholey was fended off. Nor could the board agree on any other replacement candidate for Simon than David himself. David was less enthusiastic, especially as he came under pressure to dump his outside board directorships. "My doctor says you're going to fucking kill me," he said bitterly at one stage, the first time many of those assembled could recall him swearing. "If there was one over-riding emotion," he told me later, "it was anger at the situation - and how I found myself in that situation." It was agreed that a committee of four would be appointed to support him in the chief executive role.

Outside the board meeting, the building was a hive of activity with departmental committees meeting all over the place. David Scholey had spent the morning interviewing potential candidates for the chief executive's committee to find a group prepared to work with each other. The more senior and established board members were brutally leapfrogged. The individuals selected were Michael Sargent, who had tussled with Nick Verey for control of the securities business; Colin Buchan, who ran the equity sales team; Mark Nicholls, the co-head of corporate finance and Ed Chandler, the corporate financier who had been so enthusiastic about a merger with JP Morgan. Apart from Michael Sargent, the team was new to the board. They were quickly dubbed 'The Gang of Four' after the infamous Shanghai clique in the Cultural Revolution. David Scholey introduced the fresh faces. "I'm most pleased to welcome my very good friend Raymond Chandler," he said, as he received Ed with a long-remembered slip of the tongue.

Meanwhile, it was almost light relief to get stuck back into a transaction.

"You want me to do what?" I demanded of Matt Playfair incredulously, just before a conference with the Australian financial press on the following Wednesday. Matt was one of the Warburg team running the Qantas transaction.

"Tell them that we think the Minister should raise the limit on foreign holdings in Qantas from 35% to 49%," he confirmed.

"But we're his adviser and lead manager," I pointed out.

"Exactly. We've told him privately but he won't listen. Now you have to tell him publicly."

"Won't he fire us straight away?"

"Come on, David. This is Oz. This is how we do things here."

Obediently I told the journalists that the deal would go far better if there was more room for foreign interest. Given British Airways' 25% holding, there were not enough shares available under the existing 35% limit. So it should be raised to 49%, which was the normal limit elsewhere in the world for national carriers.

The papers carried this attack on Kim Beazly, the finance minister, with some glee. "Pressure grows for higher foreign ownership levels," said the headline in the Australian Financial Review[1] . But Matt was right. We were not fired, and not long afterwards Kim Beazly announced that the limit would indeed be raised to 49%.

While I spent the next week in Australia, David Scholey set about rescuing the bank. Unlike Winston Churchill, he was not about to fight overwhelming odds to maintain the bank's independence. So despite rhetoric about cutting back costs and sorting out the succession, he knew the bank could not survive alone and set about preparing to be rescued.

"There was not a bank or investment bank in the world that did not know we were available. What we had to do was try to get our house in order and wait to see who turned up." David explained to me later. "There was no point in trying to get somebody to turn up. What I did do was appoint two advisers because over Morgan Stanley there had been a suggestion that we should have an external adviser, which had been rejected. That was despite somebody quoting the old adage that he who advises himself has a fool for a client."

David's concern to maintain morale took a heavy toll on the members of his executive committee. He insisted that they complete their normal tasks through the day so that colleagues would not be able to discern any signs of corporate stress. "We had to work a full day and then switch to running the bank late into the night and at the weekends," Colin Buchan told me later. Colin's origins lay in Scotland, although he had been brought up in South Africa and joined the equities arm there, before transferring to the Asian operation and then London earlier in the year. A fortnight after his appointment to the chief executive's committee, he flew up to his Edinburgh home for the weekend, desperate for a break from the gruelling routine. He had been home for barely half-an-hour when David rang him. "You have to come back. Barings is going under."

Barings was brought down by the rogue derivative trades of its Singapore-based employee Nick Leeson and the emergency meetings convened by the Bank of England that weekend to save it were ineffectual. "None of the people there could even spell 'derivative'," Colin told me. The collapse put immediate pressure on Warburg. Not only did it become clear that the City would not stand behind its leading institutions when they got into trouble but demands were put on Mercury Asset Management from its clients to withdraw the cash balances held with the bank. Those concerns were passed on to the parent bank by MAM with some force. Since MAM was then one of the largest suppliers of liquidity in the sterling market, this was a demand that could have sparked a serious run on the bank and its collapse. Herman van der Wyck, the board member with whom I had traveled out to see The Walt Disney Company in Burbank two years earlier, spent the weekend ensuring that we had adequate lines of funding to replace the lost cash. "The price was eye-watering," according to Colin.

The collapse of Barings had one other impact. Talks had started with the Dutch bank ING. Suddenly – bizarrely – they decided to buy the sad remnants of Barings instead, and David was back to square one. It was a few weeks later, on 23 March, that the next opportunity surfaced.

"Our old friend Georges Blum from Swiss Bank Corporation, whom I had known for a very long time, came to see me." David told me. "He brought with him someone I had never met before, although I had heard of, named Marcel Ospel. I took a tremendous shine to Ospel. I thought he was absolutely top class immediately." Swiss Bank Corporation, or SBC, was the bank we had rowed with over Eurotunnel and Enterprise Oil.

The other suitor to emerge was the British high street bank NatWest. Impressions of them were far less favourable than for the Swiss. Derek Higgs told me later, "They were planning to put Martin Owen in charge of us and there was no basis I would ever work for that man. Ospel and Blum were in a different league." Martin Owen was the former treasurer at NatWest in charge of their existing investment banking operation.

Rodney Ward was equally categoric. "NatWest made an appalling impression, shuffling in with peeping Tom-type mackin-toshes. I couldn't see any credible way to work together with them.

"My abiding memory of the Swiss was their youth, optimism and vigour. They were upbeat, very excited and enthusiastic."

There was little contest between the two, especially as SBC put in the better bid. The offer had one very appealing feature to the investment bankers - it excluded Mercury Asset Management. MAM would be separated from the investment bank and given full independence as a quoted company. "The reason they didn't want MAM was obviously because they were more trouble than they were worth." David Scholey told me later. The Morgan Stanley debacle, reinforced by the Barings fall-out, had left a deep sense of bitterness.

David went round to see the Mercury board. He sat at the end of the table, isolated apart from his former personal assistant, Andrew Dalton, who was to his right. David explained the proposed transaction. There was a long pause.

"Does that mean that there's no room for MAM?" Andrew asked.

"Yes," replied David with relish. A collective shiver went round the table. Whatever the battles, there was a deep sense of identity with the Warburg culture and the moment of rejection was a genuine shock.

The structures of authority in the investment bank were visibly eroding. The members of the chief executive's committee could not reveal the talks that were going on, leaving an impression of drift. Bankers were talking in corridors, meeting rooms and offices about the incompetence of management and the revolutionary changes required. One of the (younger) directors proposed volubly that anyone over the age of 35 should be excluded from positions of authority. For my own part, I spent no time plotting, but rather cynically took advantage of the chaos in another way. The effective closure of our fixed interest business provided me, I realised, with a great opportunity to build my resources. Until then I had found it impossible to recruit bankers prepared to take what was perceived as a major career risk by joining a sector. These were untried positions that seemed particularly vulnerable at a time of corporate dishevelment. With their jobs disappearing anyway, the risk did not seem quite so extreme to the fixed interest bankers and over the early part of the year I was able to build up my team to five executives, enough to start covering the transport market on a coherent basis. Some of the other abandoned fixed interest bankers found new homes within the investment bank. Perhaps the most significant, as far as my own immediate endeavours were to be concerned, was the appointment of Denys Firth and James Garvin from the fixed interest syndicate desk to fill the hole on the equity capital markets side.

The Deutsche Bank head-hunting team, which had scored such a breakthrough on the capital markets desk, now went on over-drive. By the last weekend of April, the senior group of four in the Continental European equity team, led by David Haysey and Joe Hall, had decided to follow Maurice and Michael to the German rival. Co-incidental attempts by Colin Buchan to contact them in order to let them know about the solution to Warburg's travails backfired. They thought that the calls were a prelude to legal action over a mass defection and resolutely switched their phones off. On Monday they resigned and attempts to turn them round failed. Next day, 2 May, Colin stood on a desk in the sales room to urge the rest of the team to stay as the bank announced that it had received an offer from the Swiss Bank Corporation and was evaluating it.

David Scholey called the corporate finance directors together to tell us the news just before the afternoon announcement went out. This time the deal was much more likely to go ahead. "We have every determination to conclude on terms agreed in principle; terms on which I and the group board are extremely satisfied." As to the sales-team which had left, he was typically robust: "We plan to comment as little as possible to avoid the laws of libel." He aimed to stop any more departures. "The announcement of our profits and the bonus payments will be made at the same time as the definitive announcement of the deal in the next two or three weeks. There will be arrangements to bind key people into the group."

There were some bitter questions. "Have we pursued all the routes to preserving our independence?" asked one director, a sentiment echoed by several others. David brushed the questioners aside.

"Well," I said afterwards to Adrian Haxby, who was working with me on Nynex Cablecomms, "we'd better put in another call to Colson Turner." The flotation was now coming to a head and absorbing the bulk of my time.

"I can't bear it," he replied.

"Nynex must think we are completely bonkers," I mused. "First we call to say we're merging with Morgan Stanley to be the biggest, most devastating bank in the world. Then we tell him it's all off, but not to worry, we're still right behind his offer with all our resources. Next we've lost our head of equity capital markets and Michael Cohrs, who's handling his deal, but everything's still under control because we have a first class replacement in the shape of David Charters. Oops, now he's gone. And by the way our chief executive has also just jumped ship."

"It's going to be a long time till we're the number one European investment bank again," sighed Adrian, as we dialed through to Colson to tell him how wonderful a merger between SBC and Warburg would be.

Piers von Simson was still running the European business in the 'Gang of Four' inter-regnum. Now he took the battle to the enemy in trying to stem the desertion of key personnel in a typically direct way. At the end of the week he had seized the opportunity of a full meeting of the syndicate involved in the privatisation of Deutsche Telekom. There were more than 60 bankers present from a full complement of the leading houses round the world. We had won a role as the head of the UK syndicate, under the overall lead of Deutsche, Dresdner and Goldman Sachs. At the end of the meeting Piers stood up to castigate Deutsche Bank's predatory behaviour in poaching Warburg's key staff. Protests that this was an inappropriate forum to air a private conflict between the two banks were swept aside by Piers, for whom this was all too appropriate an opportunity to embarrass Deutsche Bank in public. Addressing the chief financial officer of Deutsche Telekom, Dr Joachim Kröske, he described the 14 individuals who would have been directly involved in the offering and who had been "effectively taken from us by Deutsche Bank." Syndicate members, who had been preparing to leave when Piers stood up, scrabbled to retrieve their translator's headsets to catch the invective.

"In the history of investment banking we believe it to be absolutely unprecedented that in the course of a critically important offering the global co-ordinator should systematically attempt to bolster its own capacity to execute the transaction by raiding the resources of another and very senior member of the syndicate," he denounced the rival bank[2].

He concluded, "I can assure you that our own commitment to the success of this transaction, and to the smooth working of the team to bring about the result we all desire, remains undiminished. At the same time it would obviously be helpful if the Deutsche Bank could fill any other vacancies it may have from another bank, preferably not a member of the Deutsche Telekom syndicate. I hope that as issuer, Dr Kröske, you may wish to insist on this."

The attack did little to slow down the flow of people to Deutsche Bank and the most reliable estimates I have heard point to around 200 people in total abandoning Warburg for Deutsche over the course of 1995.

We only had a little over a week to wait for the deal to be finalised. Luckily the profit figures were lost behind the announcement, because they were truly appalling, with the six months to March producing a loss of £20.4m. David Scholey announced the takeover with the flamboyant statement at the press conference on May 10 that the two groups fitted together "like the clunk of a Rolls-Royce door."

The next morning Marcel Ospel, the head of SBC's international investment banking, arrived at the Warburg office. He was dressed in a sports jacket. Newspaper stories later emerged (always disavowed by him) that he had more than a little trouble convincing the security guards that he should be allowed in. The trademark distinction of SBC in those days was the wearing of informal clothes. David Scholey enthusiastically introduced the chief-executive elect of the soon to be created SBC Warburg to about 20 of the investment banking directors. We were in one of the top floor meeting rooms, sitting along each side of a long table, while he sat at its head. Marcel was almost exactly my own age, at 45. He struck me as curiously self-contained and rather imposing, talking carefully and choosing his words with care, a cigarette permanently to hand. He had spent most of his career in various departments of SBC, bar one period a decade earlier working for the US firm Merrill Lynch. He had a reputation for flamboyance in Switzerland, based in large part on his choice of red furniture for his office. In reality he had chosen this off-beat colour to make a point, a protest against bureaucratic insistence on the type of desk he should have[3]. In a British context he seemed sober, despite his relaxed clothing style, almost shy.

"You all want to know what is going to happen next, and no doubt are wondering whether you will be better off staying with SBC Warburg or responding to the pressing invitations of one of our competitors. We really want you to stay and we need you to stay to build a new kind of business with us," he was reported, accurately enough, to have said the next day by The Times.

"We look forward to co-operating with all of you in the design of the integration plan and then in the incredibly hard work of the next year. And we look forward to celebrating our joint success a year from now."[4]

His audience did not distinguish themselves. He faced a series of petulant questions, even from board members. Piers von Simson demanded how we were going to hold on to our staff. It was probably Marcel's first realisation of the depths to which morale in the investment banking division had sunk. It must have reinforced his instinct to take a tough line.

One of the last acts of the outgoing management took place after the SBC take-over was agreed. The chief executive's committee met to determine the level of bonus they should each receive, a relatively modest figure which was more honorarium than significant reward. They asked Rodney Ward to help them through their deliberations. When it came to David's own bonus, he left the room to allow the decision to be taken. Just before he returned to hear the figure, Mark Nicholls turned to Rodney and asked him to deliver the committee's views. Unprepared, Rodney launched into an impromptu expression of thanks for all David had done. "Your immense effort is on record," he said in his characteristically fulsome style, "and we want to recognise that effort . . ." He stopped, stunned, as tears started to pour down David's cheeks, realising with sudden clarity the enormous strain the chairman had been under.

The Nynex deal was now giving me real cause for concern. As we launched the book-building phase, orders were going into the book much too slowly. We knew the US market could not be relied on. Just before launch Salomon had suggested we reduce the allocation to American investors from 50% to 40%. Although we did not change the pre-agreed joint split of commissions, this step must have been hard for the bank to swallow, especially in the light of their brutal attempt to take control of the transaction half a year earlier. It underlined their lack of confidence in the demand they could generate.

On the closing day of the transaction, on 8 June, I flew out to New York and waited for the traditional rush of last-minute orders from the US investors. A few orders trickled in but there was certainly no stampede.

"What's Salomon got?" I asked Lucinda Riches, who used to run the New York syndicate desk and had picked up this transaction.

"They're sending it over now," she told me. She scanned the pages. "Doesn't look good," she said. "They'll have to do a proper analysis in London."

We waited.

Colson Turner called from Salomon's office downtown .

"We're just about to be on our way," I assured him.

Half an hour later I was on the phone to London. "What the hell's happening?" I demanded.

"I'm sorry, David," explained Denys Firth, the new head of equity syndicate . "We can't work the machine."

"What do you mean, you can't work the machine?"

"I mean, everybody who knows how to work this blasted bookbuilding programme is sitting over at Deutsche Bank. We're having to do it by hand." This was the first equity transaction of any substance after the defection of the team. It never occurred to me to check that somebody still understood our systems.

"Oh, my God. How long is it going to take? They're sticking pins in our eyes down at the World Financial Center."

"It's going to be at least an hour yet. We have to assess every name to see how much we can allocate to them. Most of the ones from Salomon are a joke. It looks to me to be favours from people whom Salomon have assured will be able to dump it straight back to them in the morning."

It wasn't till 7.00pm local time that we were able to go down to Salomon's headquarters at the World Financial Center. Our reception was extremely hostile. From Salomon it could be anticipated. Less comfortable were the bitter greetings of some 15 senior Nynex executives hyped up on the bad coffee they had consumed over the three hours they had been waiting for us.

We assembled in a large windowless room in the centre of the tower. It was over-crowded. The Nynex team packed one side, lining up against the wall as well as taking places at the table. I had four colleagues with me, in the shape of Lucinda Riches; Michiel McCarty, the co-head of US corporate finance; Jim Renwick from UK broking and; James Grigg, one of the London telecoms bankers. From Salomon there were well over 20 executives. It seemed every faction in the bank insisted on being represented in the pricing decision.

Before we got down to business, the chief executive of Salomon, Deryck Maughan, popped into the room and stood just inside the door. "Hey, you guys, I hear it's pretty tight. If you need any more I'm sure I can find a few dollars," he said, waving his cheque book.

"Thanks," chorused the Nynex team. "We'll do fine. You can fuck off." And with a cheerful wave Deryck Maughan left us to get on with it. Deryck was a British citizen who had worked for the UK Treasury before transferring to Goldman Sachs and then Salomon, where he ran the Asia operations out of Tokyo. Reputedly Warren Buffet, who became the main shareholder after the Treasury scandal, had plucked him from this relatively remote position to be chief executive of the bank because he was the only senior executive who could string together a sentence without the word 'fuck' in it.

The new head of syndicate after Bob Nau's departure, Frank Maturo, started using the whiteboard to lay out a picture of demand.

"The US orders came in late," he said, "as we expected. But there are some real quality names there."

After a few minutes of this I sensed Lucinda stiffening beside me. Suddenly she could take no more. She leapt to her feet and seemed almost to clamber onto the table "Bullshit," she shrieked at Frank. "The US demand is non-existent."

The room was stunned to silence.

Lucinda looked much younger than her experience suggested and was blond and attractive. "They thought she was a bit of fluff you had brought along," one of the London-based Nynex team explained to me later. So her full-throated attack on her counter-part shocked the Salomon bankers. The Nynex team, by now getting over their resentment of our late arrival, thoroughly enjoyed the theatre.

"Thank you, Lucinda," I said. "Shall we continue?" From now on we held the initiative, as the bargaining became more and more bitter. The dynamics of the meeting were bizarre. Normally the lead banks will work together to persuade the vendor to accept a reasonable price – one that can be successfully defended in the market when trading begins. In this case Salomon sided with Nynex, apparently in order to impress this important client with their selling efforts. They were happy for us to be the bad guys. Around 10.00pm we broke up to consult with London, hauling the team out of bed at 3.00am their local time.

"We can't go any higher than 137p," said Denys Firth, "and even then it'll probably be a disaster. We'll have to put a bloody great naked short out into the London market. All the Salomon crap will wing its way straight back at us." A naked short was jargon for allocating more shares than we owned. It meant that when shares were dumped back on us we would use them to cancel the 'short'. It was a market manoeuvre only undertaken when there was great certainty, since it could be extremely expensive not to own shares if their value took off in the after-market.

When the room re-assembled after this conference call our figure was accepted reasonably quickly, although I did not give Nynex much option.

"I'm afraid that 137p is all we are prepared to do," I informed them bluntly.

The Salomon analyst, Jack Grubman, broke in. "I just know you're being ridiculously conservative here. The right price is 145p and it will soar above that level when it starts to trade."

I glanced quickly round the room and risked a calculated put-down. "Well, I don't think that any of your team agrees with you on this and therefore I think we can safely ignore that contribution."

Luckily no-one leapt to his defence. Grubman was later to earn notoriety for continuing to push telecom stocks while they were collapsing, and in particular for his over-cosy relationship with

WorldCom. In April 2003 he was fined $15m and barred from the securities industry for life as part of a settlement with the New York State Attorney General. His earnings over the previous decade had been eye-watering.

We were done. I got to bed at about midnight, after a 21-hour day, and treated myself to the morning Concorde home. In the Concorde lounge at mid-morning I was suddenly overcome by nausea and was thoroughly sick in the toilet. It was the only time that stress – or the relief of stress – had such a physical effect on me in my banking career.

Jack Grubman's assessment of the aftermarket performance of the shares could not have been more wrong. As Denys had anticipated, stock poured back the next day and continued to return over the next fortnight, while the price fell away to 120p by the end of July.

"This stuff is appalling. We can't possibly send it out to our clients." I was sitting with a small group of corporate finance directors at the beginning of the following week. We were looking over the draft of a brochure that had been prepared by McKinsey describing the new SBC Warburg. Holding on to our client base had become a major priority. Over the last couple of months we had already lost high-profile brokerships for Glaxo and the Guardian insurance group and we knew many companies were considering whether we would be able to look after them properly. Would I write the new brochure so that we had something acceptable ready for the formal launch of SBC Warburg? I groaned inwardly as I calculated how I could juggle the tasks in the week ahead. "All right."

First stop was a meeting with George Feiger, the former McKinsey director who had advised Marcel Ospel on the strategic rationale for the purchase of Warburg. Their first contact had taken place a year earlier when George had conducted a McKinsey review of the options open to the international business of SBC. Subsequently he became a major advocate of the attractions of buying Warburg, against considerable cynicism among some other members of SBC management. Now, having left a favourable impression on Marcel, he had been persuaded to become an executive in the newly-formed investment bank. Born in South Africa, George was a lively man with a shock of dark hair. Ideas flowed from him with extraordinary fluency. I took a genuine liking to him although I suspected that the speed of his delivery might disguise the occasional lacuna in understanding.

"We have a huge advantage as a counter-party because we are rated Triple A by the credit agencies," he told me. "That means we obtain cheaper funding than virtually all other banks." He described the importance of the derivative technology that SBC had obtained through the purchase of a specialist company in Chicago called O'Connor. "We really understand risk management technology. We understand how to aggregate risk to build a big book. Based on that, we can price transactions more tightly than our rivals."

I went back to my desk with my head buzzing. Over the week I made my way round the rest of the SBC team; Andy Siciliano, who ran the foreign exchange operation; Steve Smith, who jointly ran the equity business and David Solo, responsible for the fixed interest division. Quickly I put together a rationale. SBC brought a large capital base of $12bn that it was prepared to use to support client transactions. It was a leader in debt and foreign exchange, based on its mastery of risk technology. Warburg brought leadership in European corporate finance, research and equity. In combination this meant SBC Warburg could offer "a full range of products and services to clients"[5].

The SBC team was determined to be tough on the Warburg management and only three Warburg executives were appointed to senior board positions. Mark Nicholls from corporate finance and Colin Buchan, now joint head of equities, joined the SBC Warburg board, while Rodney Ward in Asia became the only executive to join the parent SBC board. Most others in the hierarchy were regarded with deep distrust, a reaction to the very public shambles that Warburg had made of the last half-year. By contrast, the new owners were determined to promote talent lower down the organisation. I was an early beneficiary. Mark Nicholls called me into his office: "We are making a limited number of managing directors. Do you want to be one?"

"Yes," I said. Of course I did.

"It's got downside as well as upside, you know. While you'll share in the profits in good years you'll do badly in bad years."

"I'll take the risk."

In fact SBC only appointed about 20 managing directors out of the whole 4,700-strong former workforce of the Warburg group, and a number of these were courtesy titles for former board members like Nick Verey and Derek Higgs. The remainder were concentrated in the Corporate Finance Division. Only two were made up in the whole of the equities division, one of whom was Colin Buchan, the other Stephen Carr, the head of research. This presumably reflected a strategic view (which was carefully not revealed to me) that the equities division was a loss-making dinosaur that would need savage pruning to fulfill a much-reduced function. Under this it would be required to provide an adequate flow of business to support a successful trading operation.

Almost before the formal integration of the equities business took place on 3 July, it dawned on the new owners that this strategic analysis was nonsense. The Monday of the combination itself proved unexpectedly dramatic. This was the day scheduled for the SBC traders to come over to their positions on the main Warburg sales floor. Beforehand the Warburg salesforce had enquired as to the dress code that was now appropriate.

"You're working for SBC Warburg now," they were told. "We have a casual clothes policy."

So on the Monday three distinct groups of people arrived at work. The first were the SBC traders in their elegant chinos and £100 shirts. The second were the Warburg die-hards who had always worn a suit and were damned if they were going to change now. The third group had searched through their wardrobe for casual gear and selected what they could find, which was their bonfire gear. I suspect the most horrified group in the room were the SBC traders, who found themselves surrounded by tramps.

Despite the sartorial confusion, the combination was a great success almost from day one. The SBC traders were used to doing about 2% of the market. When they added the 9% or so that the Warburg sales-force was accustomed to handle they found themselves managing a much larger book much more profitably. The market share rose steadily from the 11% base and SBC quickly realised that the real jewel in the Warburg takeover lay here, in the equities division. They had bought the number one position in the European equities market effectively for peanuts. The final purchase price emerged at slightly below the value of the net assets, mainly the cash and liquid assets of the company. It reminded me of the TSB float which was like "buying a purse and getting your money back in it".

Before I left for my two-week break in August I popped in to see how Mark Nicholls was faring. He seemed extremely unhappy. He was bearing the brunt of managing the division in the style demanded by our new Swiss masters. He had to decide who were the main revenue earners and make sure they were rewarded appropriately. He also had to work out who he thought were the weaker performers, and show them the door. It was the kind of challenge that in the past had driven the old Warburg, with its collegiate style, to a standstill, as the 'night of the short penknives' so graphically illustrated. Now clear lines of decision-making were being established. "Those bastards in the SBC HR department," he said unspecifically to me. HR stood for Human Resources, the new jargon for a personnel department. Clearly Mark was not seeing much latitude from this quarter.

Then he talked about the row that had blown up when he had asked one of our corporate finance colleagues to leave. "He got to his clients before we did and now they're threatening to fire us if we don't have him back."

"You'll just have to reverse it," I consoled him. "Look, anyone's going to make a few mistakes. If you reverse them there's no damage done."

He shook his head sorrowfully. He really was not enjoying himself.

While I was on holiday he collapsed at work and was sent home to recuperate. Marcel Ospel instituted a careful review of the other senior bankers and came to the decision that none of them were up to the task of running the division. He took over Mark's role as head of corporate finance for a short period, before handing the task over to George Feiger in the autumn.

By then the trickle of departures over the summer was turning into a flood. Until 1995, Warburg had performed an incredible feat in keeping the corporate finance division intact, bribing here, coercing there, to hold onto the department. Only a handful of executives had left for a US rival until that point. The tactic meant the US banks could not use established relationship holders to work their way into the mainstream. This meant that UK bankers saw a move to their ranks as highly risky. With the collapse of Warburg, the barriers were lifted and the US banks now seemed far more attractive. It seemed that I was invited to leaving drinks almost daily.

Piers von Simson lamented the departure of one of his key young bankers in the German market, Colin Roy, to Merrill Lynch. "I took him on and trained him up into this business and just when he's in a position to put something back, he buggers off," he told me.

The first of the post-SBC departures had been Stuart Stradling's, the head of the corporate broking department and to whom I had briefly reported in 1986. David Scholey told me later: "As soon as I knew it was SBC, I phoned him up to warn him. I knew what his reaction would be." Stuart's run-in with SBC over the Eurotunnel rights issue had left him with explosive views about the bank, and he told David, "I'm not working for those buggers." Within days he had arranged a new job, leaving in August. Unfortunately for him he went to become the chief financial officer of the DIY firm Wickes, only to uncover accounting irregularities that brought the firm down.

His departure meant that I had to take responsibility for the Eurotunnel account. We had spent considerable resources in helping the company with its tangled finances and were now looking to be appointed adviser to a debt restructuring. In late August I went round to see Alastair Morton who was still chairman of Eurotunnel. He was not encouraging: "My quarrel is not with you but with SBC. The place is run by traders now and they've been consistently damaging Eurotunnel's stock for the last year. SBC executives have massacred those from Warburg in the merger process. And finally, a series of legal processes have been set in train in France, to which an investigating magistrate is about to be appointed. SBC will be one of his main targets."

I did my best. I reminded him of all our services to him in the past and told him: "Not only should we remain broker, but also we are best equipped to advise the company in the forthcoming debt negotiations."

He concluded: "We'll take the decision over the next two or three weeks."

Not promising.

When I went back to hear the verdict, in late September, I took reinforcements in the shape of Marcel Ospel. We traveled to the company's new offices high in the Canary Wharf tower. On this occasion Alastair Morton uncharacteristically took a back seat and let his French co- chairman, Patrick Ponsolle, deliver the bad news.

"Eurotunnel is effectively joined with the COB in taking legal action against SBC. It would be impossible to explain, particularly in France, that we are suing a bank which we are nevertheless happy to use as an adviser."

Marcel Ospel carried off the humiliation with considerable aplomb. "There are times when it is appropriate to take a back seat and it seems that this is one of those times. I hope that in future we can become more active again." He said. It was not to be. While we retained our broking role for a few months after the meeting, it fizzled out the following March as the French court case picked up steam.

As autumn progressed the atmosphere among the corporate financiers became more and more febrile. The majority were talking to other banks, negotiating personal packages of as much as they could. Between times they were trying to ingratiate themselves with their new masters, manoeuvring for position in a forming hierarchy. One director made a practice of going to meetings with George Feiger and Marcel Ospel wired for sound, agitating for changes in the division's organisation. When he got home he would type out the transcripts of the conversation, seeing if he could use the information to play office politics.

It was Robert Gillespie, the banker who had worked so closely with Simon Cairns on the Morgan Stanley deal, who now took the initiative to calm the atmosphere. In September he invited the corporate finance directors to a dinner at the Savoy. Other commitments meant I missed the event and am relying on others for an account of what Robert said.

"Look," one participant remembers him saying, "We can all go our separate ways or we can stick at this, remain friends and do the business as we always have." It was an appeal to their underlying loyalty to the Warburg culture. For most the dinner was enough to steady their nerves.

Piers von Simson was one who found it difficult to come to terms with the new management style. He exploded in public at Marcel Ospel at one of the 9 o'clock meetings, after it was announced that he had been appointed to some board within the group without anyone informing him in advance. "I think I am still entitled to the ownership of my name," he declared bitterly. "If it is used I expect to be consulted." It was no surprise when he left shortly afterwards. The other senior managers who had been passed over by Marcel, David Hobley and Ed Chandler, left at much the same time.

It never really occurred to me to leave. Money had something to do with it because I was given a healthy option package in the company that would be paid out three years later. In one way too, the takeover was an emotional release. Chris Reilly summarised the feeling for me.

"Under Warburg we were on a crusade to become a global bank. Every deal became a matter of life and death to prove that we were better than the Americans. Now it's just business. One just gets on with one's job."

Besides where would I go? My experience with the American banks had left me deeply suspicious about their behaviour and motivations. Deutsche Bank was making a serious effort to become a real player but its predatory behaviour had, for me, left a bitter taste. It seemed to have indulged in a campaign to damage the Warburg infrastructure and franchise that had seriously diminished the opportunities for those who remained. This was an analysis that left SBC Warburg as the only other serious contender. Already I could begin to see genuine improvements in the business, and not only in the powerhouse that was developing in equities. Somewhat to my surprise I found that my surreptitious approach to growing my resources was about to become irrelevant.

In September I sat down with George Feiger and explained how I was running my transport sector. George was like a sponge when it came to new ideas and unlike the old Warburg would act in scale on an idea that appealed to him.

"Right," he said. "I buy it. That's what we're going to do. We're going to throw all our resources into building up strong sectors across the board." Almost overnight I was transformed from a tolerated maverick in an organisation of business executors into a model of how to go about mainstream business.

The transformation of Warburg into part of Swiss Bank saw the creation of a great diaspora. David Scholey retained his links with the organisation while building a career as a non-executive director for companies such as Vodafone and Sainsbury, chairing the small local investment Bank, Close Brothers. Simon Cairns maintained a busy life-style following his resignation, chairing the tobacco company BAT as well as the Commonwealth Development Corporation and Voluntary Service Overseas. Derek Higgs went on to chair the Prudential's investment operation, before authoring the Higgs report on corporate governance, while Piers von Simson joined a boutique bank of Warburg outcasts called Soditic. Mark Nicholls ran the Scottish Royal Bank's venture capital business; David Hobley and Ed Chandler ended up working for Deutsche Bank. Meanwhile Maurice Thompson and Michael Cohrs, whose decision to leave Warburg for Deutsche was to prove such a catalytic event, were both thoroughly miserable for the next three years. They were shocked to find themselves working in an organisation which simply did not have the resources adequate to undertake deals of the scale they were used to. For a period Maurice became the head of investment banking before a shake-up of the department resulted in his resignation. It was his colleague, Michael Cohrs, who in early 2005 inherited the top job of the reorganised operation which had grown into an appreciable force in the market. Not all the stories had a happy ending.

"I've got this terrible bloody flu. Don't seem able to shake it off," Nick Verey complained as he drove me to Brentford in west London in his dark-blue Mercedes. It was 11 January, 1996, and we were travelling to a farewell party for the chief executive of Nynex Cablecomms at the Steam Museum. Nick had had a terrible year, taking undeserved blame for the Morgan Stanley adventure and being publicly demoted shortly afterwards by Simon Cairns in virtually his last act as chief executive. He had held on and by now was very much through the worst, as the Swiss Bank executives realised the great value of his string of corporate relationships through UK industry. Indeed in the last couple of months he had been throwing himself back into every-day work with renewed enthusiasm. I had asked him to be the senior speaker at the internal seminar on transport planned for the Saturday in two days time. This was an important event, at least as far I was concerned, being the opportunity to relaunch the sector under our new masters, who were promising to provide whole-hearted support for the effort. Nick had accepted the invitation with alacrity.

On the Friday evening, the day after the party, I received a terse message from Nick's secretary. "Nick can't attend the seminar tomorrow. He apologises." I was too busy with the preparations to puzzle more than momentarily. It was uncharacteristic of Nick to let a matter of flu slow him down. It wasn't till Monday that Derek Higgs summoned me to his office to tell me: "Nick has leukaemia."

Nick's wife, Dinah, had finally persuaded him to see his doctor on Friday morning to pick up an antibiotic for flu. The doctor took some tests. When the results came back at lunchtime the doctor immediately rang to say (Nick told me later): "You've got acute lymphoblastic leukaemia and it's galloping away. I've arranged for you to be taken in by the London Clinic. Go there. Now." Afterwards the clinic told him that if he hadn't attended immediately he would probably have been dead by the Monday, given the rapidity of the disease's progress.

As it was, once the initial attack was stabilised, Nick went through the full standard treatment to rid his white blood cells of the cancer, undergoing radio- and chemotherapy courses. I visited regularly, reassured to learn that the prognosis was good with a survival rate of 70% plus. These odds could only have been improved by the extremely professional care he was receiving at the clinic. In May he travelled to the US on holiday with Dinah and their daughter and was soon preparing to come back to work.

On the phone to him from a car in June, as I travelled to the airport, I briefed him on the progress of a transaction for Jarvis Hotels. "It's bloody tough," I told him. "We're being squeezed the whole time by UBS." I prattled on about our tactics to keep this bank, with which we were meant to be acting jointly, under control for the London-based hotel float. Abruptly Nick interrupted me. "It's come back." I was shocked into silence, hearing the tears in his voice. He didn't have to tell me that when the disease returned after such a short period of remission the prognosis had deteriorated alarmingly.

The next few months saw a desperate struggle against the illness which defied every treatment thrown at it. By the early autumn his immune system was so battered that he succumbed to one disease after the other, each one leaving him weaker. He died finally on 16 October, aged 53, just nine months after the illness was diagnosed.

I wept as I wrote his obituary for The Times. I had lost the man who had hired me, encouraged me, protected me. I had lost one of my closest friends. I was, and remain, convinced that the illness had been stress-induced by the events of the previous year; the most damaging fallout, as far as I was concerned, from the collapse of Warburg.

---

[1] Qantas Float: Pressure Grows for Higher Foreign Ownership Levels by Ian Thomas, Australian Financial Review, 16 February 1995

[2] Secret internal note by Piers von Simson dated 9 May 1995. Also: Warburg in Staff poaching row, by Nicholas Denton and Conner Middelmann. The Financial Times, 13 May 1995

[3] The Ospel interview, Euromoney April 1997, p36

[4] SBC Warburg - The Gospel according to Ospel, by Melvyn Marckus. The Times 13 May 1995

[5] SBC Warburg brochure, July 1995

10

Rail Britannia
Railtrack and the Channel Tunnel Railway Link
1995 - 2002

~

"This is appalling," summarised James Sassoon succinctly. It was March 1995 and James was looking over an early piece of research into attitudes to Railtrack. The research was based on a series of conversations with potential retail investors.

"Listen to this," he said at one of our internal team meetings, reading out some of the conclusions:

"'The appeal of the Railtrack offer is constrained by doubts and concerns about the rail system as a whole. In particular the seemingly fragmented structure will work against efficiency, safety, accountability;' oh dear, oh dear.

"And it goes on: 'The history of decay and failure will take many years to turn round. There's a need for massive investment . . blah, blah . . railways have been historically unprofitable . . Railtrack is over-dependent on the success of other, unproven operators'."

"There is some good news in there," I pointed out.

"Where?" James was suspicious.

"Look, it says that the main attraction of the Railtrack offer is the 'opportunity to make a quick killing.' "

Phil Raper broke in. "It was just as bad as this with the Water offer and look how well that went. If the boys think they can turn a penny they'll buy it even if they don't believe in the structure."

"Water wasn't as unpopular as this, surely?" James asked. He had not acted on the Water float, unlike Phil and me.

"Well, not quite," admitted Phil. "But it was pretty bad. We were getting a thick file of hostile press every day for a year beforehand, almost as thick as the file we're getting for Railtrack."

Three months earlier we had duly attended the formal presentation for the privatisation of Railtrack. It was held at the offices of the Department of Transport in Marsham Street, a three-tower block universally derided as the most execrable building in central London and shortly scheduled for demolition. On the way into the building for our Friday afternoon appointment on 16 December 1994, we saw the BZW team leaving, together with Francis Maude of Morgan Stanley. Somehow they had managed to revive their joint pitch following the collapse of the Morgan Warburg merger the day before. Our own written submission had referred to them with the lightest of touches. "In the event that the merger proceeds we would be able to deploy the additional resources of the enlarged firm to the successful execution of this mandate[1]." It meant we were not in the least embarrassed by the collapse of the transaction.

The senior civil servants on the other side of the table, in the shape of Nick Montagu, deputy secretary of the Department of Transport and Steve Robson, deputy secretary of the Treasury were much more concerned about the scale of the task.

"Do you think a Railtrack float is possible at all, given the deluge of hostile publicity that we're getting?" asked Nick Montagu.

"Look," I said, "we managed to float Eurotunnel, which had the worst possible image with the institutions because they had been forced to invest in its unquoted equity by the Bank of England. And we did it even after the September 1987 crash. If we could do that, we can float Railtrack." Combined with our success in selling BT3 for the Treasury, our credentials were evidently impressive enough to make our selection straightforward. We won, apparently, because we were judged the best team players and the hungriest for the transaction. After a bit a of haggling over our fees we were appointed five days later. We estimated we would earn at least £8.5m on the mandate, at which level we would probably just about cover our costs; in practice the figure would emerge at £10.9m[2]. The appointment also followed the precedent set by the BT issues; we were adviser, broker, global co-ordinator - the works. If it all went horribly wrong there would be only one institution to blame.

As we sat there in March that institution was not quite the one that the department had appointed. Clearly their judgement on our superiority as team players looked sadly misplaced. Already the team was short of Simon Cairns, who had led our pitch, while Maurice Thompson was no longer available as the global co-ordinator. Warburg itself was publicly falling apart. Whatever concerns the Government must have had, they did not let us know about them.

Railtrack was not the only piece of rail business in which I was involved. Nick Wakefield, in our project finance team, was pursuing the franchise to build the Channel Tunnel Railway Link, dubbed CTRL for short. He had already briefed me on the plan.

"It's a fabulous opportunity," he told me. "The Government has bundled up the rail service to Paris and Brussels – Eurostar – with the franchise. So the operations will provide cash flow to support the building of the high-speed link. Clever, eh?"

"How are they going to support the construction?"

"That's the other clever thing. The bidders will bid for a subsidy. The winner will be the group which wants the least subsidy."

Nick had formidable energy and enthusiasm. He would describe a project he was working on with the same infectious delight as a boy with a new tricycle. He was pursuing some strong partners and was succeeding in assembling a credible group: Bechtel, which had sorted out Eurotunnel's construction problems, and National Express, one of the biggest of the new bus companies. He also had the French railways on board.

"We'll probably need about £1bn of equity."

I jumped like a scalded cat. "Nick, after the fiasco of Eurotunnel nobody will ever raise public equity for a rail project again."

He waved the objection away. "It doesn't have to be public," he assured me. "We'll just have to structure something suitable. I'll keep you in touch."

He left me puzzling over where on earth he thought he could locate £1bn of equity outside the public markets.

Because of my role on the Railtrack mandate, acting for the Government, I had to stay at one remove from the CTRL bid, where Nick and his team were negotiating on the other side to get the best possible deal from the Department of Transport. He was as good as his word, however, about keeping me informed. "After all, David, once Railtrack is out of the way and we've won the CTRL franchise, I'll probably join the new company and you'll be responsible for all the financing," he said.

"We've chosen the name," he told me another time. "All that fruit stuff – Apple and Orange – is out of the window. It's back to descriptive titles: 'London & Continental Railways'. What do you think? Elegant, isn't it?"

The Railtrack mandate kicked off early in 1995 with a presentation from the new management team at their dreary temporary office in Bloomsbury. It was designed to allow us to start understanding the company so we could construct all the materials we would need; a prospectus, information for all the investment banking analysts (not least our own) and marketing materials. The session had been a desultory affair, led by John Edmonds, the chief executive, and his chief financial officer, Norman Broadhurst. It came to life only when John Edmonds described the early history of the railway industry. "Some of the signalling and point systems still date from the last century," he explained with an historian's enthusiasm. We sat in a gloomy airless room, surrounded by dull wood panelling trying to absorb the arcane details of the company's internal organisation. John Edmonds seemed to have too many people reporting directly to him - the heads of the 10 zones into which the business was divided as well as the normal specialist functions, such as the financial, safety and legal officers. It looked like a recipe for overload. We also were experiencing overload, albeit of a different kind. The speakers bombarded us with acronyms – roscos, bris, tocs. The names of the different parts of the rail industry seemed to go on and on. It was almost impossible to absorb any real information behind this barrage of new jargon.

Railtrack was at the heart of a radical overhaul of the UK rail system, under which British Rail had been broken up into more than 60 separate entities. The break-up was consciously modelled on the aviation industry. Railtrack itself was the equivalent of the airports, with responsibility for the tracks, main stations and signalling; it would have franchise contracts with some 25 operators who were responsible for running the trains in the same way as the airlines flew the aircraft. Their job was to maximise revenue by optimising their marketing strategy to passengers. Because the franchises were short – typically at seven years – the operating companies would lease their train sets from three specialist rolling stock owners, just as airlines often leased their aircraft from lessors.

The system was overseen by a regulator, who would set the level of charges that Railtrack was allowed to levy from the operators. The first regulator was John Swift, a barrister, who had just determined what Railtrack could charge for the next five years. He had laid down a regime under which charges would fall by 8% below the rate of inflation in the subsequent year and 2% a year thereafter. This would allow the train operators the information required to bid for their franchises – the winner would typically be the bidder that wanted the least subsidy to run the trains for the period.

The falling charges assumed that there was plenty of fat in the costs that British Rail incurred. "We reckon we can make big savings in maintenance," we were told. "We are currently in the process of letting out the contracts for maintaining and renewing track."

Soon afterwards Bob Horton, the chairman of Railtrack and former chief executive of BP, told us: "We've had our strike and now we are getting rid of all the Spanish practices that the signalmen were up to." In the summer of 1994 the signalmen had launched a series of strikes to defend their work practices, but the company had stuck to its guns and they had caved in. "We estimate big savings here," said Bob.

Everything, however, was running behind plan, which was hardly surprising given the complexity of the arrangements and the number of different companies that had to be established, before contracts could be agreed with them. We went back to our office in sombre mood.

Meanwhile the tone of the press comment we read each day continued to deteriorate.

"The unpalatable truth for Railtrack . . . is that almost no one in Britain believes that breaking up the network into more than 60 units and selling them individually will be anything other than a disaster for the customers and very possibly for investors as well," The Independent informed us on 12 April.

"If British Rail devised its timetables on the same basis of optimism employed by government ministers forecasting the progress of rail privatisations, it is doubtful whether a single train would run on time," The Financial Times wrote on 5 June, adding for good measure that Railtrack was "the most controversial and unpopular privatisation of recent years."

By 16 August the Guardian had decided that: "Privatisation of the railways, which looked bizarre . . . is now looking positively loopy."

The flood of hostile commentary was unstoppable. "Where's all this stuff coming from?" I asked Jenny Williams, the undersecretary at the Department of Transport who was in day-by-day charge of the Railtrack flotation.

"It's all the British Rail people who see their jobs disappearing," she hypothesised. Jenny was an incredibly hard-working civil servant who somehow managed to attend the key working meetings during the day and prepare all the necessary internal memoranda for the department machine in the evening.

I didn't worry about the rights and wrongs of the criticism. We were at war; and as the executive in charge of marketing the flotation, I was in the front line.

"What are you planning to do?" asked Jenny pointedly.

"Nothing," I replied. I added, "Yet.

"We have to let this stuff all come out and then launch a sustained counter-attack. And I think I know how to do it."

I explained my plan. "We've lost the transport journalists. That's over. They've written up all this negative stuff and they can hardly reverse themselves without looking idiots. So it's a waste of time trying.

"We have to switch the story towards the financial journalists, which we can do when the float process gets under way. And there are two issues they will be concerned about. Firstly, will it be cheap? We can engineer that. Second, is the flow of future earnings reliable?"

Jenny looked at me quizzically. She was a master at this kind of expression.

"Here's the point," I said. "Like all the other regulators, John Swift has got a duty to ensure that Railtrack can finance its activities. It's not a cast-iron guarantee of profits growth but it provides a lot of comfort for investors. We need to get the regulator in front of institutions to give them that comfort in person. The financial press will take their tone from the investors."

Accordingly I set about arranging a conference for investors with all the main parties of the new railway industry, The Secretary of State, Sir George Young; Bob Horton, the chairman of Railtrack; Roger Salmon, the franchising director; and John Swift, the regulator.

"Really we only need John Swift," I admitted, "but we can hardly call an investor conference with him as the sole speaker. The others provide cover." My initial plan to hold the conference in October slipped to January, as delays to the tortuous re-organisation of the railway industry pushed back the float timing from the first quarter of 1996 to May.

"What do you think about Virgin joining our consortium?" asked Nick Wakefield on the phone. He was over at the offices of London & Continental just off Oxford Street in central London.

"I'd be really against it."

"Why?"

"They're so difficult to work with," I said. I knew what I was talking about. A decade earlier we had been appointed broker to the Virgin Group. It was one of my early experiences of floating a company and it had not been particularly happy. Right from the start the relationship had been strained. Richard Branson, the charismatic owner of Virgin, had selected Roger Seelig of Morgan Grenfell, almost as glamorous, to be his adviser and Roger had directed his client towards us to handle the broking. My first meeting was with Trevor Abbott, Branson's in-house financier, from whom I was tasked with collecting enough information to put together a coherent plan for issuing stock to investors. This plan would be the base for the subsequent meeting with Branson himself, effectively our pitch to him. The initial fact-finding phase was also an opportunity to impress a potential client by the depth and understanding of the questions.

Not this time. Abbott stuttered his way through the answers and quite clearly did not have a clue about large aspects of Branson's business. A day or so later the message came back to Nick Verey from Roger Seelig that I should be kept under control. So much for making an impression.

Despite this unhappy start, a visit to the Branson houseboat in north-west London's fashionable Little Venice confirmed our appointment. We got to work. But Branson was a difficult client. His public image was that of a showman, so I was genuinely surprised by the difficulty he had in expressing himself as I prepared him for his first round of institutional visits. Nor did his comfort in answering investor questions improve after his Virgin vehicle was floated. A business style which appeared to be based on making instinctive judgements – and which he did not seem able to articulate with any precision even after the event – was the antithesis of the strategic analysis which professional investors were accustomed to hearing from other companies.

It was a relief when Branson bought back the quoted stock from investors in 1987 and took Virgin private. I had no enthusiasm to repeat the experience of working with the group.

Nick Wakefield was on the phone again. "I'm sorry, David, we've had to let Virgin join London & Continental as equal partners."

"Bloody hell," I swore. "What on earth for?"

"They were threatening to join Eurorail if we wouldn't have them. And we were frightened at what Branson's marketing muscle and Government contacts could do for the other side."

"You'll regret it," I said icily. Nick had a way of blithely pushing ahead with his own strategy, regardless of the views of any of his colleagues.

I was becoming seriously worried about London & Continental. In theory in 1995 it still wasn't my deal. But the reality, as I saw all too clearly, was that it was too big to duck. The full cost of the project was estimated at more than £4bn, representing the biggest privately-funded rail project in the world. In the new SBC Warburg the sectors would have full responsibility for all the projects which fell under their area. If I wanted to run the transport sector it was not an option (as it would have been under Warburg) to fold my arms as others attempted to secure the financing. Nor would a personal strategy of rejection be of any service to my sector plans. If London & Continental ran into trouble it would be so humiliating for the bank as a whole that any attempt to maintain a well-resourced transport sector thereafter would be a waste of time, regardless of whether or not I had been personally involved.

Better, I decided, was to involve myself fully to make sure the consortium's bid had at least some chance of being financed. In October I briefed the most experienced of my team on the task of checking that the London & Continental figures stood up. Ben Storey was a young merchant banker who had moved to us from Kleinwort Benson a couple of years earlier.

"This must not be another Eurotunnel," I insisted to him. "I want you to go through every damn figure in the model that Nick has put together. He's got deal fever. He's spent so long on London & Continental that he can't afford to lose the bid. You know how easy it is to manipulate the data if you want to flatter the returns. A quarter percent on a travel assumption here, a quarter percent off the financing cost there and pretty soon, when they're in perpetuity, you've whistled up hundreds of millions. Check every bloody line."

I was undoubtedly being unfair to Nick in my strictures. He had been battling heroically to reduce some sky-high traffic forecasts and squeeze out contracting margins. However, from my perspective the consortium projections were personified by Nick, and I brought my pressure to bear on him. Indeed, later he admitted to me that "My loyalty was to get the deal done," so my muttering about deal fever may not have been too wide of the mark.

While Ben spent the next few weeks over at the London & Continental headquarters, just off Oxford Street, we attended various presentations by the contracting team and the traffic consultants. As the adviser to the consortium it was our job to be sure that the bid we put in could be financed. This meant writing a letter to the Secretary of State for Transport that the proposals were realistic. We could only write a letter like this after an exhaustive review of the submission, independent of the working team under Nick Wakefield.

In the end it boiled down to a gut feel. The difficulty was summed up succinctly by Andrew Barker, the head of the transport research team. "Each year's revenue forecast in the London & Continental model is based on 450 assumptions (15 assumptions in each of 30 different market segments). Two of the assumptions in each market segment have some scientific basis (underlying growth rate, "generation factor"); the others (market share, distribution of traffic into 12 different fare bands) are purely subjective and based on the forecasters' personal experience of the market."

As I looked over the model I became more and more concerned that the bid we were planning to put in, for about £1.5bn of subsidy, would be inadequate to build the new link. If we bid for too little subsidy, we might win the franchise only to go bust later.

My secretary, Liz Collick, was shaking her head. "It's more difficult to set up a meeting between you and Nick than anyone external. He's out for several days; you're back and forth from Germany and the Far East." In the end we held the meeting in late November in a room at the Radisson hotel at Heathrow just before I travelled out to Hong Kong. Ben Storey kept score. It was fairly stormy.

"I've got the deepest doubts about public equity after Eurotunnel anyway," I told Nick, "and now you've set it up so that we need £800m of the stuff."

"There's no other way, David. That's the only source of funding for this kind of risk."

"And £1.5bn subsidy is much too skinny. It should be nearer £2.1bn, as best I can tell."

Nick was aghast. "We can't go back to Government with that kind of figure. There's no way we could justify a jump like that from our indicative bid back in September."

"So what?"

"At that kind of price we'll lose the bid to Eurorail." Later Nick told me that his fury with me was fuelled by some reliable inside information that we were ranking behind Eurorail.

For an hour we shouted back and forth, going over one point of detail after another as we tried to press our arguments home. The room was dispiriting and the table too small to quarrel over without spitting in each others' eyes. We spent most of the time on our feet, waving bits of paper carrying particular runs of figures. In the end I accepted the equity component in return for a 20% increase in the costs of building the link and similar cuts in the assumptions for traffic revenue as well as other changes. It would imply a subsidy of £1.8bn. After a series of internal meetings at the bank and board meetings at London & Continental the bid was submitted on 15 December. The precise figure was kept deliberately secret from all but a handful of people – to avoid any possibility of a leak to Eurorail. I was angry but not particularly surprised to learn later that Nick had used the cover offered by such secrecy to ease back our agreed level to £1.73bn. What we did not know, until later, was that the Eurorail team were being rather more successfully squeezed by their investment committee and NatWest insisted on them raising their subsidy requirement at the very last moment. As best I can establish, the Eurorail bid for subsidy came in pretty close to the £2.1bn I had been agitating for. At the time I reckoned, cynically, that if it later emerged that we were £300m short the Government would probably find some way to plug the gap, given the importance of the project. The size of the gap that did in fact emerge a couple of years later did not figure in my worst nightmares.

By the end of 1995 we were getting to grips with the new shape of the rail industry as we prepared Railtrack for flotation. In October I had arranged for Richard Holloway to move into the Department of Transport on a temporary basis. He had been in charge of press relations through the collapse of S.G.Warburg, an experience leaving him admirably equipped to handle the chaos as the rail industry was restructured. Steadily he worked with the in-house department team to develop and communicate coherent answers to the myriad questions about the industry which were acceptable to all parties. Early in the New Year, on 5 January 1996, I felt confident enough to be quoted in the Financial Times on the flotation of

Railtrack, saying: "Four years ago we might have promoted it as a symbol of the renaissance of the railways but there is not much appetite for that now. It will be a pragmatic, practical campaign emphasising the company's role in the railway system, the reliability of its earnings and the share value." I might have chosen my words more carefully, since our own analysts had put out a report entitled 'A Platform for Renaissance' only eight months earlier. I also cut across Bob Horton, the chairman's, favourite renaissance theme and had to write him a grovelling letter. Nevertheless, the quotation was a valuable base for the lowered expectations we needed to establish to float the company.

The investor conference on Monday, 29 January, was a great success despite some last-minute wobbles. At one stage during the rehearsals Bob Horton and John Swift, the regulator, rushed out of the room to argue privately, and ferociously, about an aspect of the penalty system. On the day itself more than 100 institutional investors turned up for the 10.30am kick-off, packing our ground-floor presentation room. The morning was launched by Sir George Young, the Secretary of State for Transport, followed by John Swift and then Roger Salmon, responsible for franchising out the service to operators. Bob Horton took the platform after coffee, to be succeeded by our own rail analyst, Wyn Ellis.

As I had hoped, John Swift, the Regulator, was the outstanding performer, drawing on his courtroom experience as a top QC. "Unlike other utilities, I have been involved in the industry from well before privatisation," he pointed out. This was a reference to the notorious behaviour of some regulators and a side-swipe at the electricity regulator, Stephen Littlechild, in particular, who 10 months earlier had incurred the wrath of the audience by saying he was considering tighter price controls just one day after the Government's £4bn generator sale, resulting in the prompt collapse of their share prices. "There can be no interference with the contractual matrix for the next six years," he pointed out, reassuring the audience that it would be difficult for a subsequent Labour Government to unstitch the new structure. He concluded by stating that: "Railtrack will function in a stable regulatory regime consistent with strong incentives for improvement."

It proved to be the turning point in the campaign. According to the salesman tasked with collecting feedback the institutional investors thought that although there were still plenty of questions to address and subject to a high yield: "This could be the better utility stock to go through the next election with." That positive view worked its way back through the analysts in the other investment banks to the financial journalists. Suddenly we were on the front foot.

The traditional row between Government and the privatising company ensued. How much debt could Railtrack carry? What allowance should be made for Railtrack's plans to upgrade the West Coast Main Line and widen the link through central London, Thameslink? The civil servants were reduced to their most violent threats about Bob Horton, as the stand-off reached a head in February: "No knighthood for him," one muttered angrily. "No knighthood for him." The outcome was a relatively modest level of debt for the company, at £586m, designed to allow it to take on the projects. Bob was knighted in the New Year's Honours list at the end of the year

"The investors will value the company more highly if it incorporates these projects," Robert Jennings argued at one of our internal meetings, referring mainly to Thameslink. "It means that Railtrack will have some growth." At that stage the West Coast project was budgeted at less than £1bn over normal expenditure and the Thameslink project at £600m. Robert had spent a long session with Professor Brian Mellitt, Railtrack's director of engineering and production, checking that the West Coast modernisation project in particular was under control. He was careful to ensure that the findings were documented in the prospectus. Under the plan the trackside signalling would be ripped up and replaced by an in-train control system. Railtrack acknowledged that "this is an area of technical innovation and associated risks." However a more conventional back-up would not be appreciably more expensive: "An alternative could be implemented, if necessary, within acceptable cost and time parameters[3]". We had no idea that we were dealing with one of the prime issues that was, five years later, to bring the company down.

We were much more worried that the Labour Party, increasingly certain to win the next election, would make effective threats about what it would do when it came into Government and thereby undermine the attraction of investing in the company. The news that Tony Blair, the leader of the party, had ruled out renationalisation, brought only partial relief. Despite a web of contracts that would make the new structure extraordinarily complicated to undo, there were plenty of vulnerable points.

When the Labour party discovered that we planned to publish their policy in the prospectus they responded by delivering a letter from the shadow Transport Secretary, Clare Short. This was extraordinarily lucky. Clare Short was a feisty left-winger, much beloved by Labour party stalwarts, but prone to bouts of candour which laid her open to press attack. She was distrusted by Tony Blair, particularly after calling for a review of cannabis legislation the year before. Her letter held no truck with the 'less is more' concept of communication, running to nearly 3,000 turgid words. Encouraged by us, the journalists dismissed the contents of the letter, when released at the end of March, as toothless without renationalisation.

"I'm not so sure we're off the hook," I told the team afterwards. "There's a very nasty paragraph near the bottom that could scupper us if the press gets hold of it. She's threatening to take control of the rail regulator and then cut the costs charged by Railtrack to use the railway. That could be very nasty[4]".

Clare Short, too, must have worked out the impact this threat could have and a week later we heard that she was planning to reinforce the message. We waited with trepidation. Then miraculously, on Sunday 14 April, she said on television that middle-income earners should pay more tax. Suddenly she was big news – and not for transport matters. She had put at risk the strategy at the heart of Tony Blair's election tactics: reassurance of the middle-class over Labour's tax plans. Her claims were denied outright by Labour's briefing team and she spent the rest of the week sheltering from a press desperate to obtain more damaging tax quotes from her. Once she was caught on television burying her head in a coat to deny the photographers. In these circumstances she could hardly court the press on transport matters and her planned remise of

Labour's Railtrack plan was aborted. The day after her gaffe we launched the preliminary version of the prospectus and the Railtrack roadshow got under way.

By now the press had turned genuinely positive. The Independent on Sunday told its readers on 14 April: "My view is that this is one rail journey well worth taking". The financial press took the pragmatic line that since the flotation was extremely unpopular, the Government would have to sell cheaply. There was a contradiction buried here, since the large numbers responding to this investment argument pushed the price back up. Nevertheless, as the formal sale period began in early May, demand was growing strongly and the main debate we were having with Government was whether to move the price above the initial range. In the end Railtrack was priced at the top of the range at £3.90 a share – valuing the whole company (including debt) at £2.5bn. At this level demand covered the shares available six times over, a healthy but not embarrassing oversubscription. In the immediate after-market the price behaved, going to a premium of 10% on the partly paid price (or 5% for the fully-paid equivalent). It had been a surprising success, as the press – whose role had been so critical – acknowledged. "The privatisation float has proved an outstanding success," concluded The Sunday Times on 19 May. The next day The Financial Times bestowed a rare accolade: "The flotation today of Railtrack . . .crowns one of the most complex privatisations ever attempted." And from The Times on the same day: "The response to the offer has exceeded all expectations." The bemused participants in the process, all inured to failure or worse, responded by attending a series of celebration parties, none grander than that held by Railtrack on the Thursday after the launch at the Natural History Museum in west London's Kensington.

London & Continental was declared the winner of the bid for the Channel Tunnel Rail Link on 29 February 1996. Nick Wakefield confirmed that he was moving over to the new company, leaving the project firmly in my lap as far as the bank was concerned. My first concern was to find a first-class banker who would grip the project on a day-by-day basis. Instinctively I knew there would a major crisis in the transaction at some point and a last-minute draftee would have no chance of helping me solve it.

At the end of March I approached Robert Jennings, who was in the process of winding down his full-time involvement in the Railtrack flotation. Robert was five years younger than me, at 41, from a family with historic links to the transport industry. His grandmother was reputed to have been the richest women in Scotland after inheriting the fortune of her uncle, Sir William McKinnon, based on ownership of the British India Shipping line. Robert's own upbringing in the Home Counties was rather more modest. After qualifying as an accountant with Coopers & Lybrand, he spent his early Warburg career in Tokyo, working in corporate finance, before coming back to execute transactions in the UK. He was shrewd, creative and careful.

Now he replied, "I'll do it, David, but not as a one-off. I want to join your transport team and see if I can build a global rail franchise – if there's enough business out there." Until then, I had not envisaged Robert as a marketer but I was quick to decide that I could be flexible about my preconceptions. I desperately needed a banker of Robert's calibre on London & Continental and besides, if he took an interest in the unloved rail sector we might succeed in positioning ourselves for future business. In the years to come he was to prove able to apply his under-stated style to winning a string of major mandates. It was not only the flamboyant who succeeded in drumming up business.

I was not the only one with recruitment problems. Derek Hornby, the avuncular chairman of London & Continental, realised he needed a more dynamic chief executive. Luckily the board member from National Express, Adam Mills, decided that this was a role that would interest him. Adam was the deputy chief executive of National Express, having been its finance director when it floated four years previously. He was a tough, experienced accountant, fully capable of getting to grips with the problems of a combined transport operation and construction project. In March he was seconded as the acting chief executive of London & Continental, a role which was formalised in October.

"David, for God's sake where have you been?" It was mid-morning with just over a week to go before the formal takeover of the Channel Tunnel Railway Link at the end of May. I had just returned to my desk from an external meeting when David Beever, the Warburg director on the London & Continental board, tracked me down. "Branson is attempting to do a takeover downstairs. You've got to stop him."

It so happened that London & Continental was holding its regular board meeting in our offices. I hurried downstairs with David to the large room at which the members of the board were assembled. Sitting round the table were representatives from Bechtel, National Express, the French railways, London Electricity, consultant contractors Halcrow and Arup, as well as various members of the management team. As I entered, Richard Branson stood at the head of the table, in his trademark jumper, clarifying some points in his team's presentation. They were proposing that the Eurostar rail service to Paris and Brussels was rebranded Virgin Eurostar. Whatever else, it would certainly be a stunning introduction for Richard's ambitions in the UK rail industry.

"We think it has real marketing impact," he was saying. "We've mocked up some signage so you can see how it will look." He reached over for some cardboard presentation sheets that had been lying on the table beside him. He raised the first one for us to see. 'Virgin Eurostar', it read. "We've done the Virgin in our red branding and left the Eurostar unchanged," he pointed out helpfully. There was a long pause. No one was willing to take him on. Then Derek Hornby looked down the room. "Perhaps we could have the view of our adviser on this proposition?" Across the table Adam Mills glared at me helpfully. I collected my thoughts as best I could.

"I am not in a position to comment on the branding issues," I started off carefully. "My concern is strictly with the implications for our planned flotation." I was desperately sceptical about whether a flotation could take place but this was one occasion when it could be useful. "I don't think institutional investors would accept a company that did not control its active brand. They wouldn't want the risk of the brand-name being damaged in another of your companies, Richard, and knocking the value of their quoted company. Also, we would have to work out the impact of the royalty payments on the revenue line."

"Though you are not proposing that we pay royalties for the use of the Virgin brand-name, as I understand it, Richard?" asked Derek Hornby.

Richard Branson turned a very hostile gaze from me and looked uncomfortably at the ceiling. "Well, no," he muttered. "I don't think that's the case." Vaguely he added, "We were planning to charge some fees for the licence agreement, as we always do."

Little more was said and the meeting broke up soon afterwards. Richard Branson's first attempt to capture Eurostar had failed. But he was not about to give up.

After the board meeting Adam Mills raged at the Virgin team seconded to run the Eurostar marketing and sales operation and whom he blamed for the attempt to rebrand the service. "I don't want the fucking shambles that we had yesterday at the board ever again," he was reported to have told the senior Virgin secondee, Ian Brooks. "I won't be raped at the altar and you can pass that back to your colleagues." For good measure he added, according to Ian Brooks, "Listen son, don't you try to threaten us – there're big people here and they are not going to be pushed around."

On his way to Italy, Richard Branson sent a letter to Derek Hornby complaining at this rough treatment and warning that he would remove the Virgin team if there was no a resolution to the conflict. By the following week Virgin was refusing to put up its £10m founder equity stake, due by Friday 31 May, unless it got its way.

"Well, what are we going to do?" demanded Derek Hornby at a small meeting held with Adam Mills to consider tactics. "It would be bloody difficult to go with the rebranding, even if we wanted to. The French were absolutely livid about the proposal."

We contemplated re-organising the consortium and maybe introducing British Airways in place of Virgin if they remained obdurate. We would need permission from the Government to make such a change.

"In the end he'll fold," I prophesied. "That's the style. He runs things to the edge and then he concedes."

"It's extremely wearing for the rest of us, though," sighed Derek

Hornby, as he made arrangements to talk to Colin Marshall, the chairman of British Airways.

However, the British Airways card remained unplayed on this occasion. My prediction proved accurate and Richard Branson dropped his demands at the last moment. Virgin paid over the £10m to remain a founder shareholder of the company.

Adam Mills set about organising the management of the company. His key requirement was an experienced finance director "What about Nick Wakefield?" he asked me. "He's basically been the driving force in assembling the consortium and driving through the negotiation with the Government."

We agreed that Nick did not have the background to be the finance director (as Nick himself subsequently agreed). Given the slim management structure of the company this meant that the role that Adam did find for him, as deputy chief executive, was from the beginning somewhat peripheral.

Adam's priority remained the need for a finance director. His sense of urgency had been underpinned by a phone call received immediately after the deal went through at the beginning of June. It was from Ernst & Young, the auditors of Eurostar. "We need to see you," they said. "Now."

"They told me they were going to qualify the accounts because of a failure to keep proper books and records," Adam later confided to me. "They couldn't get the results out closer than £1m to £10m a month." By then the Eurostar service had been operating for just over six months.

In early July I was introduced to the leading candidate for the finance director role. Robert Holden was a gritty northerner who had learned his trade as an audit accountant at Ernst & Young and then become the finance director of the naval shipbuilder VSEL. It was an overwhelming relief to meet some-one with such a down-to-earth, careful and methodical approach.

"You're main job," I told him at that first meeting, "will be to find the 'Wakefield gap'." This was the shorthand term I used for the hole in the bid I was sure was there. It was, of course, unfair to Nick but I could not resist the pun. I was convinced we needed to find the hole and develop ways to plug it before we could achieve any serious financing for the project. The 'Wakefield gap' became a favourite catch phrase for the team as the months progressed – albeit out of Nick's hearing.

For the time being it began to look as if my fears were misplaced. Through the autumn we established all the normal procedures for running a big flotation, planned for November 1997. We built up the float timetable, consulted the senior salesmen – who were positive, surprisingly (at least to me) – and Robert started assembling the materials for a prospectus. In mid-September the company held a briefing day, inviting the City transport analysts to a presentation on the project at the disused, but still magnificent, St Pancras Chambers. This was the red Gothic building at the front of the London terminal that was to be re-instated as a hotel. The presentation, mainly by the contractors working on the project to build the new rail link, was polished and effective. The analysts sitting under the battered but still ornate high ceiling of the former reception hall were, I could tell, extremely impressed. For a moment I allowed myself to dream that the float strategy would work after all.

The moment passed all too briefly.

Adam Mills had by now got to grips with the performance of Eurostar. "Basically the Government has sold us a bill of goods," he confessed ruefully. "We were expecting Eurostar to lose £60m in the first year. Now we've got the figures sorted out, the loss seems to be running at an annual rate of £300m." Whether the vendor, in the shape of the Government, shared the blame for this disaster, or whether it was solely the problem of an over-enthusiastic bidder was to remain unresolved despite intensive inquiry.

"Far from being the advertised flow of cash to support building the project, Eurostar is a terrible drain," concluded Adam. He was deeply unhappy about the Virgin team's attempts to drum up business by cutting prices and offering cut-price deals. The monthly deficit was simply not closing.

"Their promotions may put on a few extra passengers but they destroy the revenue line," he fumed. He was particularly upset at a promotion in The Times which sold tickets at below operating cost. The leader of the Virgin team, Ian Brooks, was transferred out of the company in October. Passenger numbers seemed to be stuck at a little over six million a year, no more than half the level predicted for this period by the traffic forecasts.

At least the marketing strategy had been in the company's hands in those early months. In late November I listened to the radio with growing dismay as reports came through about an extensive fire in the tunnel. One of the lorries on an open rail carriage caught fire during a French truck-drivers strike. Afterwards unverified stories circulated that a striker had thrown a burning torch onto the lorry before it entered the tunnel. Whatever the cause, the driver of the shuttle train stopped midway allowing the blaze to intensify to a maximum of 1100°C. The passengers were rescued by the narrowest of margins. The tunnel was damaged for a distance of 480 metres[5].

The implications soon became apparent. With only a single track operational for a stretch under the channel, the Eurostar service would be severely disrupted. Instead of three and a half hours the trip to Paris would take nearer four and a half, and fewer trains would run. Far from closing the revenue gap, Eurostar would be in limbo till the damage was repaired, which would not be till the following summer. Worst of all, the pattern of demand from passengers would be disrupted at a critical period, undermining any attempt to build long-term projections until the reintroduction of a normal service.

In December the third shoe dropped. Adam Mills discovered that only a 35% confidence factor could be attached to the £2.8bn forecast for the cost of the project. At the 95% confidence level, the capital cost expected would rise to £3.6bn. We never got to the bottom of how the misunderstanding arose. It blew all our calculations out of the water. Taken together with the running sore of Eurostar, and after offsetting various savings and other initiatives, Rob Holden reckoned that the shortfall was now running somewhere between £400m and £500m. He had found the 'Wakefield gap' with a vengeance.

"When does the money run out?" I asked.

"February 1998," said Rob.

"Just as well," I replied. We were now caught up in the political timetable with an election expected in the early summer of 1997 and Labour regarded as the certain winner. The Conservative Government, beset by daily accusations of sleaze in the media, was in no position to sort out the crisis. "Tell it to the next lot," said Sir George Young, Transport Secretary, when Adam and Derek Hornby called on him with the problems in February 1997. We would have to wait for our new political masters.

"We'll never float now," I said to Robert Jennings, as we sat together reviewing our options.

"Maybe we can sell it to Railtrack?" thought Robert.

"Yes, but how do we get ourselves off the flotation track without getting sued to hell." Both Virgin and Bechtel were known to employ tough tactics in business affairs.

"It's the consortium from hell," agreed Robert.

"We'll get a new traffic forecast," I suggested. "I'm sure that Steer Davies Gleave have been hopelessly optimistic. If it's lower we can use it to inject some reality into the process." So, together with London & Continental, we employed the consultants LEK to double-check the work produced by Steer Davies for the original bid. Their report would be ready in the late summer. Adam Mills, meanwhile, took a few steps of his own as the difficulties mounted and in March asked Nick Wakefield to resign his role as deputy chief executive. Nick was to find himself stranded, since there was no longer a coherent project finance department for him to return to at Warburg.

Robin Budenberg looked at me with some incredulity. "Are you really sure you want to do this, David?" Robin ran the business review group in the corporate finance division, which approved all the pieces of work that individual bankers took on. "We never act for political parties as a rule," he pointed out.

"I know it's unusual," I confessed. "We'd never heard of Geoffrey Robinson, but Shriti checked him out and he is genuinely on a mission from Blair and Brown." Shriti Vadera was a junior director in the department who had extremely close links with the Labour Party. "They want to have a strategy for the London Underground and Robinson has asked us to create it for them."

"Does he know we did Railtrack?"

"He doesn't seem to care. He wants our expertise"

"And how much is Mr Robinson proposing to pay us?"

"£10,000."

Robin laughed. "That'll keep the team in shoe leather for about a day," he reckoned.

"But the Underground will be a hefty piece of work. If we do this study for them and they like it, I would expect us to be rewarded with the mandate to reorganise it."

"OK, David. If you and Robert want to do it, go ahead."

Geoffrey Robinson was the MP for Coventry North West and enjoyed an independent fortune. He was one of the few senior businessmen in the Parliamentary party, having been chief executive of Jaguar, the luxury car manufacturer. His wealth was fairly evident as Robert Jennings and I went to a series of meetings with him at his flat in London's elegant Grosvenor House on Park Lane.

"We want to inject private sector expertise into the Tube, but we don't want to privatise it," he explained to us at our first session.

Robert developed a clever plan for the system.

"You can sell 49% of the infrastructure to a private group," explained Robert at the closing meeting at which we delivered our report. "That'll bring in about £1bn to modernise the system, but you'll still have control with your 51%. Then you can franchise out the train service to one or maybe two private operators. They should be able to run the service for considerably less than London Underground."

"It's a classic public/private partnership structure that Robert's developed," I added.

"Thank you very much," said Robinson. "That is excellent. Let me have some extra copies."

Later we heard that he was quick to deliver our document to his political masters, whom it evidently impressed. The payback came after Labour duly won the election in May. Much to the surprise of the party (and in particular the long-serving MP who thought he was in line for the post), the obscure Robinson was promoted to the important Treasury job of Paymaster General. He was given responsibility for public/private partnerships and for establishing a Treasury Taskforce to accelerate the process of involving private companies in the public sector.

Our reward was less satisfactory. When we formally pitched to the Government for the Underground business on 18 July, we found the outcome far from a foregone conclusion. The civil servants who interviewed us were extremely concerned that our obligations to London & Continental meant that Robert, in particular, could not make a full-time commitment to work on this mandate. It went, instead, to a rival who claimed he could devote 100% of his time to it.

"Geoffrey Robinson did not lift a single finger in our support." I said ruefully to Robert at the gloomy post-presentation lunch where we drowned our sorrows. "That's the last time we work for a political party." In fact, we learned later, the Underground portfolio had been captured by John Prescott, the Deputy Prime Minister who had overall charge of transport within a new super-Ministry. Robinson could probably not have delivered the mandate to us even if he had wanted to.

In practice it had been a lucky escape. Our plan was duly given to our rival to replicate (or so we heard later). But it was thoroughly undermined by the political imperatives of John Prescott. The train operations, with all their inefficiencies, were retained in the public sector, while the infrastructure was sold to the private sector in its entirety under extraordinarily complicated contracts. The process, disrupted by the newly arrived Mayor of London, Ken Livingstone, took some five painful years to complete.

By September 1997 London & Continental was in deep crisis. The LEK traffic projections were way below those of Steer Davies Gleave and ruled out any chance of raising debt or equity from the private markets. We had hit the wall in style. It was not a question of an underbid by £300m or £500m. By the time we were able to work out the figures comprehensively we found we needed an injection or more than £1bn to finance the project. Our only hope was to find a new investor and either sell the project to them, in whole or part, or go into partnership. The only company that could conceivably perform either role was Railtrack, and in mid-October we formally approached them.

Railtrack was a company transformed since we had floated it 15 months earlier. For the first couple of months the share price had been static. Then on 25 July 1996 Blair moved Clare Short from the shadow transport portfolio, a step taken to signal a far more positive attitude to the company from the presumptive future Government. In the autumn the share price took off, soaring through the £5 barrier in November. Wyn Ellis, our lead rail analyst was quick off the mark when it moved through £5. "I'm telling investors to sell it at £5.40p," he told me. He seized the opportunity with relief; he had been anxious at recommending the offer at all, and now he could clean the slate. The investors had bought the shares; he had told them to sell; they had made money. Unfortunately for him, the Railtrack price went soaring on up and the effect of his call was to destroy his reputation on the stock with the investors and salesforce.

Meanwhile, our relationship with the company had suffered a reverse.

"I'm sorry, we can't do it," I explained to Norman Broadhurst, the combative chief financial officer of Railtrack, three months after the float. He had asked us to take some of the Railtrack debt that Barclays Bank was trying to syndicate. The deal was badly stuck and Barclays was going to end up holding too much of it. When I checked with the credit officers they estimated that we would need an internal subsidy of several million pounds to take it. The tough stance that our parent Swiss Bank Corporation adopted to lending was a regular problem in our relationships with companies, who expected loans at low rates now that we were owned by a major bank. There was no way I could justify such a discount below the true cost of capital nor, as I explained to Norman, would our support for Barclays offer much benefit to Railtrack itself.

"Well," concluded Norman abruptly, "If you can't help out in this instance, I'm afraid you can't expect to do other, more lucrative, business with us."

The share price continued to astonish. It had a corrosive impact on the company where management saw it as market corroboration for everything it did. Soon Railtrack was earning a reputation for arrogance, especially in the way it handled the rail operators, its clients. "You can't have a dialogue with them," one of them complained to me privately. "They just tell you how it's going to be and that's that."

"David, I've got a chum who's being offered the job of chief executive of Railtrack." It was Steven Latner, one of my corporate finance colleagues, on the phone. By now it was the summer of 1997. "He's looking for advice. Should he take the job?"

"Tell him he'll need to be happy handling politicians and the media," I replied. "It simply isn't an ordinary company where you only have to worry about the customers and shareholders. If anything goes wrong the politicians will be right on your back. If he doesn't mind that, he should take it."

Whether or not Gerald Corbett appreciated my second-hand advice, he took the job in September. Gerald was immensely approachable, a short and jovial figure, full of impromptu quips relayed to the accompaniment of short barks of laughter. There could not have been a greater contrast with his predecessor, the tall and austere John Edmonds. In October Gerald received our offer to become involved with London & Continental, to which he responded with great interest. We sent the company all the information it needed to make a decision, but our negotiations were undermined as the underlying figures at London & Continental continued to deteriorate. Over the turn of the year he decided that the project's finances were simply too parlous and ended the talks. He could wait till London & Continental went under and negotiate from strength. We were on our own.

"We simply can't agree a solution right now," said David Rowlands, the senior rail civil servant at a meeting on 1 December. "It's a question of getting the attention of ministers. The Deputy Prime Minister is regularly absent from the country. At the moment he is bound up in the negotiations at Kyoto." This was the international convention held in Japan that agreed the protocol to contain global warming. John Prescott was now the head of a new super-ministry that encompassed the environment and regions, as well as transport – the DETR. We had the acute impression that civil servants were finding it hard to connect with their new political masters.

"I wouldn't want to exclude folding the project," warned David Rowlands. "It is not owned by the Labour Government. Public expenditure is heavily constrained. It is a realistic option. Nor," he added, consummate civil servant that he was, "am I saying that we are going to kill it."

The meeting was held between London & Continental and ourselves on one side and officials from the Treasury and the DETR on the other. At that stage the Railtrack option was still alive, but fading fast. Much of the meeting was spent investigating ways of funding the project through till ministers could address the problem.

Adrian Montague warned that the solutions "do not mean an open cheque book" from the Treasury. Three months earlier Geoffrey Robinson had appointed him to run the Treasury's Private Finance Initiative. He was the former project finance head at Dresdner Kleinwort Benson and was to become deeply involved in the rescue of London & Continental – his first major foray on behalf of the Government.

It was another two months before the Government – in the shape of John Prescott – was ready to see us and the events I describe at the opening of the book took place. In the early evening of 27 January 1998 Derek Hornby, Adam Mills, Rob Holden, Jeremy Candfield and I arrived at Eland House, the modern office building near London's Victoria station at which the DETR was headquartered. We were sent up to his office, which was crowded with officials and advisers. There were at least 20 in the room, sitting, standing, propped against windowsills and desks. Prescott sat in the middle of the crowd in his armchair and led the meeting. The company officials and I sat in a crescent of chairs facing him to explain the situation.

"If we are to go on we need another £1.2bn of grant, or its equivalent," said Derek Hornby. "The passenger numbers we expected have simply not materialised and the tunnel fire completely disrupted our attempts to ramp up the business at a critical time."

Prescott cross-examined us carefully. None of his entourage

uttered a word through the whole process. At the end he said, "Would you wait outside while we consider what to do?"

We sat in a pokey side office for the best part of an hour while they debated. When we were summoned back into the room, the denouement was rapid. Prescott told us the amount involved was too great and regrettably the Government could not provide support.

This was a decision too big to be taken at a single sitting. Next morning all the shareholders were summoned back to Eland House for a more formal session in the late afternoon, round a huge oval table. The star of the event was to prove the representative on the London & Continental board from Bechtel, John Carter.

Bechtel, which had responsibility for ensuring the new rail link was built, had more at stake than any other member of the consortium. John Carter, the head of this leading US contractor's European operation, was a big, tough west coast American who reminded me of no-one so much as the film star John Wayne. From a role as legal adviser to the contractor over the years, he had become the group's legal counsel and was now one of the select senior team at the Californian company. He was a master of political lobbying round the world and had been disgusted at our careful briefings of the civil servants as the crisis unfolded.

"Why the hell aren't you going to see Tony Blair to sort it out?" he demanded at one of the board meetings in late 1997. "That's the only way to sort something like this. Go straight to the top." He seemed disgusted to learn that we didn't have calling powers on the Prime Minister.

At another board meeting he flew into a histrionic rage when Robert Jennings started to talk about the cost over-runs the project had endured.

"What cost over-runs?" he shouted. "There are no cost over-runs. That's the only goddam thing that hasn't gone wrong with this project. The costs are absolutely rock solid." It was vital to his strategy to make this claim, because otherwise Bechtel too would have been one of the parties for whom official punishment was due. His fury had the desired effect. No one at the board cared to start a debate about the difference between confidence ratings in the projections of 35% and 95%.

He had evidently been hard at work to clear the lines between Bechtel and John Prescott before the formal meeting in January. Now he launched into a full-scale address into the importance of maintaining the momentum of the project despite the apparent financial difficulties

"We can change everything," he said. "We can change the transport operators; we can change the management; we can change the bank." We were in the presence of a master. He was totally unconcerned at the visible shock shown by those he was proposing to eject, who were sitting alongside him. The one change John did not suggest was to the role of Bechtel as lead contractor to the project.

That evening Prescott released a statement to Parliament stating that we had been given 30 days to find a solution to our problems. This was the contractual notice period and next morning I said to Robert Jennings, "We'd better find out how to send the keys back." It would certainly be complicated to close down the company and the project. But when we phoned the department officials it was clear that they did not interpret the meetings with Prescott in quite the same way we did. We thought it was all over; they wanted to see if there was a cheaper solution. The politics of what happened over those two evenings remain a mystery to me. John Prescott may well have been aiming to put pressure on the Treasury by such hardball tactics.

Robert and the team rapidly assembled the options and we sat down to review them.

"There are four," he said, describing them.

"Forget the others. They simply don't save enough. Don't even show them. The only one that works is for the Government to guarantee the debt."

"They specifically told us not to consider that option last year."

"That was last year." I studied the figures. "It really is amazing how much a Government guarantee would be worth. Take away expensive private equity, take away expensive private debt, substitute debt at Government rates and hey presto, we've saved

£1.2bn. Just what we need. Isn't that lucky."

"They won't want it on the Public Sector Borrowing Requirement."

"That's the challenge. We need to find a structure which keeps it off the PSBR."

Robert and I went round to the Treasury to see Adrian Montague.

"If you are going to find a solution with our support you'll have to change the structure of London & Continental," he told us. "It needs to be split up and we'd like to see new people involved both in running the Eurostar service and owning the project to build the new rail link. There's a strong view that the existing team should be suitably punished for their failure."

Quickly I made an appointment to see Bob Ayling, the chief executive of British Airways, whom I had known ever since he witnessed the humiliating ban on my research on the airline by lawyers a decade earlier.

"There's a chance for you to step in as a pure operator, replacing Virgin," I told him. Any chance to upstage Virgin was viscerally attractive to Bob, given the appalling publicity Richard Branson had heaped on the airline in the early 1990s with his law-suits alleging dirty tricks.

"How much risk is there for us in this?" he asked.

"It's limited," I explained. "You'll be the operator not the owner, so we can keep the risk/reward profile in a narrow band."

"I like it," said Bob. "We'll follow it up."

By the time we went back to see Adrian Montague a week later, we had the bones of a structure in place. British Airways would form the back-bone of a consortium to operate Eurostar. Railtrack would take over ownership of the Rail Link once it was completed. London & Continental would become a shell company till the line was complete, financed through Government-guaranteed loans. We argued that these would not score in the PSBR because the asset would be sold to a private company, Railtrack.

Adrian Montague was visibly impressed. "There are some ideas here worthy of development," he told us. "There's some interesting technology here that needs to be worked up." It was a cautious imprimatur to encourage us to pursue this solution. And it came in the nick of time.

We were not the only team manoeuvring for survival in the aftermath of the collapse of London & Continental. We didn't need John Carter's offer to change the bank to alert us to the weakness of our position. The Evening Standard came out with a hostile piece attacking Derek Hornby, the chairman, Adam Mills, the chief executive and me, the adviser to London & Continental on the morning after our second meeting with John Prescott.

"There are some mighty reputations riding on this one - Adam Mills, the plummy former venture capitalist brought in to lead Britain's most prestigious transport project; David Freud, the journalist-turned-Warburg merchant banker, who was to sell the financing to a sceptical City; Will Whitehorn, Richard Branson's ebullient right-hand man, who brought Virgin to the party; Sir Derek Hornby, the amiable but ultimately ineffectual figurehead chairman and father of lad hero Nick.

"They have 30 days to rescue the £5.4bn high-speed Channel Tunnel Rail Link. Given London & Continental Railways' reputation for hitting deadlines, the chances must be almost nil.[6]"

Anthony Hilton rubbed the point home with a comment piece mocking my roles in Eurotunnel and Euro Disney. "Euro-tunnel, Euro-Disney, Euro-loser, the City said to SBC Warburg when it tried to raise money for London & Continental Railways to build the Channel Tunnel rail link. Having been persuaded by SBC Warburg to put money into these earlier massive projects, which proved disastrous for investors, the institutions were not in the mood to fall for the sweet-talking David Freud of SBC Warburg a third time.[7]"

The attack was quite plainly instigated by the Government and felt like the initial blast of a concerted campaign to allocate blame for the company's failure. It was my first direct experience of the Labour Government's aggressive culture of personal blame and its use of the press to attack those it wished to punish.

It certainly had a disconcerting impact. A blown-up transaction on this scale would clearly have serious repercussions not just for me, but for the bank. As the bad publicity mounted, Robert and I felt we were walking round the corridors of our office in a little bubble as people shrank away from us. No one wanted to be associated with our failure.

At the end of the week following the meeting with Prescott our team arrived at London & Continental offices to a cold reception. Robert Jennings rang Adam to find out what was going on. He was apologetic. "I'm afraid we've decided to stand you down," he said.

The following Wednesday 11 February we arrived at the London & Continental board meeting to find that John Carter had a surprise in store for us. Sitting at the table was a corporate financier from Deutsche Bank, Robert Leitao.

"I've employed Deutsche Bank to help sort out this mess," John Carter explained. "I'm sure no-one will object to him joining us at the board." We held our silence. Clearly Carter expected formal confirmation that we were to be removed as the board's adviser imminently.

Robert Leitao was clearly embarrassed at our discomfiture. "I'm not sure we'll be able to do anything at this stage, given the position."

Luckily we had an ace up our sleeve. At the appropriate juncture I said, "Robert and I have just been to see Adrian Montague and he liked the structure we presented to him. He told us 'there are some ideas here worthy of development'."

Now it was John Carter's turn to look uncomfortable, as we regained the initiative. Since it was our structure and the Treasury had cleared us to pursue it, he could hardly force us out of the process. It wasn't as if he had an alternative structure.

In normal circumstances we would undoubtedly have been fired from the account much earlier than this. However we were a founder shareholder of the consortium, with 18% of the stock, and our role as adviser was protected by legal agreement. The potential of the guaranteed fees was the reason Nick Wakefield had been able to clear the project within Warburg in the first place. Even in the collapsed state of the project we could not be forcibly removed against our will. In the same way the Government was forced to work through the London & Continental structure. Any other alternative would have required the project to be bid for again, under European procurement rules, inevitably delaying it by up to a decade.

The Treasury endorsement of our rescue plan was enough to call a halt to the press campaign against the company and me. The Government had not forgiven the company officials, however, and refused to communicate through Derek Hornby and Adam Mills, the chairman and chief executive. When Adam Mills complained to David Rowlands about gross misrepresentation of the company's position in the press, he was asked, "Do you want to see the Government really have a go?" Neither Adam nor Derek were to be part of any solution.

In the desperate scramble of early February, our plan had come under extreme pressure when Gerald Corbett at Railtrack decided that the risks involved in buying both stages of the rail link were too great. We managed to restructure it to allow him to buy the first stage and take an option on the second. This stage involved the building of the line from the Thames to St Pancras and the tunnelling involved undeniably made it riskier than the first stage.

Meanwhile, Railtrack was happy to continue to use Bechtel to build the rail link, and negotiations soon began between them to share the risk of cost over-runs. John Carter's manoeuvring was clearly paying off. However, the pressure to dismiss us took some time to dissipate.

Norman Broadhurst had not forgiven us for our parsimony with the loan book. He lambasted me and a colleague from our banking division at an evening meeting with DETR officials in their new building on Marsham Street. After the meeting, he said: "We need to talk," and led the way into a side office. Gerald Corbett, Railtrack's chief executive, followed, with me close behind. The room was almost entirely dark.

"You have to resign," said Gerald. "Where the fuck is the light switch?"

"We're not resigning," I replied. "It's one of these automatic sensors."

"Well it doesn't seem to be very good at sensing four people in this room."

We stood in the semi-darkness, facing each other.

"You've made a complete bog of this and you should resign if you had any sense of decency," he shouted. Later he admitted that Norman Broadhurst had put him up to the confrontation.

"We're not resigning," I shouted back, "and that's final. The only way this mess is going to get sorted out is if we sort it."

The company put out a tender for a new operator of Eurostar. British Airways joined up with National Express and the French railways to form a consortium, with Virgin challenging on its own – and losing. Meanwhile I had gone round to see Alastair Morton, who was advising Prescott on rail matters.

"I think this structure is quite clever," I explained, "It keeps private sector disciplines, because Railtrack has every incentive to make sure that the line is built to cost, while pushing down the cost of funding through the Government guarantee."

"Well, David, it looks a bit of a cheat to me but it's probably the best that can be done in the circumstances."

Soon afterwards, on 27 March, Prescott announced that enough progress had been made for him to extend the grace period for another two months. There were plenty of caveats round the statement, but the reality was that the period was required to document the solution rather than change it dramatically. On 3 June he formally cleared the deal. We were off the hook. The Channel Tunnel Railway Link would be built and, to my relief, we would not have to try to sell dubious equity to a suspicious market.

When you are an investment banker no one ever says thank you; at least not in words. The reward comes in the form of mandates from a grateful client. In this case we were to receive rewards from two clients. The Government approved an award of the mandate to arrange the debt financing for London & Continental. We were selected (jointly with Deutsche Bank) to raise £2.65bn of bonds for the company in February the following year. We were also allowed to hedge the bonds, so that the first stage of the project would not be vulnerable to fluctuating interest rates but would lock onto a fixed annual rate for the life of the bonds. This was much more profitable for the bank than the bread and butter business of issuing the bonds themselves.

Our quarrel with Railtrack was also resolved amicably, hardly surprising given the astonishing strength of the shares through the first half of 1998, as the deal with London & Continental was hammered out in full view of the market. The shares gained more than 400p through the period and as the originator of the transaction, which had brought such investor approval, we now stood in good odour with the company. Norman Broadhurst, the finance director, said to me: "We're prepared to let you issue our convertible – if we can just sort out a reasonable lending relationship."

Hans de Gier, the chairman of the investment bank in this period, remained sceptical about allowing a loan through. "This stuff is ghastly, David. It sits around on our balance sheet losing us money year after year. Are you really sure we need to lend?"

I took him through the fees we were likely to receive if we did make the loan and finally received reluctant approval. We lent a relatively modest £50m or so directly to Railtrack, fortunately on far less aggressive terms than the Barclays loan. Norman Broadhurst was as good as his word and not only awarded us the £400m convertible to distribute to investors in February 1999 but also cleared the way for us to undertake more complex - and profitable - hedging business. This was related to Railtrack's obligation to buy the first stage of the rail link once it was built under the terms of the London & Continental rescue. Railtrack would be exposed to fluctuating interest rates up to the point when it bought the operation and issued bonds. So it decided to hedge out that risk in advance by fixing the rate for future loans worth £1.5bn. We were the bank brought in as the counter-party for the position, paying funds over to Railtrack if fixed rates rose and relying on them to compensate us if they fell. The market transactions which we conducted to support this position were highly complex. It was a transaction that was to have a vicious sting in its tail.

There was no stopping the Railtrack share price in the early months after the deal. In late September Gerald Corbett came to the annual transport conference in London that I arranged annually and exulted: "The Channel Tunnel Link is a good commercial deal. It will generate good returns for us and our shareholders. But it also symbolises the shift that has occurred in our relationship with the

Government. We've gone from being a sort of Black Pariah to being the White Knight[8]".

The shares peaked on 23 November 1998 at £17.68, four and a half times the £3.90 level we had floated the company at just 30 months before. The timing could not have been more embarrassing. A bare three weeks later, on 16 December, the Government watchdog, The National Audit Office, finally published its damning report on the flotation of the company[9]. Despite our best efforts in months of commenting on the drafts produced by the authors it concluded that we and the Department of Transport had thrown taxpayers' money away by floating the whole company at once – evidencing the subsequent run-up in the stock. "Overall sales proceeds might have been increased by at least £600 million, if the Government had been able to effect a phased sale and had retained 20% of the shares, and by £1.5 billion had they retained 40%".

"I'm not having this," I exploded at James Sassoon as we read through the final text before publication. "Why should we be screwed just because the Railtrack price is mad?"

"I'm not sure that saying that the Railtrack price is mad is an entirely credible defence," James pointed out mildly. "After all, finance professionals are meant to believe that the market is always right."

"No, we'll have to find something else," I fumed. "But the price is mad."

"By the way," warned Robert Jennings, "apparently the Audit Office is planning to talk to journalists the day before the official release. They want to hit us hard."

"Two can play at that game," I muttered, already planning a counter-ambush.

That Tuesday I spent talking to my former colleagues in the press. The outcome was far beyond my expectations and must have horrified Sir John Bourn, the Comptroller and Auditor General.

Neil Collins on The Daily Telegraph said: "The NAO report into the flotation of Railtrack is as scathing as a feather boa, delicately wrapped about an empty centre. The comptroller and his chums have tiptoed around anything which can be said to be political, and thus outside their reporting remit. The result is a ridiculous document.

"Railtrack shares went cheaply because the Conservative government was hanging by a thread, so neither delay nor a partial sale was feasible while Ms Short's hysterical threats were likely to be government policy any minute. As was pointed out here at the time, these were the conditions to create a bargain, and so it has proved. As a demonstration of how nervous investors were, the first day premium to the fully-paid price was just 5%, almost exactly on the target for most flotations, and it was not until Labour started talking sense that the shares began to rise."

He concluded magisterially: "Any more reports like this one, and the comptroller himself ought to fear an investigation into his value for money[11]".

Anthony Hilton was just as scathing in his Evening Standard comment column. He was feeling embarrassed at his attack on me over London & Continental and now he could provide a little compensation: "The NAO inevitably believes that Railtrack was sold too cheaply, but it fails to see that it was Clare Short, not S.G.Warburg, that cost the taxpayer those hundreds of millions of pounds. Indeed, its analysis is deeply flawed because it ignores this political context.

"Take its recommendation that the issue should have been sold in two tranches, a little at first to establish the price and a larger lump later. This is fine in theory, but in practice no one at the time would have believed that the larger lump would ever see the light of day, because Labour would block it. Nor in such circumstances would they have subscribed for the first slice. The NAO proposal was not an option. Indeed, it would have been disastrous."

The Independent carried the same conclusion, if expressed more bluntly: "The Railtrack report is a slipshod and feeble piece of work"[12].

We were off the hook. With the NAO report comprehensively discredited in the media I began to look forward to our attendance in front of the Parliamentary Committee of Public Accounts, the group of MPs tasked with following up the audit office's work and producing a final report.

James Sassoon and I were due to attend the committee a couple of months later on 15 February of the next year, 1999. It was only the second time that bankers had been called as witnesses before the Committee and the first occasion had been a disaster. The directors from Hambros had been thoroughly humiliated over the sale of the rolling stock leasing companies. We would be giving evidence alongside the Permanent Secretary of the DETR, Sir Richard Mottram, who had not been involved in the flotation but was representing the position of the department. A fortnight before we went over to his office to discuss how to handle the session.

Two years later Sir Richard achieved everlasting immortality by his expressively succinct – and widely quoted – analysis of the difficulties of his department following internal manoeuvring against the Transport Secretary's political adviser. "We're all fucked. I'm fucked. You're fucked. The whole department's fucked. It's been the biggest cock-up ever and we're all completely fucked."

On this occasion he was rather more restrained, while appearing much jollier than the conventional civil servant.

"Right," he said. "There's a convention with these affairs. We have to show great respect to the MPs and basically accept the criticisms in the NAO report. That's the convention. After all we have had the opportunity to make extensive comments on what goes into the report."

"I don't want to do that," I blurted out.

"Ah ha," he exclaimed, looking at me with sudden interest.

I blundered on, "I think we did a fabulous job by selling the company at all, and I'm proud of our performance, and that's what I think we should say."

Sir Richard started to smile. He rubbed his hands together briskly. "This is going to be interesting," he chuckled. "If that's what you want to say, far be it from me to stop you."

A fortnight later we assembled at 4.00pm in an upstairs corridor of the House of Commons. After twenty minutes or so we were summoned into the unprepossessing committee room to face the MPs as they sat behind tables arranged in a horse-shoe.

Early on Sir Richard kicked over the convention he had explained to us – to the evident surprise of the committee chairman, the senior Conservative MP, David Davis.

"I do not have to agree with all those things in the report that were not ascribed to the department, but were the views of the NAO," he stated. From then on it was pure knock-about.

MP after MP used their 10 minutes of question time to hit the same point. Why had we under-priced the stock?

"Why did the department not raise the price range?" demanded David Davis.

"How much personally did you make out of this sale?" asked the Labour MP Geraint Davies.

"Why did you get this one so wrong?" Richard Page (Conservative).

"Has your bank ever given any advice which has been influenced in any way whatsoever by financial incentive?" Iain Davidson (Labour).

"Taxpayers were ripped off by the sale and now the people who use the railways are subject to a declining service." Gerry Steinberg (Labour).

We hit back as hard as we got. In the political context we achieved "a miracle", I told them. I went through how the share price had responded to various political developments – in great detail. "I am on a limited time schedule," complained Richard Page, truncating me. James Sassoon indignantly denied any influence from our fee structure either corporately or personally.

Charles Wardle (Conservative) concluded his questioning by saying: "All I would like to add is a private word of advice, private to the entire listening population, to Mr Freud. On the way out of this building for heaven's sake avoid Clare Short!"

David Davis, as chairman, summed up by saying: "Can I say to Warburgs that the evidence you have given us is very clear, thank you for that. Sometimes we get evidence that is less clear in this committee; it is a pleasure to have it this clear. Sir Richard, you entertain us as always." Presumably it was the farcical tone of the exchanges rather than our clarity that explained why the session seemed to be running almost continuously on the Sky Parliamentary channel over the next fortnight.

The committee put out its report in June[13]. The accusations were fundamentally unchanged from those of the NAO report but by now the story was dead and buried. The committee had published only just in time. Within six months the atmosphere round Railtrack was to sour dramatically and the share price would hurriedly retrace its stellar trajectory. It was not long before the accusations of under-pricing the float hurled at us by the comptroller and the committee were to appear surreal.

The audience was assembling for the second day of our 1999 transport conference on 5 October at London's Savoy hotel when we heard the first reports of a serious rail crash to the west of London beyond the main Paddington terminal. The rail session of the conference, scheduled for that morning, was overlain by a flow of increasingly horrific news as the scale of the tragedy became apparent. Gerald Corbett of Railtrack and Moir Lockhead, the chief executive of FirstGroup, whose train was involved in the crash, naturally pulled out of the conference. The final death toll emerged at 31. The crash signalled the end of the 'White Knight' period for Railtrack, certainly as far as John Prescott, the Deputy Prime Minister, was concerned. His knee-jerk reaction, as blame began to focus on the awkward positioning of a red light, was to strip Railtrack of its safety role. It was the start of sustained Government criticism of the railway industry: "We always said this kind of organisation of the railway would lead to a blame culture. It was fragmented. Everybody would want to blame everybody else," he told BBC radio later that week[14].

If fragmentation had been a concern, he was now heaping fuel on the flames. Alastair Morton had ably filled the conference time slot left by Gerald Corbett and Moir Lockhead on the morning of the crash, speaking as the chairman of the Strategic Rail Authority, which was about to be incorporated. This was a new institution planned by the Government to give direction to the industry. Meanwhile the highly effective regulator John Swift had just been replaced, in July, by Tom Winsor. Winsor was a combative lawyer who initially communicated with Railtrack solely through openly published letters and documents: a semaphore technique hardly designed to encourage smooth relationships. The Labour Government had stripped Railtrack of strategic direction and safety, adding an aggressive regulator and hostile media input to the mix; all this on top of a Tory structure which had encouraged the separation of track maintenance and placed an ongoing dispute about responsibility for delays at the heart of the relationship between Railtrack and the operators. As a recipe for infighting and stasis this was hard to beat.

The fault lines that would destroy Railtrack lay exposed in painful retrospect at the next transport conference, held in early October 2000, at which Gerald Corbett and Tom Winsor both spoke. Tom Winsor led off, announcing a series of reforms, of which the most important was, "The establishment of a reliable and comprehensive register of the condition, capacity and capability of the company's assets"[15]. This reflected a growing concern that Railtrack simply did not know what it owned. How could it possibly maintain assets that it did not know?

Following on, Gerald Corbett admitted the mistake over the West Coast Main Line. "The initial numbers were done on the back of a fag packet in 1995 and it was all based on a technology that they found terribly difficult to get working between the north terminal and the south terminal at Gatwick airport. Re-doing the whole of the West Coast, 400 miles up to Glasgow, based on it was just not on. We faced up to that and we reconfigured it last year. Inevitably the costs of the reconfiguration have gone up." Quite how much they were to rise from the original £1bn-odd of extra spending outlined in the prospectus was not yet clear – but certainly reverting to a more conventional system would be much more painful than the prospectus had suggested.

Two weeks later, on 17 October, the sky fell in. The blame for a high-speed derailment just north of London at Hatfield was found to lie squarely within Railtrack's ambit, caused by a cracked rail which fragmented into 300 pieces when the London-Leeds express traveled over it at 115mph. Now the company's ignorance of its infrastructure came home to roost. A snap board decision to institute comprehensive safety checks resulted in lengthy delays across the network and general chaos for the next half-year. Passenger numbers dropped by more than a third. In its panic, the company spent more than £700m rerailing the network even though no other rail as bad as the one at Hatfield was found.

"It's a collective nervous breakdown by the whole industry," Alastair Morton told me shortly afterwards. If it was a nervous breakdown, it was one fostered by the hostile environment created by the Government. Gerald Corbett was an early casualty, with the board accepting his second offer to resign a month after the crash. The share price promptly fell back through the £10 level.

As Railtrack struggled through the spring, with new senior management, a second factor started to loom. The true cost of the West Coast main line project was emerging and every figure was higher than the one before. Estimates of £8bn in the spring would rise to £12bn and more by the late summer. Railtrack was forced to deliver by the structure of an inadvised contract it had signed with Virgin Rail, the operator on this stretch of track, which planned to operate tilting trains on it at 140mph.

We began to work intensively with the Railtrack financial team to develop structures which would allow the company to finance this desperate hole in its balance sheet.

"I think we're getting somewhere," said Robert Jennings. He was building on our experience with the London & Continental rescue. "This structure will allow them to borrow up to £10bn. They're pretty keen over at Railtrack."

"I bet they are," I replied, impressed at how high the figure was. Robert's structure used a free-standing subsidiary company of Railtrack to borrow the money from the market. 'Leasetrack', as it was dubbed, would pay the interest using the income flow from the infrastructure subsidy. The high quality of this funding, effectively guaranteed by Government, generated the borrowing power. "What does Tom Winsor reckon?"

"I think he's supportive. We've only got to persuade Alastair Morton at the Strategic Rail Authority. He doesn't like it."

"Why not?"

"It takes control of the future direction of the industry out of his hands and back into Railtrack's. Apparently he told the department that he knew where this idea came from – that means us – and didn't approve."

"I suppose he thought he let us off lightly on London &

Continental."

For whatever reason Alastair Morton remained opposed to the plan. I consoled Robert a few weeks later, with perhaps just a touch of banker's optimism. "Look, Railtrack are going to dump Rothschild and appoint us as their main adviser any day now. We'll give 'Leasetrack' another push then."

John Robinson, who formally took over as chairman in early July, rapidly disabused us of this comfortable expectation. He immediately announced that he had brought in our arch-rival, CSFB, to devise a new financial structure for the company. The announcement left the executive management team at the company almost as dismayed as ourselves.

It was not until mid-August that John Robinson deigned to see us. He sat with his feet on the desk, putting on an impressive display of confidence and bonhomie. "I've opened discussions with the Government and I'm confident we'll get the funding we need," he told us cheerfully. We decided it would be inelegant to cross-question him as to why he had not even bothered to see us before appointing CSFB. By now the share price was far below the level at which we had floated the company, at just over £3 a share.

"Well, it looks like we're being pushed out of the rail advisory business," I said to Robert, "at least in the UK. We didn't get the job advising the Government because we were too close to Railtrack and now Railtrack has slung us out on our ear." Robert at least would have some involvement in the solution. It had been arranged that he would be seconded to the Treasury for six months from early October to work on rail and other transport matters.

I was sitting in the top-floor restaurant of the Tate Modern having lunch with my father when my mobile rang. It was the first Saturday in October 2001. The call was from Sara Small, the duty officer in our press department.

"The Sunday Times are running a story tomorrow that Railtrack is being put into administration by the Government. Have we got an involvement? Are we the adviser or broker?" It was my first intimation that the Government's patience with Railtrack had finally snapped under the dual pressure of the post-Hatfield chaos and the escalating cost of the West Coast project. The £1.7bn John Robinson had so confidently demanded to keep going until March 2002 had rebounded in his face.

"My God." I paused to collect my thoughts. "No, we're not involved; neither adviser, nor broker." It looked as if John Robinson's preference for CSFB had been a blessing in disguise. I switched off the phone and continued discussing the surrealist exhibition at the Tate with my father.

It was not till a few hours later, back at home, that the true implications hit me and I started making urgent phone calls to try and collect my team and the key executives in the fixed income department. We were up to our eyes in exposure to Railtrack, thanks to the hedging structure for the first stage of the Channel Tunnel Railway Link.

It was not till mid-afternoon on Sunday, 7 October, that we assembled in the office to review where we were. It was not encouraging. We were running a position worth £1.5bn for a company which had just gone bust. Every basis point that fixed interest rates fell would cost about £1.5m and the company might not be able, or allowed, to honour its debt. We were all conscious that if the news leaked of an exposure on this scale the market professionals would tend to move prices to squeeze us as we tried to undo the position. If the market moved by 0.5%, or 50 basis points, we would be looking at a loss of £75m, for example.

"A yard and a half," said Tim Fredriksen, who ran the Government bond trading department and was responsible for the position. "That's a pretty hefty position to shift in a hurry." I gathered that a yard stood for £1bn.

We started to put in calls to every Government contact we could think of. What did they want us to do? Did they want us to hold the position on behalf of who-ever would now buy the first stage of the Rail link? Did they want us to cut? What was the plan with this huge piece of Railtrack exposure – equivalent to 60% of the total debt and equity of the company when it was floated?

The Government's lead adviser at Schroder Salomon Smith Barney, David Challen, was clearly non-plussed when we contacted him. "Avoid precipitate action," he suggested, unhelpfully. Andrew

Turnbull, permanent secretary at the Treasury, was even less helpful. After some bland and general reassurances he suggested we contact Pippa Mason at Schroder Salomon.

"She's on their capital markets desk, for Christ's sake," yelled one of the fixed interest team. "She's exactly the kind of person we have to make sure this information doesn't leak to."

By now we had gained the impression the Government didn't know what it was doing. It seemed to have rushed into action without having thought through the consequences, at least as they applied to us. We were on our own.

Early on Monday morning we re-assembled. After a brief review of the position I put in a call to Sebastian Bull. Sebastian had worked on the London & Continental rescue in our banking department with me back in 1997 and 1998. Shortly afterwards Gerald Corbett had recruited him into Railtrack and he was now the company's director of business development. He knew the value of speed and secrecy in the market-place.

"OK, you better unwind the position," he confirmed just before the market opened. We could go to work. It took the better part of two weeks, but by the end of it we had closed the hedge and the price moved against us only marginally. It had been a narrow escape.

For Railtrack and the Government, however, the furore was only just beginning as a furious shareholder response gathered steam. In the end the Government was forced to buy the shareholders out at up to 260p. It took nearly a year to wind Railtrack down, and Sebastian Bull stepped up to the finance director role over the last 10 months.

"It's fascinating to see how badly wrong investors got this company when they drove the price up to £17," he told me. "They did not seem to understand that its income was completely under the regulator's control. The strong profits of the early years meant nothing. Indeed one reason they seemed so healthy was because all the subsidy Railtrack received each year for renewing the track was called income while the actual costs were spread over several years. The market thought the company was far more profitable than it really was."

The Government's favoured replacement vehicle for Railtrack was to be a not for profit company called Network Rail. As one of the directors responsible for the float of Railtrack, I was not allowed to pitch to advise on this, but my team was. The selection of a new adviser seemed just as chaotic as the process of putting Railtrack into administration.

"This is gibberish," I told Stephen Paine in early December 2001, when he brought me the first draft of our presentation. In Robert Jennings' absence Stephen was acting as the head of my infrastructure team and was to be the day-by-day leader of the Network Rail transaction.

"We're trying to answer the RFP," he defended himself. I pulled over the RFP, the Request for Proposal, which the department had sent out to the investment banks. "This is gibberish too," I agreed. "And we've got four more days to put in our response?"

"Yes."

"Well pity the competition. At least we know what we're talking about. The problem here is that they think they can do it in one stage. But the stand-alone financing can't go ahead until the credit rating and that can't be done till the rail regulator has ruled. Let's turn the whole thing round and show how we would do it in two stages, bank debt first and then stand-alone financing. We can even revive Robert's 'Leasetrack'."

We spent the next four days rewriting the pitch almost from scratch. It meant that we were probably the only bank with a workable plan and were accordingly awarded the mandate to advise Network Rail. Once again I blessed our luck in losing the Railtrack advisory mandate, an appointment which would have excluded us from the competition.

"Well, at least we're still in the rail advisory business," I said to Robert Jennings, when he returned from his Treasury secondment in spring 2002. "How much rail business is left in this country is an entirely different matter."

---

[1] Submission to Act for HMG in the Railtrack Privatision, S.G. Warburg. December 1994

[2] The Flotation of Railtrack, 24th Report by the Committee of Public accounts, Session 1998-99, pxvii

[3] Railtrack Share Offer. Pathfinder Prospectus, SBC Warburg, 15 April 1996, p46

[4] Ibid. Letter addressed to SBC Warburg dated 29 March 1996. pp102-3

[5] Inquiry into the fire on Heavy Goods Vehicle shuttle 7539 on 18 November 1996. Department of Transport

[6] Railtrack lurks as LCR's big shots come a cropper, The Evening Standard, 29 January 1998

[7] Loser Link. City Comment by Anthony Hilton, The Evening Standard, 29 January 1998

[8] From utility to Growth Vehicle, Gerald Corbett, Chief Executive Railtrack plc. Third Annual Transport Conference: "Transport Toward 2000", 28-29 September 1998, Day 2 - Bus and Rail. Warburg Dillon Read, p8.4

[9] The Flotation of Railtrack, Report by the Comptroller and Auditor General. National Audit Office, HC 25 1998/99. 16 December 1998. ISBN 0102540993

[10] Audit Office slips with wrong kind of report on the lines. City Comment, The Daily Telegraph, 16 December 1998, p27

[11] Short on Understanding over Railtrack sell-off, by Anthony Hilton. City Comment, The Evening Standard, 16 December, p33

[12] Short-changed on Railtrack sale. Outlook, The Independent, 16 December, p15

[13] The Flotation of Railtrack, Twenty-fourth report, Committee of Public Accounts, Session 1998-99. House of Commons, 30 June 1999

[14] On the Record, BBC One, 10 October, 1999

[15] Regulatory environment in the UK Rail Industry, Tom Winsor. 2000 Transport Conference, UBS Warburg, 2-3 October 2000, Day 1, p5.3

11

High Noon
The Supremacy of the Sectors – 1996 - 1999

"You've got three choices," I said, ticking them off. "One; you can just go away and die. You'll probably read about Smedvig doing a transaction with someone else in a few months time. Two; you can go back and beg to restart the transaction. But this is hardly a strong negotiating position. Three; you can go hostile and try to buy them in the market."

I was addressing the board of Bona, the Norwegian shipping company we had floated late in 1994. The company had been planning a friendly merger with another Norwegian tanker company, Smedvig, run by Peter Smedvig. We had spent September 1995 talking to his bank, NatWest. On Friday 6 October we were due to complete the deal at an all hands session. Most of the details had been ironed out. Then, out of the blue, the process ground to a halt.

Late on Thursday afternoon, Peter Donald, the NatWest banker, called to say the deal was off. He gave no explanation. When we met later that evening the Bona management team were non-plussed and upset. It was then that I laid out their three options.

"How do you rate our chances?" asked the Bona chairman, Rudolph Agnew. He was an expert chairman of companies involved in hostile take-overs; indeed, as chairman of Lasmo, he had helped to fend off the Enterprise attack we had been advising on. Rudolph had a powerful and irreverent sense of humour. He also knew when to concentrate intently on the matter in hand.

"Reasonable," I said. "Tom's got a few ideas on how to get hold of the stock. We're not planning a long-winded affair here. We'll either get it quickly or pack up and go home."

"Give it a go," said Rudolph.

Over the weekend Tom Cooper, my deputy, pored over who the main shareholders might be. There was no list of shareholders available, so he had to make do with scraps of information based on our contacts with the investing institutions.

"I reckon," he concluded, "if we're lucky, these six institutions might hold more than 50% of the stock between them. We'll go to them on Monday and tell them we'll buy their stock at $7.50 a share if we can build the 50% by 5.00pm. If we can't we'll go away and they'll never hear from us again."

"Is that legal?" asked one of the team members.

"Sure, why not," replied Tom. "This is Norway. They don't have a take-over code or any nonsense like that. You can forget all your London Stock Exchange inhibitions here."

On Monday morning we started phoning the institutions.

"We'd like to put you inside on a situation till 5.00pm today. Are you interested?" By putting them 'inside' we were giving them non-public information that meant they could not trade in the stock for the period. When they agreed – and all six did – we told them what we were planning and arranged to go round to see each of them later in the day. Tom's list was spot on, and each of the institutions we called had a substantial holding in Smedvig.

Through the morning and early afternoon we called on the institutions with our proposal. One by one they indicated they were minded to accept. The break-through meeting was with Morgan Grenfell, where I was introduced to the new manager of the European fund, Peter Young. He was a taciturn, bespectacled, man in his late 30s with dark hair. He said not a word as we made our cash offer for his stock.

"Fine," he said, immediately we had finished. "You can have mine." And he totted through some figures on a computer print-out to find out how many shares he had. It was more than we had reckoned – some 8.4% of the company in total – and it was enough to carry us through our 50% target.

I did not learn till nearly a year later why Peter Young had been so keen to sell out. In September 1996 Morgan Grenfell announced that it had discovered irregularities in some of its funds. It emerged that Peter Young had been ploughing investors' money into a series of highly speculative unquoted companies, using secret holding companies to disguise these exposures - way beyond the limits for the funds he was managing. Presumably the cash from liquidating his Smedvig stock was just what he needed in late 1995. The scandal was estimated to cost Morgan Grenfell's parent, Deutsche Bank, £400m in fines and compensation. As for Peter Young, after arriving at the pre-trial hearings dressed as a woman and answering to the name of Elizabeth, he was found unfit to stand trial under the 1964 Insanity Act.

By 5.00pm we had five enthusiastic sellers. The last conversation took place well after 6.00pm and was with Anthony Bolton of Fidelity, one of the top fund managers in the City and the largest single holder of Smedvig. I had got to know him in my early years with Warburg Securities, when I had tried (and failed) to sell an investment trust specialising in Europe for him.

"I've done the figures now, David, and it's not enough. We would only be prepared to sell this stake for asset value, which is $8.22."

"That's unreasonable," I pointed out. "There are various options and other costs which will be triggered in a takeover. They would bring the net assets down to $8.00 a share."

We settled on that price.

When I went back to the board I said, "I've got good news and bad news. The good news is that you can take control of this company if you want it. The bad news is that it will cost you more than we planned, at $8.00."

Rudolph Agnew looked genuinely astonished. "What do you recommend?"

"I recommend you do the deal at $8.00. You've had $100m burning a hole in your pocket ever since the flotation. There isn't anything else to spend it on. This brings you up to critical scale in the medium tanker market. You should take the opportunity you have today."

The board spent more than an hour alone to debate the issue.

"They'll buy," prophesied Tom. "They're Norwegians. They couldn't turn a piece of piracy like this down for anything."

"You should know," I told him. Tom was half-Norwegian.

He was also right.

"Okay, David," said Rudolph. "We want you to go ahead and buy as much of the company as you can."

By now it was 9.00pm. We had had the foresight to collect the evening telephone numbers of the fund managers. I went onto the main trading floor and picked up a phone that would record the conversation. All trading calls were taped so that deals could be verified in cases of disagreement. "Right, we're buying so and so many Smedvig shares from you at $8.00 a share. Dealt." I agreed with each fund manager in turn. Some were sitting in pubs; others were in restaurants eating their dinner. They were delighted to find that our price had increased from $7.50 to $8.00.

We ended the evening with 65% of the company and put out an announcement that we effectively controlled the company soon after the market opened the next morning. The announcement caught Peter Smedvig off a plane from a trip to the Far East and must have been stunning. There was a long silence. Then late in the afternoon he put out an announcement that declared that Smedvig Tankships "has retained NatWest Securities to assist in evaluating all alternatives". That had me in stitches. "Tom, he has no alternatives," I said, between giggles. This was a little unkind. He could choose between selling out and remaining as an irritating minority shareholder.

As far as I can tell this was the fastest hostile take-over recorded in Europe in modern times. Two days later, on 12 October, the holding was above 75% and Peter Smedvig conceded control.

It was only a couple of months later that Rudolph Agnew confessed: "David, I only asked you to go ahead with the hostile takeover to keep up the morale of management. I never dreamt you would actually succeed."

The Smedvig coup was my first noteworthy transaction after Swiss Bank absorbed S.G.Warburg. In hindsight, the Swiss had timed their purchase with uncanny precision. Almost to the week that the takeover was completed, the bond markets turned up and the sour bear market for the industry reversed dramatically. It was the beginning of the most dramatic boom for investment banks ever seen and one that stretched through the rest of the decade. The figures for the level of activity in the industry are difficult to piece together. According to the US consulting firm, Freeman & Co, investment banking fees worldwide nearly tripled between 1995 and 2000, to $53.5bn[1]. Activity of every kind soared. Between 1995 and 2000 global M&A jumped by a factor of six, international equity issuance by five and bond issuance by three.

In many ways the figures understated the level of activity for the bankers. In the early 1990s most corporate executives had appeared uninterested in the ideas which the bankers brought to their offices. However, as the decade progressed they became increasingly infected by the spiralling market activity and responded more and more positively to the flip-books in which proposals were outlined. "Yes, why don't you look at that more closely," a chief financial officer would end a typical meeting, "and let me have your thoughts on taking over such and such a company. And, while you're about it, let me see how we might finance the deals." The next bank through the door would doubtless receive another – or even the same – set of tasks. Maybe the company would do one of the transactions, but the work involved in preparing all the different proposals represented a new order of activity compared with the past. To cope, the banks started to suck in new staff. The increase was heavily concentrated in one area, the specialist sector banker. Till the mid-1990s this breed of banker hardly existed in Europe; now virtually all the growth in numbers within the corporate finance departments was to be represented by this arriviste.

"You've got to have stuff," I lectured my colleagues at an informal get-together of 20 or so senior corporate finance directors after the Swiss Bank merger. "If you don't have stuff you can't talk to the companies. If you don't talk to the companies you won't get the deals.

"Lots and lots of stuff," I concluded to mild amusement, mixed with some suspicion. Most had been brought up in a tradition in which proposals made to companies were the hand-crafted output of a high-level team concentrating its full intellectual resource on the issues facing the client. My 'stuff', by contrast, was a volume product that could be produced by a junior banker after a quick briefing on what was required.

"Tell them how to generate the 'stuff'," urged George Feiger, head of corporate finance. We were sitting round a big table in the autumn of 1995 in one of the seventh floor presentation rooms, surrounded by windows on three sides.

"You can't wait for a request from a company to discuss a particular issue," I said. "It takes too long to assemble a good presentation from scratch. You've got to have the key data ready to roll. That way you can turn it round in a day or two, or even overnight if you have to."

I described how I had linked up with the research analysts in the equities department.

"Corporate financiers are great at accuracy." I continued. "They might not understand what the data means but they get it right to the third decimal place. Equity analysts, the good ones, know what the data is telling them, directionally, but their actual figures are all over the place. What we've done, in transport, is to introduce a data analyst funded jointly by corporate finance and equities. That way we get data that's meaningful, as well as accurate.

"The data analyst has all the information bang up to date in a format we've specified, so when we need to produce a pitch we just crank the handle and the relevant tables of comparisons print out straight away.

"We can do lots of pitches. I see companies with presentations, one, two, three times a day - day after day - always with 'stuff'. That's almost all I do, that and the transactions that result.

"And the more companies we see, the more business we win. That's the formula. That's how it works. You've got to have the 'stuff'."

My throw-away expression soon became a jokey byword in the corporate finance department as bankers called for 'stuff'. George Feiger was in no doubt of the importance of the approach as he pushed and bullied bankers into the sectors that would spear-head the pitching machines: telecoms, pharmaceuticals, financial institutions, building materials, property, paper and packaging, retailing – all were bolstered into cohesive groups initially before swelling and consolidating into stand-alone mini-departments.

I had been putting my conviction that the key to success was constant presence in front of potential clients to aggressive test from 1994 onward. The results certainly seemed to back up the theory.

In September 1995, Per Hilstrom, our Swedish coverage banker told me, "I'd like to take you to see the Swedish State railway company, SJ."

"Why?"

"They're losing money and need to sell things. You can tell them how much they could raise by selling their bus subsidiary, Swebus."

We cranked off the comparative figures and came up with a valuation together with a list of the likely buyers - mainly the British bus companies. We had slotted in a meeting after lunch in mid-October. The two executives at SJ, Bo Hamnell and his assistant Henrik de Laval, seemed delighted to see us.

"You know, you're the first people to have taken us through the figures for Swebus and we've just this morning taken the decision to sell it," said Bo Hamnell. There was a long pause. Then: "Oh, why not. We'll let you have the latest figures so you can update your valuation. If you can offer us some sensible fees, you might as well have the mandate."

Henrik de Laval was chuckling to himself as he escorted us down the stairs to the entrance next to the main Stockholm railway station. He had worked in a Swedish securities house and knew how hard it normally was to win mandates. "That's pure serendipity," he said, "the way you guys walked into our office at exactly the right time."

Sometimes you could have too much of a good thing. In Hong Kong at the end of the same month we prepared a formal presentation to Shenzhen Expressway, a state owned company which planned to raise funds to build toll motorways across the fast-growing development zone alongside Hong Kong. In the morning our six-strong presenting group traveled up to the border by train and, after passing through passport control, transferred into a hired mini-bus for the hotel where the presentation was held. Immediately after the formal presentation – full of slides and cumbersome translation into Chinese – we were invited to a ceremonial lunch with the management and the various other Chinese businessmen present. There must have been at least 20 on their side. It was an enormously jolly occasion, where we toasted each others' health again and again in a 55% strong fire-water called Maotai, a famed and expensive delicacy which packed a devastating punch. I vaguely remember standing on the main table of our banquet to make my speech, to loud applause, although no one can recollect what I actually said. Nor can I remember how I got from the venue in Shenzhen back to the Mandarin Oriental hotel in Hong Kong where I was staying.

The next week, safely back in London and sober, I was on the phone to the local coverage officer, Nicole Yuen. "Have they confirmed the mandate?" I asked.

"Well, there's a problem," she confessed.

"What?" I exploded.

"Another company, Road King, want to appoint us to manage their flotation."

"Road King?"

"They own a series of road concessions in China. Their management was at our presentation and they liked what they saw, so they want to appoint us."

"Oh," I said, relieved. "That's good isn't it?"

"Well, it's quite good," she replied. "The trouble is that Shenzhen Expressway want to appoint us too and they're pretty angry about Road King. A couple of days ago they were blaming us for bringing Road King to the presentation, but luckily they've just found out that they were the ones who invited the company along, since they are working in partnership with them on one of their roads." In the end we took the first appointment that could be confirmed, which was for Road King, and floated the company in June 1996. Shenzhen Expressway, launched nine months later, felt we could not act for them as well, despite our most persuasive efforts.

I always felt driven to make the maximum use of the time I had available. "Are there any other transport companies in Singapore then?" I asked the local coverage banker, Yee Ting Sim, in spring 1996. I was planning a tour of the Far East and wanted to make the most of the stop off in Singapore, where I was planning to visit Singapore Airlines. "Well, there's always the Port of Singapore," she pointed out. "I've never talked to them and don't know whether they'd be interested in meeting investment bankers."

"Let's give them a whirl," I said. "See if you can set something up."

A fortnight later, in late April, we were escorted into a meeting room at the authority's headquarters to meet Kevin Yap, the lively and quick-witted finance director with whom we were soon swapping repartees. He listened with mild interest to my presentation. Then, as we were standing to leave, he paused as if considering a problem. Abruptly, he seemed to take a decision.

"You know, it's highly fortuitous you're here. We're planning to turn the authority into a company and I've just asked a couple of banks to send us presentations to act as our adviser. You weren't on the list but now that I've met you I suppose I should invite you to pitch as well." It was an invitation that we took up with alacrity. As is often the way with such opportunities, we won the competition and became the port's adviser, both over how it should structure itself into a company as well as a series of other matters over the years.

Pitches did not always go so well. A little earlier, in late January 1996, the news came through that the Dutch aircraft manufacturer Fokker was in imminent danger of going bust. We threw a team together, naturally led by Hans de Gier, chairman of the SBC Warburg investment bank and a Dutch national. Six of us flew over in a private jet from Northolt airport, west of London and met with the board of the company in the evening of 29 January. This was a transaction, should we win it, that would demand considerable resource and there was only the slimmest of possibilities that we would succeed in rescuing the company. In the plane going over we rehearsed our strategy. "We'll ask for substantial monthly fees and an extremely high success fee," we agreed. Hans de Gier would handle the fee issue.

Over in the outskirts of Amsterdam, where the company was based, we found ourselves making a presentation to a depressed group of Dutch board members. They included Rob Abrahamsen, the former chief financial officer of KLM who had so enraged Piers von Simson with his demands for frugality when we were working on the Alcazar fairness opinion. We swung through our set piece and sensed a positive response from the 10 or so board members on the other side of the table. They cracked the odd joke and warmed perceptibly to our strategy for saving the company.

At the end Rob Abrahamsen asked, "So what will all this wonderful service cost us?"

Hans de Gier stuck to our agreed figures, replying in measured tones. "We would look for a monthly fee of £250,000, payable in advance, and if we save the company we would want a success fee of $10m."

There was a horrified silence. All the warmth of our reception evaporated in an instant. This was clearly many orders of magnitude beyond what they expected.

Eventually the silence was broken by Rob Abrahamsen. "Why?" he asked, in a tone that was quizzical, academically curious, "why do you quote the monthly fee in pounds and the success fee in dollars?"

I had the greatest difficulty in restraining myself from rolling off my chair onto the floor in great gouts of hysterical laughter. Hans de Gier did his best. He talked about the difference between running fees and one-off amounts, but it didn't matter. The board facing us would never contemplate such figures. It was anyway irrelevant. The company was formally declared bankrupt six weeks later on 15 March.

Building the team in those years required dogged opportunism. I became adept at taking advantage of the corporate developments that came thick and fast. I also needed to maintain focus. In late 1995 George Feiger called me to his office. By then we had spent several sessions working through the development of the firm's sector approach.

"David," he said, as we sat at his oval table, "you're one of two people I am considering to take over this department when I move on. The trouble is you don't have a deputy who can take over your transport department. You should get one. Otherwise you'll be stuck."

Though I didn't admit it to George, I was unenthusiastic about the challenge of running corporate finance. The job had exhausted and drained one holder after the other. I was, however, much keener to boost my team with a competent senior banker and was quick to recruit as my deputy Tom Cooper, with whom I had worked on the original flotation of Bona in 1994. During our discussions I told him: "If you ever catch me talking about running corporate finance, tie me to the mast, like Odysseus, and row me straight past the sirens. If I had wanted to be a manager I would have joined Unilever."

Tom was in his early thirties when he joined my team. He was above average height, with a tight head of curly hair and extremely clever. A mathematician and trained accountant, he had joined Warburg in 1988, in corporate finance, before moving over to support Ed Chandler in the Nordic region. Then he had helped start up the utilities sector (for which I had been responsible for a short period). He was intellectually curious and loved nothing better than to work out elegant solutions to a client's problem. I thought he was the smartest young banker in the organisation and formed a close working bond with him over the rest of the decade.

The other key relationship behind the growing success of the sector lay on the other side of the 'Chinese Wall', in the research department. A strong link with the research analysts was central to the sectoral approach. Through the analysts we could find out what was happening in the market as well as the critical developments in the various companies we covered. Most importantly, if we had a company we wished to float, their cooperation was vital to produce research and promote the stock to the investors. In 1992 the task of following the airline stocks round the world was allocated to Andrew Barker, an intensely intellectual 27-year old with a vivid turn of phrase. Andrew had spent his gap year on a United Nations exchange scheme attending a Japanese high school, becoming fluent in the language as a result. He had spent a year on the equity sales-desk in London before transferring in 1989 to the Tokyo research department. Here my former transport analyst, Tom Hill, who had worked with me on the British Airways and Eurotunnel transactions, handed over coverage of the transport stocks including the Japanese airlines. Now that Andrew had become responsible for the global coverage of the aviation companies, he was determined to make a major leap forward in their analysis. He was stripping the data – plentiful in the airline world – to the bone so that direct comparisons between the companies could be made. And it seemed to be taking him an awfully long time. It was well into 1993 when I asked him, not for the first time, when his *magnum opus* was due.

"It'll come soon," he promised.

By now I was sceptical. Motivational reinforcement seemed in order.

"Either it comes," I said, "Or you go."

The threat seemed to do the trick. In June 1994 Andrew produced an outstanding piece of work that was to remain the core component of his coverage for a decade and won him a consistent position as the leading global analyst of the airline sector. Nor did my clumsy attempt at encouragement do any lasting damage to our relationship. In the years that followed we worked together closely on deal after deal across five continents, from Australia to Hong Kong, Germany to South Africa to Brazil. An abiding principle of that relationship was that my team of corporate financiers would only become involved in a market-based deal that Andrew, and his growing team of research analysts, endorsed. As a result they would only be asked to market deals they believed in. After all, if a deal blew up in the immediate aftermarket it would be their reputation to be destroyed; and once an analyst's reputation was in tatters their career was effectively over.

The other element critical to producing 'stuff' was a production line manned by junior staff, known somewhat confusingly, as analysts. These had nothing to do with the research analysts in the equities department. They were some of the smartest graduates from the top universities of Europe and the US, recruited to work impossible hours for the next three years to put together the presentations required by the senior corporate financiers. I was quick to build a team of six, a number that would double as the decade progressed. Each youngster would specialise in one area of the transport universe, be it airlines, roads or bus companies. They would understand the figures; stay in touch with news developments; know the views of the research analysts on the different companies in the segment. That meant that when a presentation had to be produced they could turn it round with extreme rapidity. Some were more reliable than others.

In 1997 I was visiting companies in Turkey. In the car on the way across Istanbul to the headquarters of Turkish Airlines I pulled out the flipbook prepared for the occasion. As was typical, this was the first chance I had had to go through it. It calculated the valuation that the market might be prepared to put on the airline, using comparisons with quoted companies, should it be floated. It extrapolated from the valuation to draw lessons on how the airline might finance itself. A nagging worry seized me as I turned the pages: some kind of sixth sense. I put in a call to the Turkish office, manned by Markos Komondouros, with whom I had worked on Euro Disney.

"Markos, does Turkish Airlines have a quote, by any chance?"

"Yes, it's listed on the Istanbul market. Only a few per cent, so the price is artificially high."

"Thanks." I looked glumly at my presentation. "Artificially high, you think?"

"Yes."

Usually in these circumstances I would tear the offending pages out, but in this case our valuation – much lower than the real figure Markos had given me – was on virtually every page. The car drew up outside the offices. The chief financial officer was upstairs waiting for us. There was only one thing for it.

Upstairs, after the introductory handshakes and general chit-chat, I launched into our presentation. "Your price in the market is artificially high, because so few shares are quoted," I explained. "What we have done is to calculate the value the shares would settle at should you issue a meaningful tranche of say 20 or 30%. Then we look at your financing options in that context . . . ."

That, I thought to myself, was close.

We did not always catch the errors in time.

"I just need to pop over to see you quickly," Andrew Barker phoned one day in 1997. Settled in my office a few minutes later he explained, "We've just uncovered an error in the airport data."

"Go on," I encouraged.

"Specifically the figures for South African Airports. They're a bit flattering."

"How flattering?"

"Well, it looks as if we didn't translate the Rand figures into US dollars to compare the airport's performance with the others in the sample."

"Oh," I said, realisation dawning, "I wondered why South African Airports was the best performer across the universe."

"Yes," said Andrew mildly. "If you multiply all the revenues by four it does tend to give you a boost."

"The trouble is that Dirk Ackerman, the chief executive, has been going round the airport conference circuit using these figures to show how well he's performing," I pointed out.

"It is difficult," Andrew agreed. I thought through the implications.

"As I see it, we have three options," I said. "First, we can own up, admit we've made a mistake and never do business in South Africa, and probably the rest of the airport industry, ever again.

"Second, we can jump out of the window, all of us.

"Or third, we can try to cover it up. In the next 24 hours we can invent a completely new way to analyse airports which can't be cross-checked back to our current way."

Andrew nodded philosophically, "So it's the cover-up?"

"Yes. I suppose there's a small chance we won't be caught. We'll have to change all our tables and graphs so that nobody will be able to compare the new correct figures with the old mistaken ones."

"How will we explain that?"

"We'll just have to say that we've decided to update our approach."

To my amazement our new presentation passed without comment, apart from some irritated phone calls from junior personnel in South Africa complaining that they couldn't make direct comparisons with past statistics.

Living close to the wire was one of the hazards of the intensive meeting schedule we were maintaining. I was careful never to complain over-much about occasional mistakes. If the juniors became frightened of repercussions their productivity would decline dramatically; we were all familiar with the disproportionate effort total accuracy required. Now we were in a race - a race that had been sparked by globalisation. Until the 1990s most companies' frame of reference had been their national market. As investment flows increasingly crossed national borders, comparison with companies abroad in the same industry gained far more significance. The sector specialists emerged as the bankers with relevant information. The race was on for us to see more company executives than our competitors, more often, with better insight into developments in their industry.

In the autumn of 1996 I devised a simple measure for running the business based on the number of pitches, or presentations, we undertook. In that first quarter the rate was maintained at five a week. As the team grew so did the number of pitches – up to 25 presentations a week by the end of the decade. I compared the total with the number of mandates we won. The relationship proved extremely stable. Most years we gained a mandate for every 20 pitches we made, a rate of 5% or so. The only exception was in the peak years at the end of the decade, when the rate soared to one mandate for every seven presentations in the year 2000.

In the race to beat the other banks we would pitch first and ask questions later. In another incident involving South Africa I found myself in Cape Town in December 1997, pitching to advise the Government on the sale of South African Airways. I was already uncomfortable about this piece of business. Earlier we had undertaken an advisory mandate for the company that had thrown up disconcerting findings, so I knew the transaction would be far from straight-forward. However, Shriti Vadera, running our business with the South African public entities, had insisted that a failure to respond to the RFP, the Request For Proposal, would damage our reputation with the Government. As the interview progressed I became more and more unhappy at the thought of trying to sell the company. It was curiously liberating. One of the pilots on the interview panel flipped the pages of our proposal over to the appendices.

"I notice that every single member of the team has been to Oxford University," he sneered.

I looked at him coldly.

"I'm extremely sorry," I replied. "Next time we come, we'll bring some historically disadvantaged people from Cambridge."

The reference to South Africa's post-apartheid adjustment process was doubtless in poor taste. Shriti looked at me aghast as the table erupted in laughter. To my relief we failed to win the mandate, although Shriti assured me afterwards that this was due more to our insistence on a reasonable fee than my inability to resist delivering a high-risk repartee.

The most unexpected obstacles could be thrown against our pitch machine, particularly if we were working far from home. In the summer of 1998 Tom Cooper brought me along on one of his marketing trips to the shipping companies in Taiwan, as part of our regular bi-annual Far East tour. On the stop-over in Hong Kong we received an urgent text message from the London office.

"Taiwanese have put Erling in jail," we read. Erling Astrup, the junior specialising in shipping, had flown to Taiwan directly from London with the presentations and was due to meet us when we arrived.

"Why on earth is Erling in jail?" squawked Tom down the phone, "and has he got our presentations?"

"Because he's Norwegian."

"Surely that's not a crime?"

"He's not a citizen of the European Union so he needs a visa. Our travel department slipped up."

When we arrived at Taipei airport that evening we found that Erling's predicament had eased, thanks to vigorous lobbying by our local team. He had spent 10 hours in a cell in the airport, watched over by guards with machine guns. Our team had managed to negotiate a transfer to the airport hotel within the customs barrier, to which he was confined till the next flight to London at midday.

"It was terrible in there," he told us, having slid out through the back door, "all refugees, weeping women and children."

"There are some mistakes in the presentation which need correcting." Tom pointed out.

"Leave it with me," Erling promised. Early the next morning he slipped out of the back door again into a black Mercedes arranged by our local staff which took him to the downtown office. Here he was able to update the presentation and reprint it for us before being smuggled back into the hotel in time for his return flight.

The main lesson of survival in an investment bank I had absorbed was the importance of setting my own objectives and concentrating my energies in areas where I thought I could succeed. It was all too easy to be flattered into a difficult role and then subsequently find oneself exposed at the next of the regular management changes. As far as I was concerned, the next major change was the somewhat abrupt transfer of George Feiger from running the division in May 1997. I was sad to see him go since he had been instrumental in effecting the sector revolution at the bank and had, incidentally, provided ready support for all my schemes to make the system work effectively. It had been no easy task. When he took the department over it was full of bitterness. "Warburg was full of angry people," he wrote to me later. "They were angry at their former management. They were angry at being sold in a way that they found deceptive. Many were angry because their business model (the all-purpose generalist) was declared by me to be outmoded. Indeed you were one of the leading proponents of this view and were not exactly making headway with your colleagues.

"I had to clear out dead wood. I had to push a sector and special-knowledge based approach to banking. I had to intermediate between the corporate finance function and my colleagues who were traders and didn't understand relationship-based business. In our world, remember, the traders were on top and the corporate financiers were the puny weaklings, the opposite of the old Warburg. I served as a useful punching bag for the anger."

The occasion of George's departure was the purchase by SBC

Warburg, against his strong disagreement, of a US investment banking boutique called Dillon Read – a firm in genteel decline despite an illustrious history and name. The investment bank was renamed SBC Warburg Dillon Read and the chief executive of the US house, Fritz Hobbs, was appointed head of corporate finance. Fritz was every inch a patrician East Coast banker, tall and studiedly courteous. I was deeply relieved when he supported my team against the rival transport banker in Dillon Read's New York office, Sharyar Aziz. Nevertheless, by the end of the year I needed to respond to another siren call when Fritz called me to his office.

"David, your sector is too damn small. We can't afford to have you running around looking after 2% of world market capitalisation. I'd like you to take over the financial institutions group. That'll give you nearer a quarter of the market to play with."

"It's not as small as it looks, Fritz. The sector may be small in market cap, but I reckon it represents nearer 10% of world economic activity. There are enormous fees to be made in structuring and financing. Banks bore me and it would take years to establish a reputation in the sector."

"You'd be heavily incentivised to make the switch," Fritz grumbled, as I stood firm.

"I could pick up some more business segments to swell the business?" I suggested.

"Oh, all right," Fritz sighed. He would have to find another solution for the financial institutions group.

In November I put in a paper proposing that I start up a two-man team focusing on the leisure and hotel sector. Fritz cleared the initiative rapidly. I also started to consider how to build up the infrastructure side of the transport business. The project finance team was currently separately organised, but I could see increasing opportunities within the rail and road segments to advise on complex restructuring. The time was still not right since London & Continental was about to explode in our faces. Indeed, unless this problem could be solved I suspected that I would be faced with the rapid dismemberment of the sector rather than expansion.

As I plotted in miniature, Marcel Ospel, now chief executive of Swiss Bank, moved with typical decisiveness to engineer a reverse take-over of the largest bank in Switzerland, UBS, a bank that had lost its way and found itself without a coherent strategy. The takeover announced on 8 December 1997 was dressed up as a merger, but the best management roles were allocated to Marcel Ospel and other members of Swiss Bank, then the smallest of the Swiss Big Three. In the afternoon the investment bankers of both UBS and Warburg Dillon Read (as we were now called) were invited to a presentation of the merger on neutral ground at the City's Chiswell Street Brewery. The two teams filed into one of the ground floor function rooms to hear what management had to say. There was no disguising the brutal reality of the takeover, so far as it concerned the investment banks. The 'platform' for the new merged entity would be Warburg Dillon Read. In practice this meant – certainly in the corporate finance and equities divisions – that we would pick over those people who could be conveniently added to our existing mix. If the UBS bankers were under any illusions, their chief executive Mathis Cabiallavetta, quickly disabused them when he stood to make an emotional speech. He told them: "I don't feel sorry for you. You all have resources to cope. I feel sorry for the little people, the drivers, cooks and receptionists." Marcel Ospel, who was sitting alongside, looked up at him with an appalled expression as he spoke.

By now I was fully familiar with the take-over routine. I prepared presentations to show the strength of our performance. That was to defend against attack. Then I looked for personnel who could be useful. After all, this was a time when budgetary constraints on headcount were abandoned. Finally I looked for any opportunities thrown up in the chaos inevitably generated as hundreds of bankers jockeyed for position. The head of corporate finance at UBS, Malcolm Le May, was keen for me to take over one particular individual: "If you want to get a meeting with Gadaffi, he's your man." I did my best to disguise my bemusement as to why any banker would want to meet Libya's head of state. "I'd be very keen to welcome Robin Phillips and two of his people to continue their coverage of airports for me," I counter-proposed, and added three more to the team. By the time the merger was consummated at the end of June 1998, London & Continental had been successfully solved and in the afterglow I was able to take on four project financiers to join Robert Jennings in the rail and road segment.

I had assembled a formidable team. By the end of 1998 it had grown to 25 bankers, up from five at the beginning of 1996. In early 1999 I added a further group to cover the Business Services companies, persuading my old colleague Markos Komondouros to take charge. As activity continued to accelerate, so did the numbers, and the team eventually peaked at around 40 bankers in 2000.

The business grew with the numbers. We had created a virtuous circle. We had concentrated on the various sub-sectors, like shipping or post or roads, before the other banks. We had built up the largest team, which allowed us to market more aggressively, using the track record our early start gave us. That in turn won us more business. In Europe, in particular, we built up a very substantial market share – probably over 30% in terms of fees generated. The bank's other sector teams rarely exceeded a market share of 10%. I began to feel more comfortable with the decision to stick with the sector, despite Fritz Hobbs' urgings.

The nature of my work changed. From running individual transactions I found myself in charge of a pipeline and relationships with companies all over the world. These did not always go smoothly and when there was a problem I had to deal with it.

"Brian, I'm sorry we can't do it." I was talking to Brian Souter in late 1998 about a transaction he wished to pursue in North America. Brian Souter was the mercurial co-founder and chairman of the rapidly growing UK bus company, Stagecoach. I had inherited the brokership of the company with the UBS merger. Initially the relationship had been excellent. Brian was a witty, eloquent expansionist who dressed in jeans as he tripped round the City, carrying his papers in a plastic bag. I took to him immediately. We had got to know him before the UBS merger when we sold him Swebus in September 1996; 18 months later, in May 1998, we raised £140m for him in a rights issue, as well as selling him a 20% stake in the Chinese Road King.

Now I was telling him: "It's too big for your balance sheet. We simply can't finance the transaction. And anyway we don't think it's the right deal for you." He was forced to abandon the project – which was probably just as well since the Canadian target, Laidlaw, filed for bankruptcy less than three years later.

Brian was swift to take his revenge. We were summoned to the company's Perth headquarters in Scotland in March to repitch for the brokership, always an ominous request. It was an unpleasant encounter. I was hardly surprised when a junior from the company rang afterwards to say that Credit Suisse First Boston had been awarded the position in our place.

Brian may well have regretted the step. The day after the issue of his press release announcing our firing, his biggest UK bus rival, FirstGroup, made contact. "If Stagecoach has dumped you, we'd like to appoint you to look after us," they said.

"That's fine," we replied. "And we've got just the company for you to buy in the US." My US banker, Jim Westphal, had discovered that Ryder, a Florida-based transportation company, was looking to sell its school bus division. We had been on the verge of bringing the idea to Brian when our brokership was terminated. Instead we were to watch Stagecoach rush through the $1.2bn purchase of another North American company, Coach USA, bungling the financing miserably, and later writing off most of the purchase price as its own share price cratered. By contrast, FirstGroup's US transaction proved an outstanding success. I was to run into Brian only one more time after that, at the Regent's Park house of the US Ambassador for the Fourth of July celebrations in 2000. I suddenly found myself standing beside him in the garden next to the marquee.

"Hello," I said.

He looked me over cautiously. The value of his holding in Stagecoach had collapsed by more than two-thirds since our last encounter and was to fall considerably further before starting to recover. A proper conversation would have proved too painful. "Hello," he replied. There was a short, but meaningful, silence. Then we both moved off in different directions.

Competition with other banks remained as intense as in the early part of the decade, although ground rules had now been established. This meant that the key battles took place at the outset of a transaction to win defined roles. Once they had been awarded, the banks tended to work together much more smoothly, without the constant jockeying for position seen in the flotations of Pharmacia and Nynex Cablecomms. The initial clashes could be ferocious, however.

"We've got no cards in our hand at all," I complained to James Garvin on the flight over to New York in March 1997. James ran the syndicate desk in London. We were chasing a role in the $780m flotation of Galileo International, one of the three main airline reservation systems. Derek Stevens, the chief financial officer of British Airways, one of the owners of Galileo, had invited us to pitch for the business. We were still broker to British Airways and Derek, whom I had first encountered when he was the finance director of the TSB, had proved a staunch friend over the years.

"It looks as if it will be a purely US listing," Derek said when we met him that afternoon in New York along with the chief financial officer of Galileo, Paul Bristow. It confirmed our worst fears. Originally we had expected there to be a dual listing in Europe, probably London, as well as in the US. If, instead, Galileo was to have a purely US orientation, we were badly placed to compete with the other bank in the frame, Morgan Stanley. The timing could not have been worse. We had just closed down our New York equities desk selling US stock to US institutions, so we had no sales force to distribute the stock in its home market. (Our purchase of Dillon Read was to make good the deficiency, but this development lay two months in the future.)

"It's going to be a nasty meeting with Morgan Stanley in the morning," James Garvin said afterwards. We had been told by Paul Bristow to reach agreement with them on how we would run the transaction.

"Well, I'm staying on UK time, if we've got to be up first thing," I said. "See you in the morning." James and Charles Otton, who was also with us on the trip, planned to go out to dinner.

I got to bed at 8.00pm New York time, or 1.00am London time and fell into a profound sleep. Then the phone rang. I looked at my watch. It was an hour later, 9.00pm New York time. Paul Bristow said: "I need you over here right now. There's a problem with

Morgan Stanley." His hotel was a few blocks across to the west. I called up James and Charles but they were still out at dinner and I did not know where they were. Our European mobile phones did not work in the US. Reluctantly I took a cab across town - alone.

"Morgan Stanley don't like the terms you're talking about," said Paul Bristow as we sat in the outer room of his suite.

"If we're going to put resources into this we need to agree fixed economics upfront," I replied. "If they're bookrunner they will be able to manipulate all the orders. We need to fix our return at $5m."

Paul went through into his bedroom to phone Morgan Stanley. I felt terribly vulnerable. There was presumably a full team in their office cranking over their computers while I had even forgotten my pocket calculator.

"They're prepared to let you be joint lead manager of an international tranche and co-lead of the US tranche. But no pre-agreed economics."

We haggled for the next two hours, looking for different formulas that would give us a guaranteed share of the fees. I stuck firm to the $5m figure, to Morgan Stanley's and eventually Paul Bristow's fury. All the while I thought to myself, if Morgan Stanley just check us out properly they'll uncover the closure of our US sales desk. With that information they'll destroy my negotiating position, claiming we don't have any resources to commit to the transaction. But the blow never fell. I left Paul after midnight without conceding a penny.

By the time I was back in my own hotel bed it was approaching 5.30am London time and my circadian rhythms had moved to the next day. For the next five hours I lay there, exhausted and wide-awake.

"Thank God for their arrogance," I said to James and Charles over breakfast as I briefed them on the night's developments. "They can't even be bothered to check out the opposition any more." While we failed to reach agreement with Morgan Stanley that morning, by the end of the week they had conceded and agreed fixed terms for our role in the transaction. We got my $5m.

Our most difficult task, as sector bankers, was to maintain the trust of the companies with which we were working. British Airways knew we were handling transactions for Lufthansa, for instance, but the UK airline had to feel comfortable that none of its secrets would leak through us to their main rival. It was an uneasy line to follow, since companies would want to talk to us for our specific industry knowledge. That we had built a reputation for impartiality became evident when we started to win mandates as the intermediary between companies striving to close a transaction. These were invariably extremely painful experiences.

The first we undertook was for P&O and Stena, who wanted to merge their UK short sea channel ferry interests now that Eurotunnel was in operation.

"It's your bloody fault that Eurotunnel got built, so you can help us sort this out," was how Bruce MacPhail, the managing director of P&O put it in May 1996. Through the summer we shuttled back and forth between P&O in London and Stena's Swedish headquarters in Gothenburg. The main challenge was to strip the various counter-proposals of the rude embellishments made by each side. On one thing the two companies were agreed, however, and that was the overweight nature of our fee proposal. They managed to avoid signing our engagement letter till the deal was agreed in October. Then Bruce sent me one of the bluntest letters on pay that I ever received. Blandly he announced that each company would pay half the amount we had previously discussed, concluding, "I am sorry, but I think that in the circumstances this is fair." I was so impressed I framed the letter and put it on my office wall as a lesson to the team about the importance of signed engagement letters at the outset of a transaction.

Almost immediately we started work on our next intermediary role which was more ambitious still. Again it was in the ferry business but this time we were asked to act as an intermediary in a three-way merger between the Swedish, Danish and German railway ferry companies, shuttling round the entrance to the Baltic. We had learned our lesson well enough by now to ensure that a watertight contract was signed. I even inserted a clause stating we could only be fired by all three acting in concert. After all, one company or the other was bound to become upset with how the deal was going and wish to undermine the process by firing the intermediary.

We named the project 'Trident'. When the Swedes pulled out in July 1997 we changed the name to 'Bident'. Later the Germans sent us a letter firing us, but to little avail since the Danes did not join them in the action. So by the end of the year we had painfully put together a two-way merger between the Danish and German companies. It had been a bad tempered, difficult process.

Over these years a quiet revolution was taking place at UBS Warburg, as we were now called. It had been discreetly master-minded by Robin Budenberg, the most respected mainstream corporate financier in the bank. In the immediate aftermath of the SBC take-over he had taken over management responsibility for transaction execution and client service. With the return of stability he had eschewed further full-time management to step back into regular front-line banking. However, he also initiated a business review group, or BRG, which cleared all transactions that we undertook and in particular set the fees at which we would be prepared to act. Our fee scales were raised considerably; we adopted the levels shown to us by Morgan Stanley during the aborted merger discussions, our only benefit from the whole experience. Not only were they higher, they also had to be agreed upfront rather than afterwards as had been the case so often under the S.G. Warburg regime. Steadily the BRG transformed the bank. Obviously any banker could find a client if he under-charged. By insisting on market rates, Robin steadily identified the weaker bankers who could no longer make pretence of activity. They could then be shown the door. The income of the division increased dramatically as a direct result, which was just as well, since pay rates in the industry were going sky high.

"I have to charge you outrageous fees," I explained to a sceptical Bruce MacPhail at P&O, as we negotiated another mandate, this time upfront. "If we don't charge the market rate, I won't be able to pay these guys enough." I waved my hand round my team members sitting at the rectangular table in his office. "They will then get poached by Goldman Sachs. You'll end up forced to use Goldman, and if you think our fees are bad, you should see theirs'."

For once Bruce could not think of a convincing answer, although he remained as reluctant as ever to pay the rates that the banks were trying, usually successfully, to impose.

The bonus round held in the New Year became increasingly traumatic as the decade progressed. The one-off nature of the payment, which grew to several times the level of some individual's salaries, gave the announcement a sudden death quality. Each person built up particular expectations, often based on the alternative job offers made to them by the head-hunters who assiduously worked the industry. If the level was disappointing, the executive would, as often as not, succumb to outside blandishment the moment the money was paid over a month later and leave.

The process became more and more formalised each year. Each individual would be scored in an elaborate evaluation process; then team heads would put in claims for each of their people that would go back and forth with the division's management. By the end of the decade, the October-January period had become a ghastly bureaucratic round of report writing and pay-setting. Nor was UBS Warburg unusual in this regard. The process was essentially the same across all the investment banks.

"If the rest of the country knew what we being paid, there would be tumbrels on the street and heads carried round on pikes," I once said to Tom Cooper, my deputy, as we worked through the bonus figures we were recommending for the team. According to Freeman & Co figures, the average pay for a junior banker, or associate, rose from $125,000 in 1997 to $460,000 in the peak year of 2000. For the senior bankers, hovering below managing director level, the figures moved up from $1m to $1.6m over the same period[2]. While these figures were probably weighted to New York rates, by the end of the decade the differential between Wall Street and the City had closed appreciably. Certainly nothing I saw over the years made these figures look unrealistic.

As each autumn progressed I would come under intense pressure from members of my team anxious not to be overlooked by the system. One year I determined to limit the amount of time spent in intense interviews during the build-up phase. At our team summer dinner in July 2000 in a Cambridge restaurant I stood to make my speech.

"I know we are moving into an anxious period for you all," I opened. "And I look forward to seeing many of you to discuss pay and promotion in the months ahead. However, I do have one stipulation. As you know, I have a very low boredom threshold, so if anyone wants to come in to discuss these matters with me, I do insist on an original approach."

I went through some of the angles people had used on me, without naming the perpetrators. "I am very bored by the person who comes in saying they've just turned down a job offer from Goldman Sachs. Of course you've had a job offer from Goldman Sachs. You wouldn't be on my team if you weren't receiving regular job offers from Goldman Sachs.

"Nor do I want to hear about your housing plans; how you need a rough early indication of bonus levels to arrange the appropriate mortgage. I've also heard the one about how much your fiancée is going to be paid and that if you don't exceed her figure you'll abandon the wedding from shame. I've heard about paying back the MBA debt; the comparative figures of the flat-mate working for CSFB; the discreet inquiry as to whether you can afford to buy your wife a BMW, and; how your father will drop dead from mortification if you are not promoted.

"But if anyone can come up with a new line, I'll be delighted to hear it so I can add it to my collection." The speech left a few red faces, but it gave me an appreciably more peaceful autumn.

Our marketing efforts produced a climactic 1999, the annus mirabilis for the team. Outside the US (which I never succeeded in cracking), it felt as if we were involved in every appreciable transport deal. In the UK we bought the Ryder school bus division for FirstGroup and issued bonds for Railtrack and London & Continental. We bought a minority stake in Iberia for British Airways as well as issuing a perpetual bond, a most unusual instrument, for the UK company. In Spain we floated a second airline reservation group, in the shape of Amadeus; in Italy, the motorway giant Autostrade; in Germany, the logistics company

Stinnes. We merged our Norwegian tanker company, Bona, into the Canadian leader in medium-sized tankers, Teekay, and advised the logistics group Danzas to sell out to Deutsche Post. In Australia we privatised the State of Victoria's rail and tram services. Moreover the pipeline was filling up with transactions we would complete in the early part of the next year: the float of the Hong Kong underground system; the sale of the Mexican airports; the float of easyJet in the UK. Our total revenues for the year peaked at about $200m. Indeed, at around this time I was amused to note, in the light of Fritz Hobbs' earlier strictures, that we made more money in my little area than the bloated telecoms segment in every year except one.

It was the high noon of my career. The stresses of running the business in one of the most extraordinary booms ever seen, the Dotcom Boom, were about to explode.

---

[1] State of Investment Banking – 2001 and Beyond/2002 and Beyond, January 2001/ October 2002. Freeman & Co. p10/p10

[2] State of Investment Banking – 2001 and Beyond, January 2001. Freeman & Co. p27.

12

Deutschland AG
Germany during the Dotcom Boom – 1997-2002

"Bang Bang, you're dead," I said. "There's blood all over the floor." I rammed the point home. "It's all over."

There was a shocked silence. I had gone too far. It was October 2000 and I was rehearsing the chief executive of Deutsche Post, Dr Klaus Zumwinkel, for his meetings with investors ahead of the flotation of the company. This was not an informal, relaxed session. Deutsche Post, Germany's monopoly postal provider, was probably one of the most hierarchical companies in a country renowned for its emphasis on organisational structures. Klaus Zumwinkel - tall, elegant and imperial - was surrounded by minders and board colleagues in a large meeting room next to his office, all of whom froze at this blatant demonstration of lèse-majesté. I had visions of the time Sir John Read, the chairman of the TSB, threw me out of the rehearsal for that company's float fourteen years earlier. Then I was a disownable analyst; now I was in effective charge of the transaction and a bust-up with the chief executive would have undermined the largest German IPO of the year, not to speak of our relationship with the owner of the company, the German Government.

Similar concerns probably ran through the mind of Klaus Zumwinkel, a chief executive always fully conscious of the dignity of his position. Suddenly he smiled and the crisis was over. "So what's the right answer then?" he asked. The room relaxed. He turned to his chief financial officer, Dr Edgar Ernst, sitting next to him. "Listen to this, Edgar, my friend," he said. "You'll have to remember the right answer to this question just as much as me."

I carried on with the rehearsal, asking him one typical investor question after the other and each time invariably needing to explain why his initial answer was inappropriate. My high-risk strategy had worked – just. I had decided that a deferential approach to Klaus Zumwinkel would have had a negligible impact in changing his attitude to the financial markets – and that attitude needed a dramatic transformation if Deutsche Post was to be well-received by investors. As it was, I had won a licence to indulge in hyperbole and could get away with rebukes and corrections that would have been considered outrageous from the mouth of a German national. For weeks after the session I would catch our German colleagues from Deutsche Bank, with whom we were acting jointly, muttering 'Bang Bang, you're dead' to each other, presumably code for their exasperation at dealing with an irrational Englishman.

By the autumn of 2000, I had been involved in mainstream German transactions for nearly four years. Slowly I had worked out that the tactics of running relationships with senior German executives were very different from those in the UK, and indeed in most other countries in which I had operated. In May of the previous year I had delivered a talk in our Frankfurt office to our German team and other senior members of the investment banking department. The first portion was conventional enough, covering the transactions we had completed and the prospects for my sector. Then I flipped up a few charts to illustrate the difference between English and German executive behaviour.

"The Englishman will make a few light remarks as he approaches a topic, which will appal the German, who regards someone who treats serious matters with frivolity as a light-weight. He will also be disgusted at the delicate way an Englishman will frame his advice. It will not be taken as a sensitive way to reach agreement but as equivocation and an avoidance of an obligation to offer plainly-spoken views. By contrast the Englishman will be horrified at the rudeness of Germans in stating their position and will perceive hysteria where the German is merely offering extra emphasis.

"So my advice to my English colleagues is to say what you think and speak bluntly. No 'on the one hand, on the other' analysis. The trouble is, of course, that Germans are becoming increasingly sensitive to the peculiarities of English behaviour and if you adapt they may take you only for a rude Englishman." I concluded to general laughter, "You can't win."

I had been spending more and more time in Germany in the previous few years as the market woke up and the German Government launched a major campaign of privatisations.

"The Germans spend more on flowers than they do on equities," was the memorable summary by Miko Giedroyc, one of the more flamboyant Warburg analysts, as he described the situation in the late 1980s. A decade later that was changing fast, and German activity, in terms equity issuance, overtook that of the UK in 1998.

Our entry into the mainstream German issuing business had come about by a most circuitous route. I first visited Dr Klaus Schlede, the chief financial officer of Lufthansa, some time after the German airline had signed a co-operation agreement with the Scandinavian Airline SAS in May 1995.

"What do you think of SAS?" he asked. "We're very pleased with our arrangement with them." Klaus Schlede had a formidable reputation as the chewer-up of bankers with whom he disagreed.

"They're the worst airline in Europe," I said, to a look of astonishment. I showed him our comparative statistics on airlines. "They've got a terrible cost base and appalling problems with their workforce. There are incredible stories all round the industry about how many seats are removed from SAS planes so that the crew can work in a more comfortable galley.

"Mind you," I added as an afterthought, "they're probably quite a smart airline to do a deal with. You'll suck up all their feeder traffic and boost your own volumes. I don't see them getting much back from you, though. It seems a pretty clever deal."

By now Klaus Schlede was openly chuckling.

"Well then, tell me about South Africa. Should we do a deal to buy South African Airways?"

In the first part of 1996 we were assessing this airline's suitability for transfer to the private sector for the South African Government.

"I don't know yet," I told him. "We're looking into it." And I explained the nature of our mandate.

It was from this meeting that our relationship with Lufthansa developed, with increasing warmth on both sides, even though they knew we were also close to their European rivals British Airways and Swissair. I strongly suspect that our advisory mandate on South Africa Airways played a pivotal role, since in this period the German company was deeply interested in buying a stake in the airline when it became available. Lufthansa probably took a deliberate decision to build up a relationship with us in order to position themselves for the South African stake, given their deep-seated belief in the efficacy of trading favours. In the event, our probity was never put to the test. In a double irony, first we failed to win the disposal mandate in 1997, helped by my reference to the historically disadvantaged; then Lufthansa lost interest in the 20% stake, which was eventually bought by Swissair in the summer of 1999.

For whatever reason, by 1997 we were the investment bank most favoured by Lufthansa as the German Government moved to sell its remaining 36% stake in the company. We had also been marketing hard to the German Government, in the shape of Dr Eberhard Rolle, the relevant senior civil servant in the finance ministry. He was an utterly charming, tall man with a mop of untidy grey hair and a sincerity that was almost painful. So when our seven-strong team turned up for the beauty contest in mid-July we had prepared the ground as well as possible. All we had to do was perform on the day.

We were last to appear before the selection committee made up of representatives from the Government and Lufthansa. They had seen six banks before us and by now it was early evening. If they were feeling sleepy, they were jolted back to full wakefulness by Andrew Barker, our airline expert, in the most compelling performance by an analyst that I have ever seen, before or since.

"Lufthansa is undervalued," he declared. "It's standing way below the level of British Airways and there's no reason why the national airline of the biggest economy in Europe shouldn't be at a premium.

"The price has run up from below DM20 a share in the last

couple of months to DM36, so lots of analysts are advising their clients to take profits and sell. I'll be telling my clients that the share is worth DM50 a share or more."

"And as the No 1 European analyst they may very well follow his advice and buy the stock," I said, reinforcing this exercise in hyperbole.

The outcome was that we were appointed the sole international bookrunner of the transaction, with the German bank Dresdner Kleinworth Benson responsible for the domestic tranche. It was a breakthrough for more than my sector. The Lufthansa mandate was the first genuine lead role the bank had received from the Government in the public equity markets, giving us a seal of approval for business across the economy. It raised the equivalent of $2.7bn and was the second largest public offering in Germany seen till that time. At a stormy October meeting in Frankfurt, the shares on offer were priced at less than 1% below the level seen in the market, at DM33.3. From the German Government's point of view the transaction had gone outstandingly well. We had arrived.

It was not long before we were to earn our first reward although, as is the way of these affairs, it was not to take the shape of a German transaction but one based in Madrid. The following summer we attended a beauty contest in Zurich airport, of all places, to present to the four airlines that owned the Computer Reservation System known as Amadeus: Lufthansa, Air France, Iberia and Continental. With weak relationships with the latter three airlines and a perceived conflict from our senior role in the flotation of the rival Galileo, my expectations for winning this mandate to float Amadeus were not high.

"Leave us some crumbs," teased James Leigh Pemberton, a former Warburg banker now working for CSFB whom we met in the waiting area and who was also pitching for the business. CSFB was already acting for Amadeus in its negotiations to merge with the weakest of the four main Computer Reservation System companies, Worldspan, so they were in an infinitely stronger position to win this mandate than we were.

I was genuinely surprised when the Amadeus chief financial officer, Riswan Rahman, phoned me after the pitch, on 6 August, to say: "The decision of the owners is that you will be sole bookrunner and that Merrill Lynch will be your joint global co-ordinator. You made a striking presentation. It was well orchestrated and controlled."

He added, "The team we saw is the team we expect to carry out the transaction and I should stress that the presence of the team leader is essential." This was a dig to ensure that I did not disappear on other transactions as senior investment bankers were wont to do. Nevertheless it was a rare clear-cut victory. Typically in such circumstances a fully joint appointment would have been made. On this occasion we were absolutely senior to Merrill Lynch, given our sole control of the book. CSFB were nowhere to be seen. I learned later that Klaus Schlede, the Lufthansa chief financial officer who had been so amused by my views on SAS and who was the senior figure on the Amadeus selection committee, had insisted on a single point of responsibility for the flotation.

The transaction was to represent my first experience of the difficulties of working in the technology area – which was now beginning to take off as the US Dotcom boom crossed the Atlantic. We may have won the Amadeus flotation as transport experts; we were soon expected to achieve the kind of sky-high valuations that were increasingly to be seen in the technology area. The best proxy for the excitement in the technology area was represented by the index for the performance of stocks in the Nasdaq exchange, the composite index. This includes some 3,000 of the newer companies in the US firmament and has a bias towards the technology sectors that interested the investors as the 1990s drew to a close. Over the summer of 1998, as we talked values to the owners of Amadeus, the index had jumped nearly 30% from the beginning of the year. By the time we settled down in October with a transaction to launch, values had collapsed again – to below the levels seen in January. We scaled back our valuation of the company accordingly.

On Friday evening, on 9 October, Andrew Barker came round to my office with Neil Steer, the technology analyst.

"This deal isn't going to happen, is it?" said Andrew.

"Not at this level," I said. The markets were experiencing a sharp correction. The prices of the two main competitors, Galileo and

Sabre, had just collapsed on fears about passenger airline growth. Even Goldman Sachs was delaying its flotation.

"Do we really have to produce the research?" Neil Steer asked. He looked exhausted.

"How much do you have to do? We're meant to submit the final draft to the company on Monday."

Neil looked at the ceiling. "All of it," he admitted. "I've done some of the tables."

"Bloody hell. You've only got two days."

"I know. I just ran out of time. I'll have to work straight through the weekend."

"We've made all the other members of the syndicate produce their research by tonight," I pointed out. "It's going to look pretty peculiar if we don't have anything when the deal is still formally meant to be going ahead. We are the bookrunner, after all"

"When will you pull it, then?" asked Andrew.

"Tuesday, I should think," I guessed. "Just too late to spare our blushes." I didn't have the heart to put Neil through hell to spare our embarrassment. Besides, given his current exhaustion his output would inevitably read like gibberish if he were to work through the weekend.

"Leave it with me," I said. "We'll manage somehow."

As anticipated, the October launch plan was postponed early in the following week. However, the letter from Riswan Rahman complaining about the delinquency of our analysts later in the week was ferocious in its resentment.

"I must also express my surprise and disappointment on knowing that before the decision to postpone the IPO was taken by the shareholders, you had asked your firm's analysts to discontinue the preparation of the research report and no mention of this was made to Amadeus. On the contrary, Amadeus management has been urged to proceed with the finalisation . . ." and so on.

Back and forth went the transaction. In December we established a new timetable to launch in February. Later that month the plan was abandoned when talks re-opened to merge the company with Worldspan. Back came the timetable as these talks wavered and we assembled with the shareholders in the Sofitel hotel at Charles de

Gaulle airport in Paris on 12 January. By now the Nasdaq had soared: at 135, the composite index stood 55% higher than when we had delayed in October. Still it wasn't enough for the shareholders who decided to pursue the Worldspan option rather than a stand-alone float. We had entered the hotel in the mid-afternoon in bright sunshine. When we came out in the early evening, depressed by our lack of progress, we found ourselves in the middle of a snowstorm (of which more shortly).

With horrid inevitability the plan to merge with Worldspan collapsed, but not soon enough for us to catch the pre-summer window to float the company. Luckily technology values held firm through the summer of 1999 and when we were finally ready to float in October we achieved a level comfortably above that indicated 12 months earlier, at €5.75 a share. There were no complaints about the quality of our research on this occasion. However, in retrospect the shareholders should have prevaricated a month or two longer for suddenly the technology boom took off with a vengeance – the biggest financial bubble the world has ever seen. The Nasdaq index, standing at 156 on 19 October, the day Amadeus started trading, took off in a vertical line and finished the year at 237. This was an increase of more than 50% in the space of 10 weeks. The Amadeus share price reacted like a startled deer. First it doubled, then it soared further, touching €17 a share over the turn of the year.

By now the newspapers were stuffed with stories about opportunities in the technology area and in particular on the internet, which was set to revolutionise business dynamics round the world. We all started picking up the relevant jargon, whether it were B2B (business-to-business), or B2C (business to consumer). Within six months, Alan Greenspan, the iconic chairman of the US Federal Reserve Board, was talking about a paradigm shift as the new information technologies irreversibly increased the productivity of the 'old economy'. This was a long way from the speech he made in 1996 warning of the 'irrational exuberance' of the markets, at a time when they were standing at not much more than half their level at the end of 1999[1].

The Dotcom boom, as it became known, was to make the year

2000 one of the most difficult of my career. But before dealing with this I should revert to my second important German transaction, which took place in the previous year. This was the flotation of a transportation company called Stinnes, a subsidiary of the German conglomerate Veba.

My first encounter with Stinnes was an abrupt introduction to the brutality with which Germans could conduct their corporate affairs. In the late autumn of 1998 Richard Jaeckel, one of our relationship bankers based in Frankfurt, brought me to Mulheim in the Ruhr to meet Erhard Meyer Galow, the recently appointed chief executive of Stinnes, to discuss the plans to float. He was a tall, handsome man in his mid-fifties, with the dash of a cavalry officer. In his office, high in the Stinnes headquarters tower, we went through his strategy and examined the financial figures.

"We really should clean up and restructure two problem companies," he told us. "It will hit both the earnings and the balance sheet."

"Your balance sheet is already in bad shape," I told him. "You've got so much debt that you won't be able to do the restructuring once you are independent. You'll have to persuade Hartmann to remove some of this debt." Ulrich Hartmann was the chief executive of the parent company, Veba, whose weak share price had forced him to promise investors that he would dispose of various subsidiaries, including Stinnes.

"Do you think Hartmann will agree to reduce our debt?" asked Meyer Galow. "I'm due to see him soon."

"You're in a strong negotiating position," I pointed out.

My judgement could not have been more wrong. Richard Jaeckel rang me up shortly afterwards.

"Look at your Reuters screen," he said enigmatically.

It was a short piece. Meyer Galow had been fired with immediate effect for what were called differences in business perspective. In a German context his negotiating position had not been strong enough. A new Stinnes chief executive, in the shape of Wulf Bernotat, was appointed almost immediately.

"Well," I said to Richard later. "I suspect our chances of winning this float have just gone down the toilet."

"They're pushing ahead," he told me. "The beauty contest is set for mid-January. Make sure you can make it."

It would be tight since I was committed to addressing the Amadeus board in the late afternoon in Paris, but I juggled the itinerary to make sure I took an evening flight to Dusseldorf to be able to rehearse with the rest of the team. That was the theory.

When I walked out of the Sofitel hotel at Charles de Gaulle airport on 12 January there were already two inches of snow on the ground. I jumped into the chauffeur car to drive the mile round to Terminal Two. Cars slewed all over the road, sliding backwards as they failed to climb the steep ramp up to the terminal circulatory system. Somehow we made it up the ramp and round to the terminal.

"Cancelled," the Air France check-in attendant told me, with apparent malice. I hurried back to the car and Terminal One another mile or so away. Maybe I could catch the Lufthansa flight in an hour's time. The snow was pelting down and now lay four or five inches thick on the ground. After inching forward for half an hour our car ground to a halt, having proceeded less than a quarter of a mile. With cars strewn at random across the road, the traffic was immobile. My only chance was the last Air France flight.

"Can we go back to Terminal Two?" I asked the driver, who responded as if I had made a particularly amusing joke. I got out of the car and waded back through the blizzard to the terminal, cold, wet and muttering Captain Oates' famous last words as he left the tent in Antarctica to keep my spirits up: "I'm just going outside and may be some time."

"The airport is shut," the Air France check-in attendant told me triumphantly when I appeared at her counter.

Chaos. Twenty thousand people reached for their mobile phones and tried to book taxis or hotels or both.

I found a quiet corner and tried to phone up the Stinnes team to join their rehearsal long distance and work through the content of the next morning's presentation. It was hopeless. 'Network busy' registered on my mobile again and again. When I did get through it was only five minutes or so before I was cut off and had to start all over again. It was past 10.00pm before we had finished.

My team member Charles Otton called. He had been with me at the Amadeus meeting and was at the other terminal, his flight back to the UK equally aborted.

"We've managed to get a taxi," he told me. "Shall we pick you up?"

"Please," I said. Somehow he had managed to book a nearby hotel. Crazily we skidded through the blizzard to the hotel, watching mesmerised as a huge lorry slowly slid down a motorway slip road on the wrong side of the road. It was only when we were safely in the hotel, nursing a beer, that I suddenly realised the social revolution of the last decade.

"You know, Charles, I was sitting there huddled over my useless mobile next to banks and banks of public phones and it never occurred to me to use them. I didn't even register they were there." The new communication technology had transformed the way bankers operated over those years. I was able to run a team doing business all over the world because of the mobile phone and the increasingly ubiquitous email systems – staying in touch with companies wherever I was.

In spite – or maybe because – of my enforced absence from Dusseldorf the next morning, Veba awarded us the mandate to float Stinnes jointly with Dresdner. We were summoned to a launch session shortly afterwards. "They want to move with great speed," Richard Jaeckel told me.

Back at the Stinnes headquarters in Mulheim, the new chief executive officer, Wulf Bernotat, led the Stinnes executives in a presentation of the company to the two global co-ordinators, ourselves and Dresdner. We were a group of at least 20 clustered seminar style in the ground-floor presentation room, behind rows of tables. I sat at the front with Richard. Rothschild, the bank advising Veba on the transaction, had dressed up the presentation to impress us. Their efforts seem to have been devoted to emphasising the logistics aspect of the company. Logistics was becoming a buzzword in the market, closely connected to the supposed revolution in information technology under way. The introductory slides whizzed up in the irritating format of the Microsoft Powerpoint presentation programme, with each of the six subsidiaries renamed as a 'logistics' operation. Thus: 'Steel Logistics' for their tired steel stockholding business, or 'Wholesale Logistics' for their retail wholesaler. The catch-cry for this ragtag group of businesses was 'We link markets'. At the end there was an expectant pause as they awaited our reaction.

"I don't think the market will be fooled into thinking you are a pure logistics company by this," I pointed out. As the day progressed it became clear that nothing much had changed since our meeting with Meyer Galow in October. It was a conglomerate within a conglomerate.

"Our strategy is to become the consolidator of the industry," Wulf Bernotat summarised. This meant they wanted to take over their main rivals to build a powerful market position in their main transport business. However, since they had no money – indeed were heavily over-indebted – they simply could not afford to do this. Veba was planning to float a company in the market whose strategy was completely incoherent.

"This company is not floatable," I announced at the end of the day. Richard turned to look at me in horror. The rest of the room went deathly still. Rolf Pohlig, the senior management representative from Veba head office looked shocked.

"It will not have an investment grade rating," I added. This was not strictly relevant but the point would resonate with a bureaucratic company like Veba, deeply concerned with the attitude of the ratings agencies that assessed the debt position of companies.

"It has too much debt and the wrong strategy." These were real issues. I reckoned that unless we registered our concerns immediately Veba would assume we were content.

The shock tactics seemed to work. Stinnes and Veba started to look for ways to shore up the balance sheet and adjust to a more realistic corporate strategy. In retrospect I had been lucky to miss the beauty contest, where bankers always needed to exaggerate their enthusiasm for the prospective task. I had offered no judgements to constrain me as we got down to work. Indeed, I learned later that the Veba team assumed that I had deliberately missed the beauty contest exactly in order to retain this freedom of manoeuvre.

If only. The cock-up theory invariably fits the facts better than the conspiracy alternative.

As the flotation loomed I worried about the messages Wulf Bernotat would put out to the investors. More shock tactics were needed, I decided.

Reaching back to my former career, I wrote two sample Lex columns: Lex from Hell and Lex from Heaven. In May I handed them over to him, in order; first the Lex from Hell, which was extraordinarily rude:

"Latest to accept the urge to deconglomerate is Veba and the first set of assets to hit the block is its rambling transport plus bits and pieces subsidiary, Stinnes. The message does not seem to have penetrated the lower echelons of the empire which still thinks that sticking an embracing 'Logistics' title over the six or more different endeavours represents a business strategy. The most favourable interpretation is that this was the best that the third set of management within a 12-month period could develop in the time available."

It went on to attack the management's strategy: "Does the management have a strategy for growth? Up to now it has concentrated on the top line, with an endless series of acquisitions designed to keep a top-heavy head-office gainfully employed. The balance sheet stretch that has been the result means that this route to expansion will be denied in the medium term."

Finally it took a dig at Wulf Bernotat himself: "The CEO has been careful to retain his seat on the parent board. A formal voice with this key shareholder will clearly have some value but it smacks all too much of a personal parachute should things get tough."

Wulf Bernotat paled as he read through this litany of insults.

"That's the kind of thing you will be reading if you don't talk to the market about the importance of being careful with your capital and concentrating your efforts on getting margins up in the attractive businesses," I warned. "The investors want to hear that you intend to sort out this business, not embark on more grand strategies." I handed over the Lex from Heaven, subtitled 'Prometheus Unbound'.

"The revolution in corporate Germany is releasing the potential of some formidable competitors onto the world stage. Not least is the logistics group Stinnes, buried for so many years in the cellars of the utility group Veba.

"It emerges, blinking in the light of day, with a strategy tailor-made for success. A brand new management team is injecting vigour into operations across the board.

"Within months it has substituted DM4bn of tired revenues for growth opportunities. Looking a couple of years out, this process represents a hidden treasure chest to fund dominance in its core business."

It concluded: "With a highly incentivised management team focusing on escalating the returns on shrewdly used capital, there could not be a better time for investors to hitch a ride on this Prometheus, one of the long-term consolidators of this rapidly growing industry."

By now Wulf was looking a little more cheerful

"I prefer the Lex from Heaven," he pointed out. While he knew little about the transport business, he was a shrewd businessman. He was already beginning to grip the sprawling Stinnes empire and strip out the bureaucratic excesses. The two Lex Columns helped to focus him on how to put that message over to investors.

While the company was now in just about acceptable shape to offer to investors, the sales process was far from smooth. Just after we launched the market turned sour, with the new issue immediately preceding our own, for Agfa Gervaert, proving a failure and the price tumbling in the aftermarket. Investors smelled blood. On 10 June, 1999 - the evening before the planned close - James Garvin, head of syndicate, called a council of war. I had worked on a series of transactions with James since he had taken over the syndicate desk in 1995. He had a slightly rumpled appearance and an extremely quick, and somewhat mordant, wit which would occasionally plunge him into hot water. He had worked mainly in the debt markets before transferring to equity after the equity capital markets desk deserted to Deutsche Bank. At the time of this transaction he was aged 36. He had the ability to focus incisively on what was required to lock up a transaction and his market judgement was impeccable.

"This deal is going nowhere," he announced with characteristic bluntness. "The book is nonexistent. We have to cut. Both the amount and the price."

I put a call through to my opposite number at Dresdner, Michael Rohleder. An unpalatable message like this could only be delivered to Veba by both the global co-ordinators acting in concert.

Michael was unavailable. I tried his mobile, his office, his home. Nothing.

It was approaching midnight by the time we got hold of the head of syndicate at Dresdner, to agree a joint line. I rousted Rolf Pohlig of Veba out of bed.

"If you want the deal to go through," I explained, "We have to cut back the amount from 49% to 35% of the company and take a euro off the price."

"We'll need to consider this in the morning," he replied, "but I can tell you we can accept the reduction in size but not in price."

I put the phone down. "It looks like they've got the idea from someone that the deal will go through if they reduce the size alone," I said ruefully. "I guess that's why Michael Rohleder's been lying low."

James Garvin observed sardonically. "If we reduce the size and not the price the deal will still fail. The only difference is that it will fail to the sound of hysterical laughter from the market."

The observation stiffened my resolve next morning when I talked to the chief financial officer of Veba, Dr Hans Michael Gaul.

"You can reduce the size, but not the price," he told me.

"We are not prepared to go ahead on that basis," I replied.

"Then the deal is off."

"So be it."

It was a classic stand-off. Our only hope now was that Wulf Bernotat, the chief executive of Stinnes, might be able to persuade Hartmann to countermand Gaul.

"Where the fuck is Bernotat?" I demanded.

Nick Hughes, an Australian on secondment from our Sydney office, was working with me on the deal. "His plane got delayed in New York. Engine trouble. He's still flying over the Atlantic," he told me. Wulf Bernotat was returning overnight from the final leg of the roadshow to introduce Stinnes to investors in the US. It was mid-morning before he landed in Frankfurt.

We held a hurried telephone call. "Well," he concluded, in the measured manner with which he handled all crises, "now that we've done all this work I think it would be unfortunate to abandon the exercise for the sake of a euro a share."

His call to Hartmann clearly did the trick. Shortly after lunch the deal was back on and the salesmen of the two firms rapidly gathered orders for the stock at €14.5 a share, raising €380m.

The stress of this transaction was to leave a long trail. Hans Michael Gaul never forgave me, or Warburg, for facing him down over the Stinnes price and in my time we were never again appointed to act in a significant transaction for the company. Wulf Bernotat proved an able chief executive of Stinnes whose share price advanced steadily over the years. As a result he developed a reputation for being 'market-friendly', a rare enough attribute among German executives. This reputation meant that when the time came in May 2003 for Hartmann to retire from Veba (now renamed E.ON and the most important energy utility in Europe), Bernotat was appointed to succeed him as chief executive rather than Gaul, who had been favourite for the job. It was sometimes fascinating to give fate a helping hand.

Our roles for Stinnes and Lufthansa gave us some serious credentials to compete for the flotation of Deutsche Post which the Government planned for the year 2000. Deutsche Post was the largest postal operator in Europe and had used its financial resources to expand globally in logistics and express post as well as taking back ownership of the Postbank system. The transaction would represent the first flotation of a national postal operator and would inevitably be the largest IPO in Germany for the year.

I really did not want to go to the pitch set up for 3 February.

"Chris, I'd be really grateful if you lead the team on Thursday," I said to Chris Reilly, my close colleague from Euro Disney days.

"You have to be there," said Chris. "You're the head of transport."

"Ah yes, but they are insisting that only German speakers attend and I don't speak German."

"I'm sure they'd make an exception."

"I'd rather not ask. I'm heli-skiing in Canada in the back of beyond. I really don't want to miss it. Whichever joker put this insistence on a German-speaking team in the RFP has provided me with the perfect alibi."

I managed to keep my week's break in Canada.

The selection committee decided that their linguistic requirements were counter-productive and asked us to come back with the working team – speaking English – on the following Tuesday. By now I was back in Europe and happy to oblige. We were not out of the woods yet, though. Klaus Zumwinkel, the powerful chief executive of Deutsche Post, was determined to see his favoured bank CSFB appointed to the role of international global co-ordinator alongside the domestic Deutsche Bank.

We lobbied our friend at the finance ministry, Eberhard Rolle, as hard as we could. "Zumwinkel will get his way," I moaned to Chris as we put down the phone. "The German finance ministry is the weakest in Europe. They always get kicked around by businessmen and politicians."

We played up a hostile court judgement over the organisation of tenders for the sale of Berlin airport, in which CSFB had been peripherally involved, although the Ministry seemed to brush it aside. More telling was the publicity that emerged with impeccable timing in the German press pointing out that the former Chancellor, Helmut Kohl, had been appointed to the CSFB board. The SPD Government Ministers were sensitive to this promotion of their former CDU rival.

"Do you have a conflict of interest in advising the UK Royal Mail?" came back the counter-blow, as the shadow-boxing went on. We had recently won a formal selection process to act for the UK organisation. Now the victory came back to haunt us. Klaus Zumwinkel had established a ferocious reputation for rejecting banks with any real or imagined conflicts. Previously he had insisted that the Government fire Morgan Stanley as its adviser on postal matters when that bank was appointed the lead manager of the flotation of its bitter rival UPS in the United States. With heavy heart I signed a carefully-worded legal commitment restricting our ability to act for any competitors of Deutsche Post for the period of the mandate.

At least we had won the IPO.

James Sassoon, who was working with me on the Royal Mail

account, joined me in a painful meeting with the chief executive of the UK company, John Roberts, later in February.

"John, I am sorry but we have taken the decision to sign this commitment," I confessed. "It is too important a transaction for us to give up and we considered that over the next nine months you won't need us to work on anything material anyway."

John looked us over calmly. "I'll have to think about the implications. But I need your assurance that you will not put yourselves in this position ever again."

"You have that assurance," replied James. Later John told us that the decision on whether or not to fire us had been close. In the end the company decided that we were accurate in our judgement that little would transpire over the rest of the year. Indeed, it was not till Deutsche Post was safely floated in November that we began the major labour of preparing the UK Royal Mail to be merged with the Dutch equivalent, TNT Post Group.

Concerns over conflicts paled as the year progressed. Suddenly, the desperate issue became holding on to personnel. Until the year 2000 I had only lost one of my team involuntarily, back in 1997. Now the floodgates opened. The Dotcom boom was sucking bankers out of the industry with awesome efficiency as stories multiplied about companies being floated within a few months of creation, on the back of a vague concept and some energetic marketing. Investment banks fell to poaching each other's staff with ferocity to fill in the gaps. Headhunters would call round the team-room on a daily basis. I could almost track the telephone calls.

First to leave was Robin Phillips, the banker from UBS I had asked to lead the airport effort. He left for Salomon taking two members of his team with him. Then the youngsters started to leave. I became used to them entering my office and carefully closing the door before letting me know the bad news. One would be off to a boutique specialising in technology issues, the next to join a Dotcom company, the third to a rival investment bank to join their technology team.

I tried my best to hold on to them. I would argue that we were a dominant sector team in which they would gain experience in transactions of the highest quality; that after three or four years this kind of track record would provide the foundation for a formidable career. I might have saved my breath. They looked at me as if I were a Victorian corpse, with all this talk of careers and experience. Fortunes were being made in a matter of months. And besides, where was the risk? If their Dotcom went up in smoke they could always come back to work in a bank. It was a free option and they invariably responded to my warnings that the environment might be very different in 18 months time with a pitying smile. I did not prevent a single person from leaving. The grand total of personnel lost from my team that year, including normal transfers, was no fewer than 22.

Worst of all was the internal competition.

"We're going to set up a Chinese Army," said Robert Gillespie, now the joint head of corporate finance, early in the year. "We know we've been late into this technology boom but we're going to throw bodies at it, both in the equities division and in corporate finance. Anyone who wants to transfer into the new sector will be able to do so."

"Bloody hell," I complained a couple of weeks later as the repercussions hit home and one of the juniors requested a transfer. "He's working on Deutsche Post. It's only the biggest and most difficult IPO the bank's working on anywhere in the world. We can't afford to lose him."

All to no avail.

"I'm sorry," I told Nick Hughes, whose skills in sorting out German logistics companies, following the flotation of Stinnes, were now to be applied to the Deutsche Post issue. "They won't budge."

"Bastards."

Condemned to inadequate support by the department's strategic switch of resources into the Dotcom boom and the death of a German colleague in an autobahn accident, he was to find himself under real pressure in the months to come. In the circumstances his reaction was remarkably restrained.

As I struggled to refill the gaps left in my department, the pressure of transactional work intensified. In late May I picked up the phone to Edgar Ernst, the chief financial officer at Deutsche Post.

"Edgar," I said. "I simply don't understand your figures."

"What do you mean? They are perfectly straight-forward aren't they?"

"Not to me, they aren't," I said. "And while I may be pretty slow when it comes to German accounting, I suspect that if I have a problem, the investors will have one too."

"Well, we'd better set up some sessions to make sure you do understand them," he replied. Early in June we assembled in a hotel a little upriver from the company's headquarters in Bonn at Konigswinter on the Rhine. Nick and I, together with our Deutsche Bank colleagues, spent two separate days working through the numbers, sitting at a table facing some 15 members of the company's financial control department arranged in a horse-shoe. Slowly we plodded through.

"What's this profit, here?

"That's from the sale of real estate we don't use any more."

"Where does it appear in terms of revenue?"

"In the reconciliation line." The 'Reconciliation', or Uberleitung, category was to prove a rag-bag into which items were thrown with great abandon. German accountants boasted that they could work their birth dates into the published figures and after studying the Uberleitung category for half a day I could see why.

"There's a huge number here for negative goodwill. What on earth is that?"

"That's because we bought Postbank cheap. So we are writing it back up to its real value."

"The net assets of Postbank seem to represent two-thirds of those for the whole group," I challenged. "What capital are you running the rest of the group on?"

"Ah," said Edgar Ernst, pityingly. "You don't understand accounting."

I never did get an answer I could understand to that question.

And so it went on, for hour after hour. The company had changed its accounting approach from German to international standards; it had taken over some 50 companies over the previous three years; its figures were heavily distorted by the ownership of a bank; it was under attack from regulators at home and in Brussels for abusing its market position.

Nick Hughes had the appalling responsibility of making sense of all this confused data. I said to him afterwards, "I used to have a 'Rule of 1' that you could get away explaining just one piece of complexity to investors. If there were two they would just switch off. Here we've got to take them through about 10."

"You'll have to make up a new 'Rule of 10'," Nick suggested.

"Yes. When there are 10 or more bits of complexity, investors won't bother to investigate and buy anyway," I said hopefully.

By the time we began rehearsing Klaus Zumwinkel and Edgar Ernst on 20 October for their meetings with potential investors, we understood enough about the figures to present the underlying reality of the group's performance. We also knew the key issues that investors would pound them on.

The preparation was enough to ensure that Deutsche Bank and we were able to build a healthy book of demand over the November road-show period. Now we arrived in Frankfurt on Friday evening, 17 November, ahead of the next day's formal meeting to agree the right price for the issue. As the team worked through the night to analyse the book, Lucinda Riches and I took ourselves off to a good restaurant in the middle of Frankfurt. In the five years since her stunning intervention in the pricing meeting for Nynex Cablecomms, Lucinda had been steadily promoted and she now ran the equity capital markets operation alongside James Garvin. She remained as irreverent as ever.

Every ten minutes, as we ate, her mobile would sound off. It was invariably Michael Bednar, our German equity market specialist, reporting on the latest news from German radio.

"Demand is excellent, they're saying. The price has been set at 22 euros a share."

"We haven't even had the pricing meeting yet," she protested. "We're meant to be bloody pricing it tomorrow."

"Eichel's decided on 22 euros, according to the reports," replied Michael. Hans Eichel had been appointed German Finance Minister in April the previous year.

"I don't know why we bother to fly all the way over to this dump," she grumbled, "if it's all been agreed without us." She reached over for our bottle of wine. "At least let's enjoy the booze."

We were a long way from the UK privatisation boom of the 1980s. Just as the institutional investors had grown more sophisticated in their analysis of how companies used their capital, so had Government vendors like Hans Eichel learned how to squeeze the maximum price out of the market.

The next day it was hardly a surprise to be confronted by a demand from the Government officials to price the issue at €22. The computerised book we had built had plenty of bids for stock in it, and on the surface was covered at this price. The reality, however, was that many of the bids at this level were over-inflated, designed to obtain scarce stock as the investors played sophisticated games with us, rather than genuine demand. The price would collapse in the after-market if we set this price. Our arguments that the Government should not risk a disappointing float, which would sour the many future issues it planned, were brushed aside.

"That's what they want and nothing we can say will stop them," airily pronounced my former colleague Michael Cohrs, now in charge of the Deutsche Bank capital markets operation, in one of the many coffee breaks during that Saturday morning.

Lucinda was made of sterner stuff. "At €21.5 we will lose nearly all the German investor base," she pointed out.

"Will we?" said Eberhard Rolle, now genuinely concerned that the finance ministry might be squeezing too hard. We broke yet again to work out the sums properly. As is invariably the way, the night-long toil of the team to produce graphs breaking down the book in every conceivable way had overlooked this specific analysis – the only one that turned out to have any impact at all. We worked out the information with a pencil on a grubby sheet of paper. Lucinda was right. Nearly all the big German investors had limited their demand below €21.5.

In the end this was the decisive factor and we priced the deal at €21 a share, raising €6.6bn for the ministry. In the event the share held onto the €21 level when it started trading on the following Monday, just about, but it was swept away with the rest of the market half a year later and bottomed out below €10 in 2002.

This was not to be my last formal encounter with Deutsche Post. The second transaction proved just as painful as the first and came about through a most circuitous route – our relationship with Lufthansa.

In September 1998, shortly after ensuring our appointment to float Amadeus, Klaus Schlede retired as chief financial officer of Lufthansa to become the chairman of the supervisory board. His successor, Karl Kley, was recruited from the German pharmaceutical giant Bayer and proved just as staunch a supporter.

A year later he summoned my deputy Tom Cooper and me to a meeting in the Frankfurt offices of the airline. We were working on the purchase of a stake in British Midland for them. At the initial meeting on the topic Jurgen Weber, the Lufthansa chief executive, had told us this acquisition was the No 1 priority for the airline.

"How much do we need to pay?" Karl demanded. "I don't want any of your bullshit."

We worked out a price of around £450m.

"You should have the figure seven in it," I contributed. "All my offers end in the figure seven."

"Good, that's agreed then," said Karl. "£457m it is."

It took another couple of months, but by November a complicated transaction had been agreed in which Lufthansa obtained an initial 20% stake in the British airline. The precision of the £457m valuation placed on British Midland puzzled analysts in rival investment banks for years to come.

Six months later, in May 2000, the airline shareholders of Amadeus – Iberia and Air France as well as Lufthansa – were looking to sell more of their holdings in the computer reservation system company. We had been working on the transaction over the previous two months, but this time Merrill Lynch had played their cards better, trading in particular on their strong relationship with Iberia.

"We've decided to appoint Merrill Lynch jointly with you to handle this sale," said Adolf Rosell, the Lufthansa representative on the shareholder team at the formal meeting in Madrid on 5 May. This represented an ignominious descent from the dominant position we had been awarded in the original flotation, particularly after the recognition given to the quality of our performance on that transaction. I decided to take a flyer.

"This is not the kind of transaction in which responsibilities can be split," I responded. "It's a high speed, two-day placement of stock. There's no time for discussion, liaison, arguments with another bank. We are not prepared to act jointly on this type of issue. Choose either Merrill or us. One or the other."

This was only the second time in my career that I had taken a chance like this, the first occasion being the Nynex Cablecomms float. This was much riskier. While Lufthansa was happy to see our ploy succeed, our position with Iberia was much less favourable. Only a couple of months earlier we had been acting on British Airways' side to buy a keystone stake in Iberia, while Merrill had acted for the home team. My determination was reinforced by memories of the Euro Disney convertible, when the capital base of the bank was put at severe risk because BNP controlled half the stock. It took several days of arduous lobbying before we managed to see Merrill off and take the sole book-running role. In the event my obduracy was to save the transaction.

Less than three weeks later, on Tuesday 23 May we gathered in the equity syndicate room in the Warburg London office, known as the Belfry, with the results of the rapid sales operation. It was not pretty. We had launched into an abrupt downturn in the market, the Nasdaq composite having shed 6% in the day.

"We haven't got a fucking book," said James Garvin. "So you can't fucking well give it to them." One of the Iberia team was upstairs in a visitors' meeting room and had sent a message down to one of our juniors asking to see the book of demand. We had arranged for them to come over to London early exactly to undertake this task.

"If anyone gets the merest whiff of the real state of demand we are dead," James declared vehemently. "I don't care what you tell him. Tell him your grandmother's cat died for all I fucking care, but do not let him see the book."

It was mid-evening. There were about 20 of us in the room, salesmen, analysts, equity syndicate executives, members of my sector team. We had aimed to sell €1.5bn of Amadeus stock, but the exercise had not been a success and we had demand for less than €1bn. Now we were all in the hands of the trader, John Wall. Back and forth we debated, as John felt for the level of risk.

"The orders we do have are high quality," said James. "We can give them more or less all they ask for."

That was one problem under control.

John turned to me: "These are important clients, are they, David?"

"Yes," I said.

"We'd like to do them a favour?"

"Yes."

"OK. Let's do it. I can take a couple of hundred million on the book and if we fill these orders at 90%, we can do 750m euros for them, maybe more if we trade the shoe out later. We just need to get lucky with the markets in the next few days."

At 11.00pm I was ready to go upstairs and run the pricing meeting. Apologising for our regrettable printing problems with the book, I managed to obtain agreement from the shareholders – many of whom were joining the meeting by phone – on the smaller amount and somewhat lower price without revealing the hole we were in.

Luckily the market went our way in the next two weeks with the Nasdaq composite jumping 20%. As the share price rebounded, John Wall was able steadily to trade out of his position and even increased the transaction to €900m by issuing the shoe, as he had hoped. It was not for several weeks that we were able to come clean to the airline shareholders quite how close to disaster we had been and the amount of capital we had committed to making sure the transaction went ahead.

As soon as I could, I phoned up Karl Kley to explain our uncharacteristic silence in the later stages of the transaction. "It was just as well we were acting alone," I pointed out. "You would never have got two banks to act so decisively on a joint basis. The one would not have trusted the other to behave in the after-market."

"Just what I would have expected from you," he replied breezily. "After all, you are the best bank in the world." Then he adroitly changed the subject.

At any time in this period we would be working on one or more transactions for Lufthansa. A year later, in June 2001, we were engaged on yet another mandate based on their Amadeus stock. This time it was an exchangeable, an instrument that allowed Lufthansa to raise €250m of cheap debt that could convert into Amadeus equity. The deal closed on 14 June, when I happened to be taking Karl and his wife out to lunch at the Waterside Inn at Bray on the Thames. As we strolled side by side down one of the nearby lanes after the meal, both our mobiles rang. His deputy, Markus Ott, was offering his judgement on the terms we were recommending. My convertibles colleague told me: "We want to launch at 2.25%. The market would be pretty uncomfortable any lower." Neither team knew we were within two feet of each other.

"What's your lot saying?" Karl asked.

"2.25% is the right rate. What's Markus' view?"

"Much the same. Seems all right. Shall we tell them to get on with it?"

And we both cleared the terms of the transaction before catching up with our wives.

Karl Kley, a devotee of English word-play, quirky, charming, became a genuine friend over the years. It did not stop him throwing some vicious challenges at us. In the year after the exchangeable, he set me up with something much less straight-forward, the transaction that was to bring me back into the purlieu of Deutsche Post. Karl suggested to Edgar Ernst, the chief financial officer of the postal giant, that we provide a valuation of DHL International, the international express delivery service, to both companies. This was designed to help them reach a price at which Lufthansa would sell its 25% stake to Deutsche Post.

This was a no-win mandate in which our findings would inevitably infuriate one party or the other, if not both. With great trepidation the team launched into the complicated valuation, a process rendered particularly difficult by the fact that the DHL operation in the US was haemorrhaging losses and required a completely revised strategy to survive.

As we produced our first drafts my worst fears were confirmed.

Somehow we managed to arrive at a figure that was deeply disappointing to both parties. In early summer I travelled out to see each of the two companies. It was a riveting education in bullying techniques.

Edgar Ernst got right to the point: "Our relationship with UBS Warburg is not good, as you know, after your analyst said we were a hold. Now you have produced this very high figure for the value of DHL. You cannot expect to work for us in future if you behave like this."

Karl Kley was infinitely more subtle: "I always thought that UBS Warburg understood how to value companies. Now I see from this poor piece of work that you do not. It is a great shock for me. I will have to readjust my views on your strengths and weaknesses."

In terms of technique, Karl inflicted much deeper wounds.

Somehow we got through the process, which anyway reverted to a trial of strength between the two companies, and the sale went ahead in July at a total value of €610m, comfortably above our figure.

By now the Dotcom boom was a distant memory. In retrospect the boom peaked in March 2000, with the Nasdaq Composite standing at three and a half times the level just 18 months earlier. The UK travel agency start-up, Lastminute.com, caught the peak almost to the week when it floated. We had only a junior role in this transaction, partly perhaps because of one of my quips at our autumn leisure conference in the previous year. The charismatic joint founder of the company, Martha Lane Fox, had been volubly promoting the opportunities for her company.

"Don't worry, Martha," I reassured her from the platform, "if you beg, I'm sure we'll float you."

The over-exuberant market as Lastminute floated nearly destroyed the company. Morgan Stanley priced the stock at 380p per share, way beyond any conceivable fundamentals to reflect demand. The price soared to a top price of 487p before collapsing to 240p by the end of the month, 40% below the issue price. From there it headed south. We gave thanks that we had failed to win this emblematic transaction.

There was no relief in sight as the world stock markets retreated, slowly at first and then from September on with increasing speed. By the end of 2000 the Nasdaq Composite had more than halved from the peak.

The individuals who had thrown their careers into the Dotcom furnace found the experience deeply traumatic. Those who had joined companies would invariably discover that they had worked for empty promises – options that were worthless when the companies folded, rather than a salary. Those who had joined boutiques and venture capital companies specialising in technology found work drying up as the sector cratered. Those who had switched to this area of investment banking, either within our firm or for a rival, found themselves equally stranded.

And there was no way back, for soon the specific collapse of Dotcom mania merged into a general collapse in financial markets and activity. Investment banking suddenly became a very sour business indeed.

---

[1] The broadly based Dow Jones Industrial Index stood at 6437 when he made the speech on 5 December 1996 and 11,497 on 31 December 1999

13

Swansong
Recession and retirement – 2001-2003

~

"My mobile's stopped working," I complained.

"What do you mean, your mobile's stopped working?" demanded my colleague Robin Budenburg. "You're meant to be running our IT user committee – if you don't know who to call to get it fixed, I'm sure none of us can help you."

"No," I said. "I didn't mean that it's got a technical fault. It's much worse than that. Nobody rings me on it any more."

I was talking to a group of senior colleagues in one of our more or less formal get-togethers in early April 2001. The purpose of the evening dinner was to analyse trends in our business across Europe.

"If my phone is a lead indicator, which I suspect it is," I concluded gloomily, "we are going to see a really sharp fall in business in the next few months."

I could judge almost to the hour when the business climate for investment bankers turned. It had happened a few weeks earlier, on 14 February. I had paid a visit to the Dutch Ministry of Finance at the Hague at 11.00am, struggling out to the Netherlands on an early flight from London. When I got out of the meeting, just before lunch, I checked my mobile for messages. Typically, after a couple of hours incommunicado, there would be four or five urgent messages waiting for me: a client complaining about some shortcoming; a team-member with a problem (possibly connected with the first message); some urgent adjustment to my diary and travel arrangements. On this Wednesday there was nothing.

Obviously a slip-up, I thought, ringing my highly efficient

secretary, Sara Shipp, to check the real position.

"It's been quiet," she said. "Nothing's come up." She sounded as puzzled as me. It was as if some-one had pulled a switch. For the next two years – indeed, for the rest of my time with Warburg – my mobile phone remained a quiescent tool rather than the tyrannical destroyer of my diary it had become in the previous decade.

Until then, the broader market had held firm; indeed, in mid-February the UK market (as measured by the FTSE 100 index) was no more than 10% off its all time high, achieved at the height of the Dotcom enthusiasm at the beginning of the previous year. Now, however, the markets began to slide away, tumbling through the spring. A partial recovery in the summer was swept away by the Al Qaeda attack on the twin towers in New York in September. After this, with war in Afghanistan looming, the markets collapsed and investment banking activity froze.

"They'll pull," I warned Tom Cooper. "Bet you anything."

"They want to go ahead." Tom replied.

"You wait."

Tom was master-minding the French construction giant Vinci's hostile takeover for the small UK airport company, TBI. Already the French had seized a 14.9% stake in TBI, which owned the majority of Luton airport as well as stakes in Belfast International and Cardiff. In mid-August Vinci had made a generous bid for the outstanding stock, valuing the company at £515m, which the founders of TBI, and its management, were resisting with great ferocity.

It took some time for the full repercussions of the September Al Qaeda attack to hit home. With the skies over America cleared for the rest of the week, global airline stocks were among the worst hit, tumbling more than 35% over the rest of the month. Airports were down less, but still a vicious 17%. The Vinci bid now looked positively mouth-watering.

"You were right," said Tom when he returned from a trip to Paris. "Zacharias wants to pull." Antoine Zacharias was the powerful chairman of Vinci, and his initial determination to proceed had been reversed after some meetings with his shareholders.

"One simply cannot proceed when the shareholders are so

against the move," Zacharias told us a few days later.

The trouble for Vinci was that under the strict UK takeover code it was not permitted to withdraw an offer, once made, should all the conditions be met. At this stage the only outstanding condition was that it receive shares totalling 90% of the company. For the first nine days after the attack the Board of TBI remained resolutely opposed to the bid. Then, four days before the closing date, reality intruded and it abruptly recommended shareholders to accept the offer.

As we gathered in Paris on the Monday, 24 September, there was little we could do but await the outcome of this bizarre transaction. Normally a bidder would be desperate to win and the defending company equally keen to retain its independence. On this occasion, Vinci was desperate to lose and the TBI Board had woken up to the fact that it would be extremely foolish to miss a chance to sell out at these pre-11 September prices. Luckily for Vinci, the TBI change of heart had come too late and the effort to assemble enough shares failed, but only just. Our count showed that the shareholders were offering us 84% of the company – short of the required 90%. With some relief, Vinci put out a press notice announcing that the bid had lapsed – although it now had to nurse a paper loss of more than £35m on the shares it had already bought.

Activity levels fell to the lowest I could remember. Companies did not want to do deals or raise capital. Even when they did, all too often the markets would not let them and months of effort were wasted. From the summer of 2001 I worked extensively on a project to merge the UK Royal Mail with its Dutch counterpart, TPG. Since this transaction was never consummated, it is inappropriate for me to deal with it here. In any event, the attempt fell apart amid some trauma in early March 2002. I spent fruitless time on abortive airline mergers; the failed float of a German fish restaurant chain, Nordsee; unused financial structures for Deutsche Bahn, the German railway giant; trying to buy the state-owned National Air Traffic Services for the business services company, Serco.

We were much better off than our competitors. In the extraordinary year of 1999 my team had achieved gross revenues of more than $200m, a figure that fell to a more representative $140m in

2000. Now, in the tough years of 2001 and 2002, we held on at about $115m a year. Luckily the rail business, with several streams of regular income on which I did not now need to spend much effort, came through strongly. At the same time the growing maturity of the leisure and business services segments provided some compensation for a collapse in the bread and butter transport activity. We were still winning a healthy share of business – around 30%, according to our carefully gathered statistics, and we charged full fees for the business we did take on, unlike many other banks in our sector. We had to work much harder to win new business, however - approximately three times as hard in terms of the number of pitches required to win each mandate. Furthermore, many of the deals we did win turned sour.

The figures for the industry suggested we were doing better than average. According to Freeman & Co, global investment banking revenues fell by a quarter in 2001 from the 2000 peak of $53bn, and further in 2002 – to stand at 60% of their level two years earlier[1]. Somehow everyday business activity felt much slower, and more difficult, than the figures suggested. Partly this was because the nature of the business changed. Much of the activity in these two years involved working with venture capitalists, the new superstars of the financial firmament.

In the excited markets of the 1990s, some of the best returns were made by investors who bought companies, improved the way they operated, and then sold them – often for much more than the purchase price. In fact, the excellent returns could in part be explained by the way these new entrants geared their assets with debt in a decade that saw an unusually extended upward movement of share prices. 'Don't confuse brains with a bull market', states an old adage, meaning that any fool can get lucky if the market is moving in the right direction. Whatever the reason, investors poured money into the hands of the venture capitalists, whose annual funding soared by a factor of 10 between 1995 and 2000, to $105bn in the US[2] and €48bn in Europe[3]. As markets collapsed, the venture capitalists - with their committed funds - became the most important buyers in town.

"I just hope this is a good buy," said Marek Guimienny, one of the senior executives at the venture capital house Candover in the UK. In early 2003 Jason Katz, my young head of the leisure segment, had just helped them buy the bingo company Gala from yet another venture capitalist, CSFB.

"So do I," I said. "I think it probably is. I certainly hope so." I had phoned Marek Guimienny to congratulate him on the purchase. It was a rare success.

Pitching to win work with a venture capitalist was a messy business. They did not need much financial advice since their stock in trade was an ability to run financial models and conduct negotiations – exactly the skills brought into a transaction by an investment bank. To the extent they wanted help it was in the shape of inside knowledge of the target company and an ability to communicate effectively with its management. This had been precisely Jason's role with the chief executive of Gala, John Kelly. Jason was a natural networker who first started working in my team as an intern in 1994. Brought up in South Africa, he had a flair for the business that encouraged me to promote him as quickly as I could. For his part, he had devoted astonishing energy to the job. Once I was at a social event when I was confronted by a young lady.

"You bastard," she addressed me.

I rifled quickly through the possible transgressions I had committed to deserve this epithet.

"Who are you?" I asked cautiously.

"I'm Jason's cousin and you are a slave-driver." To my considerable shock I learned that in the previous week Jason had spent 48 hours straight at the office, incorporating two consecutive nights, to complete some work on time. After that I had regularly patrolled the analysts to make sure they were not killing themselves. Jason managed to fast-track his experience by this overload to take on responsibility much greater than his years would suggest.

For the venture capitalists, advice was secondary. What they really wanted from the investment banks was hard cash in the form of loans on which they could gear up their purchases. They were prepared to pay well for the funds, but in this business the investment banks had to make hard assessments about the quality of the business being bought. After all, if a purchase went bust, it was their own money that would be disappearing into the void.

For investment bankers, therefore, this became an excruciating business of negotiating with the credit department of their own bank to supply funding. The caution of UBS, *in abstracto* an admirable trait, became intensely frustrating for practitioners at the sharp end. Again and again decisions were taken – invariably late, because this was when all the information was available – not to participate in a loan-based transaction. There was no joy in the sterile internal committee work required to complete these transactions even when they were successful. When we had managed to pick the right venture capital house – the one which had won a particular auction to buy a business – and our role fell away because of lending restrictions, they became absolutely miserable.

Venture capital work, however unpalatable, could not fill the void as other business dried up. By the autumn of 2001 we were looking hard at reducing the number of investment bankers employed – in common with all the other houses.

Four rounds of firing were to follow. The first took place at the end of 2001, the next halfway through 2002, followed by one at the end of 2002, and the last (in which I was involved) in mid-2003. Each round was a grisly affair. Each time everyone in the bank knew what was afoot and rumours spread as the laborious process of compiling lists of 'weaker' performers was completed.

On the day itself those selected would be summoned to a meeting room on the seventh floor to be informed of their fate. Invariably they would not be let back to their desks, to protect the bank against sabotage of the computer systems. Their personal belongings would be collected in black rubbish sacks and handed over. By the later rounds the procedure became routine.

It was an intensely political process. As the management process concentrated on reducing manpower, so the power balance within the investment bank changed. The sector bosses, like me, lost much of their leverage in favour of the heads of the geographic regions who were managing the process. First to suffer were my teams abroad. I lost the head of each of my Japanese, Asian and US teams over the period as my ability to protect them within their local region declined.

In Europe I was better placed and struggled to make sure that I kept the core of my team in place. This was a matter of negotiation with Chris Brodie, now the geographic head of Europe.

"You need to fire so and so," he phoned me abruptly in early March 2002.

"I thought you agreed so and so could stay," I replied hotly.

"We need more heads."

"Chris, I am just passing Fort Lauderdale in Florida driving to a client. What the hell am I meant to do?"

"Either so and so, or someone else from your department," he insisted as I gave in.

Over the two-year period I fired, or transferred, more than 20 people – roughly the same number who resigned during the Dotcom boom. The two processes, involuntary and voluntary, were equally painful. I became utterly determined to see the recession through with the essential core of my team intact. In this frame of mind it became possible to act with a degree of callousness over the loss of particular individuals, especially when many of them were the junior analysts who could find other careers after their bracing experience in investment banking.

Nothing in my experience was atypical for the industry. According to Freeman, by autumn 2002 the industry had cut 8.8% of its workforce and was expected to shed a further 15 or 20% to reach break-even. Pay levels had roughly halved over the same period[4].

One more element was to be added to the miserable brew: regulatory overkill.

In July 2001, Andrew Barker, the senior transport analyst, and I had been invited to make a presentation on how corporate finance and equity research could and should work together. It seemed amazing to both of us that analysts and corporate financiers still had not absorbed our approach: the last time we had given this talk was back in 1997. We reprised our arrangements.

"The single most important thing we need from our analysts is that they are highly rated," I said. "That means we are better positioned to win business."

"Doing good corporate business is incredibly valuable for us," Andrew pointed out. "There is nothing that cements our relationship with the institutions more than putting them into a good corporate issue where they've bought a big stake and it's gone up. A position like that can really make a difference to the performance figures of their funds."

"We decided long ago that it's pointless to try and do business that the analysts don't want to do." I went on. "If they don't believe in it they won't push it. Besides there's always the chance that they might be right in thinking the company is a dog. So now we only chase the business the analysts want to do."

"That means we can trust them," Andrew pointed out.

Francois Guows, the head of equities who had organised the meeting, shook his head. "I get complaints all the time about corporate financiers bullying equity analysts to get behind their deal," he observed.

"It's very short-sighted of them," I replied, with the complacency that comes of being held out as a role model. I agreed to send out a general note on how the sector relationship should be structured.

The note soon became a historical curiosity as overwhelming forces overtook it moving in precisely the opposite direction.

The collapse of the Dotcom boom left a painful legacy of bankrupt companies, appalling losses for investors, lawsuits and regulatory investigations. As cheerleaders and significant beneficiaries of the boom, the investment banks were naturally the focus for much of the finger-pointing. The role of the analysts was subjected to particularly close scrutiny. Stories emerged of how some investment bank analysts in the US had become virtual hirelings of the companies whose shares their banks' were issuing. Hardly surprising, perhaps, when it also emerged that the pay of those analysts was directly based on the corporate business they undertook.

The most egregious of the stories concerned Jack Grubman, last encountered on the pricing night for Nynex Cablecomms in 1995 and even back then extremely keen to push out stock at an unsupportable price. Grubman continued to work for Salomon

Smith Barney, as the leading - and best paid - telecoms analyst on Wall Street. Having pushed the sector all the way up, he remained absurdly confident as it turned tail. The specific stock coverage which received most opprobrium was for Global Crossing, a company which Salomon took public in 1998 and whose share price peaked at over $61 a share the following year. Jack Grubman continued to recommend it in 2000 and again in April 2001, despite heavy falls in the price. Only in October, with the price at about $1 a share did he switch his recommendation from 'buy' to 'neutral', before suspending coverage in January 2002, as the company filed for bankruptcy. Grubman was banned from the industry in 2003, when investigators uncovered emails boasting that he had upgraded his rating for AT&T to curry favour with his boss (and get help to obtain places for his children at a prestigious New York pre-school.)

Other stories surrounded Henry Blodget, the Dotcom analyst at Merrill Lynch. Regulators compared his private view of the companies he was promoting, as expressed in his emails, with those published in his formal recommendations. "Such a piece of crap", he described Excite @ Home, while rating it 'Accumulate' to 'Buy'. In April 2003 he also was banned from the securities industry for life.

The most vigorous of those investigating malpractice was the New York Attorney General, Eliot Spitzer. As he uncovered more and more evidence about improper relationships between analysts and corporate financiers, talks began with the 10 biggest global investment banks (including UBS) to reach a settlement.

"Investors understand risk – but we demand honesty and integrity in the research that was delivered." Spitzer declared. "The business model had completely integrated investment and research… Everybody won, except the investor."

Chris Brodie, the European head, had given us a preview of the terms as the negotiations ground on through the spring of 2003. They looked horrific. There could be no communication between corporate financiers and equity analysts. Analysts could not help to win business, nor were they allowed to help market issues.

"Will all this apply in Europe as well as the US?" I asked Chris.

"I suspect it will, in the fullness of time at least," Chris answered.

My model of how to run a sector was now effectively destroyed.

After all, how could the corporate financiers and analysts agree on the companies which both wished to follow? They were hardly allowed to talk to each other without a compliance officer present.

How times had changed. For much of my career the regulators did not have a clue about market operations – leaving us free to make up the rules as we went along. As soon as they began to learn what was happening it seemed that they did not like it one bit. Whether the integrated structure of investment banking will hold up after the Spitzer settlement remains an open question as I write.

Amidst the miseries of business retrenchment and encroaching regulation, an interesting transaction shone out like a beacon. In October 2002 Derek Stevens, now retired from his job as chief financial officer of British Airways, phoned.

"Are you in a position to help us with NATS?" he asked. This was the UK National Air Traffic Services that we had failed to buy for Serco in 2001. The winning bidder had been the Airline Group, a consortium of seven British airlines, and Derek had been brought in to act as the chairman of this shareholder group. The airlines owned the company jointly with the Government.

"Yes," I replied cautiously. Our role with Serco had lapsed with the failure of the bid. "I thought Salomon was your adviser."

"Not for much longer," he replied. "We need help, and it doesn't look like Salomon is in a position to provide it."

"Why not?"

"The banks won't talk to them any more. Do you want to pitch for the job?"

"It'll be difficult to rescue," I warned him. The problems at NATS were hardly a state secret. The airline bid had incorporated a large amount of debt. With the collapse in air travel after the attack on New York's Twin Towers, the financial structure of the organisation had fallen apart.

"The terms are all agreed in principle," Derek promised. "It's just a question of locking them down."

"I've heard that before."

"Yes. It does sound a bit over-optimistic, doesn't it," Derek agreed cheerfully, as candid as ever.

"We'd love to do it," I confessed. "I'll bring a crack team to the pitch."

The rescue of NATS proved every bit as gloriously complicated as I had anticipated. Our first task was to take control of the rescue. This was easier said than done, since there were an unprecedented number of warring parties, all with different interests. There were four lending banks that essentially wanted their money back. Two of them – Bank of America and Abbey National – were so disgusted by their experience in this transaction that they had decided to close down their infrastructure financing business in Europe. There were seven airlines, from British Airways to British Midland to easyJet, who were fierce rivals. They had reached firm agreement on one thing: there was no way they would put more money into the company. The other owner, the Government, was becoming increasingly anxious about the political repercussions of privatising an important cog in the country's operating economy, only to see it go bust more or less immediately.

There were three other key players. The BAA, owner of Heathrow, had agreed to provide the extra capital required, albeit at an enviable rate of return. The Civil Aviation Authority, CAA for short, was the regulator. Its approval was needed to increase air traffic control charges and increases would certainly be necessary to put the system back on its feet. The CAA was just as anxious as the Government that it would not be taken for a patsy in this restructuring. It did not want to face the accusation that it allowed higher charges, which would eventually be passed on to air passengers, to bail out the original over-indebted takeover structure. Finally, any solution would need to be approved by two ratings agencies, whose seal of approval would help new debt to be raised and the banks to escape.

By the time another three investment banks were added – advising the Government, BAA and the regulator respectively – a more perfect witches brew could hardly be imagined.

"This is complete nonsense," said Stephen Paine. He was mulling over the debt structure that we had inherited. I had promised Derek Stevens a crack team and I had delivered one. Stephen Paine had been running the infrastructure segment of my team during Robert Jennings' absence and was steadily becoming recognised as an outstanding infrastructure financier.

"The debt structure has been designed for a project, with fixed spending and repayment schedules for 20 years. Look at this," he laughed, jabbing the spread-sheet. "They've got hundreds of millions to invest in new technology in 2023. How the hell is anyone meant to know the cost of uninvented technology in 20 years time?"

Stephen was always calm and methodical, and invariably said exactly what he thought.

"It's a company and we'll have to provide it with the debt structure of a company," he concluded. So much for Derek Stevens' observation that the entire structure was agreed in principle, I thought to myself, as the team hurtled into a breakneck process of rebuilding the entire spread-sheet from scratch and transforming the nature of the balance sheet. This model was to become the basic tool on which all the parties worked. It laid out the projected income flows and balance sheets for nearly 30 years so that we could all test how robust any proposed rescue package would be under different scenarios. It was also the mechanism we used to take control of the rescue. At one level NATS was merely the victim over which all the other parties fought, a bloodied corpse with no power whatsoever. By taking control of the rescue plan and the model, however, we and our client were able to become the central player in the drama, the fulcrum through which all the other parties were forced to negotiate.

Power did not transfer without protest. In mid-November we were ready to present the radically revised rescue plan to the existing shareholders, first the Airline Group and then the Government. The airlines gave their approval.

"I think it's all fine except for a couple of minor details," said Michael McGee, the banker at CSFB who was advising the Government. "I don't think we should offer the banks a structure based on short-term debt."

Luckily Michael was on the speaker-phone into our conference room. Otherwise he would undoubtedly have been spurred to greater obduracy by the visible exasperation round the table as he doggedly defended his position.

"Michael, the whole point of the new structure is the change in the nature of the debt," I pointed out. "You can hardly call reverting to long-term project debt a small detail." The tussle went on for the rest of the day. For once I was grateful to the Virgin Group, because it was Stephen Murphy, the incisive finance director from that company and adviser to the Airline Group Board, who finally bullied Michael McGee into submission.

Earlier I had gone out to lunch with Roy Griffins, the Director-General of Civil Aviation within the Department for Transport, who was responsible for overseeing the NATS rescue. Our previous involvement had taken place during the rescue of the Channel Tunnel Railway Link, while he was working in the rail section of the Department. Clearly, Roy was not a person to duck a challenge and he dealt with me with a refreshing directness.

"Look, Michael's only riding you because I've told him to," he said bluntly, as I complained at the way the CSFB team were checking us at every turn. "I could put a set of audit accountants into NATS to shadow the management if I wanted but I thought that a watching brief by CSFB the better option. What do you prefer?"

"We don't need an outside team," I said. "But we do need space. I can't have my people spending half their time talking to CSFB."

Our victory a week later in the trial of strength with Michael over the rescue plan was enough to convince Roy Griffins to pull CSFB back and we were able to move to the next stage with clear authority.

When face-to-face negotiations with the banks began, on 21 November, we had to use large conference rooms to fit everyone in, as each of the four banks brought in teams of four or more specialists. Steadily we battled our way down the long, long list of issues, trading off one concession here for a gain there. They were gruesome occasions, largely due to the sheer complexity, and interconnectedness, of the issues. After each session there would be a break of a few days as the banks sorted out their positions and assessed the impact of concessions on the model. At each of these sessions there would be fewer and fewer bank representatives, as individuals pealed off, disgusted by the sheer mind-numbing nature of the process.

One of our strategies was to break the united front of the banks, already badly undermined by the decision of Bank of America and Abbey National to pull out of infrastructure financing. The main attraction of the NATS rescue would be the opportunity for one bank or other to raise bonds to replace the bank debt. Indeed, relations with Salomon had broken down precisely because the banks suspected that it was trying to take over this profitable piece of issuing business for itself. We suggested that we would select the lead bank for the issue from among the four – and to our surprise the suggestion was accepted. Behind the scenes a tussle between Barclays and Bank of America ensued, both determined to take on the lead role. It certainly helped divide the opposition, with some considerable benefit to our negotiating position, although at the risk of adding a further level of acrimony that endangered the whole process.

"I can see why they fired you," I declared rudely to Duncan Caird of Bank of America at one stage. This was a reference to the public decision of his employers to pull out of infrastructure lending, a decision that meant he was looking for a new job. Duncan had been fighting the banks' corner with some effect and my rudeness was designed to slow him down. In that, I was successful. In the event he never came to another of the negotiating sessions.

Sometimes my rudeness backfired.

"If you had been properly organised you would have distributed the bonds before 11 September," I pointed out.

"How dare you," exploded Kevin Wall, the senior banker at Barclays. "Are you suggesting we are incompetent?"

That, of course, was exactly what I was suggesting, although the jibe was again directed at Bank of America. I had heard that it was delays in their area of responsibility that had lead to the missed opportunity. The insult looked dramatically counter-productive.

"That is not what I intended." I replied quickly. "I withdraw the remark unreservedly." Luckily Kevin accepted the apology.

By 12 December, we were down to about 10 outstanding issues in the term sheet that we were now using as a basis for negotiation. The CAA had ruled that it needed an agreement in principle between the parties before Christmas and the term sheet was designed to reflect that agreement. We knew there would be many more issues to fight over once these principles were turned into legal drafts, but that would be a challenge for the New Year. On the Thursday evening the banking team - now down to five or six - gathered in our office to continue the negotiation. In another office we corralled the Rothschild team, who were acting for BAA. As the evening progressed we shuttled between the two, sorting out the conflicts between the holders of debt and equity. We were not nearly finished by the early hours of Friday morning.

"We'll have to try again tomorrow evening," I said.

On Friday only two bankers showed up and by midnight they were slowing down.

"It's all too difficult," said Tim Treharne, who had taken over the negotiation brief for Bank of America. "We'll have to give up." He reached for his jacket.

"No, no, please don't go," I begged. "We're nearly there. Just a couple more issues."

To his credit, and to my genuine surprise, Tim stayed, even though he, like Duncan Caird, had received notice from his employer and had little incentive to see the rescue through. Indeed, as the process ground on into the small hours, Tim was the only banker left for us to negotiate with. It was a sharp contrast to the steady presence of my own team of eight, alongside the NATS' finance director, Nigel Fotherby. By three on Saturday morning we had reached agreement on the term sheet. We had a week for all the parties to turn it round internally before we could present it to the regulator.

There was one wrinkle.

"We won't sign it," said Arrington Mixon, head of global markets at Bank of America, and Tim's superior. "We want assurances that we will lead the bond issue." Now our divide and rule tactic came back to bite us.

"We can't give you that," I told her. "All I can do is tell you that we will hold an absolutely unprejudiced selection process." A last-minute meeting with the bank moved us no further.

"What are we going to do?" asked Nigel Fotherby.

"We'll just send the term sheet into the CAA regardless," I said, "telling them that one of the banks has a little cavil. I'm sure the CAA will accept it." Which, of course, they did. Bank of America had staged its protest demonstration and no one had noticed.

The transaction was far from over. I felt more sympathetic towards the banks' reluctance to agree terms when the CAA came back in the New Year with proposals that tightened them in a number of areas. Now we launched into a seemingly interminable legal process that took over the top floor of Lovells' (NATS' lawyers) office in Holborn for weeks. Pressure to complete the legal terms intensified as we moved into February.

On Monday 10 February, I laid out the timeline designed to close the transaction.

"So we should be in a position to close this on Friday," I concluded. "We can work right the way through the evening into the small hours, if we need to."

One of the younger lawyers present, Carina Radford from McKenna, eyed me coldly. "You know that Friday is St Valentine's Day," she protested. "Just because you don't have a love life, there's no way I'm working through Friday evening."

In the event it was not until mid-March that we were able to announce the rescue. NATS cut its costs and was allowed to maintain higher charges than before, while the BAA and the Government each put in fresh capital of £65m to improve the balance sheet. This took it out of the hands of its bankers. According to our painfully worked over spread-sheet the company's finances would now remain resilient in all normal trading conditions and even after a modest shock or two.

Barclays' presentation to issue the bonds that would replace the bank debt was so far superior to Bank of America's that there was no real debate in awarding them the transaction. When the £600m issue was completed in August, NATS had escaped its bankers for good.

Even the National Audit Office seemed impressed, to judge by the approving tone of its report on the rescue[5]. "NATS and other participants told us they thought UBS did a very good job." It was a far cry from their accusations that we had under-priced Railtrack.

As for me, with the transaction effectively closed, I came down to earth with a bump. Suddenly the code allocated to the NATS rescue by my colleagues appeared prophetic. Investment bankers always use project and company codes, to allow them first-level security against information accidentally leaking. The device allows team-members to avoid using company names on the telephone and other semi-public places. In this case my team had called the NATS transaction 'Project Swan'.

It is apparently a myth, widely believed by the ancients, that the swan sings beautifully before it dies. Certainly no one in modern times has come across the phenomenon. Nevertheless the expression 'Swansong' has come to mean a person's last piece of work or farewell performance. All too appropriately Project Swan was the last substantial investment transaction I was to undertake - my Swansong.

"Do you feel guilty?" It was a throw-away line right at the end of the interview, spoken with great mildness and timed to precision. "Why should you, after all?" This was almost inaudible, a muttered prompt.

I had been waiting for the trap question. I was being interviewed by the playwright David Hare about my role in the flotation of Railtrack in mid-February, 2003. David was planning a play – 'The Permanent Way' – about the privatisation and it was clearly not going to be complimentary. My colleague James Sassoon had only just started a job in the Treasury and thought better of talking to him. This left me to respond to the interview request, which I did with some reluctance. After all, in terms of the drama being planned, there were only three roles for the investment banker: that of villain, pawn or fool.

Straight rejection of guilt, as David was subtly encouraging, would have put me straight into the villain category. "Which answer do you want me to give," I asked. "The Nuremburg defence? 'I was only obeying orders.' Or the other one? 'I didn't know what was happening.' I can do either," I said.

"I do feel guilt. I do. But I didn't feel there was anything badly enough 'agley' that couldn't be fixed. So that's my defence[6]".

It was mesmerising to watch the play early in the following year at the Royal National Theatre in London, as a procession of participants in the Railtrack saga, including me, told their stories in their own words.

The thesis of the play was simple: that privatisation was a total botch resulting directly in a number of accidents that killed people. My own view about the Railtrack saga is inevitably much more complex. With hindsight there were some clear mistakes in the underlying structure of the railway industry when it was privatised. Railtrack lost control of maintenance when it contracted this function out. It lost the people who knew about the track and did not build a proper asset register to regain control. It was also a mistake to place a row about who was responsible for train delays at the heart of the relationship between Railtrack and its customers, the rail operators.

However, some of what went wrong can probably be directly attributed to the Railtrack management. Clearly it made a serious misjudgement about the cost of upgrading the West Coast Main Line, which moved from about £1bn to eight times this figure in practice, and was one of the causes of the company's collapse into administration. It also underspent on maintenance. The actions of the Labour Government, and in particular John Prescott, in egging on a hostile regulator and press, and overloading the structure with yet more bureaucracy in the shape of the Strategic Rail Authority, were also deeply unhelpful.

I suspect, with vision, some of the early flaws in the structure could have been corrected. I still cannot decide whether or not the separation of track and wheel at the heart of rail privatisation was a mistake.

The encounter with David Hare set me pondering about the financial markets and my own role within them. The central function of the City, after all, was to direct scarce capital towards the most promising recipients, where it would obtain the best return. How did it perform this central role in an open, global economy?

Certainly the City had completely confounded my original image of it from afar as an anonymous shuffler of money between faceless institutions. Quite the reverse. It proved to be a battle-ground of individualism, particularly in the corporate arena in which I mainly worked. It was dominated by powerful characters accustomed to taking tough decisions under the immediate pressure of a gossip fuelled marketplace. The currency was not cash but chaos. Transactions invariably took place at the edge of feasibility, conducted against a competitive background under great time pressure. I found few committees of experts considering all the available evidence in wise conclave. Much more typical were decisions taken on the fly, by whoever happened to be available, based on a fraction of the full information. The relentless pressure, combined with a high-risk environment, could foster close relationships between colleagues who had discovered they could rely on each other *in extremis*. It could also ferment bitter enmity where people felt they had been undeservedly let down or deserted under fire. Those intense personal relationships extended both within the specific institutions for which people worked and between them.

As the global revolution advanced, the importance of the individual grew still further. Too many financial institutions fought for a position in an integrating market, a sense of desperation fuelling extreme levels of competition. In particular they battled to obtain the services of the few individuals who knew how to function at the cutting edge of the new marketplace (or could convincingly pretend they did). Job-hopping and multi-million payouts became standard. The 1990s were an heroic age, albeit a venal one, in which individual initiative counted for more than systems and structured hierarchies.

The major challenge for the competing financial institutions in this maelstrom was to focus on identifying the key individuals who could create profitable business, to give them appropriate resources and to pay them enough to stop rivals poaching them. The indecisive, collegiate culture of Warburg found this challenge beyond it. The focused Swiss management which took over in 1995 proved up to the task. It transferred power from the intellectual and vocal corporate financiers to the traders. Within corporate finance the business winners obtained ascendancy over the technical experts. The result over the next decade was to propel the firm into the front rank of the investment banks, achieving a remarkable breakthrough into the US domestic bulge bracket.

And how had I performed in this hot-house environment? Clearly I had raised a lot of capital over my career: I had been involved in equity issues adding up to some £50bn (updated for inflation). On occasion my role had been pivotal. Alastair Morton, the chairman of Eurotunnel, wrote to me after the 1987 flotation that without me the launch would not have proceeded. On the other hand, while the tunnel was undoubtedly an extraordinary feat of engineering and a major national asset, it was also a financial disaster. As the marketer of the issue, I had successfully sold the market a pup. It was a similar story for Euro Disney. I had engineered an extremely hot issue which was consequently over-priced and encouraged a level of overspend by the Disney organisation that led to the subsidiary's collapse and rescue.

"Ah, the Fraud Squad." Miko Giedroyc, the flamboyant, witty, lead European analyst in the early 1990s delighted in greeting me. It was not just a play on my surname. It reflected the concern of the equity sales team that I would create a marketing bandwagon for my issues that led to a distortion in the level of demand and the price obtained. Already, by the early 1990s, I had absorbed the lesson. I stopped performing the dual functions of the analyst and the corporate financier responsible for the marketing programme. I was lucky to have learned the lesson early. Many of the analysts of the Dotcom boom a decade later retrod my path and became marketers in disguise. The fall-out led directly to Spitzer's draconian settlement.

I could be less equivocal about my role in some of the major restructurings in the UK. I suspect the Channel Tunnel Railway Link would have been delayed for years, if not decades, but for some of the well-prepared manoeuvring I organised in 1998. On that occasion my main motivation was precisely to avoid going to the market with a dubious prospectus. The rescue of NATS was fascinating because it could have failed solely through its sheer complexity, not because of overt hostility from any of the parties.

I could feel genuine pride in the success of the sectors I had nurtured, in particular transport. Here I had managed to build a genuinely international business with an extremely high market share. They were organised along lines that did not distort the market and, on many occasions, I had succeeded in making capital available to companies on much fairer terms than they would otherwise have received.

In spite of the Spitzer settlement I was still convinced that heavyweight sectors - which I had, after all, introduced to Warburg in the mid-1990s - remained by far the most effective way to organise investment banking activity. Not everyone agreed.

"Now that we're down to the activity levels of 1992 we really have to think hard about switching to the way we were structured then, too," Robert Gillespie, joint head of the department, observed in a one-to-one conversation in late 2002. I didn't take the remark too seriously. There had been regular mutterings about reorganisation over the previous eighteen months and none of them had come to anything.

Curiously, however, I failed to summon up any enthusiasm to take part in whatever clandestine reorganisation exercise was going on, despite the regular hints and observations from colleagues.

Rumours about my retirement had gone the rounds every six months or so over the last three years. I suspect many of them were started by rival bankers trying to undermine our position with clients. They were all based on the simple fact that I had celebrated my fiftieth birthday in 2000. Fifty is a magic number in investment banking when colleagues start to expect you to leave, either through retirement or more forcibly. As a result one becomes 'short-dated', to use the jargon of the gilt market.

"I've some spare capacity and could start up some more mini-sectors," I offered to Robert at the end of 2002. There was no response. Presumably he was reluctant to organise new initiatives around someone whose future presence was problematic.

So this is burn-out, I thought to myself. It was nothing like my vision. I had always imagined burn-out as a particular kind of exhaustion when one simply couldn't keep going at the necessary pace. This was quite different. I had simply lost interest. I was no longer challenged. I couldn't envisage future transactions more interesting than the ones I had already accomplished. Investment banking was steadily becoming just like any other business, based on systems and procedures. Not least, after years of being overpaid in terms of the outside world, I no longer needed the income. Virtually all that kept me at my desk was a somewhat perverse determination to leave a strong legacy behind me by ensuring that my team saw their way through this recession. And by mid-2003 I could already sense that the savage reductions in manpower in the investment banks were coming to an end.

"They seem to be planning to shrink the sectors quite radically," Chris Reilly, my close colleague from Euro Disney days told me. He was now based in Zurich and had popped into my office on the first Thursday in June. "They want a big central pool for the juniors to work in. They'll be allocated out as required. The senior bankers will stop running sectors and countries and purely be responsible for looking after their clients."

"They haven't told me a thing," I confessed. I went over to Robert Gillespie to see if he wanted to let me know the plans. I didn't let on that I knew them already. He kept the discussion vague with practised skill and provided little more information when I returned on the following Tuesday.

It was left to Chris Brodie, head of Europe, to confirm the structure on the following day. "We want to relieve you of all the bureaucracy, David. You'll be able to concentrate purely on your clients, like all the other senior managing directors." My team would be scattered throughout the bank.

I listened with a mixture of emotions. At least I could now leave without letting anyone down. I thought the plan itself was doomed. "If you want to break up what is probably your only world-class sector in Europe, that's up to you. But you can't expect me to hang around and watch it," I said.

"Anyway, it won't work. There's no way you can replicate the huge strength of sectors, with their incredible productivity in winning mandates and deal-doing."

I was quickly proved right. Within months it became evident that the re-organisation, pushed through with considerable pain, was a failure. Within a year it was reversed.

By then I was long gone. We agreed that I would take the sabbatical over the summer months that I had already planned before taking a final decision on my departure. When I returned in

September I was more certain than ever that I should retire. I spent the rest of the year ensuring a smooth handover of all my clients.

On my last day, in mid-December, my team took me out for a farewell lunch at the Real Greek restaurant in Hoxton Market, just north of the City. It was an extended occasion, laden with reminiscence and alcohol; too much alcohol in fact. I have always had a weak head for drink and the life-style of an investment banker had left little room for toughening it. I arrived back in my bare office on that Friday evening at 6.00pm or so feeling the worse for wear. Luckily there was still a waste-paper basket under the desk, lined with a plastic sack. I was copiously sick into it.

"This is not a fair representation of my parting views," I muttered to myself ruefully, as I contemplated the contents. I could not have had greater challenges, more drama or more sheer fun over those 20 years doing anything else. And I was profoundly grateful.

---

[1] Figure 12: Investment Banking Fees by Industry, 1997-2003, p10. Investment Banking 2002 and Beyond. Freeman & Co

[2] Capital Commitments to US Venture Funds. Figure 2.01. National Venture Capital Association 2004 Yearbook. Thomson Venture Economics, p21. 1995 figure was $10bn.

[3] Funds raised. 2003 Yearbook of European Private Equity and Venture Capital Association. PricewaterhouseCoopers. P34. 1995 figure was €4.4bn.

[4] Freeman, 2002 and Beyond. pp5 and 6

[5] Refinancing the Public Private Partnership for National Air Traffic Services. Report by the Comptroller and Auditor General. HC 157 Session 2003-2004: 7 January 2004. p27. National Audit Office. London, The Stationery Office

[6] The Permanent Way by David Hare. Part Two, p17. Faber and Faber, 2003

Appendices

Appendix 1
Main Transactions

~

IBL: £26.5m flotation (computer leasing, UK); June 1985
  Bank's role: Broker (My role: Marketing)
Singapore Airlines: S$860 privatisation (airline, Singapore);
November 1985
  Joint advisor and European bookrunner (Marketing)
TSB: £1.5bn flotation (bank, UK); September 1986
  Lead broker (Research and marketing)
Virgin Group: £240m flotation (leisure, UK); December 1986
  Broker (Team member)
British Airways: £900m privatisation (airline, UK); January 1987
  Lead broker to company (Research and marketing)
Eurotunnel: £770m flotation (rail infrastructure, UK/France);
November 1987
  *Lead UK adviser, broker and international bookrunner (Joint project
leader/marketing)*
British Steel: £2.5bn privatisation (steel, UK); December 1988
  Lead broker to issue (Project leader)
Abbey National: £1.6bn demutualisation (bank, UK); June 1989
  Broker to issue and company (Project leader)
Euro Disney: €915m flotation (leisure, France); October 1989
  International bookrunner (Joint project leader/marketing)
Water Authorities: £5.2bn privatisation (water, UK); November
1989
  Lead broker to 10 simultaneous issues (Team member)
Euro Disney: €610m convertible (leisure, France); July 1991

International bookrunner (Joint team leader)
British Telecom: £5.4bn secondary issue, BTII (telecom, UK);
December 1991
Global coordinator and bookrunner (Team member)
Thai Airways: US$240m privatisation (airline, Thailand); February
1992
Joint international adviser (Team leader)
Vienna Airport: €130m privatisation (airport, Austria); June 1992
International bookrunner (Joint team leader)
British Telecom: £5.4bn secondary issue, BT3 (telecom, UK); July
1993
Global coordinator and bookrunner (Team member)
KLM: Fairness opinion on merger with Swissair, SAS, Austrian
Airlines (airline, Netherlands); September 1993
Opinion provider (Team leader)
Bona Shipholding: US$115m flotation (shipping, Norway);
December 1993
Bookrunner (Team leader)
Euro Disney: Restructuring (leisure, France); June 1994
Adviser (Team leader)
Pharmacia: US$1.2bn privatisation (pharma, Sweden); June 1994
Joint Global co-ordinator and bookrunner (Joint project leader/marketing)
Nynex Cablecomms: £400m flotation (telecoms, UK); July 1995
UK bookrunner and joint global co-ordinator (Team leader)
Qantas: A$1.4bn privatisation (airline, Australia); July 1995
Joint bookrunner (Joint team leader)
Bona Shipholding: Takeover of Smedvig Tankships (shipping,
Norway); October 1995
Sole adviser (Team leader)
Roadking: HK$1.5bn flotation (road infrastructure, Hong Kong);
June 1996
Bookrunner (Joint team leader)
Railtrack: £1.9bn privatisation (rail, UK); June 1996
Global co-ordinator and bookrunner (Joint team leader/marketing)
Jarvis Hotels: £144m flotation (hotels, UK); July 1996
Bookrunner (Team leader)

Swebus: US$300m sale to Stagecoach (bus, Sweden); September 1996
Sole adviser (Team leader)

Galileo: US$780m flotation (airline reservation, US); August 1997
Junior lead manager of international tranche (Team leader)

Lufthansa: €2.45bn secondary issue (airline, Germany); October 1997
International bookrunner and joint global co-ordinator (Joint team leader)

Stagecoach: £140m rights issue (bus, UK); April 1998
Joint broker (Team leader)

P&O/Stena: Merger of UK ferry operations (shipping, UK); May 1998
Sole adviser to both companies (Team leader)

Scandlines Shipping: Merger of Baltic ferry companies (shipping, Denmark/Germany/Sweden); July 1998
Sole adviser to all parties (Team leader)

London & Continental Railways: £7bn restructuring (rail, UK); November 1998
Joint adviser (Team leader)

British Airways: £200m perpetual preferred securities issue (airline, UK); May 1999
Bookrunner (Joint team leader)

Stinnes: €380m flotation (logistics, Germany); June 1999
Joint bookrunner (Team leader)

Amadeus: €850m flotation (airline reservation, Spain); October 1999
Bookrunner (Team leader)

Autostrade: €4.2bn privatisation (road, Italy); December 1999
Joint bookrunner (Joint team leader)

MTR Corporation: US$1.4bn privatisation (rail, Hong Kong); February 2000
Joint bookrunner (Team member)

Mexican Airports: Restructuring and strategic sale (airports, Mexico); April 2000
Adviser (Team leader)

Amadeus: €900m secondary issue (airline reservation, Spain); June

2000
Bookrunner (Team leader)
Asur: US$386m SEC-registered flotation (airports, Mexico);
September 2000
Bookrunner (Team leader)
easyJet: £225m flotation (airline, UK); November 2000
Joint bookrunner (Team leader)
Deutsche Post: €6.6bn privatisation (Logistics, Germany);
December 2000
Joint bookrunner (Joint team leader)
Lufthansa: €250m exchangeable bond into Amadeus (airlines,
Germany); June 2001
Bookrunner (Team leader)
Vinci: £516m unsolicited offer for TBI (airports, UK/France);
September 2001
Adviser (Joint team leader)
Network Rail: £9bn takeover of Railtrack from administration (rail,
UK); October 2002
Adviser (Team consultant)
National Air Traffic Services: Restructuring (air traffic, UK);
March 2003
Adviser (Team leader)

Appendix 2
Glossary of Financial Terms

Accounting standards Common rules used by companies in preparing their accounts. These varied greatly across Europe, complicating direct comparison of performance, before gradually coming more into line through the 1990s.

Adviser Corporate finance specialist within investment bank, who provides advice to companies and governments on strategy and tactics for market operations.

Bear An investor or analyst who believes a stock price or prices will fall.

Beauty contest Competition involving a formal presentation to select an investment bank to undertake a particular transaction.

Bookbuilding The process of gathering demand for an issue, and other intelligence, from potential investors.

Book of demand (book) A record of the demand for a new issue, showing how much stock institutions would like and at what price. Casual recording became highly computerised and defined during the 1990s.

Bookrunner The house that controls the allocation of stock in a new issue to the investing institutions.

Big Bang Transformation of the UK financial markets in anticipation of the abandonment of fixed stockbroking commissions in October 1986. Brokers, jobbers, merchant banks and other financial institutions threw themselves into a frenzy of merger activity in 1983-84.

Bond Financial instruments that usually pay regular interest. The interest rate can be fixed or linked to the general level of the market.

Bulge bracket The leading US issuing houses, whose names were recorded with more white space round them at the top of the syndicate list in a prospectus. Traditionally they were Goldman Sachs, Morgan Stanley, Merrill Lynch, Salomon Bros, Lehman and Credit Suisse First Boston (CSFB).

Business Expansion Scheme UK tax relief introduced by Thatcher's Government for holding shares in qualifying unquoted companies.

Bull An investor or analyst who believes a stock price or prices will rise.

Capital markets The worldwide markets for long-term debt and equity funds. The capital markets desks manage the issuing business of the investment banks.

Chinese wall An original general concept of maintaining silence about price-sensitive client affairs which has developed into formal communication barriers between different parts of the investment banks.

City of London (City) The area in London roughly approximating the original Roman city in which the UK's financial markets have traditionally been based. Increasingly used to refer to London-wide and even UK-wide financial institutions.

Conflict of interest Where a financial institution such as an investment bank finds itself with obligations to more than one party in an actual or potential transaction. Sometimes it can continue to act if the conflicting positions are kept separate through Chinese Walls. Investment banks also use the excuse of unspecified conflicts to decline unattractive work.

Convertible bond A bond which converts into shares if these perform well and is redeemed if they disappoint. The downside protection means that the interest rate can be set at a low level.

Corporate broking Stockbroking activity (which survived Big Bang), specialising in raising money, underwriting stock and liaising with investing institutions on behalf of corporate clients.

Corporate Finance The provision of strategic advice, normally by merchant banks, to corporate clients, often involving merger and acquisition work.

Coverage banker Increasingly specialised function within expanding investment banks of individuals who are responsible for the relationship with particular corporate clients.

Covered warrant An instrument which provides the right to subscribe for stock in future at a pre-determined price, for which eventuality the seller has procured adequate stock, or cover.

Derivative products Second or third order instruments based on underlying stocks or bonds, such as futures, options or swaps, which can be traded.

Dividend Regular payments by companies to shareholders out of profits.

Equity The funds in a company's balance sheet left after deduction of its other liabilities. This residue is owned by the shareholders, so their shares are often called equity.

Eurobond A bond normally sold by an international syndicate of banks in a currency other than that of the country or market in which it is issued.

Eurodollar A dollar deposit in a US bank held outside the US.

Euro-equity Formally an issue of shares by a company on a foreign exchange and in foreign currency. Often in practice applied more generally to shares sold abroad.

Exchangeable bond Similar to a convertible in that the bond initially issued can be converted into shares when these perform satisfactorily, but the shares are those of a different company from the bond issuer.

Exchange controls Limits and controls by a Government on the exchange of currency by its citizens as well as payments to foreigners and receipts from them.

Fairness Opinion A recommendation by an investment bank, based on thorough analysis, that a transaction is fair to a company's shareholders.

Fixed Interest Securities such as bonds that pay out a rate of interest fixed at the time of issue.

Fixed Commission Standard rate charged by stockbrokers for buying and selling securities. Its abolition resulted in Big Bang.

Flotation (float) The introduction of a company onto the stock exchange by means of an issue of shares. Later the US expression Initial Public Offer (IPO) gained popularity.

Financial Times (FT) London-based business newspaper regarded as an authoritative news source for financial market professionals.

FT-Actuaries share indices Measure of price movements by all or specific segments of the market.

Fund managers Individuals and institutions which invest money into the markets on behalf of owners, usually institutions such as pension funds and insurance companies. The fund managers can provide a third-party service or be in-house teams for the owning institution.

Gilts (Gilt-edged) Deriving their name from the original gold edge on the paper certificate, these are fixed interest securities issued by the UK Government and traded on the stock exchange.

Glass-Steagall Act US legislation of 1933, passed in the aftermath of the 1929 crash, prohibiting commercial banks from trading securities and investment banking more generally. The ban was breaking down through the 1990s.

Global Co-ordinator Manipulative term invented in the early 1990s for international banks to claim overall lead position in an equity syndicate.

Global Syndicate Single syndicate selling equity in a new issue across all institutional markets.

Going public bond Bond issued by a company incorporating an option to transform on pre-agreed terms into shares on a flotation.

Green shoe First used by the Green Shoe Corporation in the US, this is an option for the lead investment bank in a syndicate to call on extra shares from the issuing company, typically a month after the issue. This allows the bank to over-allot shares in the issue and thereby assert control on the price of the stock in that period, underpinning confidence in the issuing process.

Hidden reserves Pre-Big Bang accounting convention that allowed merchant banks to maintain an unpublished reserve of funds, built up during times of healthy profitability, which could be used to boost published profits in bad times and so maintain a steady profit record and public confidence.

Initial Public Offering (IPO) A US expression for flotation, in which shares are offered for sale to the public for the first time.

Insider (insider dealing) Recipient of non-public information which legally (and ethically) prevents dealing in the relevant securities. An insider dealer breaks that requirement.

Institutional investor (institution) Bodies such as pension funds, insurance companies, charities, investment trusts and unit trusts that invest their funds into the market.

International Capital Markets See capital markets.

Investment bank Portfolio title for financial conglomerate based on the equity and debt markets.

Investment grade Higher level of ranking of company or security by the rating agencies.

Investor Relations Corporate function responsible for communication between a company and its shareholders, particularly the institutional investors.

Issue The sale of a security. A new issue is an initial sale.

Jobber (stockjobber) Pre-Big Bang specialist traders with the brokers, who would run a book at all times.

Joint economics Agreement to split all revenues from a transaction equally.

Jump ball A syndicate in which the house obtaining an order is allocated the commission.

Lead manager Title of lead bank in syndicate issuing bonds in particular. Also used in equity issuing, the term has been superceded by bookrunner and global co-ordinator.

Lex Column Financial comment on the day's events on the back page of the Financial Times.

Listed company One whose shares are listed on an official stock exchange.

Market (marketplace) Shorthand term for financial activity.

Market capitalisation The value of a company based on the price of its shares, calculated by multiplying the share price by the number of shares in issue.

Marketmaker Post-Big Bang combination of jobbing and broking function to provide continuous market in specified stocks to clients.

Merchant bank Complex financial institutions at the heart of the City which specialise, among other things, in M&A, arranging complex financial packages and investment management.

Merger and Acquisition (M&A) The most publicised activity of the merchant and investment banks in which advice is provided on buying and selling companies and their subsidiaries.

Nine o'clock meeting Regular morning meeting of directors in the Warburg corporate finance department. Other banks held equivalent meetings.

Offer for sale Main method of issuing new shares, in which stock is offered to the public under a formal timetable.

Option The right to buy or sell a security or other asset at a certain price at some future point.

Partly paid shares An issuing technique often used in privatisations in which only part of the price was required upfront. It tended to increase the potential premium of the stock in the after-market and therefore the initial demand.

Placement Direct sale of shares by broker to institution.

Position The extent to which a person, and in particular an investment bank, is short or long of a stock or other asset.

Price earnings ratio (p/e) The multiple of a company's capitalisation over its earnings, historic or prospective.

Privatisation Government sale of companies and assets. Large companies are usually floated on the Stock Exchange in a process which allows easy purchase by the general public. Originating in the UK, the practice was widely adopted round the world.

Prospectus A legal document containing all relevant information about a company making a new issue of shares.

Provisions Funds, charged against profits, set aside by a company in a specific balance sheet category to pay for charges expected in future, such as redundancy payments after a restructuring decision.

Public/private partnership (PPP) Usually a concession auctioned by Government into the private sector to provide a public service under specified conditions.

Public sector borrowing requirement (PSBR) The financial deficit of the UK Government combined with other public bodies.

Quoted company One whose shares are listed on an official stock exchange and whose prices are therefore quoted so that the shares are available to be bought and sold.

Rating agencies Independent organisations such as Standard and Poors which rank companies, Governments and other entities for their credit worthiness.

Request for Proposal (RFP) Formal invitation to apply to undertake a piece of work.

Research (analyst) Assessment of value of shares and other securities. The analysts spend much of their time explaining their findings to fund managers (and justifying them in restrospect).

Rights issue An offer of new shares to existing shareholders in proportion to their holding. Known as a pre-emptive right, this central tenet of the UK market contrasts sharply with US practice.

Roadshow Series of marketing meetings conducted by the issuer of new stock with the investing institutions.

Salesforce Team which specialises in liaising with institutional investors over stock buying and selling. Key role in placing large lines of stock rapidly.

Sectors Categorisation of businesses by main activity, ie transport, pharmaceuticals. By the late 1990s the investment banks mobilised large teams specialised in the issues relevant to particular sectors.

Securities Generic term for bonds and shares.

Share Instrument of ownership in a company, usually entitling the holder to economic and voting rights in proportion to the number of shares extant.

Share register Record of shareholders' identity and stock held.

Short (naked short) Having a future obligation to supply a security which is not owned at the time of the commitment. If prices fall profits are made and vice versa. Bookrunners can cover the exposure by exercising the green shoe; if it is greater than the shoe they are running a naked short.

Sponsor A traditional UK term for the merchant bank which arranges the issue of new shares for a company. It also implies responsibility for the success, or otherwise, of the process. The perceived identity between sponsor and company eroded significantly through the 1990s.

Stag A speculator in new issues, who subscribes with the intention of selling immediately in the aftermarket and harvesting the premium.

Stockbroker Pre-Big Bang term for individual or firm which buys and sells stocks as an agent on behalf of clients.

Stock Exchange The central market in which shares and other securities are bought and sold.

Stock Exchange Automated Quotation System (SEAQ) Screen-based system introduced into the London market in 1986 with Big Bang in which marketmakers advertise their prices and report volumes to the institutions.

Sub-underwriting The distribution of the primary sponsor's underwriting under the traditional UK system to the institutional investors by broking houses.

Syndicate desk Part of the capital markets desk which liaises, and battles, with other syndicate members in an issue.

Takeover (hostile) Acquisition of one company by another. If an approach is not agreed by the other company's board, it is termed hostile.

Tender The offer of a new issue by way of auction. A predecessor to bookbuilding, with an over-mechanistic approach.

Traded Option Instrument that allows option position to be traded.

Trader Post-Big Bang jobbing function in which large positions would be taken by the specialists within the investment banks in order to execute substantial volumes in particular stocks.

Tranche (International/domestic) The division of a financial transaction into pre-agreed sections, from the French word meaning slice.

Treasury market Invariably a reference to the US Government money market, in which Treasury bills are issued and traded.

Underwriting In the traditional UK market this is a guarantee by the sponsors to take up all the stock of a new issue. The system has remained in place mainly for rights issues. The expression is used under the bookrunning system, although the guarantee is worth little because it is provided only at the time of issue when the shape of the book is known.

Yellow Book London Stock Exchange regulations covering listing, reporting and dealing requirements for companies and directors.

Index

~